revelations

an anthology of expository essays by and about blacks

Fourth Edition

Edited by
Teresa M. Redd, Howard University

Pearson
Custom
Publishing

Cover art: *One 4 Bear Den*, by Jeff Donaldson.

Printed in the United States of America

10 9 8 7 6 5 4 3 2 1

Please visit our web site at www.pearsoncustom.com

ISBN 0–536–63236–7

BA 993154

 PEARSON CUSTOM PUBLISHING
75 Arlington Street, Suite 300, Boston, MA 02116
A Pearson Education Company

Copyright Acknowledgments

in memory of
my aunt,

Jean Camper Cahn,

lawyer,
educator,
civil rights activist
and
co-founder of national legal
services for the poor

Contents

---

*annotated

_____

*annotated

Rhetorical Index

ILLUSTRATION

Ishmael Reed, "America: The Multicultural Society"*
Henry Louis Gates, Jr., "The Debate Has Been Miscast from the Start"
Ralph Ellison, "What America Would Be Like Without Blacks"
Farai Chideya, "Homophobia: Hip-Hop's Black Eye"
John Hope Franklin and Alfred Moss, Jr., "Slave Resistance"
Karen Grigsby Bates, "Excuse Me, Your Race Is Showing"
John Rickford and Russell Rickford, "The Ubiquity of Ebonics"
Lerone Bennett, "The Black Founding Fathers"
Karen Webb, "Black English: A Discussion"
Geneva Smitherman, "White English in Blackface, or Who Do I Be?"
Michael Eric Dyson, "The Evolution of Rap Music"
Ossie Davis, "The English Language Is My Enemy"
Patricia Elam Ruff, "Private School, Private Pain"
James Baldwin, "If Black English Isn't a Language, Then Tell Me, What Is?"
Nathan McCall, "Faking the Funk: The Middle Class Black Folks of Prince George's County"
Frederick Douglass, "The Meaning of July Fourth for the Negro"
Student Essay: *Oluwatoyin Tella*, "The Comment"
Student Essay: *Shay Gilliam*, "Struggle of a Gentleman"
Student Essay: *Kenya Doyle*, "The American Dream"

COMPARISON-CONTRAST

Steve Biko, "Some African Cultural Concepts"*
Joseph White, "African Roots of the African American Family"*
Jay Ford, "20/20 Hindsight"
Kwame Ture, "Pan-Africanism"
Gerald Early, "Never African Again"
Shelby Steele, "On Being Black and Middle Class"

---

*annotated

----

*annotated

CAUSE-EFFECT

CRITIQUE

---

*annotated

SYNTHESIS

Ishmael Reed, "America: The Multicultural Society"
Henry Louis Gates, Jr., "The Debate Has Been Miscast from the Start"
Benjamin Quarles, "Black History's Diversified Clientele"
Claude Steele, "Race and the Schooling of Black Americans"
Joseph White, "African Roots of the African American Family"
Meta Carstarphen, "Black vs. Blue: Time for a Cease-Fire"
Audrey Chapman, "The Great Divide: Male vs. Female"
Farai Chideya, "Homophobia: Hip-Hop's Black Eye"
Patricia Elam Ruff, "Private School, Private Pain"
Nathan McCall, "Faking the Funk: The Middle Class Black Folks of Prince
    George's County"
Student Essay: *Kela Francis*, "A Travesty of Justice: The Diallo Trial"
Student Essay: *Shaton Sanderson*, "Living on the Razor's Edge"
Student Essay: *Daud Cole*, "The Origins and Intentions of Colorism"
Student Essay: *Harold Nyikal*, "African Ceremonies"

Preface for Instructors

Maintaining its Afrocentric focus, the fourth edition of *Revelations* expands and updates the anthology's repertoire of essays. The fourth edition offers four new features:

- **MORE STUDENT ESSAYS.** You'll find more student essays since such essays are often the easiest for students to relate to and imitate.
- **MORE ACADEMIC WRITING.** You'll find more essays that critique other works, synthesize sources, or draw conclusions based upon scientific observation.
- **MORE DIVERSE OPINIONS.** You'll find a wider range of opinions on controversial issues, to stimulate debate in your classroom.
- **MORE BACKGROUND RESOURCES.** You'll find a companion website that will link students to other webpages where they can explore the history behind terms that they encounter in the book.

This new edition includes a total of 78 essays, 58 professional and 20 student selections. These essays are *clustered around themes* so that students can enter and join the "conversation" that is the sine qua non of academic life. However, for teachers who prefer to organize their courses around the expository patterns, I have retained the unique *thematic-rhetorical organization* from the third edition. Thus, the essays in *Units I through VI are grouped according to their theme AND their dominant pattern:* illustration, comparison-contrast, classification, process analysis, cause-effect analysis, or definition. Within each thematic-rhetorical unit, at least one essay has been *annotated* to highlight its organizational pattern. To identify additional examples of each pattern, you may consult the Rhetorical Index.

Following each essay, you will also find *topics designed to prepare students for writing across the curriculum:* Some topics demand critiques and syntheses of material in the book while the other topics invite students to draw upon field research and personal observations. For students who wish to delve into outside sources for their assignments, there are *updated lists of background readings.* Students may also enjoy reading the *poetry excerpts* that introduce each thematic unit. Further details about the purpose and pedagogical apparatus of the book appear below.

Purpose

This anthology grew out of a need articulated by countless professors at my historically Black university. For years my colleagues in the English department had complained that there were not enough essays by or about Blacks in composition anthologies.[1] We needed an Afrocentric anthology, they insisted, an anthology with essays that would illuminate our students' heritage and experience. This anthology fulfills that need. Designed for a course on expository writing, it features Black men and women writing about the Black experience.

Since I published the first edition of this anthology in 1991, authors have significantly increased the number of selections by Blacks in their composition textbooks, especially in multicultural anthologies. However, too few of these selections are examples of exposition, which is the type of writing students must produce in most introductory writing courses.[2] The limited number of expository models is a drawback since studies show that analyzing model essays generally has a positive effect on students' writing.[3]

Moreover, because *Revelations* is Afrocentric, to Black student writers, this anthology offers several benefits that traditional anthologies lack. First of all, in this anthology not only the essays, but all of the writers serve as models for Black students who may have wondered whether their experiences were worth writing about or doubted whether the techniques of writing were worth mastering. Now these students can see that they are part of an intellectual and rhetorical tradition. They can see that Blacks of many backgrounds have made writing an effective tool. As the headnotes reveal, these writers represent a variety of professions, for example, playwright, minister, historian, novelist, lawyer, journalist, surgeon, poet, linguist, psychologist. Although the majority of the writers are African American, some represent other areas of the African diaspora, such as the Caribbean and Latin America, as well as Africa itself.

---

[1]In 1991, when I published the first edition of *Revelations,* some of the most disappointing texts were *The Harper & Row Reader* (1989), *The Norton Reader, Shorter Edition* (1988), and *The Little Brown Reader, Shorter Edition* (1989), where less than 5% of the essays were written by Blacks. Since then, the percentage has increased. However, there is still ample room for improvement.

[2]See, for instance, recent multicultural anthologies such as *Rereading America* (2001) and *Between Worlds* (2001). Even in *Heritage* (1997), which consists of only African American writing, a large percentage of the selections are poems, short stories, plays, or autobiographical narratives.

[3]See George Hillock's 1986 review and more recent studies by Marion Crowhurst (1991) and Peter Smagorinsky (1991). Although the analysis of model essays is no substitute for writing instruction and practice, it does contribute to writing improvement.

The content of this anthology is another positive feature for Black students. As the subtitle indicates, this anthology is not simply *by* Blacks. It is *about* Blacks. Topics range from the Civil Rights Movement to the Black Power Movement, from racist stereotypes to racial pride, from African culture on the continent to African culture a continent away. Whether the essays date from the 20th century or the 21st, they explore issues of continuing importance to Black people.

Writing about such Afrocentric topics allows Black students to tap their personal experience, giving them rich resources for writing whether they are critiquing the authors' texts or telling their own stories. As I have observed in my own composition classes, writing about such topics can also increase students' motivation and self-confidence.[4] As a result, students may develop a greater sense of authority as writers, a feeling that appears to be a prerequisite for effective writing (Epps 156; Freedman 345; Shaughnessy 85).

However, there is another reason to use this anthology in a composition course for Black students. The reason can be found in an article by Ronald Walters, a professor of political science. In "The Afrocentric Concept at Howard University," Walters reminds us that the research of W.E.B. Du Bois, Carter Woodson, Kelly Miller, Horace Mann Bond, and Charles Wesley indicates that "education is the construction of a system of information with a social purpose" (9). The question is "Whose purpose shall education serve?" Like an increasing number of educators, Walters concludes that education should serve the student, that it should "enlighten, correct, preserve and enrich the student's information about himself/herself as the first proposition" (9).[5] From this perspective, the U.S. school system has failed to serve Black students: It has perpetuated negative myths about Blacks while omitting many positive facts about Blacks' ability, culture, and history (see Van Sertima; Asante; Bennett). This anthology shatters some of those myths and fills in the gaps, for it contains a wealth of essays that can "enlighten, correct, preserve and enrich" Black students' information about themselves.

But reading the essays is only the first step. This book can serve Black students best if the essays become the focus of writing in a composition course. Because of its emphasis on writing, a composition course is an ideal vehicle for achieving the kind of self-discovery Walters describes. As Haki Madhubuti has observed, "writing is a form of self-definition and communication through which writers basically define themselves and their relationship to the world" (174).[6] Writing makes possible such self-definition because it facilitates extended

---

[4]Allen (865), Anderson (224), and Taylor and Bradford (218)—among others— have made similar observations.

[5]See Freire, Combs, and Nobles for other statements of this educational philosophy, a philosophy that is supported by Maslow's learning theory. According to Maslow, self-esteem and self-actualization are basic needs that must be fulfilled before people can reach their intellectual potential.

thinking (Bereiter 88; Emig 90; Smith 15–16). When we write, we create an object with our thoughts, an object we can distance ourselves from and reflect on, an object we can question and revise.

Since composition courses focus on writing, they promote extended thinking. Since they also introduce logical patterns of thinking, they encourage sound reasoning and systematic exploration of issues. Finally, since they develop critical reading, they stimulate careful thinking about issues raised in texts. That is why using this Afrocentric text in a composition course is so important. It gives Black students a chance to use writing to "think through" issues of importance to themselves and their communities. It makes writing a process of revelation, an act of liberation.

Instructional Aids

This edition of *Revelations* includes four types of instructional aids for each essay in addition to an *Instructor's Resource Manual* (available upon request):

1. **Reading-to-Write Questions**

    These questions help students read with a writer's eye so that they can learn how to write from reading. Covering aspects of an essay's *content, arrangement,* and *style,* the questions encourage students to notice the choices the authors have made and the rhetorical effects of those choices. I recommend assigning some of these questions to groups of students. After deliberating in groups, the students can report their findings to the rest of the class.

2. **Suggested Topics**

    Most of the topics elicit writing in the expository mode of the model essay.

    *   *Observation* topics invite students to gather data firsthand or draw upon personal experience.
    *   *Critique* topics encourage students to question or support one of the author's statements.
    *   *Synthesis* topics make connections with other essays in the book, bringing other voices into the conversation.

    For each topic, a *target audience* is suggested. Sometimes students must imagine this audience, but usually the audience is accessible inside or outside the classroom. For instance, in the classroom you could help students identify audiences such as "uninformed classmates" or "a peer interested in becoming a social worker." At the same time, you could encourage stu-

---

[6]For an extended discussion of this idea, see the article "All Writing Is Autobiography," in which Donald Murray argues that "we become what we write" (71).

dents to submit essays to audiences outside the classroom, such as "the readers of the op-ed page of the campus newspaper" or "your high school administrators." Whether inside or outside the classroom, the target audience can guide students as they write and assist you as you evaluate your students' essays. However, you may prefer to ask your students to specify their own audience on the outside of their papers.

3. **Background Readings**

Below each essay several books are listed for students who want to incorporate research in their papers and for teachers or students who simply want more background knowledge. Included are some literary works for teachers and students who wish to combine the study of literature and composition.

    The booklists are introductory reading lists consisting of the most relevant titles that I could find in databases and publishers' catalogues. When there were many books on a topic, I chose the most recent and most comprehensive. Since the books represent different (sometimes opposing) viewpoints, students should examine more than one source and read all sources with a critical eye. To make the books accessible to the whole class, you may need to put some on reserve in your campus library.

    I recommend assigning some of the headings of the booklists as journal topics for freewriting (i.e., unedited, extemporaneous writing). These freewriting assignments can not only promote writing fluency but also serve as prereading or prewriting exercises. As *prereading* exercises, the assignments can help students appreciate how the essayist chose to handle a topic that they have just tackled. As *prewriting* exercises, the assignments can help students generate and explore ideas for an upcoming draft of an essay.

    As you teach with *Revelations*, you will undoubtedly think of questions and suggestions that are not included here. Therefore, in each of the preceding categories, you will find a space for your ideas.

4. **Web Links**

Some of the writers refer to historical events or people whom today's students may not recognize or may need to know better. Therefore, encourage your students to use dictionaries, library sources, and Internet search engines to look up unfamiliar terms. However, you may also obtain an access code (available upon request) that will link students to webpages where they can learn more about the terms and authors.

Additional Suggestions

1. **Structural Models**

   If you are looking for annotated examples of expository structure, you may refer students to the following essays:

"America: The Multicultural Society"	ILLUSTRATION
"Some African Cultural Concepts"	COMPARISON-CONTRAST Point by Point
"African Roots of the African American Family"	COMPARISON-CONTRAST Subject by Subject
"Black History's Diversified Clientele"	CLASSIFICATION
"Gikuyu Industries: Hut-Building"	PROCESS
"Black vs. Blue"	CAUSE
"Black Men and Public Space"	EFFECT
"The Handicap of Definition"	DEFINITION

   You may also refer your class to student essays that model the academic purposes reflected in the "Suggested Topics":

"The Four Types of Publics"	SUMMARY
"Ebonics: A Racial Profile"	CRITIQUE
"African Ceremonies"	SYNTHESIS

   Although these essays are helpful models, they should be studied in conjunction with the most accessible models of all: *your* students' essays.

2. **Multiple Patterns**

   Several essays illustrate more than one expository pattern. Therefore you can use these essays to demonstrate how to combine patterns (see the Rhetorical Index for examples).

3. **Nonstandard Conventions**

   Some authors (e.g., Ford, Biko, Reagon, Baldwin, and Hurston) occasionally deviate from the rules of Standard Written English. Here and there you will find a comma splice, a fragment, vague pronoun reference, or idiosyncratic use of colons, semicolons, and commas. Consider challenging your students to find and report such instances. Then, the class can discuss whether the author has truly made an error or whether s/he has made an effective choice.

4. Headnotes

The headnotes include information about the author, rhetorical context, and expository structure of each essay. Students can take advantage of this information in the following ways:

(a) to acquaint themselves with an author's other works

(b) to determine how effectively an author adapted an essay to the target audience

(c) to identify an author's expository strategies as they read.

Works Cited

Allen, Michael. "Writing Away from Fear: Mina Shaughnessy and the Uses of Authority." *College English 41* (1980): 857–867.

Anderson, Edward. "Using Folk Literature in Teaching Composition." *Tapping Potential: English and Language Arts for the Black Learner.* Ed. Charlotte K. Brooks. Urbana, IL: National Council of Teachers of English, 1985. 219–225.

Asante, Molefi Kete. *The Afrocentric Idea.* Philadelphia: Temple University Press, 1987.

Bennett, Christine. *Comprehensive Multicultural Education,* 2nd ed. Boston: Allyn & Bacon, 1990.

Bereiter, Carl. "Development in Writing." *Cognitive Processes in Writing.* Ed. Lee W. Gregg and Erwin R. Steinberg. Hillsdale, NJ: Lawrence Erlbaum, 1980. 73–93.

Combs, A.W., ed. *Perceiving, Behaving, Becoming,* ASCD Yearbook. Alexandria, VA: Association for Supervision and Curriculum Development, 1962.

Crowhurst, Marion. "Interrelationships Between Reading and Writing Persuasive Discourse." *Research in the Teaching of English 25* (1991): 314–338.

Emig, Janet. "Writing as a Mode of Learning." *The Writing Teacher's Sourcebook,* 2nd ed. Ed. Gary Tate and Edward P. J. Corbett. New York and Oxford: Oxford University Press, 1988. 85–91.

Epps, Janis. "Killing Them Softly; Why Willie Can't Write." *Tapping Potential: English and Language Arts for the Black Learner.* Ed. Charlotte K. Brooks. Urbana, IL: National Council of Teachers of English, 1985. 154–158.

Freedman, Sarah. "The Registers of Student and Professional Expository Writing: Influences on Teachers' Responses." *New Directions in Composition*

Research. Ed. Richard Beach and Lillian Bridwell. New York: Guilford Press, 1984. 334–347.

Freire, Paulo. *Pedagogy of the Oppressed.* New York: Continuum, 1970.

———. *Education for Critical Consciousness.* New York: Seabury, 1974.

Hillocks, George, Jr. *Research on Written Composition: New Directions for Teaching.* Urbana, IL: National Conference on Research in English and ERIC Clearinghouse on Reading & Communication Skills, 1986.

Madhubuti, Haki R. "Hard Words and Clear Songs: The Writing of Black Poetry." *Tapping Potential: English and Language Arts for the Black Learner.* Ed. Charlotte K. Brooks. Urbana, IL: National Council of Teachers of English, 1985. 168–175.

Maslow, A. *Motivation and Personality.* New York: Harper & Brothers, 1954.

Murray, Donald. "All Writing Is Autobiography." *College Composition and Communication* 42 (1991): 66–74.

Nobles, Wade W. "The Infusion of African and African American Content: A Question of Content and Intent." *Infusion of African American Content in the School Curriculum: Proceedings of the First National Conference October 1989.* Ed. Asa G. Hilliard III, Lucretia Payton-Stewart, Larry Obadele Williams. Morristown, NJ: Aaron Press, 1990. 5–24.

Shaughnessy, Mina P. *Errors and Expectations: A Guide for the Teacher of Basic Writing.* NY: Oxford University Press, 1977.

Smagorinsky, Peter. "The Writer's Knowledge and the Writing Process: A Protocol Analysis." *Research in the Teaching of English* 25 (1991): 339–364.

Smith, Frank. *Writing and the Writer.* New York: Holt, Rinehart & Winston, 1982.

Taylor, Ethel, and Ernest Bradford. "Using the Oral History Approach to Teach Freshman Writing." *Tapping Potential: English and Language Arts for the Black Learner.* Ed. Charlotte K. Brooks. Urbana, IL: National Council of Teachers of English, 1985. 214–218.

Walters, Ronald W. "The Afrocentric Concept at Howard University: A Viewpoint." *New Directions.* 17.4 (1990): 6–9.

Van Sertima, Ivan. "Future Directions for African and African-American Content in the School Curriculum." *Infusion of African American Content in the School Curriculum: Proceedings of the First National Conference, October 1989.* Ed. Asa G. Hilliard III, Lucretia Payton-Stewart, Larry Obadele Williams. Morristown, NJ: Aaron Press, 1990. 87–109.

Acknowledgments

In many ways, this anthology is a product of the Department of English at Howard University. My colleagues in the Department made me think of creating such an anthology, they urged me to undertake the project, and then they wholeheartedly supported my efforts. Thus, I thank *all* of my colleagues in the Department—past and present. However, I owe special thanks to Eleanor Traylor and Victoria Arana, my current and former chairpersons, for providing encouragement and clerical support. I thank Freshman English Director Evora Jones and the Freshman English Committee for adopting the book at Howard. I am also grateful to Cynthia Fowler, Wade Harrell, Andre Hoyrd, Ethel Lewis, Diayyah Abdullah, Tim Ruppel, Daria Winter, Gail Yngve, Carolyn Shuttlesworth, Victoria Arana, and Mary Larkin for contributing professional or student essays to this or previous editions. I wish to thank as well Paul Fallon, Sandra Shannon, Ann Kelly, Karen Webb, Jennifer Jordan, and Victoria Arana for reviewing parts of the manuscript. In addition, I am indebted to Joshua Hehner, Ned Preston, and Victoria Tolliver-Harris for assisting me with the bibliographic research and to Renee Baron, Sandra Shannon, and Carolyn Shuttlesworth for recommending related literature. Finally, I wish to thank John Trimble for assisting me and Terry Brennan at Pearson Custom Publishing for turning an idea into a reality.

Introduction for Students

You are about to enter a Black world. Here you will find Black writers from different parts of the Black disapora, but especially from Black America. Some are famous writers of literature: novelists such as Toni Morrison, poets such as Haki Madhubuti, and playwrights such as Ossie Davis. But since writing is important in many fields, you will find Black writers from a variety of professions. For instance, you will meet historian Benjamin Quarles, neurosurgeon Ben Carson, anti-apartheid activist Steve Biko, psychologist Claude Steele, lawyer Stephen Carter, and Kenya's first president, Jomo Kenyatta.

Regardless of their background, all of the writers in this book have a great deal to say about the things that matter most to us. They write about landmark events in Black history—events such as ancient Africans' scientific discoveries, the enslavement of Africans in the U.S., the Civil Rights Movement, and the Black Power Movement. They also write about Black culture—our language, our literature, our music, our art. And they write about prejudice within the Black community as well as in society at large.

While some writers offer the viewpoint of the careful observer or inquiring scholar, others give you an insider's view:

- Bernice Reagon takes you on the marches and in the jails where she sang during the Civil Rights Movement.
- Jay Ford, an African American student, invites you into the streets and homes of Kenya to share his sense of wonder and freedom.
- Ben Carson reveals how he performed pioneering and life-saving surgery.
- Brent Staples shows how it feels to be a Black man—a continual target of white suspicion.

Reading the Essays

In the following pages, these writers explain themselves, their community, and the world from a Black perspective. They explain by illustrating, comparing, contrasting, classifying, defining terms, analyzing processes, identifying causes, and describing effects. These are the strategies of *expository* writing. They reflect the way we think, and they can guide the way we write. Used appropriately, expository strategies can help writers generate ideas and organize those ideas in a logical and meaningful way. As you read this anthology, notice how the writers employ these strategies to develop their essays. Do they *contrast* two subjects, highlighting the differences point by point or subject by subject? Do they identify discrete stages of a *process?* Or do they divide a group into categories according to a principle of *classification?*

In addition to the expository patterns, notice each writer's sentence structure, word choice, and punctuation. Do you prefer the clean, simple prose of Haki Madhubuti's essay or the long, rhythmic sentences of James Baldwin's? What do you think of the mixture of Black English and academic English in Geneva Smitherman's essay? Or the distinctive diction in Eleanor Traylor's?

Finally, think critically about the content of the essays. Compare your experiences and observations to those described here. Can you cite examples to support Clarisse Jones's thesis about dark-skinned girls? How would you compare Zora Neale Hurston's definition of "colored" in 1928 to your definition of "Black" today? Do you think that Patrice Gaines-Carter overlooks important similarities between her generation and the younger generation?

Writing Your Essays

At first, you might respond to these essays by recalling your own experience in a *journal entry* as Naomi Porterfield does or by writing a *summary* similar to Kristen Haynes's synopsis. On the other hand, following Tracy Brewington's example, you might conduct an informal survey and report your *observations*. After carefully re-examining an essay, you might compose a *critique* like Bakesta King's or Kaelie Knight's, to question or support one of the author's statements. Later, after consulting related readings from this book or the bibliographies, you might compose a *synthesis* of the opinions, facts, and examples from many sources, just as Harold Nyikal and Shaton Sanderson do so well.

Regardless of the approach you choose, take advantage of the opportunity to write about the issues raised in this book. They are important issues, which can be clarified by writing, for writing is a means of exploring ideas, of turning them inside out and looking at them slowly, carefully, thoughtfully. In other words, when you write about these issues, write in order to communicate with readers, but also—as Black author Terry McMillan advises—"write in order *to know."*

american dream:
illustration

I, too, sing America.

I am the darker brother.
They send me to eat in the kitchen
When company comes,
But I laugh,
And eat well,
And grow strong.

Tomorrow,
I'll be at the table
When company comes.
Nobody'll dare
Say to me,
"Eat in the kitchen,"
Then.

Besides,
They'll see how beautiful I am
And be ashamed—

I, too, am America.

"I, Too" by Langston Hughes

America:
The Multicultural Society
Ishmael Reed

*Ishmael Reed has distinguished himself as a nov-
elist and essayist. His novels include* The Free-
Lance Pallbearers, Mumbo Jumbo, *and* Reckless
Eyeballing. *His volumes of essays are* Shrovetide
in Old New Orleans, Writin' Is Fightin' *and*
MultiAmerica: Essays on Cultural Wars and Cultural Peace. *The following essay comes from*
Writin' Is Fightin', *which was published in 1988.
From the beginning to the end, Reed uses examples to demonstrate that American society is a
"cultural bouillabaisse" and that the Western
civilization it lays claim to is not as homogeneous or exceptional as commonly believed.*

At the annual Lower East Side Jewish Festival yesterday, a Chinese woman ate a pizza
slice in front of Ty Thuan Duc's Vietnamese
grocery store. Beside her a Spanish-speaking   example 1
family patronized a cart with two signs: "Ital-
ian Ices" and "Kosher by Rabbi Alper." And
after the pastrami ran out, everybody ate
knishes.

New York Times, June 23, 1983

1   On the day before Memorial Day, 1983, a poet called me to describe a <u>city</u> he   example 2
had just visited. He said that one section included mosques, built by the
Islamic people who dwelled there. Attending his reading, he said, were large
numbers of Hispanic people, forty thousand of whom lived in the same city.
He was not talking about a fabled city located in some mysterious region of
the world. The city he'd visited was Detroit.

2   A few months before, as I was leaving Houston, Texas, I heard it announced
on the radio that Texas's largest minority was Mexican-American, and though
a foundation recently issued a report critical of bilingual education, the taped
voice used to guide the passengers on the air trams connecting terminals in
Dallas Airport is in <u>both Spanish and English</u>. If the trend continues, a day will   example 3
come when it will be difficult to travel through some sections of the country
without hearing commands in both English and Spanish; after all, for some
western states, Spanish was the first written language and the Spanish style
lives on in the western way of life.

3   Shortly after my Texas trip, I sat in an auditorium located on the campus of
the University of Wisconsin at Milwaukee as a <u>Yale professor</u>—whose original   example 4
work on the influence of African cultures upon those of the Americas has led
to his ostracism from some monocultural intellectual circles—walked up and
down the aisle, like an old-time southern evangelist, dancing and drumming
the top of the lectern, illustrating his points before some serious Afro-American
intellectuals and artists who cheered and applauded his performance and his
mastery of information. The professor was "white." After his lecture, he joined
a group of Milwaukeeans in a conversation. All of the participants spoke
Yoruba, though only the professor had ever traveled to Africa.

4   One of the artists told me that his <u>paintings</u>, which included African and   example 5
Afro-American mythological symbols and imagery, were hanging in the local
McDonald's restaurant. The next day I went to McDonald's and snapped pictures of smiling youngsters eating hamburgers below paintings that could
grace the walls of any of the country's leading museums. The manager of the
local McDonald's said, "I don't know what you boys are doing, but I like it,"
as he commissioned the local painters to exhibit in his restaurant.

5   Such blurring of cultural styles occurs in everyday life in the United States
to a greater extent than anyone can imagine, and is probably more prevalent
than the sensational conflict between people of different backgrounds that is
played up and often encouraged by the media. <u>The result is what the Yale Pro-</u>   thesis
<u>fessor, Robert Thompson, referred to as a cultural bouillabaisse, yet members</u>
<u>of the nation's present educational and cultural Elect still cling to the notion</u>
<u>that the United States belongs to some vaguely defined entity they refer to as</u>
"<u>Western civilization,</u>" by which they mean, presumably, a civilization created
by the people of Europe, as if Europe can be viewed in monolithic terms. Is
<u>Beethoven's Ninth Symphony</u>, which includes Turkish marches, a part of   example 1
Western civilization, or the late nineteenth- and twentieth-century <u>French</u>   example 2
<u>paintings</u>, whose creators were influenced by Japanese art? And what of the
<u>cubists</u>, through whom the influence of African art changed modern painting,   example 3

or the surrealists, who were so impressed with the art of the Pacific Northwest Indians that, in their map of North America, Alaska dwarfs the lower forty-eight in size?   *example 4*

6   Are the Russians, who are often criticized for their adoption of "Western" ways by Tsarist dissidents in exile, members of Western civilization? And *example 5* what of the millions of Europeans who have black African and Asian ancestry, *example 6* black Africans having occupied several countries for hundreds of years? Are these "Europeans" members of Western civilization, or the Hungarians, who *example 7* originated across the Urals in a place called Greater Hungary, or the Irish, who *example 8* came from the Iberian Peninsula?

7   Even the notion that North America is part of Western civilization because our "system of government" is derived from Europe is being challenged by *example 9* Native American historians who say that the founding fathers, Benjamin Franklin especially, were actually influenced by the system of government that had been adopted by the Iroquois hundreds of years prior to the arrival of large numbers of Europeans.

8   Western civilization, then, becomes another confusing category like Third World, or Judeo-Christian culture, as man attempts to impose his small-screen view of political and cultural reality upon a complex world. Our most publicized novelist recently said that Western civilization was the greatest achieve- *example 1* ment of mankind, an attitude that flourishes on the street level as scribbles in *example 2* public restrooms: "White Power," "Niggers and Spics Suck," or "Hitler was a prophet," the latter being the most telling, for wasn't Adolph Hitler the archetypal monoculturalist who, in his pigheaded arrogance, believed that one way and one blood was so pure that it had to be protected from alien strains at all costs? Where did such an attitude, which has caused so much misery and depression in our national life, which has tainted even our noblest achievements, begin? An attitude that caused the incarceration of Japanese-American *example 3* citizens during World War II, the persecution of Chicanos and Chinese- *example 4* Americans, the near-extermination of the Indians, and the murder and lynch- *example 5* ings of thousands of Afro-Americans. *example 6*

9   Virtuous, hardworking, pious, even though they occasionally would wander off after some fancy clothes, or rendezvous in the woods with the town prostitute, the Puritans are idealized in our schoolbooks as "a hardy band" of *example 7* no-nonsense patriarchs whose discipline razed the forest and brought order to the New World (a term that annoys Native American historians). Industrious, responsible, it was their "Yankee ingenuity" and practicality that created the work ethic. They were simple folk who produced a number of good poets, and they set the tone for the American writing style, of lean and spare lines, long before Hemingway. They worshiped in churches whose colors blended in with the New England snow, churches with simple structures and ornate lecterns.

10   The Puritans were a daring lot, but they had a mean streak. They hated the theater and banned Christmas. They punished people in a cruel and inhuman manner. They killed children who disobeyed their parents. When they came in

contact with those whom they considered heathens or aliens, they behaved in such a bizarre and irrational manner that this chapter in the American history comes down to us as a late-movie horror film. They exterminated the Indians, who taught them how to survive in a world unknown to them, and their encounter with the calypso culture of Barbados resulted in what the tourist guide in Salem's Witches' House refers to as the Witchcraft Hysteria.

11   The <u>Puritan</u> legacy of hard work and meticulous accounting led to the establishment of a great industrial society; it is no wonder that the American industrial revolution began in Lowell, Massachusetts, but there was the other side, the strange and paranoid attitudes toward those different from the Elect.

12   The cultural attitudes of that early Elect continue to be voiced in everyday life in the United States: the <u>president</u> of a distinguished university, writing a   example 1
letter to the *Times,* belittling the study of African civilizations; the television
<u>network</u> that promoted its show on the Vatican art with the boast that this art   example 2
represented "the finest achievements of the human spirit." A modern up-tempo state of complex rhythms that depends upon contacts with an international community can no longer behave as if it dwelled in a "Zion Wilderness" surrounded by beasts and pagans.

13   When I heard a <u>schoolteacher</u> warn the other night about the invasion of   example 3
the American educational system by foreign curriculums, I wanted to yell at the television set, "Lady, they're already here." It has already begun because the world is here. The world has been arriving at these shores for at least ten thousand years from Europe, Africa, and Asia. In the late nineteenth and
early twentieth centuries, large numbers of <u>Europeans</u> arrived, adding their   example 1
cultures to those of the European, African, and Asian settlers who were
already here, and recently millions have been entering the country from <u>South</u>   example 2
<u>America and the Caribbean</u>, making Yale professor Bob Thompson's bouill-abaisse richer and thicker.

14   One of our most visionary <u>politicians</u> said that he envisioned a time when   example 1
the United States could become the brain of the world, by which he meant the repository of all of the latest advanced information systems. I thought of that
remark when an enterprising <u>poet friend</u> of mine called to say that he had just   example 2
sold a poem to a computer magazine and that the editors were delighted to get it because they didn't carry fiction or poetry. Is that the kind of world we desire? A humdrum homogeneous world of all brains and no heart, no fiction, no poetry; a world of robots with human attendants bereft of imagination, of culture? Or does North America deserve a more exciting destiny? To become a place where the cultures of the world crisscross. This is possible because the United States is unique in the world: The world is here.

Reading-to-Write Questions

1. **Content:** This essay is informative because of Reed's examples. What kinds of specifics does Reed cite?

2. **Arrangement:** Reed withholds his thesis until *after* he has presented a series of anecdotes. What are the advantages and disadvantages of this arrangement?

3. **Style:** Why does Reed pose so many rhetorical questions?

4. _____

    _____

    _____

Suggested Topics

1. **Observation:** Write an essay about the "cultural bouillabaisse" in a neighborhood or city you know. Cite specific examples. (audience = someone who does not live in your neighborhood or city)

2. **Critique:** Summarize Reed's essay, highlighting his claim that the "blurring of cultural styles" in the U.S. "is probably more prevalent than the sensational conflict between people of different backgrounds." Citing examples from history, the media, and your experience, support or question Reed's claim. (audience = skeptical classmates)

3. **Synthesis:** Reed suggests that the term "Western civilization" is not meaningful because non-Western cultures have profoundly influenced the West. Is there such a thing as "Western civilization"? Discuss the validity of the term, drawing upon statements and examples from Reed's, Gates's, and Ellison's essays. (audience = gatekeepers of "Western civilization")

4. _____

    _____

    _____

Background Readings: MULTICULTURALISM IN THE USA

Buenker, John, ed. *Multiculturalism in the United States.* New York: Greenwood Press, 1992.

Carnevale, Anthony. *The American Mosaic: An In-depth Report on the Future of Diversity at Work.* New York: McGraw-Hill, 1995.

Cose, Ellis. *A Nation of Strangers: Prejudice, Politics, and the Populating of America*. New York: Morrow, 1992.

Eddy, Robert, ed. *Reflections on Multiculturalism*. Yarmouth: Intercultural Press, 1996.

Gates, Henry Louis, Jr. *Loose Canons: Notes on the Culture Wars*. New York: Oxford UP, 1992.

Geyer, Georgie Anne. *Americans No More*. New York: Atlantic Monthly Press, 1996.

Graff, Gerald. *Beyond the Culture Wars*. New York: Norton, 1993.

Harris, Dean, ed. *Multiculturalism from the Margins: Non-Dominant Voices on Differences and Diversity*. Westport: Bergin & Garvey, 1995.

Nieto, S. *Affirming Diversity: The Sociopolitical Context of Multicultural Education*. New York: Longman, 1992.

Royal, Robert, ed. *Reinventing the American People: Unity and Diversity Today*. Washington, DC: Ethics and Public Policy Center, 1995.

Schlesinger, Arthur, Jr. *The Disuniting of America: Reflections on a Multicultural Society*. Knoxville, TN: Whittle Direct Books, 1991.

Thompson, Becky, and Sangeeta Tyagi. *Beyond a Dream Deferred: Multicultural Education and the Politics of Excellence*. Minneapolis: University of Minnesota Press, 1993.

Vecoli, Rudolph, ed. *Gale Encyclopedia of Multicultural America*. Detroit: Gale Research Group, 1995.

West, Cornel. *Beyond Eurocentrism and Multiculturalism*. 2 vols. Monroe, ME: Common Courage Press, 1993.

_____

_____

_____

Recommended Literature: Langston Hughes,
                          "Let America Be America Again"
                          from *International Workers Order* (poem)

The Debate Has Been Miscast from the Start

Henry Louis Gates, Jr.

Arguably the most prominent scholar of African American literature, Henry Louis Gates, Jr. chairs the Afro-American Studies Department at Harvard University, where he heads the W.E.B. Du Bois Institute for Afro-American Research. He is the author of The Signifying Monkey: Towards a Theory of Afro-American Literary Criticism, *which garnered an American Book Award in 1989. He has also edited several volumes, including* Africana: The Encyclopedia of the African and African American Experience *and the* Norton Anthology of African American Literature. *In the following essay, printed in the* Boston Globe Magazine *in October 1991, Gates musters quotations and examples to support his call for a new American identity—an identity shaped by "a civic culture that respects both differences and commonalities."*

1   What is multiculturalism and why are they saying such terrible things about it?

2   We've been told that it threatens to fragment American culture into a warren of ethnic enclaves, each separate and inviolate. We've been told that it

menaces the Western tradition of literature and the arts. We've been told that it aims to politicize the school curriculum, replacing honest historical scholarship with a "feel good" syllabus designed solely to bolster the self-esteem of minorities. The alarm has been sounded, and many scholars and educators—liberals as well as conservatives—have responded to it. After all, if multiculturalism is just a pretty name for ethnic chauvinism, who needs it?

3   But I don't think that's what multiculturalism is—at least, I don't think that's what it ought to be. And because the debate has been miscast from the beginning, it may be worth setting the main issues straight.

4   To both proponents and antagonists, multiculturalism represents—either refreshingly or frighteningly—a radical departure. Like most claims for cultural novelty, this one is more than a little exaggerated. For the challenges of cultural pluralism—and the varied forms of official resistance to it—go back to the very founding of our republic.

5   In the university today, it must be admitted, the challenge has taken on a peculiar inflection. But the underlying questions are time-tested. What does it mean to be an American? Must academic inquiry be subordinated to the requirements of national identity? Should scholarship and education reflect our actual diversity, or should they, rather, forge a communal identity that may not yet have been achieved?

6   For answers, you can, of course, turn to the latest <u>jeremiad</u> on the subject from, say, George Will, Dinesh D'Souza, or Roger Kimball. But in fact these questions have always occasioned lively disagreement among American educators. In 1917, William Henry Hulme decried "the insidious introduction into our scholarly relations of the political propaganda of a wholly narrow, selfish, and vicious nationalism and false patriotism." His opponents were equally emphatic in their beliefs. "More and more clearly," Fred Lewis Pattee ventured in 1919, "is it seen now that the American soul, the American conception of democracy, Americanism, should be made prominent in our school curriculums, as a guard against the rising spirit of experimental lawlessness." Sound familiar?

7   Given the political nature of the debate over education and the national interest, the conservative penchant for charging the multiculturalists with "politics" is a little perplexing. For conservative critics, to their credit, have never hesitated to provide a political defense of what they consider to be the "traditional" curriculum: The future of the republic, they argue, depends on the inculcation of proper civic virtues. What these virtues are is a matter of vehement dispute. But to imagine a curriculum untouched by political concerns is to imagine—as no one does—that education can take place in a vacuum.

8   So where's the beef? Granted, multiculturalism is no panacea for our social ills. We're worried when Johnny can't read. We're worried when Johnny can't add. But shouldn't we be worried, too, when Johnny tramples gravestones in a Jewish cemetery or scrawls racial epithets on a dormitory wall? And it's because we've entrusted our schools with the fashioning of a democratic

r/c is showing the society'l emphciis

polity that education has never been exempt from the kind of debate that marks every other aspect of American political life.

9   Perhaps this isn't altogether a bad thing. As the political theorist Amy Gutmann has argued: "In a democracy, political disagreement is not something that we should generally seek to avoid. Political controversies over our educational problems are a particularly important source of social progress because they have the potential for educating so many citizens."

10   And while I'm sympathetic to what Robert Nisbet once dubbed the "academic dogma"—the ideal of knowledge for its own sake—I also believe that truly humane learning, unblinkered by the constraints of narrow ethnocentrism, can't help but expand the limits of human understanding and social tolerance. Those who fear that "Balkanization" and social fragmentation lie this way have got it exactly backward. Ours is a world that already is fissured by nationality, ethnicity, race, and gender. And the only way to transcend those divisions—to forge, for once, a civic culture that respects both differences and commonalities—is through education that seeks to comprehend the diversity of human culture. Beyond the hype and the high-flown rhetoric is a pretty homely truth: There is no tolerance without respect—and no respect without knowledge.

Different
proponent

11   The historical architects of the university always understood this. As Cardinal Newman wrote more than a century ago, the university should promote "the power of viewing many things at once as one whole, of referring them severally to their true place in the universal system, of understanding their respective values, and determining their mutual dependence." In just this vein, the critic Edward Said has recently suggested that "our model for academic freedom should therefore be the migrant or traveler: for if, in the real world outside the academy, we must needs be ourselves and only ourselves, inside the academy we should be able to discover and travel among other selves, other identities, other varieties of the human adventure. But, most essentially, in this joint discovery of self and other, it is the role of the academy to transform what might be conflict, or context, or assertion into reconciliation, mutuality, recognition, creative interaction."

12   But if multiculturalism represents the culmination of an age-old ideal—the dream known, in the 17th century, as *mathesis universalis*—why has it been the target of such ferocious attacks? On this point, I'm often reminded of a wonderfully wicked piece of 19th-century student doggerel about Benjamin Jowett, the great Victorian classicist and master of Balliol College, Oxford:

> Here stand I, my name is Jowett,
> If there's knowledge, then I know it;
> I am the master of this college,
> What I know not, is not knowledge.

13   Of course, the question of how we determine what is worth knowing is now being raised with uncomfortable persistence. So that in the most spirited attacks on multiculturalism in the academy today, there's a nostalgic whiff of

the old sentiment: We are the masters of this college; what we know not is not knowledge.

14   I think this explains the conservative desire to cast the debate in terms of the West vs. the Rest. And yet that's the very opposition that the pluralist wants to challenge. Pluralism sees cultures as porous, dynamic, and interactive, rather than the fixed property of particular ethnic groups. Thus the idea of monolithic, homogeneous "West" itself comes into question (nothing new here: Literary historians have pointed out that the very concept of "Western culture" may date back only to the 18th century). But rather than mourning the loss of some putative ancestral purity, we can recognize what's valuable, resilient, even cohesive, in the hybrid and variegated nature of our modernity.

15   Genuine multiculturalism is not, of course, everyone's cup of tea. Vulgar cultural nationalists—like Allan Bloom or Leonard Jeffries—correctly identify it as the enemy. These polemicists thrive on absolute partitions: between "civilization" and "barbarism," between "black" and "white," between a thousand versions of Us and Them. But they are whistling in the wind.

16   For whatever the outcome of the culture wars in the academy, the world we live in is multicultural already. Mixing and hybridity is the rule, not the exception. As a student of African-American culture, of course, I've come to take this kind of cultural palimpsest for granted. Duke Ellington, Miles Davis, John Coltrane have influenced popular musicians the world over. Wynton Marsalis is as comfortable with Mozart as he is with jazz; Anthony Davis writes operas in a musical idiom that combines Bartok with the blues.

17   In dance, Judith Jamison, Alvin Ailey, Katherine Dunham all excelled at "Western" cultural forms, melding these with African-American styles to produce performances that were neither, and both. In painting, Romare Bearden and Jacob Lawrence, Martin Puryear and Augusta Savage learned to paint and sculpt by studying Western masters, yet each has pioneered the construction of a distinctly African-American visual art.

18   And in literature, of course, the most formally complex and compelling black writers—such as Jean Toomer, Sterling Brown, Langston Hughes, Zora Hurston, Richard Wright, Ralph Ellison, James Baldwin, and Gwendolyn Brooks—have always blended forms of Western literature with African-American vernacular and written traditions. Then, again, even a vernacular form such as the spiritual took for its texts the King James version of the Old and New Testaments. Toni Morrison's master's thesis was on Virginia Woolf and Faulkner; Rita Dove is as comfortable with German literature as she is with the blues.

19   Indeed, the greatest African-American art can be thought of as an exploration of that hyphenated space between the African and the American. As James Baldwin once reflected during his long European sojourn, "I would have to appropriate these white centuries, I would have to make them mine. I would have to accept my special attitude, my special place in this scheme, otherwise I would have no place in any scheme."

20   "Pluralism," the American philosopher John Dewey insisted early in this century, "is the greatest philosophical idea of our times." But he recognized

that it was also the greatest problem of our times: "How are we going to make the most of the new values we set on variety, difference, and individuality— how are we going to realize their possibilities in every field, and at the same time not sacrifice that plurality to the cooperation we need so much?" It has the feel of a scholastic conundrum: How can we negotiate between the one and the many?

21   Today the mindless celebration of difference has proven as untenable as that bygone model of monochrome homogeneity. If there is an equilibrium to be struck, there's no guarantee we will ever arrive at it. The worst mistake we can make, however, is not to try.

Reading-to-Write Questions

1. **Content:** How does Gates reproduce the academic conversation surrounding the issue of multiculturalism? Label his use of quotation, paraphrase, and "name-dropping."

2. **Arrangement:** Where does Gates introduce his opponents' views? Does this arrangement help Gates present his views?

3. **Style:** Occasionally, colloquialisms interrupt Gates's erudite prose. Underline the colloquial phrases. What effects do these shifts in style produce?

4. _____

   _____

   _____

Suggested Topics

1. **Observation:** According to Gates, "the greatest African-American art can be thought of as an exploration of that hyphenated space between the African and the American." To illustrate this statement, explain how a famous African American musician, dancer, artist, or writer blends African and European forms. See Gates's list for ideas. (audience = uninformed classmates)

2. **Critique:** Gates states, "Today the mindless celebration of difference has proven as untenable as that bygone model of monochrome homogeneity." Do you agree that contemporary political movements, educational reforms, or social events that celebrate ethnic differences have too often proven "mindless"? If so, after restating Gates's position, cite supporting examples from the national or local scene. If not, challenge Gates's position by citing counterexamples. (audience = readers of the op-ed page of a local newspaper)

3. **Synthesis:** Gates poses the question "What does it mean to be an American?" How have Gates, Reed, and Ellison—directly or indirectly—responded to this question from an African-American perspective? Do you share their views? Cite clarifying examples. (audience = international students on your campus)

4. _____

   _____

   _____

Background Readings: MULTICULTURALISM IN THE USA

See the reading list for Ishmael Reed's essay.

What America Would Be Like Without Blacks

Ralph Ellison

With his novel Invisible Man, *Ralph Ellison (1914–1994) won the National Book Award in 1952 and a place of honor in American literature. After the publication of the novel, he wrote short stories and two volumes of essays,* Shadow and Act *and* Going to the Territory. *Reprinted in* Going to the Territory, *the following essay originally appeared in the April 6, 1970 issue of* Time Magazine. *In the essay Ellison's examples reveal how Blacks have affected America "materially, psychologically, and culturally."*

---

1   The fantasy of an America free of blacks is at least as old as the dream of creating a truly democratic society. While we are aware that there is something inescapably tragic about the cost of achieving our democratic ideals, we keep such tragic awareness segregated to the rear of our minds. We allow it to come to the fore only during moments of great national crisis.

2   On the other hand, there is something so embarrassingly absurd about the notion of purging the nation of blacks that it seems hardly a product of thought at all. It is more like a primitive reflex, a throwback to the dim past of tribal experience which we rationalize and try to make respectable by dressing it up in the gaudy and highly questionable trappings of what we call the "concept of race." Yet, despite its absurdity, the fantasy of a blackless America continues to turn up. It is a fantasy born not merely of racism but of petulance, of exasperation, of moral fatigue. It is like a boil bursting forth from impurities in the bloodstream of democracy.

similie w/ imagery

15

3   In its benign manifestations, it can be outrageously comic—in the picturesque adventures of Percival Brownlee who appears in William Faulkner's story "The Bear." Exasperating to his white masters because his aspirations and talents are for preaching and conducting choirs rather than for farming, Brownlee is "freed" after much resistance and ends up as the prosperous proprietor of a New Orleans brothel. In Faulkner's hands, the uncomprehending drive of Brownlee's owners to "get shut" of him is comically instructive. Indeed, the story resonates certain abiding, tragic themes of American history with which it is interwoven, and which are causing great turbulence in the social atmosphere today. I refer to the exasperation and bemusement of the white American with the black, the black American's ceaseless (and swiftly accelerating) struggle to escape the misconceptions of whites, and the continual confusing of the black American's racial background with his individual culture. Most of all, I refer to the recurring fantasy of solving one basic problem of American democracy by "getting shut" of the blacks through various wishful schemes that would banish them from the nation's bloodstream, from its social structure, and from its conscience and historical consciousness.

4   This fantastic vision of a lily-white America appeared as early as 1713, with the suggestion of a white "native American," thought to be from New Jersey, that all the Negroes be given their freedom and returned to Africa. In 1777, Thomas Jefferson, while serving in the Virginia legislature, began drafting a plan for the gradual emancipation and exportation of the slaves. Nor were Negroes themselves immune to the fantasy. In 1815, Paul Cuffe, a wealthy merchant, shipbuilder, and landowner from the New Bedford area, shipped and settled at his own expense thirty-eight of his fellow Negroes in Africa. It was perhaps his example that led in the following year to the creation of the American Colonization Society, which was to establish in 1821 the colony of Liberia. Great amounts of cash and a perplexing mixture of motives went into the venture. The slaveowners and many Border-state politicians wanted to use it as a scheme to rid the country not of slaves but of the militant free Negroes who were agitating against the "peculiar institution." The abolitionists, until they took a lead from free Negro leaders and began attacking the scheme, also participated as a means of righting a great historical injustice. Many blacks went along with it simply because they were sick of the black and white American mess and hoped to prosper in the quiet peace of the old ancestral home.

5   Such conflicting motives doomed the Colonization Society to failure, but what amazes one even more than the notion that anyone could have believed in its success is the fact that it was attempted during a period when the blacks, slave and free, made up eighteen percent of the total population. When we consider how long blacks had been in the New World and had been transforming it and being Americanized by it, the scheme appears not only fantastic, but the product of a free-floating irrationality. Indeed, a national pathology.

6   Nevertheless, some of the noblest of Americans were bemused. Not only Jefferson but later Abraham Lincoln was to give the scheme credence. Accord-

ing to historian John Hope Franklin, Negro colonization seemed as important to Lincoln as emancipation. In 1862, Franklin notes, Lincoln called a group of prominent free Negroes to the White House and urged them to support colonization, telling them, "Your race suffers greatly, many of them by living among us, while ours suffers from your presence. If this is admitted, it affords a reason why we should be separated."

7   In spite of his unquestioned greatness, Abraham Lincoln was a man of his times and limited by some of the less worthy thinking of his times. This is demonstrated both by his reliance upon the concept of race in his analysis of the American dilemma and by his involvement in a plan of purging the nation of blacks as a means of healing the badly shattered ideals of democratic federalism. Although benign, his motive was no less a product of fantasy. It envisaged an attempt to relieve an inevitable suffering that marked the growing pains of the youthful body politic by an operation which would have amounted to the severing of a healthy and indispensable member.

8   Yet, like its twin, the illusion of secession, the fantasy of a benign amputation that would rid the country of black men to the benefit of a nation's health not only persists; today, in the form of neo-Garveyism, it fascinates black men no less than it once hypnotized whites. Both fantasies become operative whenever the nation grows weary of the struggle toward the ideal of American democratic equality. Both would use the black man as a scapegoat to achieve a national catharsis, and both would, by way of curing the patient, destroy him.

9   What is ultimately intriguing about the fantasy of "getting shut" of the Negro American is the fact that no one who entertains it seems ever to have considered what the nation would have become had Africans *not* been brought to the New World, and had their descendants not played such a complex and confounding role in the creation of American history and culture. Nor do they appear to have considered with any seriousness the effect upon the nation of having any of the schemes for exporting blacks succeed beyond settling some fifteen thousand or so in Liberia.

10   We are reminded that Daniel Patrick Moynihan, who has recently aggravated our social confusion over the racial issue while allegedly attempting to clarify it, is coauthor of a work which insists that the American melting pot didn't melt because our white ethnic groups have resisted all assimilative forces that appear to threaten their identities. The problem here is that few Americans know who and what they really are. That is why few of these groups—or at least few of the children of these groups—have been able to resist the movies, television, baseball, jazz, football, drum-majoretting, rock, comic strips, radio commercials, soap operas, book clubs, slang, or any of a thousand other expressions and carriers of our pluralistic and easily available popular culture. And it is here precisely that ethnic resistance is least effective. On this level the melting pot did indeed melt, creating such deceptive metamorphoses and blending of identities, values, and lifestyles that most American whites are culturally part Negro American without even realizing it.

11   If we can resist for a moment the temptation to view everything having to do with Negro Americans in terms of their racially imposed status, we become aware of the fact that for all the harsh reality of the social and economic injustices visited upon them, these injustices have failed to keep Negroes clear of the cultural mainstream; Negro Americans are in fact one of its major tributaries. If we can cease approaching American social reality in terms of such false concepts as white and nonwhite, black culture and white culture, and think of these apparently unthinkable matters in the realistic manner of Western pioneers confronting the unknown prairie, perhaps we can begin to imagine what the United States would have been, or not been, had there been no blacks to give it—if I may be so bold as to say—color.

12   For one thing, the American nation is in a sense the product of the American language, a colloquial speech that began emerging long before the British colonials and Africans were transformed into Americans. It is a language that evolved from the king's English but, basing itself upon the realities of the American land and colonial institutions—or lack of institutions, began quite early as a vernacular revolt against the signs, symbols, manners, and authority of the mother country. It is a language that began by merging the sounds of many tongues, brought together in the struggle of diverse regions. And whether it is admitted or not, much of the sound of that language is derived from the timbre of the African voice and the listening habits of the African ear. So there is a *de'z* and *do'z* of slave speech sounding beneath our most polished Harvard accents, and if there is such a thing as a Yale accent, there is a Negro wail in it—doubtlessly introduced there by Old Yalie John C. Calhoun, who probably got it from his mammy.

13   Whitman viewed the spoken idiom of Negro Americans as a source for a native grand opera. Its flexibility, its musicality, its rhythms, freewheeling diction, and metaphors, as projected in Negro American folklore, were absorbed by the creators of our great nineteenth-century literature even when the majority of blacks were still enslaved. Mark Twain celebrated it in the prose of *Huckleberry Finn*; without the presence of blacks, the book could not have been written. No Huck and Jim, no American novel as we know it. For not only is the black man a co-creator of the language that Mark Twain raised to the level of literary eloquence, but Jim's condition as American and Huck's commitment to freedom are at the moral center of the novel.

14   In other words, had there been no blacks, certain creative tensions arising from the cross-purposes of whites and blacks would also not have existed. Not only would there have been no Faulkner; there would have been no Stephen Crane, who found certain basic themes of his writing in the Civil War. Thus, also, there would have been no Hemingway, who took Crane as a source and guide. Without the presence of Negro American style, our jokes, our tall tales, even our sports would be lacking in the sudden turns, the shocks, the swift changes of pace (all jazz-shaped) that serve to remind us that the world is ever unexplored, and that while a complete mastery of life is mere illusion, the real secret of the game is to make life swing. It is its ability to articulate this tragic-

comic attitude toward life that explains much of the mysterious power and attractiveness of that quality of Negro American style known as "soul." An expression of American diversity within unity, of blackness with whiteness, soul announces the presence of a creative struggle against the realities of existence.

15   Without the presence of blacks, our political history would have been otherwise. No slave economy, no Civil War; no violent destruction of the Reconstruction, no K.K.K. and no Jim Crow system. And without the disenfranchisement of black Americans and the manipulation of racial fears and prejudices, the disproportionate impact of white Southern politicians upon our domestic and foreign policies would have been impossible. Indeed, it is almost impossible to conceive of what our political system would have become without the snarl of forces—cultural, racial, religious—that make our nation what it is today.

16   Absent, too, would be the need for that tragic knowledge which we try ceaselessly to evade: that the true subject of democracy is not simply material well-being but the extension of the democratic process in the direction of perfecting itself. And that the most obvious test and clue to that perfection is the inclusion—*not* assimilation—of the black man.

17   Since the beginning of the nation, white Americans have suffered from a deep inner uncertainty as to who they really are. One of the ways that has been used to simplify the answer has been to seize upon the presence of black Americans and use them as a marker, a symbol of limits, a metaphor for the "outsider." Many whites could look at the social position of blacks and feel that color formed an easy and reliable gauge for determining to what extent one was or was not American. Perhaps that is why one of the first epithets that many European immigrants learned when they got off the boat was the term "nigger"—it made them feel instantly American. But this is tricky magic. Despite his racial difference and social status, something indisputably American about Negroes not only raised doubts about the white man's value system but aroused the troubling suspicion that whatever else the true American is, he is also somehow black.

18   Materially, psychologically, and culturally, part of the nation's heritage is Negro American, and whatever it becomes will be shaped in part by the Negro's presence. Which is fortunate, for today it is the black American who puts pressure upon the nation to live up to its ideals. It is he who gives creative tension to our struggle for justice and for the elimination of those factors, social and psychological, which make for slums and shaky suburban communities. It is he who insists that we purify the American language by demanding that there be a closer correlation between the meaning of words and reality, between ideal and conduct, our assertions and our actions. Without the black American, something irrepressibly hopeful and creative would go out of the American spirit, and the nation might well succumb to the moral slobbism that has ever threatened its existence from within.

19   When we look objectively at how the dry bones of the nation were hung together, it seems obvious that some one of the many groups that compose the

United States had to suffer the fate of being allowed no easy escape from experiencing the harsh realities of the human condition as they were to exist under even so fortunate a democracy as ours. It would seem that some one group had to be stripped of the possibility of escaping such tragic knowledge by taking sanctuary in moral equivocation, racial chauvinism, or the advantage of superior social status. There is no point in complaining over the past or apologizing for one's fate. But for blacks, there are no hiding places down here, not in suburbia or in penthouse, neither in country nor in city. They are an American people who are geared to what is and who yet are driven by a sense of what it is possible for human life to be in this society. The nation could not survive being deprived of their presence because, by the irony implicit in the dynamics of American democracy, they symbolize both its most stringent testing and the possibility of its greatest human freedom.

Reading-to-Write Questions

1. **Content:** According to Ellison, what impact have Black people had upon America? Identify each effect.

2. **Arrangement:** Where is Ellison's thesis? Why do you think he postpones it?

3. **Style:** What metaphors and similes does Ellison employ? How does he extend a metaphor?

4. _____

   _____

   _____

Suggested Topics

1. **Observation:** Discuss in greater detail the African American influence in ONE of the areas mentioned by Ellison (e.g., language or politics). (audience = Ellison's *Time Magazine* readers)

2. **Critique:** Briefly summarize Ellison's essay, including his opinion that dichotomies such as black culture and white culture are "false concepts." Are they false? Or are black and white culture in America different enough to justify this distinction? Does Ellison offer enough evidence to support his view? Write your response. (audience = Ellison's readers)

3. **Synthesis:** Ellison claims that popular culture in America is a melting pot that creates "such deceptive metamorphoses and blending of identities, values, and lifestyles that most American whites are culturally part Negro American without even realizing it." Illustrate this point through examples culled from Reed's, Gates's, and Baldwin's essays. You may also add examples from your own examination of popular culture (e.g., language, fashion, music, movies). (audience = White Americans)

4. _____

   _____

   _____

Background Readings: THE AFRICAN AMERICAN CONTRIBUTION

Drotning, Phillip T. *Black Heroes in Our Nation's History; A Tribute to Those Who Helped Shape America.* New York: Cowles, 1969.

Gates, Henry Louis, Jr., and Cornel West. *The African American Century: How Black Americans Have Shaped Our Country.* NY: The Free Press, 2000.

Lanker, Brian. *I Dream a World: Portraits of Black Women Who Changed America.* New York: Stewart, Tabori & Chang, 1989.

Quarles, Benjamin. *The Negro in the Making of America.* 3rd ed. NY: Touchstone Books, 1996.

Roucek, Joseph S., and Thomas Kiernan, eds. *The Negro Impact on Western Civilization.* New York: Philosophical Library, 1970.

Van Sertima, ed. *Blacks in Science: Ancient and Modern.* New Brunswick, NJ: Transaction, 1983.

_____

_____

_____

Recommended Literature: George Schuyler, *Black No More* (novel)

Douglas Turner Ward, *Day of Absence* (play)

Student Essay:
A TRAVESTY OF JUSTICE:
THE DIALLO TRIAL

Kela Francis

(2000)

. . . Give me your tired, your poor
Your huddled masses yearning to breathe free,
The wretched refuse of your teeming shore.
Send these, the homeless, tempest-tost, to me,
I lift my lamp beside the golden door.

---

1   The Statue of Liberty raises her torch in welcome for all to see. Even today, millions of immigrants still flock to these shores. After all, they were promised never to be turned away. America was created this way. The very essence of American culture is the immigrant, not one specific ethnicity, but all kinds. Not everyone recognizes this; most simply choose to ignore the truth. Instead, they insist on a "lily-white" America, a monoculture that does not exist. It has been so for generation upon generation. Today, America still suffers from the fantasy of a lily-white America formed from its puritanical roots, an unwillingness to accept its multiculturalism.

2   America's value systems were formed by the Puritans. They are still considered the first "American" settlers, even revered for their ethics. The Puritans were hard-working honest people. They were "a 'hardy band' of no-nonsense patriarchs," according to our textbooks, "virtuous . . . pious" who "brought order to the New World" (Reed 5). From their determination to conquer and control their environment through hard work, America got its work ethics. Their religious fervor influenced American morals and attitudes. However, America's penchant for persecuting groups classed as foreign or

"other" is also a retention of Puritan Politics, their "mean streak," according to Ishmael Reed. At fault is their "bizarre and irrational" behavior towards those they considered "aliens" (6). Their fear of outsiders is deeply engraved in America, a fear directed especially towards people who look "alien," i.e., those people whose ideals and appearance are not European. The fear is seen today when white women clutch their purses in response to a black man's approach. This irrational stereotyping was founded in Puritan beliefs.

3   Arising from this foundation is America's need to segregate, the need for an "us" and "them" manifested in the racism that exists today. The obviously "alien" Black Man, therefore, could not have contributed to the mainstream. As Ralph Ellison suggests, White Americans claim that they have "resisted all assimilative forces," believing that Black Americans are not part of the mainstream, the monoculture such people think exists in America (17). Therefore, the Black Man, the "alien," is the "other," the "them," a separate class subordinated and xenophobically oppressed. To support this separation, to enhance segregation, the descendants of the Puritans—the white ethnic groups of America—established stereotypes about the rest of the melting pot. They classified all non-whites as lazy and unproductive, to be frank, as non-Puritans. As a result of such stereotypes, the Black Man is neither appreciated nor protected. As a result of such derogatory classifications, the Black Man is feared; he appears to threaten the White Man's status and identity. White America projected all negative aspects of human nature onto the Black Man. Even today, in the media and in White America's subconscious, the Black Man, any and every Black Man, is threatening. Such stereotypes are continually passed down, as common lore, from fathers to sons.

4   So when a black man, Amadou Diallo, standing in the vestibule of his apartment building, trying to get inside, is stopped by four "plain clothes" policemen; when he reaches into his back pocket for his wallet and is shot at 41 times and hit 19 times; when these four white police officers are acquitted of the crime, it could only be explained by this common lore (Harkavy).

5   Therefore, the question cannot be whether the four young officers were explicitly racist or not. They suffer from the same malady as the mainstream that refuses to acknowledge its major tributary. The assumption that Diallo was not one of "us," that he was an alien threat, stems from the stereotype of the Black Man. The mere fact that the officers claimed that he resembled a rapist they were looking for (not to mention the fact that the jury believed that these officers should have been genuinely worried about Diallo's wallet being a gun) is an example of the reigning stereotype of the threatening Black Male. Like the Puritans who persecuted "others" before questioning, these four officers opened fire without questioning. It is as though these four young men were on a witch-hunt. They are expressions of monoculturalism to the extreme. They maintained, like the rest of the American "mainstream," "strange and paranoid attitudes toward those different from the Elect" (Reed 6). Perhaps the fantasy of "getting shut" of the Black Man, as described by Ellison, is still prevalent in America today (16). Even if their desire is not as extreme as that of

the Ku Klux Klan or white supremacists, most white Americans still prefer to "get shut" of the Black Man via these stereotypes, via their xenophobia, to preserve "lily-white" America.

6   Despite the calls by Ralph Ellison, Ishmael Reed, Henry Louis Gates, Jr., Martin Luther King, Jr., Jesse Jackson, and so many others, for America to embrace its multiculturalism, the fantasy of a "lily-white" America persists. Those four officers would never have been acquitted if the stereotype of the Black Man had not been perpetuated in America's subconscious. The Diallo decision is a step backwards, away from America accepting its true heritage, both black and white. Perhaps then, the words inscribed on the Statue of Liberty should be amended.

Works Cited

Ellison, Ralph. "What America Would Be Like Without Blacks." *Revelations*. Ed. Teresa M. Redd. 3rd ed. Needham Heights, MA: Simon & Schuster, 1997. 15–22.

Harkavy, Ward. "The Diallo Index." *Village Voice* 9 Feb. 2000. 15 Oct. 2000. <http://www.villagevoice.com/issues/0006/harkavy.shtml>.

Reed, Ishmael. "America: The Multicultural Society." *Revelations*. Ed. Teresa M. Redd. 3rd ed. Needham Heights, MA: Simon & Schuster, 1997. 3–8.

Student Essay:
THE AMERICAN DREAM
Kenya Doyle
(2000)

1   Growing up relatively poor in Brooklyn (we were on welfare and our back-yard was the train track), my family has only recently begun to realize the American dream. Certain changes that have occurred within the last ten years contributed to our realization of the dream. The year 1990 marked my parents' separation and the beginning of our American dream. My mother returned to school and received her master's degree from Columbia University Teacher's College, proving that, through hard work and sacrifice, one can succeed in this country. Only one decade after leaving our one-bedroom, roach-infested, Flat-bush apartment, my mother purchased a new car, took our family to Brazil for summer vacation, and enrolled a daughter in college. Clearly, it appears as though my mother has fulfilled some aspect of the dream.

2   The typical American ideal has traditionally been thought of as having a house in the suburbs, three children, and a dog. Jay Ford's dream, for example, was this ideal, in addition to travelling to Europe, getting a college degree, and marrying a white or light-skinned black woman (33). However, this is not all that the dream entails. The goal is to become middle to upper middle class. This status can be characterized by having money for the children's college education as well as extra-curricular activities like ballet, karate, and violin lessons, one or two cars, leisure vacations, a summer home, a retirement fund, and most importantly, social mobility. Education is viewed as the most impor-tant aspect of the American dream because it provides social mobility. The aspiration is to have each successive generation build on the wealth and increase social status.

3   Aside from social and material status, a key part of the American dream is cultural assimilation. America has been called the "melting pot," where many different cultures come together and become American. Whether one's ances-try is Irish, Italian, or English, one becomes American after successive genera-tions. Many immigrants desire assimilation so that they are not in the margins of American society and they can gain cultural acceptance.

4   Since I grew up in America, my values and ideals for the American dream
are very similar to those of white Americans. I want to have the best there is to
offer in terms of housing, education, occupation, and travel. However, I also
feel an immense obligation to use my talent and opportunity to help others
who are less fortunate. For many black families (and this is also true for many
white families), it has only been the first, second, or third generation that has
become college-educated. Therefore, many of us do not have a strong hold on
middle-class status. If *we* are unstable in this aspect, conditions are many times
worse for those without a college education. This is why I feel obliged to help
other blacks who are less fortunate. I also feel that it is necessary to teach my
children to reject the ideal of materialism and focus on more important and
pressing ideals like humanism. Part of my American dream is to ensure that
my children are exposed to the wide range of human struggles throughout the
world and to have them realize that there are more pressing issues than material wealth and material things. This is the ideal that Ford believes Kenyans
have and Americans lack (39). It is true to some extent because many Americans tend to focus on individual achievement and wealth rather than community achievement. My American dream is to combine all of the positive aspects
and opportunities of American society with a value for people and life.

5   My goal differs from the typical American dream in that I do not want to
achieve assimilation. Blacks will probably continue to be seen as African
Americans and not as just American. For these reasons, as well as cultural reasons, I have no desire to become part of the "melting pot." To assimilate is to
lose sight of one's cultural heritage, and I think it is very important for blacks
to keep sight of their cultural heritage. It is especially important for them
because they were told for so long that they had no culture or history. I think
it is important for my children to be aware of the black struggle and their cultural past.

6   Today, the term *white* American dream may no longer be appropriate
because it has become the standard for most Americans, regardless of color.
Most new immigrants have the same goal of getting jobs, providing a good
education for their children, buying a house, and being socially mobile. This
has become the dream of many Americans and the ideal to which many aspire.
This was the ideal that my mother aspired to and succeeded in fulfilling. However, while embracing the American dream, Americans should keep sight of
their cultural values and ideals and integrate them into their dream.

Works Cited

Ford, Jay. "20/20 Hindsight." *Revelations.* Ed. Teresa M. Redd. 3rd ed. Need-
      ham Heights, MA: Simon & Schuster, 1997. 33–39.

african roots: comparison-contrast

What is Africa to me:
Copper sun or scarlet sea,
Jungle star or jungle track,
Strong bronzed men, or regal black
Women from whose loins I sprang
When the birds of Eden sang?
One three centuries removed
From the scenes his fathers loved,
Spicy grove, cinnamon tree,
What is Africa to me?

from "Heritage" by Countee Cullen

Some African Cultural Concepts
Steve Biko

South African activist Steve Biko (1946–1977) studied medicine and law, worked in the Black Community Programs of South Africa, and helped found the South African Students Organization (SASO), which advocated a philosophy of Black Consciousness. Because of his political activities, Biko was arrested, tortured, and beaten to death by four policemen. The following selection is a paper he read at a conference of Black cultural, educational, and religious organizations in Natal, South Africa in 1971. In this paper, Biko contrasts African and Western culture, sometimes implicitly referring to Western beliefs by saying what Africans do not believe.

---

1   One of the most difficult things to do these days is to talk with authority on anything to do with African culture. Somehow Africans are not expected to have any deep understanding of their own culture or even of themselves. Other people have become authorities on all aspects of the African life or to be more accurate on BANTU life. Thus we have the thickest of volumes on some of the strangest subjects—even "the feeding habits of the Urban Africans," a publication by a fairly "liberal" group, Institute of Race Relations.

2   In my opinion it is not necessary to talk with Africans about African culture. However, in the light of the above statements one realises that there is so much confusion sown, not only amongst casual non-African readers, but even

31

amongst Africans themselves, that perhaps a sincere attempt should be made   thesis
at emphasising the authentic cultural aspects of the African people by Africans
themselves.

3   Since that unfortunate date—1652—we have been experiencing a process of
acculturation. It is perhaps presumptuous to call it "acculturation" because
this term implies a fusion of different cultures. In our case this fusion has been
extremely one-sided. The two major cultures that met and "fused" were the
African Culture and the Anglo-Boer Culture. Whereas the African culture was
unsophisticated and simple, the Anglo-Boer culture had all the trappings of a
colonialist culture and therefore was heavily equipped for conquest. Where
they could, they conquered by persuasion, using a highly exclusive religion
that denounced all other Gods and demanded a strict code of behaviour with
respect to clothing, education, ritual and custom. Where it was impossible to
convert, fire-arms were readily available and used to advantage. Hence the
Anglo-Boer culture was the more powerful culture in almost all facets. This is
where the African began to lose a grip on himself and his surroundings.

4   Thus in taking a look at cultural aspects of the African people one
inevitably finds himself having to compare. This is primarily because of the
contempt that the "superior" culture shows towards the indigenous culture.
To justify its exploitative basis, the Anglo-Boer culture has at all times been
directed at bestowing an inferior status to all cultural aspects of the indigenous people.

5   I am against the belief that African culture is time-bound, the notion that
with the conquest of the African all his culture was obliterated. I am also
against the belief that when one talks of African culture one is necessarily talking of the pre-Van Riebeeck culture. Obviously the African culture has had to
sustain severe blows and may have been battered nearly out of shape by the
belligerent cultures it collided with, yet in essence even today one can easily
find the fundamental aspects of the pure African culture in the present day
African. Hence in taking a look at African culture I am going to refer as well to
what I have termed the modern African culture.

6   One of the most fundamental aspects of our culture is the importance we   point 1
attach to Man. Ours has always been a Man-centred society. Westerners have   subject A
on many occasions been surprised at the capacity we have for talking to each
other—not for the sake of arriving at a particular conclusion but merely to
enjoy the communication for its own sake. Intimacy is a term not exclusive for
particular friends but applying to a whole group of people who find themselves together either through work or through residential requirements.

7   In fact in the traditional African culture, there is no such thing as two
friends. Conversation groups were more or less naturally determined by age
and division of labour. Thus one would find all boys whose job was to look
after cattle periodically meeting at popular spots to engage in conversation
about their cattle, girlfriends, parents, heroes etc. All commonly shared their
secrets, joys and woes. No one felt unnecessarily an intruder into someone
else's business. The curiosity manifested was welcome. It came out of a desire

to share. This pattern one would find in all age groups. House visiting was always a feature of the elderly folk's way of life. No reason was needed as a basis for visits. It was all part of our deep concern for each other.

8   These are things never done in the <u>Westerner's</u> culture. A visitor to someone's house, with the exception of friends, is always met with the question "what can I do for you?". This attitude to see people not as themselves but as agents for some particular function either to one's disadvantage or advantage is foreign to us. We are not a suspicious race. We believe in the inherent goodness of man. We enjoy man for himself. We regard our living together not as an unfortunate mishap warranting endless competition among us, but as a deliberate act of God to make us a community of brothers and sisters jointly involved in the quest for a composite answer to the varied problems of life. Hence in all we do we always place Man first, and hence all our action is usually joint community oriented action rather than the individualism which is the hallmark of the capitalist approach. We always refrain from using people as stepping stones. Instead we are prepared to have a much slower progress in an effort to make sure that all of us are marching to the same tune.   *subject B*

9   Nothing dramatises the eagerness of the African to communicate with each other more than their love for song and rhythm. <u>Music</u> in the <u>African</u> culture features in all emotional states. When we go to work, we share the burdens and pleasures of the work we are doing through music. This particular facet strangely enough has filtered through to the present day. Tourists always watch with amazement the synchrony of music and action as Africans working at a road side use their picks and shovels with well-timed precision to the accompaniment of a background song. Battle songs were a feature of the long march to war in the olden days. Girls and boys never played any game without using music and rhythm as its basis. In other words with Africans, music and rhythm were not luxuries but part and parcel of our way of communication. Any suffering we experienced was made much more real by song and rhythm. There is no doubt that the so called "Negro spirituals" sung by Black slaves in the States as they toiled under oppression were indicative of their African heritage.   *point 2*
    subject A

10   The major thing to note about our songs is that they <u>never were songs for individuals.</u> All African songs are group songs. Though many have words, this is not the most important thing about them. Tunes were adapted to suit the occasion and had the wonderful effect of making everybody read the same things from the common experience. In war the songs reassured those who were scared, highlighted the determination of the regiment to win a particular encounter and made much more urgent the need to settle the score; in suffering, as in the case of the Black slaves, they derived sustenance out of a feeling of togetherness, at work the binding rhythm makes everybody brush off the burden and hence Africans can continue for hours on end because of this added energy.   *subject B*
    (implied)

11   Attitudes of <u>Africans</u> to <u>property</u> again show just how unindividualistic the African is. As everybody here knows, African society had the village commu-   *point 3*
    subject A

nity as its basis. Africans always believed in having many villages with a controllable number of people in each rather than the reverse. This obviously was a requirement to suit the needs of a community-based and man-centred society. Hence most things were jointly owned by the group, for instance there was <u>no such thing as individual land ownership.</u> The land belonged to the people and was merely under the control of the local chief on behalf of the people. When cattle went to graze it was on an open field and <u>not on anybody's specific farm.</u>

subject B
(implied)

12   Farming and agriculture, though on individual family basis, had many characteristics of joint efforts. Each person could by a simple request and holding of a special ceremony, invite neighbours to come and work on his plots. This service was returned in kind and <u>no remuneration was ever given.</u>

13   Poverty was a foreign concept. This could only be really brought about to the entire community by an adverse climate during a particular season. It <u>never was considered repugnant to ask one's neighbors for help</u> if one was struggling. In almost all instances there was help between individuals, tribe and tribe, chief and chief etc. even in spite of war.

14   Another important aspect of the African culture is our mental <u>attitude</u> to problems presented by life in general. Whereas the <u>Westerner</u> is geared to use a problem-solving approach following very trenchant analyses, <u>our</u> approach is that of situation-experiencing. I will quote from Dr. Kaunda to illustrate this point:

point 4
subject B
subject A

> The Westerner has an aggressive mentality. When he sees a problem he will not rest until he has formulated some solution to it. He cannot live with contradictory ideas in his mind; he must settle for one or the other or else evolve a third idea in his mind which harmonises or reconciles the other two. And he is vigorously scientific in rejecting solutions for which there is no basis in logic. He draws a sharp line between the natural and the supernatural, the rational and non-rational, and more often than not, he dismisses the supernatural and non-rational as superstition. . . .
>
> Africans being a prescientific people do not recognize any conceptual cleavage between the natural and supernatural. They experience a situation rather than face a problem. By this I mean they allow both the rational and non-rational elements to make an impact upon them, and any action they

may take could be described more as a response of the total personality to the situation than the result of some mental exercise.

15   This I find a most apt analysis of the essential difference in the approach to life of these two groups. We as a community are prepared to accept that nature will have its enigmas which are beyond our powers to solve. Many people have interpreted this attitude as lack of initiative and drive, yet in spite of my belief in the strong need for scientific experimentation, I cannot help feeling that more time also should be spent in teaching man and man to live together, and that perhaps the African personality with its attitude of laying less stress on power and more stress on man is well on the way to solving our confrontation problems.

16   All people are agreed that <u>Africans</u> are a deeply <u>religious</u> race. In the various forms of worship that one found throughout the Southern part of our Continent there was at least a common basis. We all accepted without any doubt the existence of a God. We had our own community of saints. We believed—and this was consistent with our views of life—that all people who died had a special place next to God. We felt that a communication with God could only be through these people. We <u>never knew anything about hell</u>—we do not believe that God can create people only to punish them eternally after a short period on earth.

point 5
subject A

subject B
(implied
at first)

17   Another aspect of religious practices was the occasion of worship. Again we did <u>not believe that religion could be featured as a separate part of our existence on earth.</u> It was manifest in our daily lives. We thanked God through our ancestors before we drank beer, married, worked etc. We would obviously find it artificial to create special occasions for worship. <u>Neither did we see it logical to have a particular building</u> in which all worship would be conducted. We believed that God was always in communication with us and therefore merited attention everywhere and anywhere.

18   It was the <u>missionaries</u> who confused our people with their new religion. By some strange logic, they argued that theirs was a scientific religion and ours was mere superstition in spite of the biological discrepancies so obvious in the basis of their religion. They further went on to preach a theology of the existence of hell, scaring our fathers and mothers with stories about burning in eternal flames and gnashing of teeth and grinding of bone. This cold cruel religion was strange to us, but our forefathers were sufficiently scared of the unknown impending anger to believe that it was worth a try. Down went our cultural values!

19   Yet it is difficult to kill the African heritage. There remains, in spite of the superficial cultural similarities between the detribalised and the Westerner, a number of cultural characteristics that mark out the detribalised as an African. I am not here making a case for separation on the basis of cultural differences. I am sufficiently proud to believe that under a normal situation, Africans can

comfortably stay with people of other cultures and be able to contribute to the joint cultures of the communities they have joined. However, what I want to illustrate here is that even in a pluralistic society like ours, there are still some cultural traits that we can boast of which have been able to withstand the process of deliberate bastardisation. These are aspects of the modern African culture—a culture that has used concepts from the white world to expand on inherent cultural characteristics.

20   Thus we see that in the area of music, the African still expresses himself with conviction. The craze about jazz arises out of a conversion by the African artists of mere notes to meaningful music, expressive of real feelings. The Monkey Jive, Soul etc. are all aspects of modern type African culture that expresses the same original feelings. Solos like those of Pat Boone and Elvis Presley could never really find expression within the African culture because it is not in us to listen passively to pure musical notes. Yet when soul struck with its all-engulfing rhythm it immediately caught on and set hundreds of millions of black bodies in gyration throughout the world. These were people reading in soul the real meaning—the defiant message "say it loud! I'm black and I'm proud". This is fast becoming our modern culture. A culture of defiance, self-assertion and group pride and solidarity. This is a culture that emanates from a situation of common experience of oppression. Just as it now finds expression in our music and our dress, it will spread to other aspects. This is the new and modern black culture to which we have given a major contribution. This is the modern black culture that is responsible for the restoration of our faith in ourselves and therefore offers a hope in the direction we are taking from here.

21   Thus in its entirety the <u>African</u> Culture spells us out as people particularly close to <u>nature</u>. As Kaunda puts it, our people may be unlettered and their physical horizons may be limited yet "they inhabit a larger world than the sophisticated <u>Westerner</u> who has magnified his physical senses through inverted gadgets at the price all too often of cutting out the dimension of the spiritual." This close proximity to Nature enables the emotional component in us to be so much richer in that it makes it possible for us, without any apparent difficulty to feel for people and to easily identify with them in any emotional situation arising out of suffering.   point 6
    subject A

    subject B

22   The advent of the Western Culture has changed our outlook almost drastically. No more could we run our own affairs. We were required to fit in as people tolerated with great restraint in a western type society. We were tolerated simply because our cheap labour is needed. Hence we are judged in terms of standards we are not responsible for. Whenever colonisation sets in with its dominant culture it devours the native culture and leaves behind a bastardised culture that can only thrive at the rate and pace allowed it by the dominant culture. This is what has happened to the African culture. It is called a sub-culture purely because the African people in the urban complexes are mimicking the white man rather unashamedly.

23   In rejecting Western values, therefore, we are rejecting those things that are not only foreign to us but that seek to destroy the most cherished of our beliefs—that the cornerstone of society is man himself—not just his welfare, not his material well being but just man himself with all his ramifications. We reject the power-based society of the Westerner that seems to be ever concerned with perfecting their technological know-how while losing out on their spiritual dimension. We believe that in the long run the special contribution to the world by Africa will be in this field of human relationship. The great powers of the world may have done wonders in giving the world an industrial and military look, but the great gift still has to come from Africa—giving the world a more human face.

Reading-to-Write Questions

1. **Content:** Where do you think Biko overgeneralizes? How could he limit his generalizations?

2. **Arrangement:** Biko follows a point-by-point pattern of organization, but sometimes he implicitly refers to Western beliefs by saying what Africans do NOT believe. What are the advantages and disadvantages of indirectly referring to the West?

3. **Style:** In the concluding paragraph, how does Biko employ the conjunctions "not only . . . but" and "but" to dramatize the major differences between African and Western beliefs?

4. _____

    _____

    _____

Suggested Topics

1. **Observation:** Interview an African student on your campus. Compare and contrast his/her cultural values with yours. (audience = class)

2. **Critique:** Summarize Biko's claims about Western society. Then, comparing his claims to your views of the West, consider whether Biko presents a distorted or realistic picture of Western culture. (audience = defenders of Western culture)

3. **Synthesis:** Biko looks at Africa and the West through African eyes, while Ford looks at them through African American eyes. How do their perspectives differ? (audience = African American readers)

4. _____

    _____

    _____

Background Readings: AFRICAN CULTURAL CONCEPTS

African Systems of Thought Series. Bloomington: Indiana UP, 1980–1997.

Asante, Molefi Kete and Kariamu, eds. *African Culture: Rhythms of Unity.* Trenton, NJ: Africa World Press, 1989.

Diop, Cheik A. *Cultural Unity of Black Africa.* 2nd ed. Chicago: Third World Press, 1978.

Lamb, David. "Culture Shock." *The Africans.* New York: Random House, 1982. 226–242.

Mazrui, Ali. *The Africans: A Triple Heritage.* Boston: Little, Brown, 1986.

Osei, Gabriel Kingsley. *The African Philosophy of Life.* London: The African Publication Society, 1971.

Sofola, J.A. *African Culture and the African Personality.* Ibadan, Nigeria: African Resources, 1973.

_____

_____

_____

Recommended Literature: Chinua Achebe, *Things Fall Apart* (novel)

African Roots of the African American Family
Joseph White

A professor of psychology and psychiatry, Joseph White has written extensively about the mental health of African Americans and adolescents. Among his publications are the books Black Man Emerging, The Troubled Adolescent, *and* The Psychology of Blacks: An Afro-American Perspective. *The latter, published in 1984, is the source of the following excerpt on the Black family. Here White, proceeding subject by subject (instead of point by point), contrasts two models of the African American family to demonstrate that the African American family must be seen in relation to its African roots.*

The Deficit-Deficiency Model

1 <u>The view of the core structure of the Black family as an extended family grouping is not shared by all observers.</u> The traditional view of the Black family, which has evolved from the works of Frazier (1939), Elkins (1968), Moynihan (1965), and Rainwater (1970), is one of a disorganized, single-parent, subnuclear, female-dominated social system. This is essentially the deficit-deficiency model of Black family life. The deficit-deficiency model begins with <u>the historical assumption that there was no carry-over from Africa</u> to America of any sophisticated African-based form of family life and communal living. Viable patterns of family life either did not exist because Africans were incapable of

subject A
thesis

point 1

creating them, <u>or they were destroyed beginning with slavery and the separa-</u>   point 2
<u>tion of biological parents and children, forced breeding, the master's sexual</u>
<u>exploitation of Black women, and the accumulative effects of three hundred</u>
<u>years of economic and social discrimination</u>. As a result of this background of
servitude, deprivation, second-class citizenship, and chronic unemployment,
<u>Black adults have not been able to develop marketable skills, self-sufficiency,</u>
<u>future orientation, and planning and decision-making competencies, instru-</u>
<u>mental behaviors thought to be necessary for sustaining a successful two-</u>   point 3
<u>parent nuclear family</u> while guiding the children through the socialization
process.

2   In a society that placed a premium on decisive male leadership in the family, <u>the Black male was portrayed as lacking the masculine sex role behaviors</u>
<u>characterized by logical thinking, willingness to take responsibility for oth-</u>
<u>ers, assertiveness, managerial skills, achievement orientation, and occupa-</u>
<u>tional mastery</u>. The Black male in essence had been psychologically castrated
and rendered ineffective by forces beyond his control. He is absent within the
family circle and unable to provide leadership and command respect when
he is present. After generations of being unable to achieve the ideal male role
in the family and in American society, the Black male is likely to be inclined
to compensate for his failure by pursuing roles such as the pimp, player, hustler, and sweet daddy, which are in conflict with the norms of the larger society. The appearance of these roles in male behavior in the Black community,
rather than being interpreted as a form of social protest, reinforces the majority culture stereotypes of Black males as irresponsible, lazy, shiftless, and
sociopathic.

3   <u>The Black woman</u> does not fare much better in terms of how she is portrayed in the deficit-deficiency model of Black family life. <u>She is regarded as</u>
<u>the head of the household,</u> a matriarch who initially received her power
because the society was unwilling to permit the Black male to assume the
legal, economic, and social positions necessary to become a dominant force
within the family and community life. Having achieved this power by default,
the Black female is unwilling to share it. Her unwillingness to share her power
persists even when the Black male is present and willing to assume responsibility in the family circle, since she is not confident of the male's ability to follow through on his commitments. Confrontation over decision making and
family direction is usually not necessary because the Black male is either not
present in the household on any ongoing basis or is regarded as ineffective by
the female when he is present.

4   The proponents of the pathology-oriented, matriarchal family model did
not consider the possibility that a single-parent Black mother could serve as an
adequate role model for the children of both sexes. The notion that the mother
could reflect a balance of the traditional male and female roles, with respect to
mental toughness and emotional tenderness, was largely ignored because of
the rigid classification of psychosexual roles in American society. In the Black
community, however, the categorization of social role behaviors based on gen-

der is not as inflexible. It is conceivable that a Black mother could project a combination of assertive and nurturant behaviors in the process of rearing children of both sexes as nonsexist adults.

5   With the reality of accelerating divorce rates, in recent years the single-parent family headed by a woman has become a social reality in Euro-America. This reality has been accompanied by an attempt on the part of social scientists to legitimate family structures that represent alternatives to the nuclear family while reconceptualizing the social roles of males and females with less emphasis on exclusive behaviors. The concept of androgyny has been introduced to cover the vast pool of human personality traits that can be developed by either sex (Rogers, 1978). A well-balanced person reflects a combination of both instrumental and expressive traits. The latter include feeling-oriented behaviors formerly considered feminine, such as tenderness, caring, and affection. Thus, it is conceptually possible for a white, single, and androgynous female parent to rear psychologically healthy, emotionally integrated children. It is interesting how the sociology of the times makes available to white Americans psychological concepts designed to legitimize changes in the family, in child-rearing patterns, and in relationships between the sexes. Yet, these same behaviors when first expressed by Afro-Americans were considered as pathological.

The Extended Family Model   subject B

6   The extended family, in contrast to the single-parent subnuclear family, consists of a related and quasi-related group of adults, including aunts, uncles, parents, cousins, grandparents, boyfriends, and girlfriends linked together in a kinship or kinlike network. They form a cooperative interface with each other in confronting the concerns of living and rearing the children. This model of family life, which seems able to capture not only the strength, vitality, resilience, and continuity of the Black family, but also the essence of Black values, folkways, and life styles, begins with a different set of assumptions about the development and evolution of Black family life in America.

7   The Black extended family is seen as <u>an outgrowth of African patterns of</u>   point 1
<u>family and community life</u> that survived in America. The Africans carried with them through the Mid-Atlantic passage and sale to the initial slave owners a well-developed pattern of kinship, exogamous mating, and communal values, emphasizing collective survival, mutual aid, cooperation, mutual solidarity, interdependence, and responsibility for others (Nobles, 1974; Blassingame, 1972). These values became the basis for the Black extended family in America. They were retained because they were familiar and they allowed the slaves to have some power over destiny by enabling them to develop their own styles for family interaction. A consciousness of closeness to others, belongingness, and togetherness protected the slave from being psychologically destroyed by feelings of despair and alienation and the extended family provided a vehicle to pass the heritage on to the children (Fredrickson, 1976;

Gutman, 1976). Slaves in essence created their own communal family space, regardless of whether the master was paternalistic or conducted a Nazi-like concentration camp.

8   To understand the cultural continuity, <u>it is necessary to depart from the tra-</u>   point 2
<u>ditional hypothesis that slave masters and their descendants exercised total</u>
<u>psychological and social control over the development of Black family life and</u>
<u>community institutions</u>. The slaves were much more than empty psychologi-
cal tablets on which the master imprinted an identity. These early Blacks were
able to find ways of creating psychological space and implementing African
cultural forms that whites were unaware of and did not understand. Once in
the New World the African recreated a sense of tribal community within the
plantation milieu through a series of extended kin and kinlike family networks that carried on the cultural values of responsibility for others, mutual
aid, and collective survival. First- and second-generation American slaves
who were separated from biological kin by continued activity at the auction
block and newly arriving slaves who were sold to different plantations were
incorporated into the extended family structures of existing plantations. It was
not essential for the survival of African conceptions of family life that biological or legal kinship ties be maintained. When a people share a philosophy
of interdependence and collective survival, persons who are not biologically
or legally related can become interwoven into newly created and existing kinlike networks. Cultural patterns once established seem to endure, especially
if they work. The extended family survived because it provided Afro-Americans a support system within the context of a shared frame of reference. Along
with other African customs and beliefs, an African family identity was
passed along to the children as the link between generations through the oral
tradition.

9   Once the philosophy of collective survival and interdependence was set
into place as the foundation for community living, the extended family
evolved through a series of cycles of formation, breakup, and reformation as
the slaves who were without the recourse to legal rights to protect kinship
structures and conjugal unions were transferred from place to place. Much
later, with the beginnings of the Industrial Revolution after the Civil War, the
pattern of Black family life based on combinations of kinship and kinlike networks continued, despite the emergence of the nuclear family among Euro-
Americans. The growth of the individual nuclear family in Euro-America
seemed to correspond with the competitive and individualistic values of the
market place. The cycles of formation, breakup, and reformation of the
extended family continued as Blacks migrated farther north and west towards
the cities at the turn of the century during the pre and post periods of the two
world wars and into the modern age.

10   The Black extended family, with its grandparents, biological parents, conjugal partners, aunts, uncles, cousins, older siblings, boyfriends, girlfriends, and
quasi-kin, is <u>an intergenerational group</u>. The members of this three-generation   point 3
family do not necessarily reside in the same household. Individual house-

holds are part of a sociofamilial network that functions like a minicommunity. The members band together to share information, resources, and communal concern (Stack, 1974). There is no central authority, matriarchal or patriarchal. Decisions are made on an equalitarian model with input and outcomes determined by who is available at a given time, who has expertise with reference to a given problem, and one's prior experience and track record in decision making. This is likely to give some edge to the tribal elders. They are looked up to within the extended family network as resource people and advisors because they have the life experience that is highly valued in the Black community. As in the past, the family is held together over time and across geographical space by a shared experience frame and a common set of values involving interdependence, mutual aid, resilience, communalism, and collective responsibility (Nobles, 1978). These values transcend sex roles and allow both men and women to participate in and contribute to the management of economic resources, child rearing, community activism, and other issues of family life without being categorically restricted on the basis of gender. The fluid distinction between social sex roles offers both men and women in the Black family network the opportunity to emerge as decision makers, influence molders, and household managers.

11   It could be argued that the Black extended family exists and persists primarily because Black people face the common fate of oppressive economic and social conditions, that it exists out of necessity as a way of surviving in an oppressive class system. Politically and economically oppressed people have historically banded together for survival, whether it be in internment camps, labor unions, or women's movements. It would follow from this argument that the Black extended family would disappear as Black people moved up the socioeconomic ladder. Yet the extended family does not appear to be disappearing with rising economic fortunes. McAdoo's (1979) work with upwardly mobile middle and upper-middle class Black families suggests that not only does the extended family model persist when Blacks move up the socioeconomic ladder but the Afro-American values of mutual aid, interdependence, and interconnectedness also remain as the guiding ethos of family existence.

12   Being part of a close-knit extended family group is a vital part of Afro-American life. Wherever Blacks appear in numbers of two or more, whether it be on predominantly white college campuses, professional baseball teams, fraternal groups, street corners, storefront churches, automobile factories, or professional conferences, they soon seem to form a quasi-family network, share information and resources, get together, git down, rap, and party. White folks don't know what to make of this. The idea of sharing closeness, and interdependence expressed in sociofamilial groups is so deeply ingrained in the fabric of the Afro-American ethos that it is not likely to give way to the nuclear family with its stress on isolation, competition, and independence. If anything, the traditional nuclear family may be moving toward becoming more like the Afro-American extended family.

Works Cited

Blassingame, John. *The Slave Community*. New York: Oxford University Press, 1972.

Elkins, Stanley. *Slavery: A Problem in American Institutions and Intellectual Life*. Chicago: University of Chicago Press, 1968.

Frazier, E. Franklin. *The Negro Family in the United States*. Chicago: University of Chicago Press, 1939.

Fredrickson, George. "The Gutman Report," *The New York Review*, September 30, 1976, pp. 18–22, 27.

Gutman, Herbert. *The Black Family in Slavery and Freedom, 1750–1925*. New York: Vintage Books, 1976.

McAdoo, Harriet. "Black Kinship," *Psychology Today*, May 1979, pp. 67–69, 79, 110.

Moynihan, Daniel Patrick. *The Negro Family: The Case for National Action*, Washington, D.C.: U.S. Government Printing Office, 1965.

Nobles, Wade. "Africanity: Its Role in Black Families," *The Black Scholar*, June 1974, pp. 10–17.

———. "Toward an Empirical and Theoretical Framework for Defining Black Families," *Journal of Marriage and Family*, November 1978, pp. 679–688.

Rainwater, Lee. *Behind Ghetto Walls: Black Family Life in a Federal Slum*. Chicago: Aldine, 1970.

Rogers, Dorothy. *Adolescence: A Psychological Perspective*, 2nd Edition. Monterey, Calif.: Brooks/Cole, 1978.

Stack, Carol. *All Our Kin: Strategies for Survival in a Black Community*. New York: Harper & Row, 1974.

Reading-to-Write Questions

1. **Content:** What type of evidence does White rely upon? Why?

2. **Arrangement:** Within the larger subject-by-subject contrast of the family models, can you find another subject-by-subject contrast?

3. **Style:** Notice the academic terminology in this essay. Underline at least ten terms derived from the field of psychology. Is this useless jargon?

4. _____

   _____

   _____

Suggested Topics

1. **Observation:** Does your family resemble the Extended Family Model? Explain. (audience = your classmates)

2. **Critique:** White claims that in the Black extended family "there is no central authority, matriarchal or patriarchal." Are you persuaded by his argument? How does White's analysis of power relationships in the Black extended family compare to your analysis? (audience = White's readers)

3. **Synthesis:** Apply White's Extended Family Model to Naylor's description of her family. (audience = students who wish to major in the social sciences)

4. _____

   _____

   _____

Background Readings: THE BLACK FAMILY

Billingsley, Andrew. *Climbing Jacob's Ladder: The Future of the African-American Family*. New York: Simon & Schuster, 1993.

Coll, Cynthia, Janet Surrey, Kathy Weingarten, eds. *Mothering Against the Odds: Diverse Voices of Contemporary Mothers*. New York: Guilford Press, 1998.

Coner-Edwards, Alice F., and Jeanne Spurlock, eds. *Black Families in Crisis: The Middle Class*. New York: Bruner/Mazel, 1988.

Davis, Richard A. *The Black Family in a Changing Black Community*. New York: Garland, 1993.

Hare, Nathan, and Julia Hare. *The Endangered Black Family*. San Francisco: Black Think Tank, 1984.

Jewell, K. Sue. *Survival of the Black Family*. New York: Praeger, 1989.

Martin, Elmer, and Joanne Martin. *The Black Extended Family*. Chicago: University of Chicago Press, 1978.

McAdoo, Harriette, ed. *Black Families*. 2nd ed. Newbury Park, CA: Sage, 1988.

Sudarkasa, Niara. *The Strength of Our Mothers: African and African American Women and Families*. Trenton, NJ: Africa World Press, 1996.

_____

_____

_____

Recommended Literature: Mary Helen Washington, *Memory of Kin* (short stories and poetry)

Lorraine Hansberry, *A Raisin in the Sun* (play)

Paule Marshall, *Brown Girl, Brownstones* (novel)

August Wilson, *Fences* (play)

20/20 Hindsight
Jay Ford

While he was a junior at Wesleyan University, Jay Ford enrolled in a student exchange program that sent him to Kenya for a semester in 1989. Below, he describes his experience, recalling (a) the events that caused him to go to Kenya, (b) the differences between Kenya and the U.S., and (c) the profound effect that his trip had on his feelings and perceptions.

---

1   Born in a middle class African-American family on the upper west side of Manhattan, I have spent most of my life chasing the (white) American dream. Absorbing the rhetoric brewed by the media, school curricula, and, more important, my teachers, I was graduated from high school with the goal of travelling to Europe, achieving a college degree, becoming a corporate lawyer and, eventually, marrying a spouse who would be most likely white or a light-skinned black. We would have two homes and probably three children. This was my rough sketch of my future, one with which I was satisfied. I would be a success and this was very important because I clearly represent what W.E.B. Du Bois coined as the "talented tenth." Therefore, I had a responsibility to my people to succeed, to vanquish the disabilities associated with my color and earn my place in white America, my America.

2   In starting off on my journey to success, I met my first obstacle as I neared the end of my sophomore year in college. The student body had taken over the administration building in hopes of persuading the University to divest monies invested in corporations in South Africa. A meeting between the students and the administration had been arranged during which the administration had thoroughly explained its position on divestment. Now it was the students' turn to respond. As student after student approached the microphone,

explaining what he/she believed to be the most important reasons for disin-vesting, an unsettling feeling began to overwhelm me. Although all of the explanations were more than legitimate reasons to disinvest, none of them had touched my personal reasons for protesting the University's position on divestment.

3   When it was my turn, I did not actually know what I wanted to say, but I was determined to say something. "My name is Julius J. Ford. I am an Afro-American. Inherent in my title is the word African, meaning "of Africa." My ancestry is from Africa. Africans are therefore my people, my history. So as long as you continue to oppress my people through violence or investment or silence, you oppress me. And as long as you oppress me, I will fight you! I will fight you!" As I returned to my seat, my friend leaned over, patted me on the back and said, "That was great, I never really knew you felt that way." I turned to him and said, "Neither did I."

4   It was this event that made me question myself. How could I be satisfied with my sketch of success when it had no background or depth? Why had I not felt this strongly about Africa or Africans before? Why was I more attracted to women who possessed European features (straight hair, light skin, thin nose) than those who possessed African features? Why did I feel that Europe was so great and Africa so primitive? Why did I choose to call myself an African-American when I knew virtually nothing about Africa? These questions would trouble my soul for the remainder of the year. In fact, they would push me to apply to a student exchange program in East Africa, Kenya.

5   Called "An Experiment in International Living," the program would offer me travel throughout the country, during which time I would live in both rural and urban areas, in both huts and hotels, for approximately four months from February through mid-May, 1989. I would be equipped with two academic directors with numerous university and government contacts and ensured a variety of learning opportunities, as I would stay with native families and be allowed to venture off on my own.

6   Even though this program seemingly presented an optimum opportunity to find answers to all my pending questions, I was still apprehensive about my decision to go. But, perhaps if there was one specific incident that canceled any wavering on my part, it was that Friday afternoon at drama class. On Fridays, I taught drama to about twenty 9–14-year-old kids from predominantly black families with low incomes at a community center about twenty minutes from my college. On this particular day I had decided to ask the class what they thought about my taking a trip to Africa. They shot off these responses: "Why would you want to go to Africa to get even blacker than you are now?", "Why don't you take a trip somewhere nice like Paris, London, Rome?", "But they say in Africa every one is backwards, they can't teach you anything," "People are so black and ugly there." And, although some of the comments from the children were said specifically to make the other children laugh, many of them were exemplifications of how our educational system and other forms of external social propaganda affect a black child's mind.

7   When I first arrived in Kenya, we stayed in its capital city, Nairobi. Surprisingly enough, my first impression of Nairobi was that it was just like any American city: skyscrapers, movie theatres, discos, and crime. In fact, I was a bit disappointed, feeling that I had travelled fifteen hours in a Pan Am jet just to come back to New York City. But upon more detailed observation, I realized that this city was quite different from any other I had visited before. This city was black and, when I say black, I'm not talking your coffee-colored Atlanta, Oakland, Harlem black people. I mean black! I mean when you were small and used to play games and chose to embarrass the darkest kid on the block by calling him "midnight," "shadow," and "teeth black."

8   But the lesson to be learned in Nairobi was that all shades of black were equally attractive and the small children did not penalize attractiveness according to shade of skin, or length of hair, or size of nose. Furthermore, being in a black city, knowing I was in a mostly black country that sits on a predominantly black continent, enhanced my confidence and hence my actions. For the first time in my life I felt as though I could do anything, fit in anywhere, be welcomed by everyone because of my color. This was the feeling I had often assumed blacks felt during the Twenties, the period of the Harlem Renaissance. It was wonderful! I would go for days without being aware of my color. It did not seem to matter.

9   It was only a few weeks into the program, however, when I began to notice social insecurities developing within my peer group (of twenty-four I was the only black). As many as half a dozen of the other students declared that they had begun to view black children as more beautiful than white, that black women and black features were more pleasing to the eye than white ones. Others simply segregated themselves from the black society as much as possible, refusing to stay with families without another white person present. Perhaps, then, inherent in the role of minority come feelings of inferiority, a certain lack of confidence, insecurity.

10   Because there is much tribalism in Kenya, the first title I had to drop was African-American. When people around me refer to themselves as Masai or Kikuyu as opposed to Kenyan or East African, then how could I refer to myself as an African? Furthermore, the language I spoke, my values, morals and education were not African. So this put me in an awkward position. No one could question my ancestry as African because of my color, so I enjoyed most benefits of majority status. Yet, to many Kenyans, I was much more similar to a white American than an African so there was a wide gap between us.

11   It was here I realized that to be an accepted descendant of Africa I had a lot of work to do. I needed to learn a new language and a new culture. I needed to assimilate, and I figured that that shouldn't be too hard as I had twenty years of experience in that in the United States. But, the difference between my American and Kenyan assimilations is that in Kenya it seemed to be welcomed if not encouraged by the majority. The more knowledge I attained of Kenya and the more I left my English at home and spoke Swahili or another tribal language, the more cultural doors opened to me. For example, as I

became increasingly familiar with Gidiam tribal customs and my use of Kiswahili improved, I was able to travel along the coast for days never worrying about food or lodging. I was often given the opportunity to sit and discuss with elders, and take part in tribal ceremonies and had responsibilities bestowed on me by elder men, *Mzees,* or my temporary *Mama.* In fact, toward the end of my trip, when travelling alone, it was often difficult for me to convince people that I was African-American. They would tell me, *"Una toka Africa qwa sababo una weza kusema Kiswahili na una fambamu Africa life"* (You are from Africa because you are able to speak Kiswahili and you understand African life). The more I learned, the more comfortable I was with the title African-American.

12   I also took more pride in myself. Here it was important to learn that the black empowerment was not from sheer numbers, it was from the fact that the blacks in Africa possess a communal sense of self, a shared past that is to never be forgotten, that has passed through generations, and is used as a reference for modern-day experiences. An exemplification of this concept is the way in which Kenyans and Africans in general treat their elderly. In Kenya you are told that you never grow to equal your parents' authority or knowledge. Your elders will forever be your elders and respected as such. In Kenya, elderly people are cherished, not forgotten.

13   As we visited small villages in the areas of Kisumu, Nakru, and on the coast, villages which by American standards were far below the poverty line, we were welcomed with feasts of foods, drinks, people and music. To them we were guests paying them the honor of visitation. Even on a more individual level, most Kenyan families were extraordinarily hospitable. To be welcomed into a stranger's home and be offered food, wine, and a bed for an unlimited number of days is shocking to Americans and even more so to a New Yorker.

14   This humanistic view was very difficult to adapt to because it affected every level of Kenyan society. For example, Kenyans have a very limited concept of personal space (but in a country with a population growth rate of 4.3 percent that is quite understandable). So it was often difficult for me to discover that my four newly acquired brothers were also my newly acquired bedmates, to change money at the bank while the people behind me were looking over my shoulder examining my passport and money exchange papers, and, to learn not to tell your family that you would like to be left alone because crazy people stay by themselves.

15   Also, Americans are lost outside of a linear society. We are taught from kindergarten to stay in line. Order for us is symbolically represented by the line, and we therefore choose to see all other forms of non-linear collective activity as chaotic. Kenyans, however, do not have this same view of order. They choose to mass together, aggressively seeking out their desires and bringing new meaning to the words "organized chaos." Mobs catch buses, herds are seen at ticket counters, and, unfortunately, until your adjustment period is complete, you stand apart from the chaos, "jaw dropped," staring at

the stampede of people. As a result, you do not obtain a ticket or get on the bus.

16   This conception of order plus the Kenyan view of personal space make for exciting moments in the public sphere. For example, there is a type of Kenyan public transportation called *matatus*. Matatus are small privately owned mini-vans that serve as buses for local citizens. To ride a matatu is like taking the most crowded New York City subway car during rush hour, placing that car on Broadway, and allowing a taxicab driver to control the wheel. Matatus do not actually stop at designated bus stops; in fact, they do not actually stop at all. Instead, they simply slow down and those who need to get off push and shove their way to the front of the van and jump out. And as for those who wish to board, they simply chase the matatu down and shove and push their way onto the van. As with circus clown cars, there is always room for one more.

17   Another linear concept I was introduced to was time. In rural areas there would sometimes be days when we would have no activities planned. It was at these moments when I would curse my directors for poor planning. But I was soon to learn that doing nothing was not necessarily wasted time. This time to think, relax, conversationalize was most important for a peaceful state of mind. I finally understood that it is not imperative even in America to eat breakfast, read the paper in the street while you are running to the subway, or to work two jobs just to pay off your life insurance bill. Here there was not "so much to do and so little time"; here there was a great deal to do but also the belief that that which is supposed to get done will get done in time.

18   For example, during the last month of my stay in Kenya I visited a small farm in Kisumu Kaubu, Uganda, with a woman and her three sons. I was only to stay for a day and one night. I had come to visit just prior to the time the rains were expected, so I had assumed that the family was going to spend very little time relaxing with me because it was imperative that the soil and seeds for the year be prepared for the rains which could come at any moment.

19   However, once I arrived, we did very little field work. We talked instead—about the history of her people, about America, and about American percep-tions of Kenya. Of course this was hard work since their English was very limited and my Swahili is fair at best. And as the day crept on to the night, I asked her how she could afford to give her attentions to me when the threat of the rains could come at any day now. "*Pole Pole, bwana*," she replied (We have not neglected our work to the fields. We have only delayed our work so to wel-come our new son, who by joining us will ease our workload). I then asked her, "But, Mama, it is already 11:00 and I leave tomorrow at 9:00." She replied, "Don't worry, bwana, we start to work the cattle (plow) at 2:00 A.M. Good night."

20   It seemed as though Kenyan culture chose to be humanistic rather than materialistic. The value placed on human life and interaction is much greater than in the States. To shake hands, to share a meal or even your home with a foreigner is an honor, not a burden. And, for you as a guest to turn down that

hand, meal, or bed is an insult. How wonderfully strange to travel to a foreign land where people who can hardly understand what language you speak are ready to take you home and make you part of the family. They wouldn't last too long in New York, I thought.

21   In most places in Kenya, it was common knowledge for one to know his/her environment. People could name the types of trees along the roads, tell you animals indigenous to the area, and explain which types of soil were best for growing specific crops. They could tell you the staple foods of different parts of Kenya *or* even the U.S. In fact, their world geography was superior to that of most American college students. Access to information, whether at home or in schools, was a privilege to be appreciated by those involved and then passed down to younger generations orally. I wonder why I did not feel this way. My country offers more educational opportunities than any other in the world and yet seldom are these opportunities fully exploited. American students go to school, but they do not go to learn. They go to get A's and move up economically. They go to play the game, the educational game of success that I like to refer to as DT (Diploma Training), a process that verifies one's intelligence by certificate as opposed to action or common sense.

22   Furthermore, along with this overwhelming appreciation for knowledge, Kenyans show reverence for everyday simplicities which we in America take for granted: the appreciation for candlelight, running water, a toilet with a seat cover, a long hot shower every day. Learning to live is to stay in Kenya and survive with twenty-three other people living mostly off rain water, sleeping in huts, and eating many fruits and vegetables with only the occasional beef meal. I felt as though Kenya taught me a new dimension of life, a rebirth of sorts. It put objectives, time, goals, values into a new perspective. It did not tell me, "Please be aware of how much water you use because a drought warning is in effect." It gave me a gallon of water and told me to drink and bathe for an undetermined period. It did not tell me of the beauties of nature, rather it revealed them to me by greeting me in the morning with the sights of Mt. Kenya, Kilimanjaro, and Lake Victoria. I saw no need for National Geographic or wildlife television, for when it wanted to introduce me to animals, a monkey, leopard, or family of raccoons would become my fellow pedestrians. There was no urge to tell me of the paradox of zoos when it could show me national parks with hundreds of acres of land.

23   In Kenya I felt more free than I have ever felt before. The only thing holding me captive was the earth which would grow the food, the sky which would quench the earth of its thirst, and the sun which would warm and help all things to grow. But these masters were sure to give back all that you have put in. When you worked hard, your rewards were great and if you chose to relax so would your crop and cattle. And with a give-and-take relationship like this, one learns that it is okay to take time, time for others, for oneself, time to enjoy and appreciate all that life and earth offer. Some choose to call this type of relationship religion, a covenant with the Lord and her divinity (sky, earth, and

animals and I will not deny that there was a strong sense of God or Allah or Sa or Buddha).

24   A forest burning to the ground germinates the soil, allowing new life to grow. The omnipotence of nature—floods, lightning, hurricanes, earthquakes, the beauty of a cheetah or giraffe running, an open field, the sky, the mountains, the sea—is overwhelming and foreign to me living so long in a concrete jungle. When all of this engulfed me and I took the time to embrace it, I became convinced that there exists a master craftsperson of this creation, that there exists a God.

25   Kenya has more than (just) given me a new perception of the world; Kenya has widened my world view. I now realize that there are other significant cultures in the world besides a western one. I no longer think of the world in First, Second, and Third World terms. There are aspects of Kenyan values which should be regarded as more First World than American: humanistic sentiments, importance of family, pride of ancestry, appreciation and respect for other peoples' differences.

26   Also, whereas I ventured off to Kenya to learn about a new culture and its new people, I found that most of the more important discoveries and evaluations were about myself. Upon leaving Kenya I feel that I have grown more confident about my African-Americanness, my perceptions of the world around me, and my expectation of 21/21 vision and beyond. I do not believe I could have gone anywhere else on earth and been as personally challenged.

Reading-to-Write Questions

1. **Content:** Reread Ford's paragraph about the *matatus*. What makes his description so vivid?

2. **Arrangement:** Where does Ford make point-by-point contrasts between Kenya and the U.S.?

3. **Style:** Find places where Ford adopts a humorous tone. How does his word choice contribute to the humor?

4. _____

   _____

   _____

Suggested Topics

1. **Observation:** If you have traveled to Africa, compare and contrast your expectations with your observations. If not, consider a different place. (audience = African Americans who would like to visit Africa or the place you substitute)

2. **Critique:** Ford suggests that certain aspects of Kenyan culture are more First World than aspects of American culture. Has Ford drawn a fair comparison of Kenya and America? (audience = Ford's readers)

3. **Synthesis:** Compare Ford's and Biko's interpretations of African cultural values. (audience = students who would like to learn about African culture)

4. _____

   _____

   _____

Background Readings: AFRICAN AMERICAN PERSPECTIVES ON AFRICA

Berghahn, Marion. *Images of Africa in Black American Literature*. Totowa, NJ: Rowman and Littlefield, 1977.

Diawara, Manthia. *In Search of Africa*. Cambridge, MA: Harvard University Press, 1998.

Jenkins, David. *Black Zion: Africa, Imagined and Real, as Seen by Today's Blacks*. New York: Harcourt Brace Jovanovich, 1975.

Magubane, Bernard. *The Ties That Bind: African American Consciousness of Africa.* Trenton, NJ: Africa World Press, 1990.

Mezu, Sebastian, ed. *The Meaning of Africa to Afro-Americans.* Buffalo, NY: Black Academy Press, 1972.

Redd, Larry Ukali Johnson. *The Black Expatriate in Africa.* San Jose, CA: Afroan Publishers International, 1982.

Uya, Okon Edet, ed. *Black Brotherhood: Afro-Americans and Africa.* Lexington, MA: Heath, 1971.

Weisbord, Robert G. *Ebony Kinship: Africa, Africans, and the Afro-American.* Westport, CT: Greenwood Press, 1973.

Recommended Literature: Countee Cullen, "Heritage" from *Color* (poem)

Langston Hughes, "Afro-American Fragment" in *Selected Poems* (poem)

Claude McKay, "Outcast" from *Harlem Shadows* (poem)

Adam David Miller, "The Africa Thing" from *Dices or Black Bones* (poem)

Pan-Africanism
Kwame Ture

Kwame Ture (1941–1998) was a leading spokes-
man for the All-African People's Revolutionary
Party. Born Stokely Carmichael, he began his
life of political activism in the Civil Rights Move-
ment of the 1960s. As National Chairman of the
Student Non-Violent Coordinating Committee
(SNCC), he issued a call for "black power" that
was heard from coast to coast and was recorded
in his book Black Power: The Politics of Liberation in America. *However, by 1969, he had left*
SNCC and the U.S. for Guinea, where he became
an advocate for the Pan-African Movement. His
first treatise on Pan-Africanism appeared in
the journal The Black Scholar *in 1969, two*
years before he wrote Stokely Speaks: Black
Power Back to Pan-Africanism. *Below is the*
introduction to the essay, which he entitled
"Pan-Africanism—Land and Power." Here, he
contrasts the way we refer to people of African
descent with the way we identify other ethnic
groups.

------

1   Whether we want it or not, there are divisions among black Africans living
in the United States, the Caribbean and on the African continent, divisions

which have been imposed on us by Europeans. There are geographical divisions, countries such as Senegal and Mauritania, Mozambique and Guinea, created by Europeans as they struggled for the wealth of Africa. Then there are political divisions and economic divisions, again imposed on us by Europeans.

2   Now they are planning to impose on us grave cultural divisions and, most of all, to divide us by naming us different things. If you are in San Francisco, for example, and you see a Japanese or a Chinese walking down the street you do not say that there goes an American Japanese or a Japanese American. You say simply that there goes a Japanese—period. Yet probably that Japanese cannot speak Japanese at all; he may be the third or fourth generation in America. But no one calls him a Japanese American. The first thing you call him is a Japanese, because a person is defined, really, at first by his physical presence, or in terms of his ancestral stock. Whether he is Chinese, Japanese or African. The same is true of the Indians. Even in America, when you see a red Indian, you do not say he is an American; you say he is an Indian. The same is true for East Indians; the same for Filipinos. Wherever you see them, in any part of the world, you call them Chinese or what not.

3   The same is not true for Africans.

4   Let's ask ourselves why.

5   If you see an African in Europe, you do not say that he is an African. If you see him in America you do not call him an African. He may be Negro; he may be West Indian; he may be everything else but African. That is because Europe took its time to divide us carefully, quite carefully. And they gave us different names so that we would never, always never, refer to ourselves by the same name; which helped ensure that there would always be differences. If you say you are West Indian, it is fairly obvious that you are something different to be set apart from an African. An American Negro and an African also obviously are not the same thing.

6   One of the most important things we must now begin to do is to call ourselves "African." No matter where we may be from, we are first of all and finally Africans. Africans. Africans. Africans. The same also happens to be true of North Africa. When they say "Algerians" or "Egyptians" they are talking about Africans, because Africa happens to be one solid continent. Among Africans there will and must be no divisions. They are just Africans—period.

Reading-to-Write Questions

1. **Content:** What kind of support does Ture rely upon?

2. **Arrangement:** How does Ture use classification as well as comparison-contrast to organize his thoughts?

3. **Style:** Why does Ture address his readers as "you" and "we" instead of using the third person (i.e., "one" or "a person")?

4. _____

   _____

   _____

Suggested Topics

1. **Observation:** Test Ture's claims by asking a random sample of people to identify the ethnicity of American celebrities of Chinese, Japanese, Native American, East Indian, Filipino, and African descent. Then write an essay comparing or contrasting your findings with Ture's claims (audience = readers of *The Black Scholar*)

2. **Critique:** Ture maintains that Europeans call Africans in the disapora different names in order to divide and thus weaken them as a people. Write an essay in which you explain why you have a similar or different point of view. (audience = Pan-Africanists)

3. **Synthesis:** Contrast Ture's and Early's concepts of the "Africanness" of African Americans. (audience = African Americans)

4. _____

   _____

   _____

Background Readings: PAN-AFRICANISM

Abdul-Raheem, Tajudeen, ed. *Pan-Africanism: Politics, Economy, and Social Change in the Twenty-First Century.* New York: New York UP, 1996.

Esedebe, P. Olisanwuche. *Pan-Africanism: The Idea and Movement, 1776–1991.* 2nd ed. Washington, DC: Howard UP, 1994.

Lemelle, Sidney, and Robin Kelley, eds. *Imagining Home: Class, Culture, and Nationalism in the African Diaspora.* London and New York: Verso, 1994.

Nkrumah, Kwame. *Africa Must Unite.* New York: International Publishers, 1970.

_____. *Class Struggle in Africa.* London: Panaf Books, 1975.

Padmore, George. *Pan-Africanism or Communism.* Garden City, NY: Anchor Books, 1972.

PAIGC, ed. *Unity and Struggle: Speeches and Writings of Amilcar Cabral.* New York: Monthly Review Press, 1979.

Sekou-Toure, Ahmed. *Africa on the Move.* London: Panaf Books, 1979.

Thompson, Vincent Bakpetu. *Africa and Unity: The Evolution of Pan-Africanism.* Harlow: Longmans, 1977.

Walters, Ronald. *Pan Africanism in the African Diaspora: An Analysis of Modern Afrocentric Political Movements.* Detroit: Wayne State UP, 1997.

_____

_____

_____

Never African Again
Gerald Early

When students protested against his appointment as the university's Director of African and Afro-American Studies, they accused Gerald Early of not being "Black enough." In response, Early explored the African roots of his Blackness in an essay in Harper's Magazine *in December 1992. Referring to the ideas of Malcolm X and W.E.B. Du Bois, he contrasts the "Americanness" and the "Africanness" of African Americans in this excerpt, the closing section of the essay. Other essays by Early are collected in the volumes* Lure and Loathing, The Culture of Bruising, *and* Tuxedo Junction. *Early has also published books about Miles Davis, Sammy Davis, Jr., and Muhammad Ali.*

---

1   Despite the unrealistic romanticism of Malcolm's back-to-Africa preachings, he offers an important message for today's young blacks: that blacks are, indeed, as Du Bois argues, a people of "double-consciousness"; that both blackness and Americanness are real options, each having meaning only when measured against the other. Malcolm would not have argued with such passion and virulence against the validity of any kind of black *American* experience if he did not suspect that assimilation, that *being* American, was truly a rooted desire, if not a fulfilled reality, for most blacks. Yet he also knew that blacks in America cannot think about what their Americanness means without thinking about what it means to be of African descent: the two are inextricably

bound together. As the historian Sterling Stuckey has argued, black people did not acquire a sense of what being African was until they came to America. They, like most people who came to this country, achieved their initial sense of identity through their clan—that is, slaves thought of themselves more as members of specific tribes or nations than as "Africans." Slavery compressed the diversity of African experience into one broad African identity, forcing blacks, in turn, to invent a collective sense of an African memory and an African self.

2   But Africanness is relevant to American blacks today only as a way of helping us understand what it means to be American. While it is necessary that we recognize our African ancestry, and remember that it was, in varying degrees, stripped away by slavery, we must acknowledge, finally, that our story is one of remaking ourselves as Americans. My world is shaped by two indelible ideas: first, that I was once an African, that I grew, generations ago, from that ancestral soil; and, second, that I will never be African again, that I will, like Joseph, not be buried in the soil of my long-ago ancestors.

3   Malcolm preached the necessity of being African at the complete expense of our American selves, a love of the misty past at the cost of our actual lives, our triumphs, our sufferings in the New World and as modern people. In this way, Malcolm merely increased our anxiety, further fueled our sense of inadequacy, and intensified our self-hatred and feelings of failure by providing us with a ready excuse: America is the white man's country, and the whites don't want you here and will never give you equal citizenship.

4   But it must always be remembered that our blood is here, our names are here, our fate is here, in a land we helped to invent. By that I have in mind much more than the fact that blacks gave America free labor; other groups have helped build this and other countries for no or for nominal wages. We have given America something far more valuable: we have given her her particular identity, an identity as a country dedicated to diversity, a nation of different peoples living together as one. And no black person should care what the whites want or don't want in the realm of integration. The whites simply must learn to live as committed equals with their former slaves.

5   Our profound past of being African, which we must never forget, must be balanced by the complex fate of being American, which we can never deny or, worse, evade. For we must accept who and what we are and the forces and conditions that have made us this, not as defeat or triumph, not in shame or with grandiose pride, but as the tangled, strange, yet poignant and immeasurable record of an imperishable human presence.

Reading-to-Write Questions

1. **Content:** How does Early's Biblical allusion to Joseph contribute to the essay?

2. **Arrangement:** How does Early set up his contrasts between "Africanness" and "Americanness"?

3. **Style:** Underline effective uses of repetition.

4. _____

    _____

    _____

Suggested Topics

1. **Observation:** Take notes during a class discussion about this essay. Contrast your opinion of the essay with an opposing view voiced by a classmate or group of classmates. (audience = class)

2. **Critique:** Early states that "Africanness is relevant to American blacks today only as a way of helping us understand what it means to be American." Do you agree? After summarizing Early's supporting points, compare or contrast his view with yours. (audience = subscribers to an African American Studies discussion group on the Internet)

3. **Synthesis:** Contrast Ture's attitude toward Africa with Early's. (audience = people who read Early's article in *Harper's Magazine*)

4. _____

    _____

    _____

Background Readings: AFRICAN AMERICAN PERSPECTIVES ON AFRICA

See the reading list for Jay Ford's essay.

Student Essay:

TWO TALES, ONE COMMUNITY

Rosoloc Henderson

(1996)

1   Can you imagine a land of peace? A land inhabited by kind and caring spirits? A land singing the harmony of man? This type of land seems impossible with violence running loose, spreading malice, fear, and strife; however it has existed. In my short lifetime, I have experienced both worlds without changing locations.

2   In "Some African Cultural Concepts," Steve Biko speaks about the differences between African and Western relationships. In general, the African unites to uplift the others, while the Westerner struggles to lift himself (45). As I read each of Biko's comparisons, I began thinking of the swift change from African to Western concepts in my community. In the eighties, I remember a bond of unity among my neighbors. Steve Biko termed this love "the modern African culture" (44). In my community, on the outskirts of Washington, D.C., everyone united as a single family. All the children went to the same schools, played the same games, and came in the house at the same time. We shared a "deep concern for each other" (Biko 45). When locked out of the house, I treasure that I could go to any of the neighbors' houses. Even if they were going to an important engagement, they would dress me with their children and take me along. They would never send me home without dinner. Because my parents knew I was in safe hands, they would not be concerned with time. Out of this deep concern came "a desire to share" (Biko 45). Ample communication flourished between neighbors. As a child, I remember if I got caught doing something wrong by neighbors, I would be scolded by the catchers and my parents. Support was given if someone was struggling. For instance, I recollect if we ran out of milk, we could go next door and they would give us their whole jug. Aid was rendered benevolently with "no remuneration . . . ever given" (Biko 46). There just was not any concern for violence. On Halloween, every house gave out candy. One Halloween—I think I was eight—I remember going trick or treating with a group of twenty kids. That night we went to every house in the neighborhood. At the end of our journey, we met about

thirty other kids at this really haunted house. We faced this haunted house together, as well as ran out of the yard together.

3   The happiness and love was so great that it must have blinded all to the change brought on by our new neighbors. Their names were violence and insolence, their children's names were fear, belligerence, and haughtiness. The exact time they moved in, I know not. They must have been disguised, hidden like thieves in the night. Although they shook the community like an earthquake, separating and destroying the family bond, no one felt the actual event but only recognized the aftermath. The trauma can be seen in the present attitudes of the community. Conversation between neighbors becomes less and less each year. Today, I can see my neighbors ten times a day, never bothering to say hello. Communication only stems from status competition. For example, if the Langleys get a new car, then the Johns must have a better one, etc. until the street is lined with new cars. My parents often argue about "Such-and-such did this to their house. Why can't we do this to ours?" Because of competition, no one wants to ask for help. My mother always tells me, "To see you struggle will make their day."

4   With the increase in violence, fear cannot be avoided. While neighbors were sitting in their houses, their cars were stolen. Another neighbor's house was robbed of large furniture. A close friend was killed on his front porch as he went into the house. All of the above events occurred during broad daylight; nobody saw anything. Day and night, drug dealers stand on corners while drug users wander the streets. Everyone totes a gun, for good reasons I believe, to be safe. People are apprehensive to come out of their own doors. As people walk on the sidewalks at night, their paths are lighted with the multiple motion sensory lights on houses. Parents don't let their young children outside. The community owner decided to remove the playgrounds because they were not being used by young children. Instead the playgrounds had become hang-outs and target ranges for teenagers. The influence of fear can be seen at Halloween. For the past several Halloweens, the majority of families have not given out candy. They are afraid to open the doors. Halloween has become a trick night with the older youth blowing up trash cans, egging houses, and scaring the few children left to trick or treat.

5   But how, in this community, did "the African begin to lose a grip on himself and his surroundings" (Biko 44)? This sickness can be attributed to many elements. Many diagnosed the current state as an overflow, a contagious leprosy, of violence from a sick, neighboring community. A road had been built connecting the neighboring areas. Designed while drawing up the plans of the area, this merging project had been overlooked and forgotten. Neighbors complained about having one exit and entrance, so the project was resurrected. As a result of opening the road, many feel the neighborhood was infected with the agitation running rampant in the heart of the adjacent areas. People saw their protection against the dangers lurking behind the woods destroyed, as the fortress of trees was knocked down.

6   This problem is centered not only in my community, but in about every black community in America. The story of Pandora's box was a myth; this story of unleashed misfortunes is real. Where did the love and respect go? Where is the strength, but, more importantly, where is the hope? Biko states in his essay, "It is difficult to kill the African heritage" which "emanates from a situation of common experience of oppression" (47). The black community must stand up by taking care of what is theirs, immortalizing Biko's words. We cannot sit around watching all that our ancestors worked for turn to dust. Wise men say "history has a way of repeating itself." For the sake of the black community, I hope this statement is a true prophecy, for I love my neighborhood. Like a mother with her child, I shall never disown my neighborhood no matter what it may do to me or to itself. For it is part of me, and I am part of it.

Works Cited

Biko, Steve. "Some African Cultural Concepts." *Revelations*. Ed. Teresa M. Redd. 3rd ed. Needham Heights, MA: Simon & Schuster, 1997. 43–49.

Student Essay:

WHAT IS THE MEANING OF A "TRUE" AFRICAN-AMERICAN?

Tracy Brewington

(2000)

1   I am an African-American student attending a predominantly African-American university. I live in a dormitory on a floor with a predominantly African-American population of young women. While preparing to write this essay, I asked several of the young women on my floor, "In filling out an application for employment, what nationality do you check off as your own?" The general response was "I check off 'black or African-American.'" I also asked, "Would you ever consider living in Africa?" The general response to this question was "No, it's way too hot over there!" or "No, I don't like their way of living!" I now ask, how can we, as a people, claim to be proud of our African ancestry, but have such negative views about our place of origin? It is sad to say that many African-Americans know little or nothing about Africa and the people of Africa. Sure, many of us know that Africa is the birthplace of civilization and who Nelson Mandela is, but in many cases, our knowledge about Africa extends no further. Therefore, the second question at hand is "Does our lack of knowledge about our ancestry mean that we are not 'true' African-Americans?"

2   Some may believe that in order to satisfy the definition of a "true" African-American, one must have complete knowledge of the cultural background of one's African ancestors. Some may even believe that one must experience, firsthand, the African way of life. As he explains in his essay "20/20 Hindsight," Jay Ford felt that in order to satisfy this definition, he would go on a four-month pilgrimage to Africa. It was during this time that he experienced African life and gained knowledge about his African heritage, in addition to developing a clear perspective about his "African-Americanness." Ford received from this experience a better understanding of himself and his life goals, in addition to his heritage (34–39).

3   Should we all (African-Americans) be like Jay Ford and go on a four-month pilgrimage to Africa in order to discover ourselves and learn more about our

ancestry? If we do not, are we any less African? Perhaps our lack of knowledge about Africa stems from being part American as well as part African. We are African because of our ancestry, but we are American because of our culture. Consequently, there are several significant differences between our culture and the African culture of our ancestors. For example, Africans tend to have a very limited concept of personal space, while we tend to value and demand ours. The same is true for property. Most Africans believe in "What's mine is yours," but most of us believe in "What's mine is mine." Also, many Africans will take care of strangers in need; it is an honor. Many of us, on the other hand, would consider it a burden. Furthermore, Africans usually find order in congregating into one large group; we usually find order in forming lines. We view the African method as chaotic (Ford 36–38). It is because of major differences like these that we differ from our ancestors in respect to our cultures. However, we are the same in respect to our blood.

4   I believe that deep down inside, we, as a race, are all truly African, regardless of what amount of knowledge we have about Africa or what culture traits distinguish us from our African ancestors. We are African in our blood, in our genes, and—despite certain differences—in our culture. We do not have to go to Africa in order to experience our African culture. It is all around us, whether we know it or not. Even though, through the process of slavery, our culture has been assimilated into that of the white American, "there remains, in spite of the superficial cultural similarities between the detribalized and the Westerner, a number of cultural characteristics that mark out the detribalized as an African" (Biko 47). Thus, as South African Steve Biko points out, "we see that in the area of music, the African still expresses himself with conviction. The craze about jazz arises out of a conversion by the African artists of mere notes to meaningful music, expressive of real feelings" (48).

5   I am an African-American. I know a fair amount about Africa, and I have neither been nor plan to go on any pilgrimage to Africa. In addition, I value my privacy, my personal property, and I would not necessarily take care of a stranger in need. This does not mean that I am any less *African*-American than Jay Ford. It simply means that I am an American of African descent. We, as a race, must keep in mind that we are indeed African-American. We must remember and be proud of where we came from, but we have adopted American culture. As Gerald Early writes, "while it is necessary that we recognize our African ancestry, and remember that it was, in varying degrees, stripped away by slavery, we must acknowledge, finally, that our story is one of remaking ourselves as Americans" (62).

Works Cited

Biko, Steve. "Some African Cultural Concepts." *Revelations.* Ed. Teresa M. Redd. 3rd ed. Needham Heights, MA: Simon & Schuster, 1997. 43–49.

Early, Gerald. "Never African Again." *Revalations.* Ed. Teresa M. Redd. 3rd ed: Needham Heights, MA: Simon & Schuster, 1997. 61–62.

Ford, Jay. "20/20 Hindsight." *Revelations.* Ed. Teresa M. Redd. 3rd ed. Needham Heights, MA: Simon & Schuster, 1997. 33–39.

visions of the past: classification-division

You may write me down in history
With your bitter, twisted lies,
You may trod me in the very dirt
But still, like dust, I'll rise.

from "Still I Rise"
by Maya Angelou

Black History's Diversified Clientele
Benjamin Quarles

A pioneer in the study of Black history, Benjamin Quarles (1904–1996) chronicled the history of African Americans, especially from the Revolutionary War through the Civil War. Among his many books are titles such as Frederick Douglass, The Negro in the Civil War, The Negro in the Making of America, *and* Black Abolitionists. *The following essay was published in 1977 in a collection of essays entitled* Africa and the Afro-American Experience. *In the essay Quarles classifies the uses of Black history according to the group it serves: the Black rank and file, Black revolutionary nationalists, Black academicians, and white scholars or laypersons. Within each category, he identifies the aims, content, and style of Black history for that particular clientele.*

---

1   Along with many other denials since he arrived on these shores, the Black American has until recently been denied a past. The consequent damage to his psyche can hardly be imagined. In a poem entitled "Negro History," appearing in the volume *From the Ashes: Voices of Watts* (Budd Schulberg, editor), young Jimmie Sherman depicts the past as his grandfather viewed it:

> A ship
> A chain
> A distant land
> A whip
> A pain
> A white man's hand
> A sack
> A field
> of cotton balls—
> The only things
> Grandpa recalls.

2   Such an outlook on the past has a stultifying effect, making for apathy and despair. Hence Black leaders since the birth of the republic have been advocates of Negro history, obviously envisioning a far broader coverage of it than Jimmie Sherman's grandpa had come to know. Black scholars, led by Carter G. Woodson in 1915, began to remove the layers of ignorance and distortion that had encrusted the Afro-American past. One of these scholars, W. E. B. Du Bois, in the closing line of his autobiography, written during his last months, bespoke anew his lifelong devotion to history: "Teach us, Forever Dead, there is no Dream but Deed, there is no Deed but Memory." A quarter of a century earlier Du Bois fired back a sharp rejoinder to a magazine editor who had rejected a Du Bois essay because it had touched upon the past. "Don't you understand," Du Bois wrote, "that the past is present; that without what was, nothing is."

3   During the past decade the cry for Black history has been stronger than ever before. Numbered among the proponents of such history are the newer Black militants. "We Blacks," writes Imamu Amiri Baraka (LeRoi Jones), "must learn our collective past in order to design a collective destiny." Of his period of confinement at the Norfolk (Massachusetts) Prison Colony, Malcolm X wrote: "I began first telling my Black brother inmates about the glorious history of the Black man—things they had never dreamed." On another occasion he referred to history as "a people's memory" without which "man is demoted to the lower animals." In his assessment of the past, Malcolm X did not ignore the less glorious aspects of the Black pilgrimage in America. Speaking to a ghetto audience in Detroit in 1953 he evoked a deep response with the words: "We didn't land on Plymouth Rock, my brothers and sisters—Plymouth Rock landed on us!"

4   Eldridge Cleaver, who, like Malcolm X, became a serious student of history while serving time in prison, spoke its praises. In his essay "To All Black Women, From All Black Men," in *Soul on Ice*, he writes:

> Be convinced, Sable Sister, that the past is no
> forbidden vista upon which we dare not
> look, out of a phantom fear of being, as the
> wife of Lot, turned into pillars of salt. Rather

the past is an omniscient mirror: we gaze and
see reflected there ourselves and each other—
what we used to be and what we are today,
how we got this way, and what we are
becoming. To decline to look into the Mirror
of Then, my heart, is to refuse to view the
face of Now.

5   One of the sable sisters who has needed no convincing about history's role
is poet Sarah Webster Fabio, who writes:

Now at all costs, we must heal our history.
Or else our future rots in the disease of our past.

6   Although Black history is now coming into its own as never before, not all
of its proponents are in pursuit of the same goal. Indeed, today Black history
is being called upon to serve an increasing variety of publics, four of whom we
may scrutinize briefly. These are the Black rank and file, the Black revolutionary nationalists, the Black academicians, and the white world, both scholarly
and lay. Not mutually exclusive, these groups often overlap. But this fourfold
typology enables us to illustrate the major contemporary uses of Black history.
We may take these in turn, first describing their aims and then noting their
general content and style.

7   For the Black rank and file, the man in the street, the laity, Black history's
main objective is to create a sense of racial pride and personal worth. To the
rank and file the new Black history is good therapy, its end result an improved
self-image. In a world that has traditionally equated blackness with inferiority,
Black history serves as a balm to make the wounded whole. In a world that has
traditionally equated blackness with low aim, Black history serves as a stimulus to success. To a Black person seeking to resolve an identity crisis, Black history is ego-soothing; it places one in the thick of things, thereby diminishing
his sense of alienation, of rootlessness. Black history is a search for the values
and the strengths imbedded in the Black subculture. Black history strikes at
the Black American's legacy of self-rejection, the burden of shame that he
had been taught was his to bear going back to the curse of Cain. "I always
wanted to be somebody," runs the title of the autobiography of a Black tennis
champion. Black history tells the Black reader that he is somebody, however
vicariously.

8   In its content Black history for the masses reflects somewhat "the great
man" theory of history. White or Black, the typical American, himself individualistic, conceives of his country's past as the achievements of a group of outstanding characters, pushing on against Herculean odds. History is a tableau
of heroes set in bold relief. To the generality of blacks their men of mark con-
stitute their history, the bulk of their attention falling upon individual achiev-
ers—an underground railroad conductor like Harriet Tubman, a dedicated
bishop like Daniel E. Payne, an educator like Mary McLeod Bethune, a sports

(margin notes: thesis categories; traits; Category 1, 1st trait; 2nd trait)

celebrity like prize fighter Peter Jackson or jockey Isaac Murphy, and a singer like Elizabeth Taylor Greenfield (the "Black Swan") or Bessie Smith. The list is endless, ranging from an early African king to a present-day ghetto leader.

9   Upbeat and achievement-oriented, Black history for the rank and file   3rd trait
stresses victories—the peak that was scaled, the foe that was vanquished, the deep river that was crossed. Moreover, to the masses, youth makes a special appeal, the younger Frederick Douglass arousing more interest than the Sage of Anacostia. Local Black historical figures likewise meet with a readier response than out-of-staters, however more nationally important the latter may be. Moreover, history designed for the laity will of necessity devote as much attention to popular culture and the lively arts as to the more traditional staples, politics and economics, particularly since the Black stamp on the former is more readily discernible.

10   The emphasis on the lively arts and popular culture lends itself to the mass media. Hence Black history for laymen has found a natural ally in television, commercial as well as educational, but obviously of far greater proportions in the latter. Radio, too, especially in the Folkways recordings, lends itself to Black cultural history. Other mass media such as newspapers and magazines are increasingly carrying Black history articles, biographical sketches, and pictorial materials. Sensing the growing interest in Black history, commercial firms have brought out coloring books, alphabet books, Black history games, and Black history in comic-book format.

11   History as hero worship is hardly the kind of history espoused by the second Black group under survey—the Black revolutionary nationalists. This   Category 2
group focuses upon exploiters and oppressors, a case study in man's inhumanity to man. This group views history as grievance collecting, a looking back in anger. Black nationalist history is essentially the story of a powerful white majority imposing its will upon a defenseless Black minority. Black nationalists hold that American society needs to be reconstructed and that Black history is, or should be, a means of ideological indoctrination in the rev-   1st trait
olutionary cause of Black liberation.

12   Black nationalist history is not without its traces of paranoid thinking, one which holds that the forces of evil are banded in an eternal conspiracy to maintain their oppressive sway. Of very ancient origin, this devil theory of history is deeply rooted in the human psyche and hence should occasion no surprise when met in any of its multiple guises.

13   Like so much else in American life, Black nationalism has, as it has always had, a variety of forms—cultural, religious, and economic, among others. Revolutionary nationalism moves a step beyond the others in its goals and does not rule out violence in achieving them. Revolutionary Black nationalists, having carefully examined the almost unbelievable pervasiveness of color prejudice in our society, have, in essence, given up on America. Estranged from the land of their birth, they ponder its dismantlement.

14   As to content, revolutionary Black history is not as interested in historical   2nd trait
spadework as in providing new interpretations of that which is already

known. Black nationalist history emphasizes racial contrast, physical and cultural. It propounds a Black aesthetic and implies a Black mystique. It bespeaks
the essential kinship of Black people on whatever continent they be located or
in whatever walk of life. Its central theme is oppression, slavery in one guise
or another. Rebelliousness against the oppressor likewise looms large in
nationalist lore.

15   A compound of Black rage and white guilt, revolutionary Black history
makes much of the analogy of colonialism, holding that Black Americans live
in a state of vassalage to white Americans. Black America is a semicolony of
white America.

16   Going further, the revolutionary school of thought stresses separatism,
insisting that Black Americans have always constituted a nation. To those who
hold these views, Black history has one overriding purpose, namely, to promote nation-building.

17   In tone, Black revolutionary history is judgmental, with overtones of   3rd trait
recrimination, moral condemnation, and prophetic warning. Apocalyptic and
polemical in temper, it scorns objectivity, which it equates with a defense of
the status quo. Revolutionary Black history may, on occasion, read like social
commentary, sometimes taking on a man-the-barricades urgency.

18   Selective in content, Black revolutionary history ignores as irrelevant those
aspects of the past which do not relate to its philosophy. As will be noted in
just a moment, however, this tendency to pick and choose is nothing new in
the historical profession.

19   The third group under survey are the Black academicians—the intellectu-   Category 3
ally sophisticated, the college and university trained, the well-read. Like the
revolutionary nationalists, they operate on a more studious level. They
would concur with the revolutionary nationalists in holding that history is a
weapon in the warfare. But to the academically oriented mind the basic foe is   1st trait
ignorance, be it willful or otherwise. It hardly need be added that ignorance
is a somewhat impersonal foe and hence less easily pinpointed, less starkly
isolated.

20   To the Black academician, history is a discipline, an attempt to recapture
and mirror the past as accurately as possible. Admittedly this is a tall order,
considering the nature of the evidence and the unreliability of so many of the
witnesses. Black academicians hardly need to be reminded that history, as we
know it, is not neutral, not value-free. Who can tell the Black academician anything new about the insensitivity of past generations of white scholars, of their
neglect or distortion of the role of Black peoples? But the Black academician
would question the viewpoint that prejudiced history must be met with prejudiced history; he would doubt that the best way to strike at the mythmakers
of history is to imitate them. In *The Fire Next Time,* James Baldwin has observed
that "an invented past can never be used; it cracks and crumbles under the
pressures of life like clay in a season of drought." As we have noted, however,
white Americans have made some use of an invented past. But Black Americans must realize that a powerful majority may for a time be able to afford the

luxury of fantasy. Such indulgence on the part of a minority is a species of living beyond its means, a minority having to husband carefully its limited resources.

21   Like the layman and the nationalist, the Black academician finds in Black history a deepening sense of racial worth and of peoplehood. He, too, reads Black history with pride. The Black academician views America as a civilization upon which his ancestors have left their stamp. Hence he does not regard America as a white civilization exclusively; to him it also has its Black, red, and yellow components. The Black academician holds that his forebears helped to build America, and this being the case no one should sensibly expect him to pack his belongings and leave for other shores.

22   In addition to personal and racial gratification the Black academician reads Black history because he feels that it will contribute to his knowledge and understanding of mankind, of his fellow travelers in time and space.

23   For academicians, <u>the content of Black history would be more selective</u> than   2nd trait
for the laymen, in an attempt to avoid the obvious or the well known. Black history for the academician would deal less with persons and more with processes, less with general Black history than with selected topics in Black history. It would include comparative studies and pose methodological problems. On the grounds that academicians do not shy away from the unpleasant, Black history for them would not ignore the less glorious aspects of the Black past—the African tribesmen who engaged in the slave trade, the slave drivers on the Southern plantations, the Black informers who divulged the slave conspiracies or those who revealed the hiding place of a runaway slave. History has its share of those blacks who turned out to be all too human.

24   The academician would grant that, more often than not, the truth makes one sick. But he believes the New Testament adage about truth also making one free. The academician holds that truth, including the search for it, has a liberating effect. To be truly free is to be free first and foremost in the great franchise of the mind. To a group like Black Americans, who have been subjected to so much falsehood by others, it would seem that the quest for truth should be held in high favor, having a relevance never failing.

25   Black history written for the academic fraternity will in the main take on a <u>reflective, judicial tone,</u> taking its cue from the careful winnowing and sifting   3rd trait
that preceded it. The style will be sober, the rhetoric restrained. Passionate and deeply emotional language is highly necessary and desirable in human affairs, but such expression is more the province of the poet, the orator, and the charismatic leader than of the professional historian. An orator may give full vent to his innermost feelings, and to the innermost feelings of his audience, but a social scientist works in a discipline which has imperatives of its own, imperatives which may point to conclusions that run counter to his private wishes.

26   The codes of his discipline bring the Black academician face to face with one of the major problems confronting every social scientist, namely, whether his citizen role should overshadow his professional role, whether he should give

priority to social action or to scientific inquiry. Should an academician strive for competence in his discipline or should he seek primarily to become personally involved and relevant? To the Black academician this dilemma takes on an unusual urgency inasmuch as he is fully aware of the long-standing discrimination against Black people in the American social order. Addressing himself to this question of citizenship role versus professional role, sociologist Ernest Q. Campbell comes to the conclusion that "there is no intrinsic reason why the roles of scientific inquirer and staunch advocate are incompatible" ("Negroes, Education, and the Southern States," *Social Forces,* March 1969). But to play these two roles simultaneously would seem to require unusual abilities and energies. In their absence each Black academician must come to some hard choices as to his own major commitment.

27   To the final audience under survey, <u>the white community</u>—academic and lay—Black history has an important message. Black history should not be confined to blacks alone—this would be like confining the Gospel to those already converted, to use a familiar figure. Black history, like other phases of Black studies, is no longer a matter of limited concern. Whites need to know Black history. As Theodore Draper points out in *The Rediscovery of Black Nationalism* (New York, 1970), "In the interest of the entire society, white students need Black Studies as much or even more than Black students." At a meeting of the Organization of American Historians in 1969, C. Vann Woodward voiced much the same sentiment in his presidential address, "Clio with Soul." Woodward spoke of Black history as being "too important to be left entirely to Negro historians."   *Category 4*

28   To begin with, whites should realize that the major reason for the long neglect of Black history falls upon the historical guild itself. As Carl Becker has pointed out, "The historian selects from a number of particular facts certain facts which he considers most important to be known." Historians, continues Becker, "unconsciously read the objective facts of the past in the light of their own purposes, or the preoccupations of their own age." To point out that written history has a subjective element is certainly nothing new—Becker's observations were made in 1910. But to mention this matter at the outset makes for the open-mindedness so essential to a proper perspective on the Black American. Whites who read history should know by now that white historians have until recently dealt with the American past in such a way as to ignore the Black presence or to minimize its importance in the making of America.

29   <u>The aim of Black history for white readers is twofold: first, to eliminate the myth that our country's past was rosy and romantic, a new Eden "with liberty and justice for all," and second, to illustrate the centrality of the Black American in our national experience.</u> White historians have until recently tended to play down the somber aspects of Black-white relationships in America—the deeply ingrained sense of white superiority dating back to Jamestown and Plymouth, the brutality of slavery, the mockery of post-Reconstruction, and the twentieth-century offshoots of these persistent pathologies. The American   *1st trait*

past has a tragic component which cannot be brushed away. White Americans must take a second thought as they sing the familiar lines, "Thine alabaster cities gleam,/Undimmed by human tears."

30   Black history would enable whites to more realistically appraise some of our country's boasted achievements and some of its acclaimed public figures. For example, whites generally view the age of Andrew Jackson as one in which the right to vote was extended to the common man. But whites need to know that it was during this period that states like North Carolina and Pennsylvania were explicitly prohibiting blacks from exercising this privilege. White readers of American history have thought highly of Woodrow Wilson for his espousal of the "New Freedom" and for his doctrine of "making the world safe for democracy." But white readers need to know that during Wilson's presidency, and with his acquiescence, Black federal workers in the District of Columbia were systematically segregated and were given inferior working conditions and restroom facilities such as had not existed up to this time in the federal government.

31   Black history would be remiss if it did not call attention to these sobering aspects of the American past. But Black history does not consist solely of white denial and discrimination. Hence Black history for whites would indicate the myriad ways in which this country's history and culture would have been different without the presence of the Black man. Many of these ways—economic, political, constitutional, and military—are more quickly spotted than others. In some fields—art, literature, music, the dance, and popular culture in general—the Black contribution centers in the common core, making its stamp more difficult to isolate. But whether obvious or subtle, the Black man's gifts to America have been freely received if slowly acknowledged. To this extent all Americans are part Black in their cultural patrimony. Blacks in general would concur in the sentiment expressed by a stanza from James Weldon Johnson ("Fifty Years, 1863–1913," in his *Fifty Years and Other Poems*, Boston, 1921):

> This land is ours by right of birth,
>   This land is ours by right of toil;
> We helped to turn its virgin earth,
>   Our sweat is in its fruitful soil.

32   The acceptance of Black history by whites has been greatly facilitated by the current emphasis on social history. "It is a good moment to be a social historian" writes E. J. Hobsbawn (*Daedalus*, Winter 1971), history professor at the University of London. This branch of history pays particular attention to the anonymous common man and to the manners and customs of everyday life. And even more importantly for a Black orientation, this branch of history emphasizes social movements and the phenomena of social protest.

33   For the white reader of Black history <u>the content would, at least initially, suggest the centrality of the Negro American and his identification with this country's great, professed goals.</u> Therefore such history would comprise a   2nd trait

general presentation of the American past with the Black component inter-woven throughout, appearing at its proper chronological juncture and not separately, somewhat like a disjointed subtheme for the curious, Clio's underworld.

34   <u>In style and technique Black history for whites would differentiate between</u>   3rd trait
<u>the white layman and the white intellectual.</u> For the white layman the approach would be much the same as for his Black counterpart, that is, an emphasis on biographical sketches and on the lively arts and popular culture, including sports. Again, as for the Black layman, books would be greatly sup-plemented by the mass media. Indeed, of course, the mass media outlets used to reach Black people will inevitably reach many whites.

35   For the white academician the approach to Black history might be broader than the biographical and less fearful of the recipient's short attention span. Black studies for white intellectuals would back assertion with documenta-tion, presenting proof and citing authorities. A footnote is not an end unto itself. But those of an academic bent have been trained to look for the hard evi-dence; to them a statement must be intellectually tenable, its sources as trust-worthy as possible. For the open-minded scholar—the seeker after truth—the will to believe is not an acceptable substitute for the data that corroborates.

36   We have dealt with Black history for four different audiences. But in written history the use of different approaches and viewpoints need come as no sur-prise. No one category of events, no single interpretation, can furnish the cloth for that seamless garment we call history. There is no single compass by which to unravel the course of historical causation. Written history, in form and con-tent, is many-sided, however much this may disconcert the doctrinaire types.

37   This short excursion into Black history has taken note of varying view-points as to its function. Although varied, these approaches are often comple-mentary rather than contradictory. More than anything else they demonstrate that there are alternate ways of looking at the past. The viewpoints of the rev-olutionary nationalist and the academic historian are not necessarily antago-nistic. The academician, for example, may disavow an activist role and say that he is dealing with ideas for their own sake. But ideas are weapons and, as a rule, action is germinated by ideas.

38   In the formation of the new Black history the academician—the traditional-ist—will continue to be of major importance. But if Black history is to come of age, revolutionary Black nationalists will also have much to contribute. The nationalist historians will force a reexamination of the historic patterns of color prejudice in America, not only in its grosser, more obvious manifesta-tions, but in its manifold subtle forms, its protective coloration, one might say. The nationalists will bring into purview the blacks of the so-called Third World, comparing and contrasting them with their counterparts in America. The tone of moral outrage that characterizes the nationalist school has its value, too, a healthy anger often acting as a social catalyst.

39   And finally the revolutionary Black nationalist has made it clear that to properly assess the Black past we need newer, nontraditional techniques. A

multidisciplinary approach is called for, one not relying so largely on written records. Historical inquiry is already profiting from the methodology of the behavioral sciences—sociology, anthropology, and psychology. Interdisciplinary history opens vistas across and beyond the traditional chronological and geographic boundaries. These widening approaches to appraising the past have led to such newer periodicals as the *Journal of Interdisciplinary History*, its first issue appearing in the autumn of 1970 and its avowed purpose to "stimulate historians to examine their own subjects in a new light, whether they be derived from psychology, physics, or paleontology."

40   This is the age of ideological cross-fertilization. It is to be noted, for example, that today in the study of early man on this planet no fewer than twelve different special skills are necessary—six field skills and six laboratory skills. In properly assessing the Black role in American history a comparable if less numerous list of skills is needed. Without the use of these newer tools the past will remain an incomplete past. In fine, historians of the Black past must take into consideration "the changing character of historical evidence, the development of new techniques and concepts in related disciplines, and the growing body of research by non-historians into historical problems," to borrow a phrase from David S. Landes and Charles Tilly ("History as Social Science," in Social Science Research Council *Items*, March 1971).

41   The newer Black history, looking afresh down the corridors of time, has a revolutionary potential of its own. For blacks it is a new way to see themselves. For whites it furnishes a new version of American history, one that especially challenges our national sense of smugness and self-righteousness and our avowal of fair play. Beyond this the new Black history summons the entire historical guild—writers, teachers, and learners—to higher levels of expectation and performance. History, as all of its disciples know, is both continuity and change. Change stems from our readiness to challenge the current order, using the best tools of our trade. A new Black history would revitalize education, quickening whatever it touches.

42   In 1925 in the foreword to his pathbreaking volume *The New Negro*, Alain Locke, one of the many illustrious Howard University scholar-humanists, said many things that have a contemporary ring: "Negro life is not only establishing new contacts and founding new centers, it is finding a new soul. There is a fresh spiritual and cultural focusing. . . . There is a renewed race-spirit that consciously and proudly sets itself apart." Locke, of course, was speaking primarily of creative expression in the arts, but his words aptly characterize the current Black thrust in history. In its work of restoring history's lost boundaries, the Black history of today is establishing new contacts and finding a new soul.

Reading-to-Write Questions

1. **Content:** In his introduction how does Quarles support his claim that interest in Black history has increased since the 1950s?

2. **Arrangement:** This is a well-organized essay. Where does Quarles preview the structure of the essay?

3. **Style:** Quarles occasionally uses metaphorical language, e.g., "to remove the *layers* of ignorance and distortion that had *encrusted* the Afro-American past." Can you find other examples in the essay?

4. _____

_____

_____

Suggested Topics

1. **Observation:** Using Quarles's criteria of aims, content, and style, classify contemporary Black music. (audience = overseas Internet correspondents)

2. **Critique:** Quarles was an academic historian. In this essay, does he describe the other types of historians fairly? (audience = students who intend to major in history)

3. **Synthesis:** Where do O'Bryant's, Reed's, Malcolm X's, Bennett's, Franklin and Moss's, and Ellison's selections fit in Quarles's classificatory scheme? (audience = class)

4. _____

_____

_____

Background Readings: BLACK HISTORIOGRAPHY

Black History. New York: Institute for Research in History and the Haworth Press, 1980.

Cimbala, Paul A., and Robert F. Himmelberg. *Historians and Race: Autobiography and the Writing of History.* Bloomington: Indiana UP, 1996.

Conyers, James L. *Africana Studies: A Disciplinary Quest for Both Theory and Method.* Jefferson, NC: McFarland, 1997.

Jewsiewicki, Bogumil, and David Newbury, eds. *African Historiographies: What History for Which Africa?* Beverly Hills: Sage, 1986.

Meier, August, and Elliott Rudwick. *Black History and the Historical Profession, 1915–1980.* Urbana, IL: University of Illinois Press, 1986.

Walker, Clarence. *Deromanticizing Black History.* Knoxville: University of Tennessee Press, 1991.

_____

_____

_____

Ancient Egyptians: Innovators of the Past
Richard O'Bryant

Tapping the knowledge of Dr. Aziz Batran, a history professor at Howard University, Richard O'Bryant composed the following summary of ancient Egyptian contributions to the world's civilizations. The article, which appeared in a 1993 issue of the Howard Engineer Magazine, *highlights Egyptian accomplishments in three fields: fine art, science, and engineering. At the time of publication, O'Bryant was a computer systems engineering major and the managing editor of the magazine.*

———————————

1   Art, science and engineering have a history that is deep in human existence. Often, people have little knowledge of the origins of the techniques and ideas in use today. Many of the techniques and innovations in use today originate from the times of ancient Egypt. These contributions are often overlooked by historians. The Egyptians contributed many things to the arts, sciences and engineering. These contributions include many of the building, mathematical and creative arts techniques we use today. Many people are aware of the great pyramids and ancient artifacts of Ancient Egypt. However, they are unaware that this African civilization may have provided the basic building blocks for civilizations to follow, such as the Greek and Roman civilizations. Dr. Aziz Batran, Associate Professor of History here at Howard University, shared his knowledge on a few of the many Egyptian contributions to fine art, science and engineering.

2   To understand the Egyptian contribution to these fields, one must understand the time in which [the Egyptians] lived. About 4000 B.C. the Kingdoms
of Upper Egypt and Lower Egypt were born. These Kingdoms grew very quickly.
During this period, buildings began to be made of bricks, the 365 day calendar
was invented, architecture styles developed and a writing system, hieroglyphics, was developed.

3   The unification of Egypt occurred in 3200 B.C. after a long period of intense
growth. Throughout the Nile Valley, new and improved methods of agriculture, domestication of animals and food production were developed. The
potential of the rich and fertile Nile Valley was being tapped. Thus village life
developed rapidly along the Nile River.

4   For about 3000 years, the black people of Ancient Egypt, heirs to the
Neolithic Revolution in the Nile Valley, built a civilization that surpassed in its
splendor any other civilization of that time. It predated the civilizations of the
Middle East, Greece and Rome. It may have provided the foundation on
which these civilizations were developed. Ancient Egypt was an authentic
African civilization, developed by Africans on African soil.

Fine Art

*"skill acquired by experience, study or observation: the conscious use of skill and cre-
ative imagination esp. in the production of aesthetic objects; also: works so produced"*

5   The Egyptians made a great deal of contributions to the field of arts and
crafts. They explored and utilized the various natural resources of their country
as well as neighboring countries to create their art. The Egyptians mastered the
techniques of metal working such as forging, hammering, casting, stamping,
soldering and riveting. They built factories where gold and silver were fashioned into jewelry, and copper into weapons and large statues. They also mastered wood-working. Egyptian carpenters used saws, pliers, hammers and
drills to manufacture many kinds of beautiful furniture. The carpenters who
had the most significant effect on the Egyptian lifestyles were those who spe-
cialized in boat making. The boats were used all along the Nile to transport food,
people, and stone blocks weighing between 8 and 10 tons each. These blocks
were used for building temples, statues and pyramids. The boats were also used
in trading expeditions to Syria, Palestine and down the Red Sea to Somalia.

6   The Egyptians were among the first to perfect the techniques of spinning
and linen making, which were used in the textile industries. Spinning was
done by the women, who produced a variety of fine fabrics. The finest cloth of
all, byssus, was woven in the temples. It was sold abroad and brought huge
revenues to the Egyptian Kingdom. In addition to textiles, Egyptians are credited with the invention of glass making techniques for both transparent and
non-transparent glass. They manufactured vases, beads, mirrors and, later,
colored glass.

7   Another of their great contributions was the making of Papyrus, from which the word paper is derived. The fibers of this plant were used for boat making, wicks for oil lamps, mats, baskets and ropes. Papyrus or paper was made by placing crosswise layers of fine strips taken from the stem of the Papyrus plant. After pressing and drying, the woven strips formed a large sheet of paper. Ancient Egypt was the source of many of the materials and methods that are used today in the field of fine arts.

Science

"knowledge covering general truths or the operation of general laws esp. as obtained and tested through scientific method: such knowledge concerned with the physical world and its phenomena"

8   In the field of science perhaps the most outstanding contribution of the Ancient Egyptians is mummification. Their perfection of mummification shows their precise knowledge of the sciences, including physics, chemistry, medicine and surgery. Mummification involves soaking the body of a deceased person in a chemical called Natron. This chemical was found in certain areas in Egypt, particularly in the Wadi el Natron (Wadi means Valley). The compounds of Natron are a mixture of sodium carbonate, sodium bicarbonate, salt and sodium sulphate. After having soaked the body in Natron for 70 days, [the Egyptians] drew the brain out through the nostrils and removed the intestines through an incision made in the side of the body. Operations as delicate as these necessitated an accurate knowledge of anatomy and surgery.

9   The Egyptians' medical knowledge can be considered as one of the most important early contributions of the Ancient Egyptians to the history of man. One of the most significant personalities in the history of medicine was Imhotep, the prime minister, architect and physician of King Zoser of the Third Dynasty. Imhotep was adopted by the Greeks. They called him Askelepios, the God of Medicine.

10   [The Egyptians] also had a vast knowledge of herbs, minerals and various chemical substances. The Egyptian doctor, like modern doctors, examined his patient and determined the symptoms of his ailment. Among the ailments identified and treated by the doctors were gastric disorders, stomach swelling, skin cancer, laryngitis, diabetes, bilharzia, opthalmia, bronchitis, and constipation. Doctors would treat their patients with ointments, syrups, potions, oils and inhalants.

11   Egyptian surgeons developed their surgical techniques at a very early period in their history. From the surgical pamphlets which survived from the old kingdom, historians have come to learn about the Egyptians' mastery of bone surgery, external pathology, dentistry and medicine.

Engineering

"the application of science and mathematics by which the properties of matter and the sources of energy in nature are made useful to man in structures, machines, products, systems and processes"

12   Engineering is a technical activity that specifies means for altering the physical environment to create utility. The genius of the Egyptians in the field of engineering can be seen today in the magnificent statues, obelisks, pyramids, sphinxes and temples which they constructed. The Egyptians were also very proficient in math. Their method of numeration is based on the decimal system. They did not use zero but used fractions such as ½, ⅓, ¼, etc. Egyptian administrative organization required the knowledge of arithmetic and the need to survey the area of land eroded or added each year by the flooding of the Nile. This led them to invent geometry. The Egyptians knew perfectly well how to calculate the area and volume of several geometric shapes. Their greatest mathematical success was the calculation of the area of a circle. They have been credited with approximating the value of pi to be 3.1605.

13   The Egyptians applied their mathematical knowledge to the extraction, transportation and positioning of the huge blocks of stone used in their massive architectural projects. They had a long tradition in using mudbricks and various kinds of stone from very early times. Their first use of heavy granite was during the period of the First Dynasty at which time it was used for flooring the tombs belonging to Al-Abydos. In the Second Dynasty, they used limestone to construct the walls of tombs.

14   The Egyptians used their mechanical engineering abilities in the construction of boats, vehicles and ramps, which were used to build pyramids, sphinxes and temples. They applied the principle of leverage to transport the large pieces of stone for very long distances.

15   The Egyptian architectural triumphs are among the best known. The most vital development in Egyptian architecture took place during the Third Dynasty. It was during this time [the Egyptians] constructed the first complete building of stone, the step pyramid of King Zoser.

16   The greatest of all pyramids was erected by Pharoah Khufu and remains number one on the list of the seven wonders of the ancient world. Its great proportions and longevity stand today as proof of the engineering, architectural and administrative expertise of the Egyptians. The exact proportions, measurements and orientation of the chambers and corridors of the Giza pyramid, not to mention the cutting and erection of giant obelisks in solid stone, indicate their great technical skills.

17   The pyramids built for the dead pharaohs were considered to be houses where they spent their immortal life. By their great height, the pyramids were meant to join earth with the heavens.

18   Khufu's pyramid stands 481 feet high; each of its square sides is 175 feet in length; 2,300,000 blocks of granite, each weighing between 8 and 10 tons, were used in its construction.

19   The cutting of stone and construction of the pyramids were accomplished solely through the strength of human hands. Every year, after the harvest season, some 100,000 peasants worked on the construction of the pyramids. Contrary to what many European historians believe, no slave labor was used. The labor was provided willingly and freely by the Egyptian peasants to immortalize the pharaohs who were thought to embody and symbolize the whole nation.

20   In addition to pyramids, the Egyptians built numerous Sphinxes out of solid rock. Sphinxes have the head of a man and body of a lion and symbolize power and strength. The Great Sphinx of Giza is believed to be the image of Khufu. The Sphinx, which was meant to commemorate Pharaoh Chephren, is believed to have been shot at and damaged as ordered by Napoleon because of its distinct black male features.

21   The Ancient [Egyptians were] ahead of their time. Their contributions, to what many consider to be European advancements, are innumerable. Only a few of their many developments were discussed by Dr. Batran. This cursory introduction to Ancient Egyptian advancements does not do justice to the greatness of their civilization. Their civilization warrants study by all people. For although their contributions are often overlooked, it is clear that their great civilization was an incubator for many of the techniques we use to this day.

Reading-to-Write Questions

1. **Content:** What role do numbers (e.g., dates and measurements) play in O'Bryant's effort to document Egypt's contributions to the world's great civilizations?

2. **Arrangement:** Imagine reading this essay without its subheadings. List two reasons that the subheadings are helpful.

3. **Style:** O'Bryant opens each of his sections with a dictionary definition of the field. Is the telegraphic style of the definitions appropriate? Would you prefer a definition in O'Bryant's words?

4. _____

    _____

    _____

Suggested Topics

1. **Observation:** Using his categories, compare what O'Bryant has taught you about Africans with what you learned about Africans in secondary school. (audience = your secondary high school teachers)

2. **Critique:** O'Bryant draws all of his evidence from one source: Dr. Aziz Batran. After consulting some of the background readings, cite evidence that O'Bryant could add to each of his categories. (audience = history majors)

3. **Synthesis:** Search the library and/or Internet to find out what African *Americans* have contributed to each of the fields that O'Bryant describes. Write an essay that opens with a summary of the ancient African achievements and then classifies more recent African American accomplishments. (audience = African American high school students)

4. _____

    _____

    _____

Background Readings: REWRITING AFRICAN HISTORY

Ben-Jochannan, Yosef. *New Dimensions in African History.* Trenton, NJ: Africa World Press, 1991.

Bernal, Martin, *Black Athena: The Afroasiatic Roots of Classical Civilization.* Rutgers, NJ: Rutgers UP, 1987–91.

Clarke, John Henrik. *African People in World History.* Baltimore, MD: Black Classic Press, 1993.

———. *Christopher Columbus and the African Holocaust.* Brooklyn, NY: A & B Books, 1992.

———. *A Search for Africa.* New York: Times Books, 1994.

Davidson, Basil. *African Civilization Revisited: From Antiquity to Modern Times.* 2nd ed., Trenton, NJ: Africa World Press, 1990.

Diop, Cheikh Anta. *The African Origin of Civilization: Myth or Reality?* New York: Lawrence Hill Books, 1974.

Gates, Henry Louis, Jr. *Wonders of the African World.* New York: Knopf, 1999.

Hamilton, Paul. *African People's Contributions to World Civilization.* 2nd ed. Denver: R. A. Renaissance, 1995.

James, George G. M. *Stolen Legacy.* New York: Philosophical Library, 1954.

Poe, Richard. *Black Spark, White Fire: Did African Explorers Civilize Ancient Europe?* Rocklin, CA: Prima, 1997.

Snowden, Frank M., Jr. *Blacks in Antiquity: Ethiopians in the Greco-Roman Experience.* Cambridge, MA: Belknap/Harvard UP, 1970.

Van Sertima, Ivan, ed. *Blacks in Science: Ancient and Modern.* New Brunswick, NJ: Transaction Books, 1983.

———. *They Came Before Columbus: The African Presence in Ancient America.* New York: Random House, 1976.

Williams, Chancellor. *The Destruction of Black Civilization.* Chicago: Third World Press, 1987.

Slave Resistance
John Hope Franklin

John Hope Franklin is the grandson of an escaped slave. A distinguished historian, he has written numerous books about the Black experience, including the Emancipation Proclamation, Reconstruction: After the Civil War, Race and History, *and* The Color Line: Legacy for the Twenty-First Century. *The following selection was taken from the eighth edition of his classic,* From Slavery to Freedom *(2000), co-authored by Alfred Moss, Jr. In this passage Franklin describes the brutality of slavemasters and overseers and then classifies the ways slaves reacted.*

---

1   It cannot be denied that as old as the institution of slavery was, human beings had not, by the nineteenth century, brought themselves to the point where they could be subjected to it without protest and resistance. Resistance could be found wherever slavery existed, and slavery in the United States was no exception. Too frequently, misunderstanding, suspicion, and hatred were mutually shared by master and slave. Indeed, they were natural enemies, and on many occasions they conducted themselves as such. There are, of course, numerous examples of kindness and understanding on the part of owners as well as docility—which may be more accurately described as accommodation—and tractability on the part of slaves. But this master-slave relationship was an unnatural relationship and was not, by the nature of things, inherent in the system.

2   The brutality that apparently was inherent in a system of human exploitation existed in every community in which slavery was established. The wastefulness

and extravagance of the plantation system made no exception of human resources. Slaves were for economic gain, and if beating them would increase their efficiency—which was generally believed—then the rod and lash should not be spared. Far from being a civilizing force, moreover, the plantation bred indecency in human relations, and the slave was the immediate victim of the barbarity of a system that commonly exploited the sex of the women and the work of everyone. Finally, the psychological situation that was created by the master-slave relationship stimulated terrorism and brutality because masters felt secure in their position and interpreted their role as calling for that type of conduct. Many masters as well as slaves got the reputation of being "bad," which contributed to the tension that seemed to be mounting everywhere as the institution developed.

3   Laws for the purpose of protecting slaves were few and were seldom enforced. It was almost impossible to secure the conviction of a master who mistreated a slave. Knowing that, the owner was inclined to take the law into his or her own hands. Overseers were generally notorious for their brutality, and the accounts of abuse and mistreatment on their part as well as on the part of those who hired slaves are numerous. Masters and mistresses were perhaps almost as guilty. In 1827 a Georgia grand jury brought in a true bill of manslaughter against a slave owner for beating his slave to death, but he was acquitted. Several years later Thomas Sorrell of the same state was found guilty of killing one of his slaves with an axe, but the jury recommended him to the mercy of the court. In Kentucky a Mrs. Maxwell had a wide reputation for beating her slaves, both men and women, on the face as well as the body. There is also the shocking account of Mrs. Alpheus Lewis, who burned her slave girl around the neck with hot tongs. Drunken masters had little regard for their slaves; the most sensational example of which is a Kentucky man who dismembered his slave and threw him piece by piece into the fire. One Mississippi master dragged from the bed a slave whom he suspected of theft and inflicted more than 1,000 lashes. Repeated descriptions of runaways contained phrases such as "large scar on hip," "no marks except those on his back," "much scarred with the whip," and "will no doubt show the marks of a recent whipping." They suggest a type of brutality that doubtless contributed to the slave's decision to abscond.

4   To the demonstrations of brutality as well as to the very institution of slavery itself, slaves reacted in various ways. Thanks to the religion of their masters they could be philosophical about the whole situation and escape through ritual and song. The emphasis on otherworldliness in slave songs certainly suggested grim dissatisfaction with their worldly status. "Dere's a Great Camp Meetin' in de Promised Land," "Look Away in de Heaven, Lord," "Fo' My Soul's Goin' to Heaven Jes' Sho's You Born," and "Heaven, Heaven, Everybody Talkin' 'Bout Heaven Ain't Goin' There" are only a few of the songs that slaves sang in the hope that their burdens would be relieved in the next world. As long as they were in this world they had to make the most of a bad situation by loafing on the job, feigning illness in the fields and on the auction block, and engaging in an elaborate program of sabotage. Slaves were so

hard on farming tools that special ones were developed for them. They drove the animals with a cruelty that suggested revenge, and they could be so ruthless in destruction of the fields that the most careful supervision was necessary to ensure survival of the crops until harvest time. Forests, barns, and homes were burned to the extent that members of the patrol were frequently fearful of leaving home lest they be visited with revenge in the form of destruction of their property by fire.

5   Self-mutilation and suicide were popular forms of resistance to slavery. Slaves cut off their toes and hands and mutilated themselves in other ways so as to render themselves ineffective as workers. One Kentucky slave carpenter, for example, cut off one of his hands and the fingers of the other when he learned that he was to be sold down the river. There were several instances of slaves having shot themselves in the hand or foot, especially upon being recovered from running away. The number of suicides seems relatively high, and certainly the practice was widespread. Slaves fresh from Africa committed suicide in great numbers. In 1807 two boatloads of Africans newly arrived in Charleston starved themselves to death. When his slave woman was found dead by her own hanging in 1829, a Georgia planter was amazed since he saw no reason why she should want to take her own life. When two Louisiana slaves were returned to their owner after having been stolen in 1858, they drowned themselves in the bayou. One of the South's wealthiest planters, Charles Manigault, lost a slave by a similar act when the overseer threatened him with punishment. Sometimes slave mothers killed their own children to prevent them from growing up in slavery.

6   Much more disturbing to the whites of the South were the numerous instances of slaves doing violence to the master class. Poisoning was always feared, and perhaps some planters felt a real need for an official taster. As early as 1761 the Charleston *Gazette* remarked that the "Negroes have begun the hellish act of poisoning." Arsenic and other similar compounds were used. Where they were not available, slaves are known to have resorted to mixing ground glass in the gravy for their owners' tables. Numerous slaves were convicted of murdering their owners and overseers, but some escaped. In 1797 a Screven County, Georgia, planter was killed by his newly imported African slave. Another Georgia master was killed by a slave who stabbed him sixteen times. The slave was later burned alive. The slave of William Pearce of Florida killed his owner with an axe when Pearce sought to punish him. Carolina Turner of Kentucky was choked to death by a slave whom she was flogging. Though the citizenry had long complained of the woman's merciless brutality in dealing with her slaves, her killer was summarily hanged for his deed. The times that overseers and owners were killed by slaves in the woods or fields were exceedingly numerous, as the careful reading of almost any Southern newspaper will reveal.

7   Every Southern community raised its annual crop of runaway slaves. Both federal and state legislation aided in their recovery, but many slaves escaped forever. The practice of running away became so widespread that every state

sought to strengthen its patrol and other safeguards to little avail. Hardly a newspaper went to press without several advertisements listing runaways, and sometimes there were several columns of such advertisements. The following is typical:

> Absconded from the Forest Plantation of the late William Dunbar, on Sunday the 7th instant, a very handsome Mulattress called Harriet, about 13 years old, with straight back hair and dark eyes. This girl was lately in New Orleans, and is known to have seen there a man whom she claims as her father and who does now or did lately live on the Mississippi, a little above the mouth of the Caffalaya. It is highly probable some plan has been concocted for the girl's escape.

8   Long before the Underground Railroad was an effective antislavery device slaves were running away: men, women, and children, singly, in pairs, or in groups. At times they went so far as to organize themselves into groups called Maroons and to live in communities, on the order of Palmares in Brazil. The forests, mountains, and swamps of the Southern states were their favorite locations, and they proved to be troublesome to the owners who sought to maintain strict order on their plantations.

9   Some slaves disguised themselves or armed themselves with free passes in their effort to escape. Others simply walked off, apparently hoping that fate would be kind and assist in their permanent escape. Some were inveterate runaways, such as the North Carolina woman who fled from her owner's plantation no less than sixteen times. Others were not as daring and gave up after one unsuccessful attempt. While there is no way of even approximating the number of runaways, it is obvious that fleeing from the institution was one of the slaves' most effective means of resistance. It represented the continuous fight that slaves carried on against their masters.

10   The most sensational and desperate reaction of slaves to their status was the conspiracy to revolt. Those slaves who could summon the nerve to strike for their freedom in a group, that is, who could engage in "carrying the fight to the enemy," hoped that insurrection would end, once and for all, the degradation of human enslavement. To whites rebellion was a mad, sinister act of desperate savages, in league with the devil, who could not appreciate the benign influences of the institution and who would dare shed the blood of their benefactors. Inherent in revolts was bloodshed on both sides. Blacks accepted this as the price of liberty, while whites were panic-stricken at the very thought of it. Even rumors of insurrections struck terror in the hearts of slaveholders and called forth the vigorous efforts to guard against the dreaded eventuality.

11   Revolts, or conspiracies to revolt, persisted until 1865. They began with the institution and did not end until slavery was abolished. It can, therefore, be

said that they were a part of the institution, a kind of bitterness that whites had to take along with the sweetness of slavery. As the country was turning to Jeffersonian Republicanism at the beginning of the nineteenth century, many people believed that a new day had arrived for the common person. Some blacks, however, felt that they would have to force their new day by breaking away from slavery. In Henrico County, Virginia, they resolved to revolt against the institution under the leadership of Gabriel Prosser and Jack Bowler. For months they planned the desperate move, gathering clubs, swords, and the like for the appointed day. On August 30, 1800, more than 1,000 slaves met six miles outside of Richmond and began to march on the city, but a violent storm almost routed the insurgents. Two slaves had already informed the whites, and Governor Monroe, acting promptly, called out more than 600 troops and notified every militia commander in the state. In due time scores of slaves were arrested, and 35 were executed. Gabriel Prosser was captured in late September, and after he refused to talk to anyone he too was executed.

12   Whites speculated extravagantly over the number of slaves involved in this major uprising. The estimates ran all the way from 2,000 to 50,000. The large numbers, together with the total disregard slaves seemed to have for their own lives, caused the whites to shudder. The high ground that slaves took in maintaining silence added to the stark terror of the whole situation. When one was asked what he had to say, he calmly replied:

> I have nothing more to offer than what General Washington would have had to offer, had he been taken by the British officers and put to trial by them. I have ventured my life in endeavouring to obtain the liberty of my countrymen, and am a willing sacrifice to their cause; and I beg, as a favour, that I may be immediately led to execution. I know that you have predetermined to shed my blood, why then all this mockery of a trial?

13   The unrest among slaves, even in Virginia, continued into the following year, and plots were reported in Petersburg and Norfolk and in various places in North Carolina. The latter state became so alarmed that many slaves were lashed, branded, and cropped, and at least 15 were hanged for alleged implication in conspiracies. In the subsequent years, before the war with England, there were reports of insurrection up and down the Atlantic seaboard. Conspiracy had crossed the mountains, for in 1810 a plot was uncovered in Lexington, Kentucky. The following year, more than 400 rebellious slaves in Louisiana had to be put down by federal and state troops. At least 75 slaves lost their lives in the encounter and in the trials that ensued. There was another uprising in New Orleans in the following year.

14   Following the War of 1812 the efforts of slaves to revolt continued. In Virginia in 1815 a white man, George Boxley, decided to attempt to free the slaves.

He made elaborate plans, but a slave woman betrayed him and his conspirators. Although Boxley himself escaped, six slaves were hanged and another six were banished. When the revolutions of Latin America and Europe broke out, Americans could not restrain themselves in their praise and support of the fighters for liberty. The South joined in the loud hosannas, while slaves watched the movements for the emancipation of the slaves in Latin America and the Caribbean. Perhaps all these developments had something to do with what was the most elaborate, though not the most effective, conspiracy of the period: the Denmark Vesey insurrection.

15   Vesey had purchased his freedom in 1800 and for a score of years had made a respectable living as a carpenter in Charleston, South Carolina. He was a sensitive, liberty-loving person and was not satisfied in the enjoyment of his own relatively comfortable existence. He believed in equality for everyone and resolved to do something for his slave brothers and sisters. Over a period of several years he carefully plotted his revolt and chose his assistants. Together they made and collected their weapons: 250 pike heads and bayonets and 300 daggers. Vesey also sought assistance from Haiti. He set the second Sunday in July 1822 for the day of the revolt; and when the word leaked out, he moved it up one month, but his assistants, who were scattered for miles around Charleston, did not all get the word. Meanwhile, the whites were well aware of what was going on and began to round up suspects. At least 139 blacks were arrested, 47 of whom were condemned. Even 4 white men were fined and imprisoned for encouraging the revolt. Estimates of the number of blacks involved in the plot ran as high as 9,000.

16   The following decade saw the entire South apprehensive over possible uprisings. The revival of the antislavery movement and the publication of such incendiary material as David Walker's *Appeal* put the South's nerves on edge. Several revolts were reported on Louisiana plantations in 1829, and in 1830 a number of citizens of North Carolina asked their legislature for aid because their slaves had become "almost uncountroulable." The panic of the 1820s culminated in 1831 with the insurrection of Nat Turner. This slave from Southampton County, Virginia, was a mystical, rebellious person who had on one occasion run away and then decided to return to his owner. Perhaps he had already begun to feel that he had been selected by some divine power to deliver his people from slavery.

17   Upon the occasion of the solar eclipse in February 1831, Turner decided that the time had come for him to lead his people out of bondage. He selected the Fourth of July as the day, but when he became ill he postponed the revolt until he saw another sign. On August 13, when the sun turned a "peculiar greenish blue," he called the revolt for August 21. He and his followers began by killing Turner's master, Joseph Travis, and his family. In rapid succession other families fell before the blows of the blacks. Within twenty-four hours 60 whites had been killed. The revolt was spreading rapidly when the main group of blacks was met and overpowered by state and federal troops. More than 100 slaves were killed in the encounter, and 13 slaves and 3 free Negroes were immedi-

ately hanged. Turner was captured on October 30, and in less than two weeks, on November 11, he was executed.

18   The South was completely dazed by the Southampton uprising. The situation was grossly exaggerated in many communities. Some reports were that whites had been murdered by the hundreds in Virginia. Small wonder that several states felt it necessary to call special sessions of the legislature to consider the emergency. Most states strengthened their Slave Codes, and citizens literally remained awake nights waiting for slaves to make another break. The uprisings continued. In 1835 several slaves in Monroe County, Georgia, were hanged or whipped to death because of implication in a conspiracy. In the following decade there were several uprisings in Alabama, Louisiana, and Mississippi. In 1853 a serious revolt in New Orleans involving 2,500 slaves was aborted by the informing of a free black. In 1856 the Maroons in Bladen and Robeson counties, North Carolina, "went on the warpath" and terrorized the countryside. Up until and throughout the Civil War, slaves demonstrated their violent antipathy for slavery by continuing to rise against it.

Reading-to-Write Questions

1. **Content:** How would you characterize the examples Franklin and Moss use as supporting evidence?

2. **Arrangement:** What do you notice about the order in which Franklin and Moss present the types of slave reactions?

3. **Style:** How do Franklin and Moss employ the dash?

4. _____

    _____

    _____

Suggested Topics

1. **Observation:** Interview an elderly African American about racial discrimination during his or her era. Then classify the ways that African Americans reacted to the discrimination. (audience = African American high school students)

2. **Critique:** Franklin and Moss state, "Resistance has been found wherever the institution of slavery existed." Support their claim by citing three types of slave resistance that have occurred outside the U.S. (audience = an international audience)

3. **Synthesis:** Consult one of the background readings. Then use examples from the source to illustrate three types of slave resistance that Franklin and Moss describe. (audience = a general audience)

4. _____

    _____

    _____

Background Reading: RESISTANCE TO SLAVERY

Aptheker, Herbert. *American Negro Slave Revolts*. New York: International Publishers, 1983.

Best, Felton. *Black Resistance Movements in the United States and Africa, 1800–1993*. Lewiston, ME: E. Mellen Press, 1995.

Carroll, Joseph C. *Slave Insurrections in the United States, 1800–1865*. 1938. New York: Negro Universities Press, 1968.

Cheek, William F. *Black Resistance Before the Civil War*. Beverly Hills, CA: Glencoe, 1970.

Coffin, Levi. *Reminiscences of Levi Coffin, The Reputed President of the Underground Railroad*. 1876. rpt. Salem, NH: Ayer, 1968.

Higginson, Thomas Wentworth. *Black Rebellion*. 1888. rpt. Trenton, NJ: Ayer, 1969.

James, C.L.R. *A History of Negro Revolt*. New York: Haskell House, 1969.

Lofton, John. *Denmark Vesey's Revolt: The Slave Plot That Lit a Fuse to Fort Sumter*. Kent, OH: Kent State UP, 1983.

McDougall, Marion Gleason. *Fugitive Slaves (1619–1865)*. 1891. rpt. New York: Bergman, 1967.

Owens, William A. *Black Mutiny: The Revolt on the Schooner Amistad*. New York: Plume, 1997.

_____

_____

_____

Recommended Literature: Robert Hayden's "Middle Passage" from *A Ballad of Remembrance* (poem)

The Black Founding Fathers
Lerone Bennett

Journalist and historian, Lerone Bennett, Jr. made his name as a senior editor of Ebony Magazine. *He has authored more than ten books about African Americans, including* Wade in the Water: Great Moments in Black History, Before the Mayflower: A History of Black America, *and* The Shaping of Black America. *From the 1975 edition of* Shaping *comes the current selection, which originally appeared in* Ebony Magazine. *This excerpt describes the types of institutions African Americans established during the nineteenth century to build an independent and united Black community.*

---

1   Institutions are mirrors, sounding boards, communication channels, and deposits of energy. They are mediations between man and man, between man and things, between man and the past, between man and the unknown. Without institutions, men cannot see themselves or be themselves. Without institutions, without rituals, without structures of relationship and meaning, men cannot communicate with their dead or pass on their experiences to the unborn. In order to be and in order to become, men must have institutions.

2   It was in obedience to that primal law that the white founding fathers gathered in Independence Hall to create a structure and an order. And it was in obedience to that same law that the excluded came together in the same year to create an order of another kind. Perhaps the key move in the second ingathering was made in Philadelphia in the same year of the Constitutional Convention. In that year Richard Allen and Absalom Jones, two former slaves, withdrew

from the St. George's Methodist Episcopal Church and created a germinal black institution. The immediate cause of the withdrawal was the rising tide of racism in the church. But there were other and deeper causes. Richard Allen and Absalom Jones and their followers already had a new sense of themselves and of what they wanted and of what they would accept. In their minds, in a larval state, was the idea of an African-American personality. They felt, they said, *cramped* in the exclusionist and whitened atmosphere of white institutions. They did not want, they said, to be *under* the government of whites but an integral part of that government. An admirable formulation, as you can see, and one which would form the dominant thrust of the African-American personality for years to come.

3   When whites transgressed the line Allen and his colleagues had defined as inviolable, they marched out of St. George's Methodist Episcopal Church in the first mass demonstration in black American history. Richard Allen was there. Let him speak:

> "A number of us usually attended St. George's church in Fourth street; and when the colored people began to get numerous in attending the church, they moved us from the seats we usually sat on, and placed us around the wall, and on Sabbath morning we went to church and the sexton stood at the door, and told us to go in the gallery. . . . We expected to take the seats over the ones we formerly occupied below, not knowing any better. . . . Meeting had begun and they were nearly done singing and just as we got to the seats, the elder said, 'Let us pray.' We had not been long upon our knees before I heard considerable scuffling and low talking. I raised my head up and saw one of the trustees . . . having hold of the Rev. Absalom Jones, pulling him up off his knees, and saying, 'You must get up—you must not kneel here.' Mr. Jones replied, 'Wait until the prayer is over.' [The trustee] said, 'No, you must get up now, or I will call for aid and force you away.' Mr. Jones said, 'Wait until prayer is over, and I will get up and trouble you no more.' With that [the trustee] beckoned to one of the other trustees. . . . to come to his assistance. He came, and went to William White to pull him up. By this time prayer was

over, and we all went out of the church in a
body, and they were no more plagued with
us in the church."

4   They were no more plagued with black people in a great many places. The
Philadelphia demonstration was the focal point of a spontaneous movement
that erupted in city after city. Without premeditation or plan or design, blacks
in Boston, New York, and other Northern centers walked out of white institutions and created counter-institutions. Here again the key move was made in
Philadelphia, where, on April 12, 1787, Richard Allen and Absalom Jones created the Free African Society, which DuBois called "the first wavering step of
a people toward a more organized social life." The society was a mutual aid
society, an embryonic church, and a political structure. It also contained the
germ of a major black business, the insurance company.

5   Similar societies were formed in New York City, Boston, and Newport,
Rhode Island. In the formation and rapid spread of these societies we have
irrefutable proof of the growth of an independent black consciousness. The
product of a new consciousness, the free African societies engendered an even
higher level of consciousness, creating links between the isolated free Northern colonies. Through the medium of these societies, free blacks exchanged
information, ideas, and programs.

6   The formation of the African societies was a crucial and formative educational experience for the pioneer leaders. In these organizations pioneer leaders learned how to resolve and how to bring collective pressure to bear. They
learned to see their lives in a time-line which extended from Africa to the Day
of Judgment they believed would vindicate them.

7   From this fount concentric circles of commitment spread to all of the communities of the North, leading to the creation of a second level of organization,
the independent Black Church. Out of the Free African Society of Philadelphia
came two of the first black churches; the First African Church of St. Thomas,
the first black Episcopal church, and Bethel AME Church, the mother church
of the African Methodist Episcopal Church. In 1796 the first congregation of
the AME Zion Church was organized in New York City. Around 1809 black
Baptist churches were organized in Boston, Philadelphia, and New York. By
the War of 1812, there were black churches of every conceivable description,
including a black Dutch Reformed church in New York City.

8   A further development of these organizational acts was the founding of
national church bodies. In 1816, sixteen ministers met in Philadelphia and
formed the African Methodist Episcopal Church. Five years later nineteen
ministers representing six churches formed the African Methodist Episcopal
Zion Church.

9   A third level of organization consisted of lodges and fraternal orders. In
1787 Prince Hall, the Revolutionary War veteran and Methodist minister, organized African [Masonic] Lodge No. 459 in Boston. Five years later a Grand

Lodge, the first black interstate organization, was launched with Hall as the Grand Master.

10   Less dramatic but no less relevant was the fourth level of educational and cultural institutions. In 1787 Boston leaders, led by Prince Hall, sounded one of the dominant themes of black concern by petitioning the state legislature for equal educational facilities. The plea was denied; and in 1798 the black parents of Boston opened a school in Prince Hall's home. The school was transferred later to the African Meeting House and was operated for some twenty-nine years. A similar course of development was roughly characteristic of other Northern centers, including Philadelphia, where Richard Allen opened a day school for black children and a night school for black adults.

11   Substantial help came from white organizations, in particular the New York Manumission Society, which was largely responsible for the organization of the famous African Free Schools of New York City. According to some authorities, the opening of the first African Free School in November, 1787, marked the beginning of free secular education in New York. James Weldon Johnson called the school, which received aid from the city and state, the "precursor of the New York Public School System."

12   The Free African Schools were run with dispatch and efficacy. Males were taught "reading, writing, arithmetic, English grammar, composition, geography, astronomy, use of the globe, and map and linear drawing." Females were taught reading, writing, arithmetic, grammar, geography, sewing, and knitting.

13   According to contemporary accounts, the black students were models of industriousness and seriousness. In its issue of May 12, 1824, the *Commercial Advertiser* commented:

> We had the pleasure on Friday of attending the annual examination of the scholars of the New York African Free School, and we are free to confess that we never derived more satisfaction, or felt a deeper interest, in any school exhibition in our life. The male and female schools. . . . were united on this occasion, and the whole number present was about six hundred. . . . The whole scene was highly interesting and gratifying. We never beheld a white school of the same age (of and under the age of fifteen) in which, without exception, there was more order, and neatness of dress, and cleanliness of person. And the exercises were performed with a degree of promptness and accuracy which was surprising. . . . We were particularly struck with the appearance of the female school. . . .

> There was a neatness of dress and person, a
> propriety of manner, and an ease of carriage,
> which reflected great credit upon themselves
> and their teacher.

14   The work of the schools for children and adults was supplemented by study circles, reading groups, and benevolent organizations. By 1831 there were more than forty-three benevolent organizations in Philadelphia alone. Among the groups listed were the African Friendly Society of St. Thomas, Sons of Africa, United Brethren, Humane Mechanics, African Female Band Benevolent Society of Bethel, Female African Benevolent, and the Daughters of Ethiopia.

15   Perhaps the best known of the black cultural institutions was the African Theater of New York City, which presented performances of *Othello*, *Richard III*, and other European fare. One observes with interest that the theater, at the African Grove, corner of Bleecker and Mercer streets, had a partitioned section in the back for white patrons. The managers said whites were segregated because they "do not know how to conduct themselves at entertainments for ladies and gentlemen of color."

16   With the organization of the first newspapers and magazines, the different organizations and colonies of black America began to coexist in the same time zone. The first edition of the first black newspaper, *Freedom's Journal*, was published on Friday, March 16, 1827, under the editorship of Samuel E. Cornish, a minister and writer, and John B. Russwurm, the first black college graduate (Bowdoin). Russwurm later withdrew from the editorship and settled in Liberia, where he edited the *Liberia Herald*, a pioneer newspaper, and served as governor of the colony of Maryland. Cornish continued to edit the paper under a new name, *Rights for All*. He later edited another newspaper, the *Colored American*. David Ruggles, another pioneer New York leader and one of the most radical men of his times, was editor of the first black magazine, *Mirror of Liberty*, which appeared in August, 1838, one month before the publication of William Whipper's *National Reformer*.

17   The appearance of the first newspapers and magazines brought the black community closer together and focused its thinking.

Reading-to-Write Questions

1. **Content:** Bennett frequently quotes contemporary accounts, letting the people of the time speak for themselves. How do these eyewitness reports enhance Bennett's work?

2. **Arrangement:** In what order does Bennett place his categories?

3. **Style:** Why does Bennett repeat the prepositions *between* and *without* in his introductory paragraph?

4. _____

   _____

   _____

Suggested Topics

1. **Observation:** In your hometown, what types of institutions can African Americans call their own? Classify and describe them. (audience = an African American who is planning to move to your hometown)

2. **Critique:** Bennett maintains, "In order to be and in order to become, men must have institutions." If you agree, what types of institutions should African Americans possess in order to succeed? (audience = Urban League)

3. **Synthesis:** How does Tony Brown's philosophy reflect Bennett's concern about institution-building in the African American community? What types of institutions would Brown want African Americans to build? Do you agree with him? (audience = African American investors)

4. _____

   _____

   _____

Background Readings: AFRICAN AMERICAN INSTITUTIONS

Detweiler, Frederick. *The Negro Press in the United States.* Chicago: University of Chicago Press, 1922.

Holmes, Dwight. *Evolution of the Negro College.* New York: AMS Press, 1970.

Nash, Gary. *Forging Freedom: The Formation of Philadelphia's Black Community, 1720–1840.* Cambridge, MA: Harvard UP, 1988.

Penn, Garland. *The Afro-American Press and Its Editors.* Salem, NH: Ayer, 1988.

Upton, William. *Negro Masonry.* 1902. Rpt. New York: AMS Press, 1975.

Williams, Loretta. *Black Freemasonry and Middle-Class Realities.* Columbia: University of Missouri Press, 1980.

Wilson, Clint. *Black Journalism in Paradox: Historical Perspectives and Current Dilemmas.* New York: Greenwood, 1991.

Woodson, Carter. *History of the Negro Church.* Washington, DC: Associated Publishers, 1972.

_____

_____

_____

Student Essay:
THERE ARE FOUR TYPES OF PUBLICS
Kristen Haynes
(2000)
Summary

1   America has given Black history not only its own month and classes in
institutions of higher learning, but also its own place in society's pool of controversial topics. In his 1997 essay "Black History's Diversified Clientele,"
Benjamin Quarles examines the four types of "publics" that have different
opinions on how to interpret Black history. Group one, the black rank and file,
chooses to "create a sense of racial pride and personal worth" using black history (345). The second group, the black revolutionary nationalists, "focuses
upon exploiters and oppressors, a case study in man's inhumanity to man"
(346). The third group, the black academicians, sees history as "an attempt to
recapture and mirror the past as accurately as possible" (347). The final group,
the white world, believes that black history should not be limited to blacks,
but also expanded to the white community because whites need to learn black
history as much as blacks do, if not more. Beginning with the rank and file,
Quarles describes the purpose, content, and style of Black history from these
four different perspectives.

Works Cited

Quarles, Benjamin. "Black History's Diversified Clientele." *Revelations.* Ed.
     Teresa M. Redd. 3rd ed. Needham Heights, MA: Simon & Schuster, 1997,
     343–352.

Student Essay:
THE COMMENT
Oluwatoyin Tella
(1996)

1 "There was no civilization in the deep, dark jungles of Africa" were the beastliest words ever uttered. I felt sick and disgusted as the words "deep, dark jungles of Africa" rolled off his spotty, pale tongue. Dr. Physicist had a reputation for making obscene and racist remarks among colleagues and students. He made remarks about the Chinese and how they have to hold books close to their face since they squint constantly. Such remarks would slip from one class period to another; however, making a racist statement about Africa was going too far.

2 Ignorance is not only an epidemic among the uneducated; it also exists among the educated. This was proven to me by Dr. Physicist one cold December day in physics class. He was showing a video on the supposed "discovery" of gravity by the scholar Sir Isaac Newton, and confusion came over me. Through outside class readings by Cheikh Anta Diop, Ivan Van Sertima, Ben-Jochannan, and others, I had learned that Sir Isaac Newton was not the scholar that he is proclaimed to be. As I recalled this, I told Dr. Physicist that the history he was forcing down our throats was false. He then became red in the face and asked me to prove it. I mentioned the Egyptologists' and historians' works that I had read. He claimed that my proof was invalid. "INVALID," these noted scholars and historians invalid? I was puzzled by his remark.

3 We argued back and forth, and then I humbly "schooled" him. I mentioned that Newton, Aristotle, Plato, and other Greek "scholars" of the sort had received their knowledge in the Rift Valley area or Ancient Egypt. He could not believe that the people he despised the most were, in fact, the originators of astronomy, geometry, trigonometry, and botany (Van Sertima, *Blacks* 10–24). He could not believe that almost everything he learned in his upscale American institutions was false. Confused and struck by the plague of ignorance which had mutated him into the racist he was, Dr. Physicist shouted, "There was no civilization in the deep, dark jungles of Africa!" He continued, "Since knowledge and schooling originated in Europe, it is and always will be the

center of civilization." He sounded like the textbooks that I had read through-out school. He did not know that Egyptians "schooled" the Greeks since Greek scholars traveled to the Rift Valley area to learn math, science, and other arts.

4   After he made the comment, he kicked me out of class. But before I left, I "schooled" the students. I stated that if they believed anything that this racist said, they would remain deaf, dumb, and blind to the truth.

5   According to my history professor, racism can be defined as follows: "Racism is that belief system in which there are privileges and premiums attached to whiteness. The attachments are institutionalized into every facet of American life and culture because whites hold the power. The goal of racism is to perpetuate white supremacy." Dr. Physicist, a white man, held the power in the classroom. He wanted to perpetuate his superiority in a facet of my aca-demic environment. The cause of Dr. Physicist's racist ways seems clear to me now. It is the American school curriculum. There is insufficient recognition given to anyone other than European scholars in school textbooks. The text-books tend to make it seem as though nothing happened in the rest of the world without European influence. For instance, the "discovery" of America by Europeans and the trade between Asia and Europe barely brought Asia "on the map" in textbooks. The textbooks do not mention that the ethnocentric Chinese had their own culture and customs and that in America there was African influence on clothing and customs within the Olmec society centuries before Columbus arrived (Van Sertima, *They Came* 27–29). In addition, it is often hinted that Africa was a deep, dark jungle until Europe "imperialized" it. The authors do not mention the fact that while Europe was in its "dark" ages, Ancient Egypt had a centralized pharaonic government.

6   Every group of people has a distinct and unique culture; however, Euro-pean culture is emphasized greatly in the schooling of America's students. This is a fault in the school curriculum, which inspired me to go outside of class to read books about other cultures and civilizations. As an educator, Dr. Physicist should take it upon himself not to limit his awareness. He should broaden his horizons just as I did so that I would not be ignorant of other cultures as well as my own. His ignorance and narrow-mindedness "dis-eased" him, and it festered into racism.

7   Beyond the text itself and those that "learn" from it, the underlying source of the racist school curriculum must be focused on also. It is those that control the pen, the racist writers, who are at fault for institutionalizing white supremacy. To promote their superiority, racist writers have written falsely for centuries. The diction that is used in some of the works can only lure one into the trap of believing that Africans are less human since they hold no place in world history and development. This is evident since this falsehood has become part of the American ideology. For instance, take the statement "If you're white, you're right. If you're black, go back!" "Go back" where? To the deep, dark jungles of Africa?

Works Cited

Ben-Jochannan, Yosef. *New Dimensions in African History.* Trenton, NJ: Africa World Press, 1991.

Diop, Cheikh Anta. *The African Origin of Civilization: Myth or Reality?* New York: Lawrence Hill Books, 1974.

Van Sertima, Ivan, ed. *Blacks in Science.* New Brunswick, NJ: Transaction Books, 1983.

———. "They Came Before Columbus." *Revelations.* Ed. Teresa M. Redd. 3rd ed. Needham, Heights, MA: Simon & Schuster, 1997. 27–29.

the magic of black art and science: process

We are black magicians, black art
s we make in black labs of the heart.

from "State/Ment" by Amiri Baraka

Gikuyu Industries: Hut-Building

Jomo Kenyatta

*Raised in Kenya, Jomo Kenyatta (circa 1894-1978) grew up among the Kikuyu (Gikuyu) people when Kenya was under British rule. Although Kenyatta received his training in anthropology, he was active in politics. After serving time in jail for his political activities, he negotiated his country's independence and became its first president in 1964. His publications include two collections of speeches (*Harambee! *and* Suffering without Bitterness) *as well as his anthropological study* Facing Mount Kenya, *which was published in 1938. The following excerpt from the study describes the collective process of building a hut among the Kikuyu.*

---

1   It is a common ambition of every Gikuyu young man to own a hut or huts, which means implicitly to have a wife or wives. The establishment of a homestead gives a man special status in the community; he is referred to as *muthuri* (an elder), and is considered capable of holding a responsible position in tribal affairs. Thus, it is the desire of every Gikuyu man to work hard and accumulate property which will enable him to build a homestead of his own. There is a proverb in Gikuyu which says: "*Wega uumaga na mocie,*" that is, the quality

of a man is judged by his homestead. With these few remarks we will proceed to describe how a hut is built.

2   Gikuyu huts are of the round type, with wooden walls and grass thatched roofs. The actual building of a hut takes only one day; and as soon as it is completed, a new fire is drilled from sacred fire-sticks, "*githegethi na Geka kia Igongona.*" But in case of rebuilding, the fire from the old hut is preserved to be transferred to the new hut. The fire is ritually lit in the new hut, and after a short ceremony of communing with the ancestral spirits the owner moves into the new homestead. Sometimes two or more huts are built simultaneously, as in the case of a man having more than one wife or a large family which could not be housed in one hut. But general custom requires that even a man with one wife should have two huts, one for his wife's private use and one for himself for general use. The woman's hut is called *nyomba*. Here it is taboo for a mere stranger to enter, because *nyomba* is considered as the traditional sacred abode of the family and the proper place to hold communion with their ancestral spirits. All aspects of religious and magical ceremonies and sacrifices which concern the family are centered around the *nyomba*. It is for fear of defilement and ill-luck that strangers are not allowed to cross this sacred threshold. The man's hut is called *thingira;* in this, friends and casual visitors are entertained.

3   Nowadays the system of having two huts for a man with only one wife is dying out, owing to the heavy burden of hut taxes imposed on the people by the British Government. The result has been congestion, whole families being crowded in one hut, for many such families can hardly maintain their livelihood and at the same time afford to find money for hut taxation.

4   We have mentioned that a hut is built and occupied in the same day; this statement may puzzle those who are not acquainted with the Gikuyu method of building. To avoid this, let us at once explain how the work that expedites the putting up of a hut is organized. Most important of all is the Gikuyu collective method of working. A few days before the erection of a hut or huts the building materials are collected. In doing this the division of labour according to sex plays an important role. The work of cutting wood necessary for building falls on men; women take the responsibility of providing thatching grass and other materials.   *thesis / stage A*

5   When a family is engaged in the work of building a hut or huts, the help of neighbours and friends is necessary in order to expedite the work. A man goes round asking his friends to help him, and at the same time telling them what kind of building materials he would like them to supply him with. In the same manner the wife visits her women friends, requesting them to help in various ways. Those who cannot take part in collecting building materials are asked to help in providing food and drink for the builders' feast, which is called "*iruga ria mwako.*" On the day appointed many of these friends will turn up, bringing with them the required materials for building. The man and his wife or wives receive their helpers joyfully and bid them to sit down and rest. After all have arrived a feast is provided, consisting of a variety of food and drink. During   *step 1 / step 2 / step 3 / step 4*

the feasting this group of men and women entertain themselves with tradi-   step 5
tional songs relating to teamwork. Before they part, <u>a day is appointed</u> when
the actual building of a hut or huts will take place.

6   It is obvious that without this system of teamwork it would take a man a
 long time to complete the work, especially in a community where the system
of paid labour is traditionally unknown. In its place, mutual help guided by
the rules of give and take plays a significant part. In every branch of work rec-
iprocity is the fundamental principle governing the relationship between a
man and his neighbours, and also between various groups or clans and the
tribe. If a man, after having been asked to give his service, absents himself
without a good reason, especially when his neighbour has urgent work, such
as building a hut or a cattle kraal, which has to be completed in one day (for it
is feared that should a hut or a kraal be left unfinished and unoccupied, evil
spirits might dwell therein and, therefore, cause constant misfortune to the
future occupants and their herd), the result will be that the defaulter will find
himself socially boycotted for his individualistic attitude. When a man has
thus been ostracised, "*kohingwo*," he will have to pay a fine of one sheep or a
he-goat to his neighbours for his bad behaviour. When the fine is paid, the animal is slaughtered for a feast, and then, after a short ceremony of reunion, the
man's status as a good and helpful neighbour is reacknowledged.

7   After the building materials have been collected, <u>the head of the family</u>   stage B
<u>selects a plot</u> where he wishes to establish his new homestead. In selecting the
plot care is taken to see that the land is not associated with any ancestral curse
or taboo. The plot must also be one that has been lawfully acquired. The homestead must not be built on or near a graveyard, or on a place where a fierce battle has taken place, resulting in loss of lives. Such places are considered as the
resting homes for the departed spirits, and to disturb them would mean to
invoke their anger.

8   When these preliminary arrangements have been made, <u>the man prepares</u>   stage C
<u>sugar-cane or honey beer for the foundation ceremony</u>. Early in the morning,
on the day of building a hut or huts, a small quantity of <u>the beer is taken to the</u>   step 1
<u>selected plot</u> and, in communion with the ancestral spirits, it is sprinkled on
the ground where the new home is to be built. Sometimes milk or uncooked
gruel, "*gethambio*," is preferred for this ceremony, according to the custom of
the clan to which the individual belongs. After the ancestral spirits have been
summoned to join in the work of building, <u>the friends who have gathered to</u>
<u>help their neighbour start to clear and to level the ground</u>. Then the <u>founda-</u>   step 2
<u>tion is marked</u> according to the size of the hut which a man wants. To make a   step 3
good circle a kind of string compass is employed. A stick is put in the centre of
the circle and a string tied to it, then a man holds one end of the string and, after
measuring the required paces, he holds the string tight and then goes round,
marking the ground until the circle lines meet. This is called "*gokurura kiea*."
When this is done <u>the builders start digging holes</u> in the ground for the outer   step 4
wall. The holes are about one foot deep and about six inches in diameter. After
this <u>the inner circle is marked</u>, which divides the hut into several apartments.   step 5

Immediately <u>the wall is erected</u> and <u>the roof put on</u>. This completes the men's   steps 6 & 7
work in building, leaving the thatching to the womenfolk.

9   While the women are engaged in thatching, <u>the men retire to a feast</u> which   stage D
has been awaiting them. During the feasting the <u>men sing songs</u> relating to the   step 1
art of building; those who are clever and hard workers are highly praised in
these songs; at the same time contemptuous phrases are uttered for laziness. In
some of the phrases <u>men call on the women in teasing tones</u>, saying: "Look on   step 2
those lazy-bones who are working like chameleons, the sun is going down; do
you want us to make torches for you? Do hurry up and join us in feasting, and
let us utter blessings for the homestead before the sun is completely gone
down." To this <u>the women answer in chorus</u>, saying: "You men, you lack the   step 3
most important art in building, namely, thatching. A wall and an empty roof
cannot protect you from heavy rain, nor from burning sun. It is our careful
thatching that makes a hut worth living in. We are not chameleons, but we do
thatch our huts like '*nyoni ya nyagathanga*' (this is the name of a small bird in
Gikuyu which is well known by its sweet songs and the neatness of its nest)."
In many of the Gikuyu cradle stories and legends *nyoni ya nyagathanga* and its
work is highly praised. This acts as an encouragement to both boys and girls
to become industrious in their future activities in life. It is characteristic of the
Gikuyu people to sing inspiring songs while performing a task, for it is said:
"to work in a happy mood is to make the task easier, and to relieve the heart
from fatigue." ("*Koruta wera na ngoro theru ni kohothia wera na konyihia minoga.*")

10   When the women have finally finished thatching <u>they join the men in feast-</u>   stage E
<u>ing</u>. Before the party comes to a close <u>the owner of the homestead brings the</u>   step 1
<u>remainder of the beer or the milk</u> which has been sprinkled on the foundation;
<u>he hands it to a ceremonial elder</u>, who after pouring the liquid into a ritual   step 2
horn, calls upon those present to stand up. Then the ceremonial elder, with his
hands raised holding the horn, turns towards Kere-Nyaga (Mount Kenya). In
this position <u>he chants a prayer</u>, calling for a blessing for the homestead and its   step 3
future prosperity. The following is the form of the prayer used for such an
occasion:

> *"Wee Githuri oikaraga Kere-Nyaga; kerathimo*
> *geaku nikeo getomaga mecie ethegee. Namo*
> *marakara maku, nemo mahukagia mecie. Togogo-*
> *thaitha tweturaneire ohamwe na ngoma cia aciari*
> *aito. Togokoria ate orinderere mocie oyo na otome*
> *wethegee. Reke atumia ona mahio mathathare.*
> *Thaaai, thathayai Ngai, thaaai."*

11   The following is the translation of the above prayer: "You, the Great Elder,
who dwells on the Kere-Nyaga, your blessing allows homesteads to spread.
Your anger destroys homesteads. We beseech You, and in this we are in harmony with the spirits of our ancestors: we ask You to guard this homestead
and let it spread. Let the women, herd, and flock be prolific. (Chorus) Peace,
praise, or beseech ye, Ngai (God), peace be with us."

12   After this <u>the homestead is declared open</u>. The next thing is to light the fire   stage F
which we have mentioned in our earlier description. Two children, male and
female, are selected for this ritual; they are looked upon as a symbol of peace
and prosperity for the homestead. <u>The ceremonial elder hands the fire</u> to the   step 1
children and instructs them how to light it; at the same time he gives them
the ritual words to be used in this connection. <u>The children enter the hut</u>, with   step 2
the elder following behind them, to see that the ritual is correctly carried out.
Behind this small procession <u>the owner of the homestead and his wife follow</u>   step 3
carrying firewood to kindle the fire, for it is considered as a bad omen for such
a fire to go out. After <u>the fire has been properly lit</u>, <u>things are moved in</u> with-   steps 4 & 5
out any further ceremony.

Reading-to-Write Questions

1. **Content:** Where does Kenyatta explain why a step is taken? Why does he devote so much time to the significance of the steps?

2. **Arrangement:** Kenyatta groups steps into stages. What would happen to readers if Kenyatta did not group the steps?

3. **Style:** Why does Kenyatta use the Kikuyu language in an essay written for English-speaking readers?

4. _____

   _____

   _____

Suggested Topics

1. **Observation:** Describe a collective process with which you are familiar. (audience = students who have never seen or participated in the process)

2. **Critique:** Evaluate Kenyatta's instructions. Has he provided enough details for you to carry out the process? Has he presented each required step in a logical sequence? (audience = someone who is trying to write clear instructions)

3. **Synthesis:** Explain how each stage of the hut-building process reflects the values described by Biko in his essay. (audience = students interested in learning more about Africa)

4. _____

   _____

   _____

Background Readings: AFRICAN TRADITIONS

Imasogie, Osadolor. *African Traditional Religion*. Ibadan, Nigeria: Ibadan UP, 1982.

Larlham, Peter. "Traditional Zulu Rites and Ceremonies." *Black Theater, Dance, and Ritual in South Africa*. Ann Arbor, MI: UMI Research Press, 1985. 1–19.

Makinde, M. Akin. *African Philosophy, Culture, and Traditional Medicine*. Athens, OH: Ohio University Center for International Studies, 1988.

Mazrui, Ali A. *The Africans: A Triple Heritage*. Boston: Little, Brown, 1986.

Schneider, Harold K. *The Africans: An Ethnological Account*. Englewood Cliffs, NJ: Prentice-Hall, 1981.

_____

_____

_____

Recommended Literature: Chinua Achebe, *Things Fall Apart* (novel)
Camara Laye, *The Dark Child* (autobiography)

Saving a Life
Ben Carson

Ben Carson's odyssey from the depths of inner-city Detroit to the heights of the medical field still inspires those who read his autobiography, Gifted Hands *(1990). At age 33, he became Director of Pediatric Neurosurgery at the prestigious Johns Hopkins Hospital, where he performed the hemispherectomy (removal of a hemisphere of the brain) that he describes below. In this excerpt from* Gifted Hands, *he takes readers step by step through the medical drama.*

----

1   Surgeons had recorded so few cases of full functional recovery that most doctors wouldn't consider a hemispherectomy as viable.

2   I was going to do my best. And I went into the surgery with two things clear. First, if I didn't operate, Maranda Francisco would worsen and die. Second, I had done everything to prepare myself for this surgery, and now I could leave the results in God's hands.

3   To assist me I asked Dr. Neville Knuckey, one of our chief residents, whom I had met during my year in Australia. Neville had come to Hopkins to do a fellowship, and I considered him extremely capable.

4   Right from the beginning of the surgery we had problems, so that instead of the expected five hours we stayed at the operating table exactly twice that long. We had to keep calling for more blood. Maranda's brain was very inflamed, and no matter where an instrument touched, she started to bleed. It was not only a lengthy operation but one of the most difficult I'd ever done.

5   The dramatic surgery began simply, with an incision drawn down the scalp. The assisting surgeon suctioned away blood with a hand-held tube while I cauterized small vessels. One by one, steel clips were placed on the edge of the incision to keep it open. The small operating room was cool and quiet.

6   Then I cut deeper through a second layer of scalp. Again small vessels were sealed shut, and a suction tube whisked away blood.

7   I drilled six holes, each the size of a shirt button, in Maranda's skull. The holes formed a semicircle, beginning in front of her left ear and curving up across her temple, above and down behind the ear. Each hole was filled with purified beeswax to cushion the saw. Then with an air-powered saw I connected the holes into an incision and lifted back the left side of Maranda's skull to expose the outer covering of her brain.

8   Her brain was swollen and abnormally hard, making the surgery more difficult. The anesthesiologist injected a drug into her IV line to reduce the swelling. Then Neville passed a thin catheter through her brain to the center of her head where it would drain off excess fluid.

9   Slowly, carefully, for eight tedious hours I inched away the inflamed left hemisphere of Maranda's brain. The small surgical instruments moved carefully, a millimeter at a time, coaxing tissue away from the vital blood vessels, trying not to touch or damage the other fragile parts of her brain. The large veins along the base of her brain bled profusely as I searched for the plane, the delicate line separating brain and vessels. It was not easy to manipulate the brain, to ease it away from the veins that circulated life through her small body.

10   Maranda lost nearly nine pints of blood during the surgery. We replaced almost twice her normal blood volume. Throughout the long hours, nurses kept Maranda's parents up-to-date on what was happening. I thought of their waiting and wondering. When my thoughts turned to God, I thanked Him for wisdom, for helping to guide my hands.

11   Finally we were finished. Maranda's skull was carefully sewed back in place with strong sutures. At last Neville and I stood back. The OR technician took the last instrument from my hand. I allowed myself the luxury of flexing my shoulders, rotating my head. Neville and I and the rest of our team knew we had successfully removed the left hemisphere of Maranda's brain. The "impossible" had been accomplished.

Reading-to-Write Questions

1. **Content:** What sort of information do you think Carson omitted to adapt this explanation to his lay readers?

2. **Arrangement:** Number the stages in the surgical procedure described by Carson.

3. **Style:** How does Carson tailor his style to his lay readers?

4. _____

    _____

    _____

Suggested Topics

1. **Observation:** Explain a technical process that you know well. (audience = novice)

2. **Critique:** How does Carson attempt to build suspense? Does he succeed? (audience = aspiring journalists and creative writers)

3. **Synthesis:** Like Gikuyu hut-building, surgery is a collective process. Comparing Carson's and Kenyatta's accounts, highlight the cooperative nature of these "primitive" and "hi-tech" processes. (audience = pre-med students)

4. _____

    _____

    _____

Background Readings: BLACKS IN SCIENCE

Carwell, Hattie. *Blacks in Science: Astrophysicist to Zoologist.* Hicksville, NY: Exposition Press, 1977.

Diop, Cheikh Anta. *Cheikh Anta Diop: On Science, History and Technology.* New York: ECA Associates, 1990.

Driver, Paul. *Black Giants in Science.* New York: Vantage Press, 1978.

James, Portia. *The Real McCoy: African-American Invention and Innovation 1619–1930.* Washington, DC and London: Smithsonian Institution Press, 1989.

Klein, Aaron. *The Hidden Contributions: Black Scientists and Inventors in America.* Garden City, NY: Doubleday, 1971.

Sammons, Vivian O. *Blacks in Science and Medicine.* Bristol, PA: Taylor & Francis, 1990.

Van Sertima, Ivan. *Blacks in Science: Ancient and Modern.* New Brunswick, NJ: Transaction Books, 1983.

Hard Words and Clear Songs: The Writing of Black Poetry
Haki Madhubuti

A leading figure in the Black Arts Movement of the 1960s, Haki Madhubuti (formerly Don L. Lee) is not only a writer but a publisher, having founded Third World Press. Among his own publications are nonfiction works such as Dynamite Voices *and* Black Men: Obsolete, Single, Dangerous? *as well as several volumes of poetry (e.g.,* Think Black, Black Pride, Don't Cry, Scream, We Walk the Way of the New World, Heartlove, Groundwork, *and* Earthquakes and Sunrise Missions*). In the following essay, Madhubuti explains how to write Black poetry. The essay was published in 1985 in* Tapping Potential, *a collection of essays for teachers of Black students.*

Prologue

1   Writers write. What they write about tells the reader to what extent they are involved with the real world.

2   Writing for me is a difficult process. I write best under pressure, under a deadline set for me by someone or one that I set for myself. I am not a professional or leisure writer. I do not earn my livelihood from writing, nor do I allot special time in the day just to write. Much of my writing is notetaking. I take

an abundance of notes and these notes, at a later time, are developed into poems, essays and occasional fiction. Writing for me is also a form of life-therapy, but it is not my life. My life is too complex to be limited to one stimulus.

3   Writers are questioners of the world and doers within the world. They question everything and are not satisfied with quick surface answers. Richard Wright was a questioner. We can see it in his works—the fiction and nonfiction. W.E.B. Du Bois was a questioner—his output was triple that of the "average" writer, but he always maintained a high level of quality and content. Both men were of the world, but in their own way refused to be subordinated to the world. They were fighters, always aware of the war, and writing was a war weapon. And writing at its best for them was a tool, a vocation, a hammer to be used for the survival and development of the Race.

Aims

4   The writer is also the lively but lonely investigator, the seeker of unknowns, the wanderer along back alleys, through power corridors, and into the far reaches of her or his own mind and that of his or her people. Essentially, the loneliness comes from the demands of the writing form; although there are exceptions, one usually does not write in a group. Writing is a personal occupation, one man or woman, one pen or typewriter. Once the writer leaves the research, the study, she or he does battle with the blank sheet of paper. The writer is alone. It is a lonely vocation that is bound to affect the writer and those closest to him or her. When the writer begins to work, the most important concern is the relationship between the writer and the subject. The central question becomes: How to bring life to the subject?

5   This process, above all, requires discipline. The creative process is a disciplined process which most writers have had to teach themselves. In most cases, as soon as the writing begins, the interruptions seem to multiply—these interruptions are both real and unreal. Each phone call is attacked or ignored because the writer is more, or less, sensitive to the uses of his or her time. Family relationships are altered during this period. Also, the book that could have been read easily two months ago becomes a *priority* now—not because the book is essential to the writer's subject, but because it becomes a part of the writer's internal interruptions. These types of interference are often rationalized as direct contributions to the writing. Nonsense. Writers waste time, as do most people; this is why discipline is so important.

6   In many ways all writers are re-creators. They take in the world and retell it, reinterpret it for others in a form and style that should be unique for them, the readers, and the times. These times are space age times, and words come and go like Chicago's weather. The way the writer uses the words tells as much about him or her as a word-user as anything else can. The major distinction that can be made between writers (other than forms they work in) is their ability to say the same thing differently, originally using and "misusing"

the language at will. The language is the tool, the weapon, and writers must train themselves to use it as a carpenter trains to use wood and nails, or as a farmer trains to use the earth.

Writer and Teacher

7   Just as I am a writer, I am also a teacher, and one of the most important tasks that I have as a teacher is to demystify the act of writing, particularly as it applies to the writing of poetry. I have discovered through years of experience that one of the best ways to teach young people how to develop their interests in poetry is to use music and recorded poems as they engage in the writing act. Both of these approaches I find personally rewarding, and as a result, I am able to heighten the students' interests not only in content but in the poet's craft as well. By increasing their awareness of the form and structure of poetry, through a rigorous examination and discussion of poems, students are better able to understand that the poet—like other writers—does more than record first impressions. The students also come to recognize that the writing of poetry is a complicated process requiring all the skills needed by writers of other forms, plus additional ones as well. Most important, these students begin to perceive that the poet, just as other writers, must develop—or rather possess—a keen eye, catching and questioning everything, the largest and the smallest detail, and reproducing it in a condensed form that challenges the readers' minds and emotions.

8   I have found that many poems written by Afro-American poets can be used to serve this purpose. I find that as a teacher, I can take the best of these writers and use their works as examples of how young people can begin to fashion language into a memorable experience, a form that challenges the reader on several levels. After all, that is what poetry does.

9   The writers who provide the best examples are not necessarily the best. Yet most do have something to say and say it in a way that people can understand and relate to. Langston Hughes's work is an excellent example of style and content that black people can relate to. His jazz poetry and "simple" folk tales not only established him as a "professional" writer of the very best order, but earned him the title "Dean" of black writers from his own people. Sterling Brown also comes to mind in terms of original style and content; his poetry and essays exemplify the highest tradition of black oral communication combined with scholarly research. For me, the content is as important as the style. Beautiful writing that does not say anything is only that—beautiful writing. Yet, bad writing containing the most revolutionary ideas is equally—first and last—bad writing. A standard must be met if the writer is to communicate effectively. The ability to develop a style that is clear, original, and communicative is what separates writers from nonwriters.

10   There are many ways to make a poem "a memorable experience," Gwendolyn Brooks says. One can use images, that is pictures, visible pictures, which

carry the characteristics of the subject or which suggest the meaning and mood the writer is trying to create. One of the strengths of using images and metaphors is that often they carry the weight of symbols; that is they suggest multiple levels of meaning to the reader as well as allow the reading of his or her own experience into the image or metaphor. Another important technique for making the poem a "memorable experience" is to create characters, real people with whom the reader can feel and empathize. In poetry, however, when creating characters, the poet should search for only those crucial characteristics which symbolize what the character is most essentially about. Images, metaphors, characters take on visibility and become memorable by the use of concrete details. The following are examples of what I mean.

> . . . Prophet Williams, young beyond St. Julia,
> and rich with Bible; pimples, pout; who reeks
> with lust for his disciple, is an engine
> or candid steel hugging combustibles.

11   Gwendolyn Brooks created this character in the poem *In the Mecca*. She is able to establish through suggestion the real character of Prophet Williams. She does this in part through concrete choice of metaphor. When she compares the prophet's passion (for his disciples) to an "engine of candid steel hugging combustibles," she is able to suggest, on the one hand, the great power, probably physical power, of the prophet, and on the other, the coldness and real dispassion or lack of passion of the prophet. In this case, then, the metaphor allows her to make several statements at the same time, using very few words (simple words).

12   In the long poem *In the Mecca*, Ms. Brooks chooses those select, concrete details which are crucial to an intimate understanding of that character. She says of Briggs, a young brother intimate with the neighborhood gang, "Briggs is adult as a stone." The stone as an image or metaphor for Briggs's development is most appropriate as it allows her to make several profound statements with only six simple words. A stone is hard as Briggs is hard. A stone does not grow as organic matter as human beings grow, thus suggesting Briggs has reached a point beyond which he cannot go. It also suggests a certain one-dimensional aspect of Briggs's character.

The Use of Words

13   The raw materials of the poet are the words and sounds. The right, most appropriate, most exact choice of words is part of what makes the experience of the poem memorable. The following examples from Ms. Brooks illustrate how the right word is specific and concrete in nature, yet often carries the massive power of the symbol (allowing each reader to be consciously directed into a myriad of experiences, emotions, and meanings). We see also from Sister Brooks (again, *In the Mecca*) that this appropriate choice of the exact word need not be a long, multisyllabic, "difficult" word.

> Conduct your blooming in the noise and
> whip of whirlwind

14   *Blooming* and *whirlwind* are concrete, visible, physical realities, and because of their concreteness, we immediately recognize that each belongs to opposite categories of reality; in fact, the nature and purpose of the whirlwind is to destroy all blooming. Thus Sister Brooks is able to make a very strong political comment without resorting to trite political clichés. The use of words which have physical, visible existence is often more powerful, more clear than abstractions like "the universe" and "the cosmos."

15   St. Julia, a character described by Sister Brooks in the poem *In the Mecca*, is a "good" church-going sister who dearly loves Jesus. Ms. Brooks has St. Julia cry out:

> He's the comfort and wine
> and piccalilli for my soul

16   Piccalilli here is another extremely concrete word, a simple word that reveals Sister Brooks's intimate knowledge of the black community's eating habits (piccalilli being just the right topping for black-eyed peas and rice, she didn't say "relish"). Through this word, we can make some very concrete deductions about where and how St. Julia grew up as well as how she feels about Jesus.

17   Sometimes the beginning poet will use complete grammatical sentences (using connectives like "and," etc.) when often just an elliptical phrase will do. It is just as important for the poet to know what to take out as to know what to put in. The following example from Johari Amini ("Let's Go Somewhere") shows how effective the use of only those words (carefully chosen) necessary to create the intense moment of message and mood can be.

> I am too past youth
> too strong
> too black
> to cry
>   still. . . .
> need
> comes: a steadied,
> profuseness; insensitive
> spreading
> spreading

18   The problem of triteness—that of using words and phrases which have been used over and over again and are no longer fresh and vivid—usually falls into the category of street rap or in the form of imitating nineteenth-century European phrases (personifying the sun and moon, "thou," etc.). The problem with the rap is that it is a potentially very powerful form. To exert its power, the writer who uses it must do more than copy or imitate the vocabulary

of the rap. He or she must create an originality and a tension on the printed page; using the words of the rap alone on a piece of paper cannot of itself carry the nuance and rhythm of a brother on the corner rapping out his mouth. In the same way, for example, Langston Hughes in his blues poems—because he only "copied" the superficial form of the blues lyric—could not really reach the power of a Blind Lemon or a Muddy Waters. The printed page imposes limitations that sound does not.

A Sense of Direction

19   Actually, a sense of direction comes from the world that students are involved in every day. If a student's work is putting comic books together or is being a professional student, he or she will see the world differently than a person working on the line at Ford Motor Company. If students question what they see, a whole new world opens up.

20   If what young people write about is to be meaningful, it must have some relationship to reality. And reality is not the same to the doer as it is to the sayer. There are four areas in which students should concentrate much of their efforts if they are to develop as a person and a writer:

1. Study and Research: This is of the utmost importance for writers of nonfiction and certain kinds of fiction such as historical fiction. Margaret Walker's research for her novel, *Jubilee*, took almost a lifetime, and Chancellor William's research for his monumental study, *The Destruction of Black Civilization*, took eighteen years. The two books mentioned will live because they are packed with life-giving and stimulating information written in a readable style.

2. Writing: The major endeavor for the beginning writer must be writing. The writer should at first put him or herself on a schedule in order to acquire discipline. Discipline in doing anything that is important is a must for the writer. The writer is his or her own whip. Self-discipline is the hardest to achieve but if achieved is the writer's most important asset. He or she should keep a small notebook in which to jot down all ideas. Writers should never rely solely on memory. They should not throw any of the notes away but keep the unused ones for later. Though students may want to concentrate in one area of writing, they should gain knowledge of all kinds of writing—fiction, nonfiction, children's, radio and television, magazine-journalism, poetry, and drama.

3. Revision: Writers never accept a first draft of their work. The art of writing is frequent revising. Writers must be their own worst critics. Writers must be their own editors.

4. Workshop: For the beginning and the inexperienced writer, workshops are good mostly for the associations that are formed with other writ-

ers. Also, workshops are probably one of the few places a young writer can get competent and truthful direct criticism. Many good writers have been involved in workshop experiences.

Final Words

21   Writing is a form of self-definition and communication through which writers basically define themselves and their relationship to the world. The writer is essentially always searching for the core of the definition, looking for the gut—the truth. There are few good writers who lie; there are a lot of liars who try to write, and unfortunately, they are in the majority. But they come and go, passing through like a European wind penetrating the African heat only to be eliminated by the warmth of reality.

22   A writer is a questioner, always asking, always seeking the bottom line, always looking for the essences within the essence—always looking for the enemies of the world. When writers stop questioning, they stop having anything to say. When writers question, they are doing more than admitting that they don't know everything, they're assuming a posture, a relationship with the world that is conducive to creativity. Writers who humble themselves before knowledge of any kind generally end up wiser and as voices with something meaningful to say.

References

Amini, Johari. *Let's Go Somewhere*. Chicago: Third World, 1973.

Brooks, Gwendolyn. *In the Mecca*. New York: Harper & Row, 1968.

_____. *Riot*. Detroit: Broadside, 1969.

_____. *Report from Part I*. Detroit: Broadside, 1970.

_____. *To Disembark*. Chicago: Third World, 1981.

Brown, Sterling A. *Southern Road*. New York: Harcourt Brace Jovanovich, 1932.

Hughes, Langston. *Montage of a Dream Deferred*. New York: Holt, Rinehart & Winston, 1951.

_____. *Selected Poems*. New York: Alfred A. Knopf, 1959.

_____. *The Best of Simple*. New York: Hill & Wang, 1961.

Lee, Don L. (Haki R. Madhubuti). *Book of Life*. Detroit: Broadside, 1975.

_____. *Earthquakes and Sunrise Missions*. Chicago: Third World, 1983.

Reading-to-Write Questions

1. **Content:** Madhubuti discusses three ways to make a poem "a memorable experience." What are the three ways, and how does Madhubuti SHOW you the ways?

2. **Arrangement:** Look at the fifth paragraph of the essay ("The process, above all, requires discipline . . ."). How is this paragraph constructed? How does Madhubuti arrange specifics and generalizations?

3. **Style:** Madhubuti's style is clear and crisp with a sprinkling of metaphors and similes. Where does he place the grammatical subject in many sentences? What do you notice about the sentence structure and length? Where are the metaphors and similes?

4. _____

    _____

    _____

Suggested Topics

1. **Observation:** Discuss the steps in a creative process that you know well, such as painting, dancing, or playing the piano. Present the instructions in essay form. (audience = a beginner)

2. **Critique:** Following Madhubuti's directions, write a poem. Were the directions adequate? In an essay, describe your attempt to follow Madhubuti's advice and the results. (audience = students who have never written a poem but would like to)

3. **Synthesis:** The central question Madhubuti faces when he begins to write is "how to bring life to the subject." How does Langston Hughes bring life to his subject in "I, Too" (reprinted on page 1 of this book)? (audience = class)

4. _____

    _____

    _____

Background Readings: POETRY OF THE BLACK ARTS MOVEMENT

Chapman, Abraham, ed. *New Black Voices.* New York: New American Library, 1972.

Flowers, Sandra Hollin. *African American Nationalist Literature of the 1960s: Pens of Fire.* New York: Garland, 1996.

Gilyard, Keith, ed. *Spirit and Flame: An Anthology of Contemporary African American Poetry.* Syracuse, NY: Syracuse UP, 1997.

Henderson, Stephen, ed. *Understanding the New Black Poetry: Black Speech and Black Music as Poetic References.* New York: Morrow Quill Paperbacks, 1973.

Jones, LeRoi (Amiri Baraka), and Larry Neal, eds. *Black Fire: An Anthology of Afro-American Writing.* New York: Morrow, 1968.

Jordan, June, ed. *Soulscript: Afro-American Poetry.* Garden City, NY: Doubleday, 1970.

Redmond, Eugene B. *Drumvoices: The Mission of Afro-American Poetry.* Garden City, NY: Anchor, 1976.

_____

_____

_____

Recommended Literature: Amiri Baraka (LeRoi Jones) "State/Ment" in *Home* (poem)

Haki Madhubuti, "But He Was Cool Or: He Even Stopped for Green Lights" from *Don't Cry, Scream* (poem)

Sonia Sanchez, "to all sisters" in *Black Fire* (poem)

Nikki Giovanni, "Adulthood" from *Black Feeling, Black Talk* (poem)

Black Music in Our Hands
Bernice Reagon

As a member of the Student Nonviolent Coordinating Committee (SNCC), Bernice Reagon sang her way through the Civil Rights confrontations of the 1960s. Since then she has researched Black music for the Smithsonian Institution and published If You Don't Go, Don't Hinder Me: The African American Sacred Song Tradition. *She has also sung in Sweet Honey in the Rock, an acappella group she founded. In the essay below she describes, stage by stage, how her perceptions of Black music changed during the Civil Rights Movement. This essay first appeared in a collection of essays entitled* In Her Own Image: Women Working in the Arts (1980).

1   In the early 1960s, I was in college at Albany State. My major interests were music and biology. In music I was a contralto soloist with the choir, studying Italian arias and German lieder. The black music I sang was of three types:

2   1) Spirituals sung by the college choir. These were arranged by such people as Nathaniel Dett and William Dawson and had major injections of European musical harmony and composition. 2) Rhythm'n'Blues, music done by and for Blacks in social settings. This included the music of bands at proms, juke boxes, and football game songs. 3) Church music; gospel was a major part of Black church music by the time I was in college. I was a soloist with the gospel choir.

3   Prior to the gospel choir, introduced in my church when I was twelve, was many years' experience with unaccompanied music—Black choral singing, hymns, lined out by strong song leaders with full, powerful, richly ornate congregational responses. These hymns were offset by upbeat, clapping call-and-response songs.

4   I saw people in church sing and pray until they shouted. I knew *that* music as a part of a cultural expression that was powerful enough to take people from their conscious selves to a place where the physical and intellectual being worked in harmony with the spirit. I enjoyed and needed that experience. The music of the church was an integral part of the cultural world into which I was born.

5   Outside of church, I saw music as good, powerful sounds you made or listened to. Rhythm and blues—you danced to; music of the college choir—you clapped after the number was finished.

6   The Civil Rights Movement changed my view of music. It was after my first march. I began to sing a song and in the course of singing changed the song so that it made sense for that particular moment. Although I was not consciously aware of it, this was one of my earliest experiences with how my music was supposed to *function*. This music was to be integrative of and consistent with everything I was doing at that time; it was to be tied to activities that went beyond artistic affairs such as concerts, dances, and church meetings.

7   The next level of awareness came while in jail. I had grown up in a rural area outside the city limits, riding a bus to public school or driving to college. My life had been a pretty consistent, balanced blend of church, school, and proper upbringing. I was aware of a Black educated class that taught me in high school and college, of taxi cabs I never rode in, and of people who used buses I never boarded. I went to school with their children.

8   In jail with me were all these people. All ages. In my section were women from about thirteen to eighty years old. Ministers' wives and teachers and teachers' wives who had only nodded at me or clapped at a concert or spoken to my mother. A few people from my classes. A large number of people who rode segregated city buses. One or two women who had been drinking along the two-block stretch of Little Harlem as the march went by. Very quickly, clashes arose: around age, who would have authority, what was proper behavior?

9   The Albany Movement was already a singing movement, and we took the songs to jail. There the songs I had sung because they made me feel good or because they said what I thought about a specific issue did something. I would start a song and everybody would join in. After the song, the differences among us would not be as great. Somehow, making a song required an expression of that which was common to us all. The songs did not feel like the same songs I had sung in college. This music was like an instrument, like holding a tool in your hand.

10   I found that although I was younger than many of the women in my section of the jail, I was asked to take on leadership roles. First as a song leader and

then in most other matters concerning the group, especially in discussions, or when speaking with prison officials.

11   I fell in love with that kind of music. I saw that to define music as something you listen to, something that pleases you, is very different from defining it as an instrument with which you can drive a point. In both instances, you can have the same song. But using it as an instrument makes it a different kind of music.

12   The next level of awareness occurred during the first mass meeting after my release from jail. I was asked to lead the song that I had changed after the first march. When I opened my mouth and began to sing, there was a force and power within myself I had never heard before. Somehow this music—music I could use as an instrument to do things with, music that was mine to shape and change so that it made the statement I needed to make—released a kind of power and required a level of concentrated energy I did not know I had. I liked the feeling.

13   For several years, I worked with the Movement eventually doing Civil Rights songs with the Freedom Singers. The Freedom Singers used the songs, interspersed with narrative, to convey the story of the Civil Rights Movement's struggles. The songs were more powerful than spoken conversation. They became a major way of making people who were not on the scene feel the intensity of what was happening in the south. Hopefully, they would move the people to take a stand, to organize support groups or participate in various projects.

14   The Georgia Sea Island Singers, whom I first heard at the Newport Festival, were a major link. Bessie Jones, coming from within twenty miles of Albany, Georgia, had a repertoire and song-leading style I recognized from the churches I had grown up in. She, along with John Davis, would talk about songs that Black people had sung as slaves and what those songs meant in terms of their struggle to be free. The songs did not sound like the spirituals I had sung in college choirs; they sounded like the songs I had grown up with in church. There I had been told the songs had to do with worship of Jesus Christ.

15   The next few years I spent focusing on three components: 1) The music I had found in the Civil Rights Movement. 2) Songs of the Georgia Sea Island Singers and other traditional groups, and the ways in which those songs were linked to the struggles of Black peoples at earlier times. 3) Songs of the church that now sounded like those traditional songs and came close to having, for many people, the same kind of freeing power.

16   There was another experience that helped to shape my present-day use of music. After getting out of jail, the mother of the church my father pastored was at the mass meeting. She prayed, a prayer I had heard hundreds of times. I had focused on its sound, tune, rhythm chant, whether the moans came at the proper pace and intensity. That morning I heard every word that she said. She did not have to change one word of prayer she had been praying for much of

her Christian life for me to know she was addressing the issues we were facing at that moment. More than her personal prayer, it felt like an analysis of the Albany, Georgia Black community.

17   My collection, study, and creation of Black music has been, to a large extent, about freeing the sounds and the words and the messages from casings in which they have been put, about hearing clearly what the music has to say about Black people and their struggle.

18   When I first began to search, I looked for what was then being called folk music, rather than for other Black forms, such as jazz, rhythm and blues, or gospel. It slowly dawned on me that during the Movement we had used all those forms. When we were relaxing in the office, we made up songs using popular rhythm and blues tunes; songs based in rhythm and blues also came out of jails, especially from the sit-in movement and the march to Selma, Alabama. "Oh Wallace, You Never Can Jail Us All" is an example from Selma. "You Better Leave Segregation Alone" came out of the Nashville Freedom Rides and was based on a bit by Little Willie John, "You Better Leave My Kitten Alone." Gospel choirs became the major musical vehicle in the urban center of Birmingham, with the choir led by Carlton Reese. There was also a gospel choir in the Chicago work, as well as an instrumental ensemble led by Ben Branch.

19   Jazz had not been a strong part of my musical life. I began to hear it as I traveled north. Thelonious Monk and Charlie Mingus played on the first SNCC benefit at Carnegie Hall. I heard of and then heard Coltrane. Then I began to pick up the pieces that had been laid by Charlie Parker and Coleman Hawkins and whole lifetimes of music. This music had no words. But, it had power, intensity, and movement under various degrees of pressure; it had vocal texture and color. I could feel that the music knew how it felt to be Black and Angry, Black and Down, Black and Loved, Black and Fighting.

20   I now believe that Black music exists in every place where Black people run, every corner where they live, every level on which they struggle. We have been here a long while, in many situations. It takes all that we have created to sing our song. I believe that Black musicians/artists have a responsibility to be conscious of their world and to let their consciousness be heard in their songs.

21   And we need it all—blues, gospel, ballads, children's games, dance, rhythm, jazz, lovesongs, topical songs—doing what it has always done. We need Black music that functions in relation to the people and community who provide the nurturing compost that makes its creation and continuation possible.

Reading-to-Write Questions

1. **Content:** How does Reagon make readers feel the music she describes?

2. **Arrangement:** Where and how does Reagon introduce her stages of awareness?

3. **Style:** Here and there Reagon suddenly injects a short sentence (e.g., "I liked the feeling"). What do you think of these short sentences?

4. _____

   _____

   _____

Suggested Topics

1. **Observation:** Did you, like Reagon, pass through certain levels of awareness as you listened more and more to a particular type of music (e.g., rap, jazz, or classical)? Explain. (audience = an Internet site for fans of that music)

2. **Critique:** Reagon declares, "I believe that Black musicians/artists have a responsibility to be conscious of their world and to let their consciousness be heard in their songs." In other words, Reagon does not believe in "art for art's sake." If you agree, explain why and how art should make listeners socially conscious. (See not only Reagon's essay but Dyson's and Madhubuti's as well.) If you disagree, identify weaknesses in Reagon's position. (audience = people attending a panel discussion on art and propaganda)

3. **Synthesis:** Read what Biko says about the function of music in African culture, both traditional and modern. As Reagon became increasingly aware of the functions of African American music, was she also becoming more aware of the *African* functions of African American music? (audience = class)

4. _____

   _____

   _____

Background Readings: BLACK MUSIC

Donovan, Richard X. *Black Musicians of America*. Portland, OR: National Book Co., 1991.

Floyd, Samuel A. *The Power of Black Music: Interpreting Its History from Africa to the United States*. New York: Oxford UP, 1995.

Jones, LeRoi. *Black Music*. New York: William Morrow, 1967.

Kebede, Ashenafi. *Roots of Black Music: The Vocal, Instrumental, and Dance Heritage of Africa and Black America*. Trenton: Africa World, 1995.

Nelson, Angela, ed. *"This Is How We Flow": Rhythm in Black Cultures*. Columbia: University of South Carolina Press, 1999.

Petrie, Gavin, ed. *Black Music*. London and New York: Hamlyn, 1974.

Roach, Hildred. *Black American Music: Past and Present*. 2nd ed. Malabar, FL: Krieger, 1994.

Roberts, John Storm. *Black Music of Two Worlds*. New York: Praeger, 1972.

Rublowsky, John. *Black Music in America*. New York: Basic Books, 1971.

Spencer, Jon Michael. *Re-searching Black Music*. Knoxville: University of Tennessee Press, 1996.

Recommended Literature: James Baldwin, "Sonny's Blues" from *Going to Meet the Man* (short story)

Langston Hughes, *Montage of a Dream Deferred* and *The Weary Blues* (poetry)

Ted Joans, *Black Pow-Wow: Jazz Poems by Ted Joans* (poetry)

August Wilson, *Ma Rainey's Black Bottom* (play)

George C. Wolfe, *Jelly's Last Jam* (play)

The Evolution of Rap Music
Michael Eric Dyson

Winner of the 1992 National Magazine Award for Black Journalists, Michael Eric Dyson is an ordained minister as well as a professor of communication and African American studies. He has earned a reputation for candor and eloquence through his articles as well as his books Making Malcolm: The Myth and Meaning of Malcolm X, I May Not Get There With You: The True Martin Luther King, Jr., Between God and Gangsta Rap, *and* Reflecting Black: African American Cultural Criticism. *The following selection, excerpted from an essay in* Reflecting Black *(1993), traces the evolution of rap music in three stages and considers the negative reactions to rap.*

---

1   Trying to pinpoint the exact origin of rap is a tricky process that depends on when one acknowledges a particular cultural expression or product as rap. Rap can be traced back to the revolutionary verse of Gil Scott-Heron and the Last Poets, to Pigmeat Markham's "Here Come de Judge," and even to Bessie Smith's rapping to a beat in some of her blues. We can also cite ancient African oral traditions as the antecedents to various contemporary African-American cultural practices. In any case, the modern history of rap probably begins in 1979 with the rap song "Rapper's Delight," by the Sugarhill Gang. Although there were other (mostly underground) examples of rap, this record is regarded as the signal barrier breaker, birthing hip-hop and consolidating the

infant art form's popularity. This first stage in a rap record production was characterized by rappers placing their rhythmic, repetitive speech over well-known (mostly R & B) black music hits. "Rapper's Delight" was rapped over the music to a song made by the popular seventies R & B group Chic, titled "Good Times." Although rap would later enhance its technical virtuosity through instrumentation, drum machines, and "sampling" existing records—thus making it creatively symbiotic—the first stage was benignly parasitic upon existing black music.

2   As rap grew, it was still limited to mostly inner-city neighborhoods and particularly its place of origin, New York City. Rap artists like Funky 4 Plus 1, Kool Moe Dee, Busy Bee, Afrika Bambaata, Cold Rush Brothers, Kurtis Blow, DJ Kool Hurk, and Grandmaster Melle Mel were experimenting with this developing musical genre. As it evolved, rap began to describe and analyze the social, economic, and political factors that led to its emergence and development: drug addiction, police brutality, teen pregnancy, and various forms of material deprivation. This new development was both expressed and precipitated by Kurtis Blow's "Those Are the Breaks" and by the most influential and important rap song to emerge in rap's early history, "The Message," by Grandmaster Flash and The Furious Five. The picture this song painted of inner-city life for black Americans—the hues of dark social misery and stains of profound urban catastrophe—screeched against the canvas of most suburban sensibilities:

> You'll grow up in the ghetto living second
> rate / And your eyes will sing a song of deep
> hate / The places you play and where you
> stay, / Looks like one great big alleyway /
> You'll admire all the number book takers /
> Thugs, pimps, and pushers, and the big
> money makers / Drivin' big cars, spendin'
> twenties and tens, And you want to grow up
> to be just like them / . . . It's like a jungle
> sometimes / It makes me wonder how I keep
> from goin' under.

"The Message," along with Flash's "New York, New York," pioneered the social awakening of rap into a form combining social protest, musical creation, and cultural expression.

3   As its fortunes slowly grew, rap was still viewed by the music industry as an epiphenomenal cultural activity that would cease as black youth became bored and moved on to another diversion, as they did with break-dancing and graffiti art. But the successes of the rap group Run-D.M.C. moved rap into a different sphere of artistic expression that signaled its increasing control of its own destiny. Run-D.M.C. is widely recognized as the progenitor of modern rap's creative integration of social commentary, diverse musical elements, and uncompromising cultural identification—an integration that pushed the music into the mainstream and secured its future as an American musical

genre with an identifiable tradition. Run-D.M.C.'s stunning commercial and critical success almost single-handedly landed rap in the homes of many black and nonblack youths across America by producing the first rap album to be certified gold (five hundred thousand copies sold), the first rap song to be featured on the twenty-four-hour music video channel MTV, and the first rap album (1987's *Raising Hell*) to go triple platinum (3 million copies sold).

4   On *Raising Hell*, Run-D.M.C. showcased the sophisticated technical virtuosity of its DJ Jam Master Jay—the raw shrieks, scratches, glitches, and language of the street, plus the innovative and ingenious appropriation of hard-rock guitar riffs. In doing this, Run-D.M.C. symbolically and substantively wedded two traditions—the waning subversion of rock music and the rising, incendiary aesthetic of hip-hop music—to produce a provocative musical hybrid of fiery lyricism and potent critique. *Raising Hell* ended with the rap anthem, "Proud to Be Black," intoning its unabashed racial pride:

> Ya know I'm proud to be black ya'll, And that's a fact ya'll / . . . Now Harriet Tubman was born a slave, She was a tiny black woman when she was raised / She was livin' to be givin', There's a lot that she gave / There's not a slave in this day and age, I'm proud to be black.

5   At the same time, rap, propelled by Run-D.M.C.'s epochal success, found an arena in which to concentrate its subversive cultural didacticism aimed at addressing racism, classism, social neglect, and urban pain: the rap concert, where rappers are allowed to engage in ritualistic refusals of censored speech. The rap concert also creates space for cultural resistance and personal agency, loosing the strictures of the tyrannizing surveillance and demoralizing condemnation of mainstream society and encouraging relatively autonomous, often enabling, forms of self-expression and cultural creativity.

6   However, Run-D.M.C.'s success, which greatly increased the visibility and commercial appeal of rap music through record sales and rap concerts, brought along another charge that has had a negative impact on rap's perception by the general public: the claim that rap expresses and causes violence. Tipper Gore has repeatedly said that rap music appeals to "angry, disillusioned, unloved kids" and that it tells them it is "okay to beat people up." Violent incidents at rap concerts in Los Angeles, Pittsburgh, Cleveland, Atlanta, Cincinnati, and New York City have only reinforced the popular perception that rap is intimately linked to violent social behavior by mostly black and Latino inner-city youth. Countless black parents, too, have had negative reactions to rap, and the black radio and media establishment, although not as vocal as Gore, have voted on her side with their allocation of much less airplay and print coverage to rap than is warranted by its impressive record sales.

7   Such reactions betray a shallow understanding of rap, which in many cases results from people's unwillingness to listen to rap lyrics, many of which

counsel antiviolent and antidrug behavior among the youths who are their avid audience. Many rappers have spoken directly against violence, such as KRS-One in his "Stop the Violence." Another rap record produced by KRS-One in 1989, the top-selling *Self-Destruction*, insists that violence predates rap and speaks against escalating black-on-black crime, which erodes the social and communal fabric of already debased black inner cities across America:

> Well, today's topic is self-destruction, It
> really ain't the rap audience that's buggin' /
> It's one or two suckers, ignorant brothers,
> Tryin' to rob and steal from one another / . . .
> 'Cause the way we live is positive. We don't
> kill our relatives / . . . Back in the sixties our
> brothers and sisters were hanged. How could
> you gang-bang? / I never, ever ran from the
> Ku Klux Klan, and I shouldn't have to run
> from a black man, 'Cause that's / Self-
> destruction, ya headed for self-destruction.

8   Despite such potent messages, many mainstream blacks and whites persist in categorically negative appraisals of rap, refusing to distinguish between enabling, productive rap messages and the social violence that exists in many inner-city communities and that is often reflected in rap songs. Of course, it is difficult for a culture that is serious about the maintenance of social arrangements, economic conditions, and political choices that create and reproduce poverty, racism, sexism, classism, and violence to display a significant appreciation for musical expressions that contest the existence of such problems in black and Latino communities.

Reading-to-Write Questions

1. **Content:** Why does Dyson quote so many lyrics? Would a description of each song suffice?

2. **Arrangement:** Number the three stages of evolution. Notice that Dyson does not introduce each stage with the words "The next stage . . ." Which phrases or sentences signal a new stage?

3. **Style:** Dyson's diction is noteworthy. Underline ten of the adjectives and verbs that trigger your thoughts or emotions.

4. _____

   _____

   _____

Suggested Topics

1. **Observation:** Analyze how rap music affects you. (See, for example, how Hurston responds to jazz.) (audience = people who don't listen to much rap music)

2. **Critique:** According to Dyson, the rap concert "creates space for cultural resistance and personal agency, loosing the strictures of the tyrannizing surveillance and demoralizing condemnation of mainstream society and encouraging relatively autonomous, often enabling, forms of self-expression and cultural creativity." Are these nothing more than high-sounding words? Or is there some truth in Dyson's statement? To support or challenge Dyson's view, explain how you think rap concerts affect the musicians and spectators. (audience = Dyson's readers)

3. **Synthesis:** Dyson refers to "the social violence that exists in many inner-city communities and that is often reflected in rap songs." Borrowing Madhubuti's and Reagon's perspectives on the function of art, can you justify the violent lyrics in some rap songs? (audience = rap's opponents)

4. _____

   _____

   _____

Background Readings: RAP MUSIC

Baker, Houston. *Black Studies, Rap, and the Academy*. Chicago: University of Chicago Press, 1993.

Fernando, S.H. *The New Beats: Exploring the Music Culture and Attitudes of Hip-Hop*. Edinburgh: Payback Press, 1995.

Perkins, William Eric. *Droppin' Science: Critical Essays on Rap Music and Hip Hop Culture*. Philadelphia: Temple UP, 1996.

Rose, Tricia. *Black Noise: Rap Music and Black Culture in Contemporary America*. Hanover, NH: University Press of New England, 1994.

Stavsky, Lois. *A 2 Z: The Book of Rap & Hip-Hop Slang*. New York: Boulevard Books, 1995.

Toop, David. *The Rap Attack: African Jive to New York Hip-Hop*. Boston: South End Press, 1984.

_____. *Rap Attack 2: African Rap to Global Hip Hop*. London and New York: Serpent's Tail, 1991.

_____

_____

_____

Student Essay:
AFRICAN CEREMONIES
Harold Nyikal
(2000)

1   Traditional African culture is under threat of oblivion as Western culture permeates the Eastern world in the name of globalization. Being part of the transitional generation into the modern age, I feel that it is my duty as a native of Africa to preserve the African heritage and profess its intrinsic beauty. One unique aspect of traditional African culture is the ceremonial status of events that would be considered everyday casual activity in Western culture.

2   For instance, one sees this difference in the steps taken by an African man in establishing a home as compared to the Westerner. It is the desire of virtually every person in the world to own some form of a house—something one can call "home." The Western trend is to simply buy or build a dream house once one has enough money. This can be done at any time, anywhere. In traditional African culture it was not that simple. For a man to establish a home, some rituals had to be conducted. Kenya's first president, Jomo Kenyatta, in his anthropological study of the Kikuyu people in Kenya, gives an account of the process of hut building for a Kikuyu man. For the process to begin, there had to be a feast, and all those involved would be invited. Special sugar cane or honey beer had to be brewed for the foundation ceremony. When the building was complete, a special prayer had to be chanted, and a ceremonial fire had to be lit before the prospective occupant moved in. If all these rituals were not done, the house would be considered uninhabitable, and in some cases, "evil spirits might dwell therein" (115). In addition, the rituals were important because, Kenyatta states, "the establishment of a home gives a man a special status in the community; he is referred to as 'muthuri' (an elder)" (113). In Western culture, there is no established social status for a man who owns a house.

3   One attribute common to both traditional African and Western cultures is the value attached to jeweled ornaments and the social status attached to wearing them. In Western culture the status is derived from the mere cost of the materials used in the making of the ornaments. In traditional African culture, however, the manufacturing of ornaments involved some ritual. These

rituals alone, so complex and divine, earned the maker of the ornaments special social distinction. In traditional African culture a goldsmith was viewed as having some divine calling, and his work was venerated. Renowned African writer Camara Laye, in his autobiography *The Dark Child,* describes the divine process of making golden ornaments. To start the process, a praise singer had to summon the services of the goldsmith with special songs of tribute. During the working of the gold, it was forbidden for anyone apart from the goldsmith to make a sound. Throughout the process, the goldsmith had to perform special chants to appease the "spirits of fire and gold, of fire and air . . . of fire born of air, of gold married with fire" (128). Apart from this, he also had to be clean and pure: "The craftsman who works in gold must first purify himself" (129). All of this was deemed necessary. Otherwise, the ornaments would not come out right.

4   Even in modern times some traditional practices still live on. A prominent aspect is the ceremonies involved in the reception of guests. Western people think of guests as "agents for some particular function," and visitors are greeted with "what can I do for you?" (Biko 45). I have experienced this firsthand. I had an uncle whom I was very fond of, and I would go to his house any time I wanted to. Then he married a European woman who was very hostile when I went there unannounced. In Africa people welcome guests all the time. People take joy in entertaining guests. It is considered an honor when one is visited by guests, especially from distant lands. The guests are received with ceremony. Jay Ford, in his essay "20/20 Hindsight," narrates how he was welcomed with "feasts of foods, drinks, people and music" when he visited some villages in Kenya (36).

5   Such are the practices that adorn life and make sure emphasis is given to the right things. Such are the beauties of African culture that Western culture despairingly lacks. Such are the strengths that will keep Africa alive.

Works Cited

Biko, Steve. "Some African Cultural Concepts." *Revelations.* Ed. Teresa M. Redd. 3rd ed. Needham Heights, MA: Simon & Schuster, 1997. 43–49.

Ford, Jay. "20/20 Hindsight." *Revelations.* Ed. Teresa M. Redd. 3rd ed. Needham Heights, MA: Simon & Schuster, 1997. 33–39.

Kenyatta, Jomo. "Gikuyu Industries: Hut Building." *Revelations.* Ed. Teresa M. Redd. 3rd ed. Needham Heights, MA: Simon & Schuster, 1997. 113–117.

Laye, Camara. "The Dark Child." *Revelations.* Ed. Teresa M. Redd. 3rd ed. Needham Heights, MA: Simon & Schuster, 1997. 125–131.

Student Essay:
HER GARMENT IN ALL ITS GLORY
Michael Jackson
(2000)

1   Mother's birthday was just a little over a month away, and I had long since been saving my pennies, nickels, and dimes for the upcoming expense. I had already decided that I wanted to give her a blouse. I could have made my life much easier and bought a nice blouse from Elder Beerman's or Parisian's, but that would have been far too predictable. If the party for her was to be a surprise, I thought my gift for her should be a surprise as well. Someone at the party would probably give her the same type of gift; it was inevitable, so my blouse would have to be different from any others. The blouse would have to be genuine—genuinely crafted, genuinely fashioned, and genuinely designed by my own hands. I remembered how I used to watch my mother sewing clothes for me when I was a child. I thought, perhaps, that I had at least learned the basics and could work my way from there. The more I thought about it, however, the memories of mom's sewing days were not enough to get me through; an hour and a checked-out book from the library would better equip me for the job.

2   Miss Mays was a sweet old lady. She had been a friend of my family for years and lived just down the street from our house. I knew for sure that she had a sewing room because I had seen it many times on my family's visits to her home for dinner. She wouldn't hesitate to let me use her machine for my project. So as to avoid intruding on her privacy too often, I resolved to work there only on Wednesdays after school and Saturdays. On the first Saturday, with my trusty, thick, yellow guide in hand—*Sewing for Dummies*—I intrepidly strolled down the street toward Miss Mays' house. After all of the preliminary greetings and hugs, I explained to her my project and situation. Just as I had expected, she heartily agreed to let me work in her sewing room.

3   Having established a work place at a friendly neighbor's, I went home, got on my bike, and pedaled to the local fabric store. There I spent almost two months of savings on materials: needles, thread, seam rippers, buttons, cloth, pattern, measuring tape, decorations, and other things that the book suggested. I returned to Miss Mays' house and got started. I spent half of the time

I was there reading and the other half working. Before I knew it, seven o'clock in the evening had come and gone, and I was still pinning the pattern to the fabric. I didn't even finish that first step that night. The next day I spent reading the book in my spare time and planning ahead for the forthcoming days.

4   Time passed quickly. Each Wednesday and Saturday I went back to the small sewing room and labored away. I did finish pinning on the pattern. I must have pricked every one of my fingers in the process. Then I moved on to cutting the fabric around the pattern, which I executed fairly well. After a few more checks in the book, I moved on to the sewing machine.

5   First, I had to sew in the seams, next was the hem, and last was the neckline. I wore thimbles on all of my fingers for safety, which affected the length of time it took to make each seam. Sometimes I worked until dinnertime had passed. Miss Mays would bring me a snack on those nights to encourage me. My deadline drew closer and closer, and I felt as if I was falling farther and farther behind. I was probably using the seam ripper a bit too much, but I wanted all of my seams to be perfect. By the third Wednesday of the month, I had finished sewing the seams and hems, but the end product didn't look too favorable. The cloth was wrinkled and worn in some areas. If I held the blouse up, I could see places where my seams were crooked. It also looked a lot smaller than I had expected: too small. I threw it on the floor and sat back in my chair with a heavy sigh. Mother's birthday was in four days! I had no blouse. I had no money. I had no time. I thought it was hopeless.

6   Miss Mays must have seen me slouched in my chair and came in to ask how the blouse was coming along. I pray every day that I didn't offend the sweet woman because I unintentionally vented all of my frustrations right then and there. I told her how I had made my bruised fingers porous with needle pricks. I moaned and complained about the uneven seams, the extra sags of fabric, and the cursed ends of the fabric, which seemed to unravel constantly. I whined about how my brilliant idea of thimble-covered fingers had backfired to produce the hideous pile of cloth that lay on the floor. I was wretched, but the woman took pity on me.

7   "Why didn't you ask me for help, sweetie?" she asked.

8   I went through the motions of explaining my reasoning, which probably made me look even more pitiful. I thought it was all over, but Miss Mays, the fountain of generosity that she was, offered to help me. I graciously accepted the offer. She picked up the raggedy garment and surveyed it for a few minutes, and then she turned to me and set up our plan. She dictated a short list of additional materials I would need and told me to return that following and last available Saturday, ready to work.

9   I borrowed some money from my father, bought the supplies, and returned on Saturday as she had asked. Little did I know that Miss Mays, with her broad and toothy smile, was going to transform my ideas of sewing. Her sewing room became a classroom that weekend. She threw her head back and laughed when I showed her the yellow book. We wouldn't be needing it.

10   We immediately set to work. Miss Mays showed me some of the follies I had made in following the book. Then she taught me some tricks of the trade that made things a whole lot easier. She showed me how to use regular white soap instead of pins to mark the pattern—which the second time was sized appropriately. She taught me how to use "stitch-witchery" and iron-on fabric tape to seal down the seams and hems, making them easier to sew. That Saturday we finished the entire blouse together. Not only was I able to decorate the front of the blouse with the satin flowers I had purchased, but Miss Mays also taught me how to embroider. I stitched the message "To Mom from Michael" on the hem of the blouse. I practically worshipped her for her masterful assistance. The blouse was ready for wrapping.

11   I chuckled as I placed the book in the library's drop-off box Saturday morning: I'd learned more from Miss Mays in a weekend than a month's worth of reading. That evening at the party, I presented the gift to my mother. Miss Mays was watching. With tears filling her eyes, Mom held the blouse up for everyone to see. She ran out of the room to change into it. People complimented me all night about how beautiful the blouse was, but I made sure I gave Miss Mays her credit. Mom wore her garment in all of its glory all that night. I was so proud! I'd learned a valuable lesson that weekend: It's okay to want to do something yourself, but should your efforts fail, never hesitate to ask a friend for help.

blackness: definition

ah, this hurt, this hate, this ecstasy before I die,
and all my love a strong cathedral!
My blackness is the beauty of this land!

from "My Blackness Is the Beauty of This Land"
by Lance Jeffers

The Handicap of Definition
William Raspberry

Syndicated columnist William Raspberry has written hundreds of articles for The Washington Post. *This commentary appeared in 1982. Through illustration, comparison-contrast and cause-effect analysis, Raspberry reveals how some people define "Black" and how that narrow definition hurts Black people.*

1   I know all about bad schools, mean politicians, economic deprivation and racism. Still, it occurs to me that <u>one of the heaviest burdens black Americans—and black children in particular—have to bear is the handicap of definition: the question of what it means to be black.</u>   thesis

2   Let me explain quickly what I mean. If a basketball fan says that the Boston Celtics' Larry Bird plays "black," the fan intends it—and Bird probably accepts it—as a compliment. Tell pop singer Tom Jones he moves "black" and he might grin in appreciation. Say to Teena Marie or The Average White Band that they sound "black" and they'll thank you.   illustration and contrast

3   But name one pursuit, aside from athletics, entertainment or sexual performance in which a white practitioner will feel complimented to be told he does it "black." Tell a white broadcaster he talks "black," and he'll sign up for diction lessons. Tell a white reporter he writes "black" and he'll take a writing course. Tell a white lawyer he reasons "black" and he might sue you for slander.

4   What we have here is a tragically limited definition of blackness, and it isn't only white people who buy it.

5   Think of all the ways black children can put one another down with <u>charges of "whiteness."</u> For many of these children, hard study and hard work are "white." Trying to please a teacher might be criticized as acting "white."   contrast

Speaking correct English is "white." Scrimping today in the interest of tomorrow's goals is "white." Educational toys and games are "white."

6   An incredible array of habits and attitudes that are conducive to success in business, in academia, in the non-entertainment professions are likely to be thought of as somehow "white." Even economic success unless it involves such "black" undertakings as numbers banking, is defined as "white."

illustration and contrast

7   And the results are devastating. I wouldn't deny that blacks often are better entertainers and athletes. My point is the harm that comes from too narrow a definition of what is black.

8   One reason black youngsters tend to do better at basketball, for instance, is that they assume they can learn to do it well, and so they practice constantly to prove themselves right.

9   Wouldn't it be wonderful if we could infect black children with the notion that excellence in math is "black" rather than white, or possibly Chinese? Wouldn't it be of enormous value if we could create the myth that morality, strong families, determination, courage and love of learning are traits brought by slaves from Mother Africa and therefore quintessentially black?

illustration and cause-effect

10   There is no doubt in my mind that most black youngsters could develop their mathematical reasoning, their elocution and their attitudes the way they develop their jump shots and their dance steps: by the combination of sustained, enthusiastic practice and the unquestioned belief that they can do it.

11   In one sense, what I am talking about is the importance of developing positive ethnic traditions. Maybe Jews have an innate talent for communication; maybe the Chinese are born with a gift for mathematical reasoning; maybe blacks are naturally blessed with athletic grace. I doubt it. What is at work, I suspect, is the assumption, inculcated early in their lives, that this is a thing our people do well.

illustration

12   Unfortunately, many of the things about which blacks make this assumption are things that do not contribute to their career success—except for that handful of the truly gifted who can make it as entertainers and athletes. And many of the things we concede to whites are the things that are essential to economic security.

contrast

13   So it is with a number of assumptions black youngsters make about what it is to be a "man": physical aggressiveness, sexual prowess, the refusal to submit to authority. The prisons are full of people who, by this perverted definition, are unmistakably men.

comparison

14   Somehow the real problem is not so much that the things defined as "black" are negative. The problem is that the definition is much too narrow.

15   Somehow, we have to make our children understand that they are intelligent, competent people, capable of doing whatever they put their minds to and making it in the American mainstream, not just in a black subculture.

16   What we seem to be doing, instead, is raising up yet another generation of young blacks who will be failures—by definition.

Reading-to-Write Questions

1. **Content:** Why does Raspberry compare and contrast in order to define "Black"?

2. **Arrangement:** How would you paragraph this newspaper article for a book?

3. **Style:** In which paragraphs does Raspberry use repetition and parallel structure to tie together examples?

4. _____

_____

_____

Suggested Topics

1. **Observation:** What does "acting white" mean to your peers? To find out, conduct a survey on campus or in the surrounding neighborhood. Then report your findings. (audience = class)

2. **Critique:** Raspberry contends that "one of the heaviest burdens black Americans—and black children in particular—have to bear is the handicap of definition: the question of what it means to be black." Does Raspberry attribute too much power to the "tragically limited definition of blackness"? (For additional ideas, see Naylor's, Davis's, and C. Steele's essays.) (audience = readers of the *Washington Post*)

3. **Synthesis:** Gathering ideas from Trent or Biko as well as Raspberry, redefine "Black" as you think it ought to be defined. (audience = an auditorium filled with African American high school students)

4. _____

_____

_____

Background Readings: BLACK ACADEMIC ACHIEVEMENT

Berry, Gordon Lavern, and Joy Keiko Asamen, eds. *Black Students: Psychosocial Issues and Academic Achievement.* Newbury Park, CA: Sage, 1989.

Brooks, Charlotte K., ed. *Tapping Potential: English and Language Arts for the Black Learner.* Urbana, IL: National Council of Teachers of English, 1985.

Focus on Black Males and Education. Washington, D.C.: Howard UP, 1992.

Foster, Herbert L. *Ribbin', Jivin', and Playin' the Dozens: The Persistent Dilemma in Our Schools.* 2nd ed. Cambridge, MA: Ballinger, 1986.

Herrnstein, Richard, and Charles Murray. *The Bell Curve: Intelligence and Class Structure in American Life.* New York: Free Press, 1994.

Irvine, Jacqueline Jordan. *Black Students and School Failure: Policies, Practices, and Prescriptions.* New York: Greenwood Press, 1990.

Jencks, Christopher, and Meredith Phillips, eds. *The Black-White Test Score Gap.* Washington, DC: Brookings Institution Press, 1998.

Lomotey, Kofi. *Going to School: The African American Experience.* Albany, NY: SUNY Press, 1990.

McWhorter, John. *Losing the Race: Self-Sabotage in Black America.* New York: The Free Press, 2000.

Smith, Willy DeMarcell, and Eva Wells Chunn, eds. *Black Education: A Quest for Equity and Excellence.* New Brunswick, NJ: USA Transaction, 1989.

Willie, Charles V., Antoine Garibaldi, and Wornie L. Reed, eds. *The Education of African-Americans.* New York: Auburn House, 1991.

_____

_____

_____

Recommended Literature: Gwendolyn Brooks, "We Real Cool" from *Selected Poems* (poem)

The English Language
Is My Enemy

Ossie Davis

A famous actor and playwright, Ossie Davis has performed in countless shows on stage and film and has written several plays, including Purlie Victorious, Escape to Freedom, *and* Langston. *In 1966, he gave a speech at a meeting of the American Federation of Teachers. In the following excerpt, published in the* Negro History Bulletin, *he exposes the biased definitions of "blackness" and "whiteness."*

---

1   A superficial examination of Roget's *Thesaurus of the English Language* reveals the following facts: the word WHITENESS has 134 synonyms, 44 of which are favorable and pleasing to contemplate, i.e., purity, cleanness, immaculateness, bright, shining, ivory, fair, blonde, stainless, clean, clear, chaste, unblemished, unsullied, innocent, honorable, upright, just, straightforward, fair, genuine, trustworthy (a white man's colloquialism). Only ten synonyms for WHITENESS appear to me to have negative implications—and these only in the mildest sense: gloss over, whitewash, gray, wan, pale, ashen, etc.

2   The word BLACKNESS has 120 synonyms, 60 of which are distinctly unfavorable, and none of them even mildly positive. Among the offending 60 were such words as: blot, blotch, smut, smudge, sully, begrime, soot, becloud, obscure, dingy, murky, low-toned, threatening, frowning, foreboding, forbidden, sinister, baneful, dismal, thundery, evil, wicked, malignant, deadly, unclean, dirty, unwashed, foul, etc. . . . not to mention 20 synonyms directly related to race, such as: Negro, Negress, nigger, darky, blackamoor, etc.

3   When you consider the fact that *thinking* itself is sub-vocal speech—in other words, one must use *words* in order to think at all—you will appreciate the enormous heritage of racial prejudgment that lies in wait for any child born into the English Language. Any teacher good or bad, white or black, Jew or Gentile, who uses the English Language as a medium of communication is forced, willy-nilly, to teach the Negro child 60 ways to despise himself, and the white child 60 ways to aid and abet him in the crime.

4   Who speaks to me in my Mother Tongue damns me indeed! . . . the English Language—in which I cannot conceive my self as a black man without, at the same time, debasing myself . . . my enemy, with which to survive at all I must continually be at war.

Reading-to-Write Questions

1. **Content:** This selection is an excerpt from a speech that Davis gave at a meeting of the American Federation of Teachers in 1966. How does Davis attempt to meet his audience's scholarly standards?

2. **Arrangement:** Where are the topic sentences? What do they accomplish?

3. **Style:** Where does Davis coordinate words and phrases to create balance and rhythm? What purpose does the coordination serve?

4. _____

   _____

   _____

Suggested Topics

1. **Observation:** Conduct an informal survey among Blacks and Whites to determine what they associate with the words "black" and "white." Then use the data to support a thesis about Black and White attitudes toward the words. (audience = Black and White parents)

2. **Critique:** Summarize Davis's argument and then consider his complaint that none of the synonyms for "blackness" are "even mildly positive." Can you, nonetheless, find some positive meanings of "black"? What about "in the black," for instance? Think of other exceptions to discuss in your essay. (audience = class)

3. **Synthesis:** Following Davis's example, use a thesaurus to expose the bias associated with another word that is applied to a group of people (e.g., "handicapped"). Then, following Raspberry's example, consider the impact the word's definitions may have on that group. (audience = readers who do not belong to the affected group)

4. _____

   _____

   _____

Background Readings: RACISM IN LANGUAGE

Herbst, Philip. *The Color of Words: An Encyclopedic Dictionary of Ethnic Bias.* Yarmouth, ME: Intercultural Press, 1997.

McPhail, Mark Lawrence. *The Rhetoric of Racism.* Lanham, MD: University Press of America, 1994.

Moore, Robert B. *Racism in the English Language.* New York: Council on Interracial Books for Children, 1976.

Smitherman-Donaldson, Geneva, and Teun A. Van Dijk, eds. *Discourse and Discrimination.* Detroit: Wayne State UP, 1988.

Van Dijk, Teun A. *Communicating Racism: Ethnic Prejudice in Thought and Talk.* Newbury Park, CA: Sage, 1987.

_____. *Elite Discourse and Racism.* Newbury Park, CA: Sage, 1993.

_____

_____

_____

Mommy, What Does "Nigger" Mean?
Gloria Naylor

Winner of the American Book Award, Gloria Naylor has written four novels: Linden Hills, Mama Day, Bailey's Café *and the award-winning book* The Women of Brewster Place. *She wrote the following essay in 1986, and it was published that year in* The New York Times. *In the essay she explains that "nigger" has many meanings—meanings determined by its use among Blacks as well as among whites.*

———————————

1   Language is the subject. It is the written form with which I've managed to keep the wolf away from the door and, in diaries, to keep my sanity. In spite of this, I consider the written word inferior to the spoken, and much of the frustration experienced by novelists is the awareness that whatever we manage to capture in even the most transcendent passages falls far short of the richness of life. Dialogue achieves its power in the dynamics of a fleeting moment of sight, sound, smell and touch.

2   I'm not going to enter the debate here about whether it is language that shapes reality or vice versa. That battle is doomed to be waged whenever we seek intermittent reprieve from the chicken and egg dispute. I will simply take the position that the spoken word, like the written word, amounts to a nonsensical arrangement of sounds or letters without a consensus that assigns "meaning." And building from the meanings of what we hear, we order reality. Words themselves are innocuous; it is the consensus that gives them true power.

171

3   I remember the first time I heard the word nigger. In my third-grade class, our math tests were being passed down the rows, and as I handed the papers to a little boy in back of me, I remarked that once again he had received a much lower mark than I did. He snatched his test from me and spit out that word. Had he called me a nymphomaniac or a necrophiliac, I couldn't have been more puzzled. I didn't know what a nigger was, but I knew that whatever it meant, it was something he shouldn't have called me. This was verified when I raised my hand, and in a loud voice repeated what he had said and watched the teacher scold him for using a "bad" word. I was later to go home and ask the inevitable question that every black parent must face—"Mommy, what does 'nigger' mean?"

4   And what exactly did it mean? Thinking back, I realize that this could not have been the first time the word was used in my presence. I was part of a large extended family that had migrated from the rural South after World War II and formed a close-knit network that gravitated around my maternal grandparents. Their ground-floor apartment in one of the buildings they owned in Harlem was a weekend mecca for my immediate family, along with countless aunts, uncles and cousins who brought along assorted friends. It was a bustling and open house with assorted neighbors and tenants popping in and out to exchange bits of gossip, pick up an old quarrel or referee the ongoing checkers game in which my grandmother cheated shamelessly. They were all there to let down their hair and put up their feet after a week of labor in the factories, laundries and shipyards of New York.

5   Amid the clamor, which could reach deafening proportions—two or three conversations going on simultaneously, punctuated by the sound of a baby's crying somewhere in the back rooms or out on the street—there was still a rigid set of rules about what was said and how. Older children were sent out of the living room when it was time to get into the juicy details about "you-know-who" up on the third floor who had gone and gotten herself "p-r-e-g-n-a-n-t!" But my parents, knowing that I could spell well beyond my years, always demanded that I follow the others out to play. Beyond sexual misconduct and death, everything else was considered harmless for our young ears. And so among the anecdotes of the triumphs and disappointments in the various workings of their lives, the word nigger was used in my presence, but it was set within contexts and inflections that caused it to register in my mind as something else.

6   In the singular, the word was always applied to a man who had distinguished himself in some situation that brought their approval for his strength, intelligence or drive:

7   "Did Johnny really do that?"

8   "I'm telling you, that nigger pulled in $6,000 of overtime last year. Said he got enough for a down payment on a house."

9   When used with a possessive adjective by a woman—"my nigger"—it became a term of endearment for husband or boyfriend. But it could be more than just a term applied to a man. In their mouths it became the pure essence

of manhood—a disembodied force that channeled their past history of struggle and present survival against the odds into a victorious statement of being:
"Yeah, that old foreman found out quick enough—you don't mess with a
nigger."

10   In the plural, it became a description of some group within the community
that had overstepped the bounds of decency as my family defined it: Parents
who neglected their children, a drunken couple who fought in public, people
who simply refused to look for work, those with excessively dirty mouths or
unkempt households were all "trifling niggers." This particular circle could
forgive hard times, unemployment, the occasional bout of depression—they
had gone through all of that themselves—but the unforgivable sin was lack of
self-respect.

11   A woman could never be a "nigger" in the singular, with its connotation of
confirming worth. The noun girl was its closest equivalent in that sense, but
only when used in direct address and regardless of the gender doing the
addressing. "Girl" was a token of respect for a woman. The one-syllable word
was drawn out to sound like three in recognition of the extra ounce of wit,
nerve or daring that the woman had shown in the situation under discussion.

12   "G-i-r-l, stop. You mean you said that to his face?"

13   But if the word was used in a third-person reference or shortened so that it
almost snapped out of the mouth, it always involved some element of communal disapproval. And age became an important factor in these exchanges. It
was only between individuals of the same generation, or from an older person
to a younger (but never the other way around), that "girl" would be considered a compliment.

14   I don't agree with the argument that use of the word nigger at this social
stratum of the black community was an internalization of racism. The dynamics were the exact opposite: the people in my grandmother's living room took
a word that whites used to signify worthlessness or degradation and rendered
it impotent. Gathering there together, they transformed "nigger" to signify the
varied and complex human beings they knew themselves to be. If the word
was to disappear totally from the mouths of even the most liberal of white
society, no one in that room was naive enough to believe it would disappear
from white minds. Meeting the word head-on, they proved it had absolutely
nothing to do with the way they were determined to live their lives.

15   So there must have been dozens of times that the word "nigger" was spoken in front of me before I reached the third grade. But I didn't "hear" it until
it was said by a small pair of lips that had already learned it could be a way to
humiliate me. That was the word I went home and asked my mother about,
and since she knew that I had to grow up in America, she took me in her lap
and explained.

Reading-to-Write Questions

1. **Content:** To define, where does Naylor adopt narration, comparison, contrast, and cause-effect strategies?

2. **Arrangement:** Reread the introductory and concluding paragraphs. How does Naylor "come full circle" by the end of the essay?

3. **Style:** Study the style of the first paragraph. Can you imitate the paragraph, clause for clause and phrase for phrase, preserving the repetition and coordination?

4. _____

    _____

    _____

Suggested Topics

1. **Observation:** Explore the many meanings of "Negro." (audience = international students)

2. **Critique:** Naylor announces, "I don't agree with the argument that use of the word nigger at this social stratum of the black community was an internalization of racism." Unlike Naylor, do you agree with that argument? (audience = participants in a class debate)

3. **Synthesis:** Naylor considers "the written word inferior to the spoken word" because "whatever we manage to capture in even the most transcendent passages falls far short of the richness of life." Drawing support from Naylor's and Smitherman's essays, show how the oral tradition of African Americans captures "the richness of life." OR, citing Madhubuti's and Traylor's essays, demonstrate that African American writing does not necessarily "fall short" of capturing "the richness of life." (audience = students intending to major in English)

4. _____

    _____

    _____

Background Readings: BLACK SEMANTICS

Abrahams, Roger. *Talking Black.* Rowley, MA: Newbury House, 1976.

Claerbaut, David. *Black Jargon in White America.* Grand Rapids, MI: Eerdmans, 1972.

Dillard, J.L. *Lexicon of Black English.* New York: Seabury, 1977.

Fab 5, Freddy (aka Fred Braithwaite). *Fresh Fly Flavor: Words and Phrases of the Hip-Hop Generation.* Stamford, CT: Longmeadow, 1991.

Holt, Grace. "Inversion in Black Communication." *Rappin' and Stylin' Out: Communication in Urban Black America.* Ed. Thomas Kochman. Chicago: University of Illinois Press, 1972. 152–159.

Major, Clarence, ed. *Juba to Jive: A Dictionary of African-American Slang.* New York: Penguin, 1994.

Smitherman, Geneva. *Black Talk: Words and Phrases from the Hood to the Amen Corner.* Boston: Houghton Mifflin, 1994.

_____. *Talkin' and Testifyin': The Language of Black America.* Detroit: Wayne State UP, 1977.

Stavsky, Lois. *A 2 Z: The Book of Rap and Hip-Hop Slang.* New York: Boulevard Books, 1995.

Recommended Literature: Clarence Major, "Vietnam #4" in *Chapman's New Black Voices* (poem)

How It Feels to Be Colored Me
Zora Neale Hurston

Best known for her novel Their Eyes Were Watching God, *Zora Neale Hurston (1891–1960) was a folklorist and anthropologist as well as a fiction writer. Among her works are* Mules and Men *(a narrative based on her folklore research) and her autobiography* Dust Tracks on a Road. *In 1979, Alice Walker collected some of Hurston's writings in* I Love Myself When I Am Laughing. *Although the following essay comes from that collection, it was first published in 1928 in* The World Tomorrow. *The essay is an autobiographical definition of the term "colored."*

———————

1   I am colored but I offer nothing in the way of extenuating circumstances except the fact that I am the only Negro in the United States whose grandfather on the mother's side was *not* an Indian chief.

2   I remember the very day that I became colored. Up to my thirteenth year I lived in the little Negro town of Eatonville, Florida. It is exclusively a colored town. The only white people I knew passed through the town going to or coming from Orlando. The native whites rode dusty horses, the Northern tourists chugged down the sandy village road in automobiles. The town knew the Southerners and never stopped cane chewing when they passed. But the Northerners were something else again. They were peered at cautiously from behind curtains by the timid. The more venturesome would come out on the

porch to watch them go past and got just as much pleasure out of the tourists as the tourists got out of the village.

3   The front porch might seem a daring place for the rest of the town, but it was a gallery seat to me. My favorite place was atop the gate-post. Proscenium box for a born first-nighter. Not only did I enjoy the show, but I didn't mind the actors knowing that I liked it. I usually spoke to them in passing. I'd wave at them and when they returned my salute, I would say something like this: "Howdy-do-well-I-thank-you-where-you-goin'?" Usually the automobile or the horse paused at this, and after a queer exchange of compliments, I would probably "go a piece of the way" with them, as we say in farthest Florida. If one of my family happened to come to the front in time to see me, of course negotiations would be rudely broken off. But even so, it is clear that I was the first "welcome-to-our-state" Floridian, and I hope the Miami Chamber of Commerce will please take notice.

4   During this period, white people differed from colored to me only in that they rode through town and never lived there. They liked to hear me "speak pieces" and sing and wanted to see me dance the parse-me-la, and gave me generously of their small silver for doing these things, which seemed strange to me for I wanted to do them so much that I needed bribing to stop. Only they didn't know it. The colored people gave no dimes. They deplored any joyful tendencies in me, but I was their Zora nevertheless. I belonged to them, to the nearby hotels, to the county—everybody's Zora.

5   But changes came in the family when I was thirteen, and I was sent to school in Jacksonville. I left Eatonville, the town of the oleanders, as Zora. When I disembarked from the river-boat at Jacksonville, she was no more. It seemed that I had suffered a sea change. I was not Zora of Orange County any more, I was now a little colored girl. I found it out in certain ways. In my heart as well as in the mirror, I became a fast brown—warranted not to rub nor run.

6   But I am not tragically colored. There is no great sorrow dammed up in my soul, nor lurking behind my eyes. I do not mind at all. I do not belong to the sobbing school of Negrohood who hold that nature somehow has given them a lowdown dirty deal and whose feelings are all hurt about it. Even in the helter-skelter skirmish that is my life, I have seen that the world is to the strong regardless of a little pigmentation more or less. No, I do not weep at the world—I am too busy sharpening my oyster knife.

7   Someone is always at my elbow reminding me that I am the granddaughter of slaves. It fails to register depression with me. Slavery is sixty years in the past. The operation was successful and the patient is doing well, thank you. The terrible struggle that made me an American out of a potential slave said "On the line!" The Reconstruction said "Get set!"; and the generation before said "Go!" I am off to a flying start and I must not halt in the stretch to look behind and weep. Slavery is the price I paid for civilization, and the choice was not with me. It is a bully adventure and worth all that I have paid through my ancestors for it. No one on earth ever had a greater chance for glory. The world to be won and nothing to be lost. It is thrilling to think—to know that

for any act of mine, I shall get twice as much praise or twice as much blame. It is quite exciting to hold the center of the national stage, with the spectators not knowing whether to laugh or to weep.

8   The position of my white neighbor is much more difficult. No brown specter pulls up a chair beside me when I sit down to eat. No dark ghost thrusts its leg against mine in bed. The game of keeping what one has is never so exciting as the game of getting.

9   I do not always feel colored. Even now I often achieve the unconscious Zora of Eatonville before the Hegira. I feel most colored when I am thrown against a sharp white background.

10   For instance at Barnard. "Beside the waters of the Hudson" I feel my race. Among the thousand white persons, I am a dark rock surged upon, overswept by a creamy sea. I am surged upon and overswept, but through it all, I remain myself. When covered by the waters, I am; and the ebb but reveals me again.

11   Sometimes it is the other way around. A white person is set down in our midst, but the contrast is just as sharp for me. For instance, when I sit in the drafty basement that is The New World Cabaret with a white person, my color comes. We enter chatting about any little nothing that we have in common and are seated by the jazz waiters. In the abrupt way that jazz orchestras have, this one plunges into a number. It loses no time in circumlocutions, but gets right down to business. It constricts the thorax and splits the heart with its tempo and narcotic harmonies. This orchestra grows rambunctious, rears on its hind legs and attacks the tonal veil with primitive fury, rending it, clawing it until it breaks through to the jungle beyond. I follow those heathen—follow them exultingly. I dance wildly inside myself, I yell within, I whoop; I shake my assegai above my head, I hurl it true to the mark *yeeeeooww*! I am in the jungle and living in the jungle way. My face is painted red and yellow and my body is painted blue. My pulse is throbbing like a war drum. I want to slaughter something—give pain, give death to what, I do not know. But the piece ends. The men of the orchestra wipe their lips and rest their fingers. I creep back slowly—to the veneer we call civilization with the last tone and find the white friend sitting motionless in his seat, smoking calmly.

12   "Good music they have here," he remarks, drumming the table with his fingertips.

13   Music! The great blobs of purple and red emotion have not touched him. He has only heard what I felt. He is far away and I see him but dimly across the ocean and the continent that have fallen between us. He is so pale with his whiteness then and I am *so* colored.

14   At certain times I have no race, I am *me*. When I set my hat at a certain angle and saunter down Seventh Avenue, Harlem City, feeling as snooty as the lions in front of the Forty-Second Street Library, for instance. So far as my feelings are concerned, Peggy Hopkins Joyce on the Boule Mich with her gorgeous raiment, stately carriage, knees knocking together in a most aristocratic manner, has nothing on me. The cosmic Zora emerges. I belong to no race nor time. I am the eternal feminine with its string of beads.

15   I have no separate feeling about being an American citizen and colored. I am merely a fragment of the Great Soul that surges within the boundaries. My country, right or wrong.

16   Sometimes, I feel discriminated against, but it does not make me angry. It merely astonishes me. How *can* any deny themselves the pleasure of my company! It's beyond me.

17   But in the main, I feel like a brown bag of miscellany propped against a wall. Against a wall in company with other bags, white, red and yellow. Pour out the contents, and there is discovered a jumble of small things priceless and worthless. A first-water diamond, an empty spool, bits of broken glass, lengths of string, a key to a door long since crumbled away, a rusty knife-blade, old shoes saved for a road that never was and never will be, a nail bent under the weight of things too heavy for any nail, a dried flower or two, still a little fragrant. In your hand is the brown bag. On the ground before you is the jumble it held—so much like the jumble in the bags, could they be emptied, that all might be dumped in a single heap and the bags refilled without altering the content of any greatly. A bit of colored glass more or less would not matter. Perhaps that is how the Great Stuffer of Bags filled them in the first place—who knows?

Reading-to-Write Questions

1. **Content:** How do Hurston's anecdotes contribute to her definition?

2. **Arrangement:** Why does Hurston close her essay with a question?

3. **Style:** Where does Hurston employ imagery to express her thoughts and emotions?

4. _____

   _____

   _____

Suggested Topics

1. **Observation:** Like Hurston, write an autobiographical definition of a term. (general audience)

2. **Critique:** Hurston muses, "The position of my white neighbor is much more difficult." Do you also believe that the descendants of slavemasters carry greater burdens than the descendants of the slaves? If your argument hinges upon any abstract or controversial terms, define them. (audience = African Americans)

3. **Synthesis:** Hurston's comment "Slavery is the price I paid for civilization" reflects her 1920s view of Africa. Based on her description of the jungle, explain what Africa must have symbolized to Hurston and what definition of "civilization" underlies her remark. Then compare Hurston's assumptions to your understanding of African culture and your own definition of "civilization." Before you construct your definition, consult Ford's and Biko's essays. (audience = students studying the Harlem Renaissance)

4. _____

   _____

   _____

Background Readings: RACIAL IDENTITY IN THE 1920s

Baker, Houston, Jr. *Afro-American Poetics: Revisions of Harlem and the Black Aesthetic.* Madison, WI: University of Wisconsin Press, 1996.

Bronz, Stephen H. *Roots of Negro Racial Consciousness, The 1920s: Three Harlem Renaissance Authors.* New York: Libra, 1964.

Huggins, Nathan. *The Harlem Renaissance.* New York: Oxford UP, 1971.

_____, ed. *Voices from the Harlem Renaissance.* New York: Oxford UP, 1994.

Hutchison, George. *The Harlem Renaissance in Black and White.* Cambridge, MA: Belknap Press of Harvard UP, 1995.

Johnson, Eloise. *Rediscovering the Harlem Renaissance: The Politics of Exclusion.* New York: Garland, 1997.

Locke, Alain. *The New Negro: An Interpretation.* 1925. rpt. New York: Atheneum, 1968.

Wall, Cheryl. *Women of the Harlem Renaissance.* Bloomington: Indiana UP, 1995.

Wintz, Cary D. *Black Culture and the Harlem Renaissance.* Houston: Rice UP, 1988.

_____. *The Emergence of the Harlem Renaissance.* New York: Garland, 1996.

_____

_____

_____

Recommended Literature: Countee Cullen, *Color* (poetry)

Langston Hughes, *The Weary Blues* (poetry)

Black and Latino
Roberto Santiago

Born to Puerto Rican parents—a dark-skinned mother and a white-skinned father—Roberto Santiago maintains that he is Black and Latino. In this essay, published in Essence Magazine *in 1989, Santiago wrestles with American and Latino definitions of race. In addition to this selection, Santiago has written newspaper columns, magazine articles, drama, screenplays, and fiction.*

————————————

1   "There is no way that you can be black and Puerto Rican at the same time." What? Despite the many times I've heard this over the years, that statement still perplexes me. I *am* both and always have been. My color is a blend of my mother's rich, dark skin tone and my father's white complexion. As they were both Puerto Rican, I spoke Spanish before English, but I am totally bilingual. My life has been shaped by my black and Latino heritages, and despite other people's confusion, I don't feel I have to choose one or the other. To do so would be to deny a part of myself.

2   There has not been a moment in my life when I did not know that I looked black—and I never thought that others did not see it, too. But growing up in East Harlem, I was also aware that I did not "act black," according to the African-American boys on the block.

3   My lighter-skinned Puerto Rican friends were less of a help in this department. "You're not black," they would whine, shaking their heads. "You're a *boriqua* [slang for Puerto Rican], you ain't no *moreno* [black]." If that was true, why did my mirror defy the rules of logic? And most of all, why did I feel that there was some serious unknown force trying to make me choose sides?

4   *Acting black. Looking black. Being a real black.* This debate among us is almost a parody. The fact is that I am black, so why do I need to prove it?

5   The island of Puerto Rico is only a stone's throw away from Haiti, and, no fooling, if you climb a palm tree, you can see Jamaica bobbing on the Atlantic. The slave trade ran through the Caribbean basin, and virtually all Puerto Rican citizens have some African blood in their veins. My grandparents on my mother's side were the classic *negro como carbón* (black as carbon) people, but despite the fact that they were as dark as can be, they are officially not considered black.

6   There is an explanation for this, but not one that makes much sense, or difference, to a working-class kid from Harlem. Puerto Ricans identify themselves as Hispanics—part of a worldwide race that originated from eons of white Spanish conquests—a mixture of white, African, and *Indio* blood, which, categorically, is apart from black. In other words, the culture is the predominant and determinant factor. But there are frustrations in being caught in a duo-culture, where your skin color does not necessarily dictate what you are. When I read Piri Thomas's searing autobiography, *Down These Mean Streets,* in my early teens, I saw that he couldn't figure out other people's attitudes toward his blackness, either.

7   My first encounter with this attitude about the race thing rode on horseback. I had just turned six years old and ran toward the bridle path in Central Park as I saw two horses about to trot past. "Yea! Horsie! Yea!" I yelled. Then I noticed one figure on horseback. She was white, and she shouted, "Shut up, you f—g nigger! Shut up!" She pulled back on the reins and twisted the horse in my direction. I can still feel the spray of gravel that the horse kicked at my chest. And suddenly she was gone. I looked back, and, in the distance, saw my parents playing Whiffle Ball with my sister. They seemed miles away.

8   They still don't know about this incident. But I told my Aunt Aurelia almost immediately. She explained what the words meant and why they were said. Ever since then I have been able to express my anger appropriately through words or action in similar situations. Self-preservation, ego, and pride forbid men from ever ignoring, much less forgetting, a slur.

9   Aunt Aurelia became, unintentionally, my source for answers I needed about color and race. I never sought her out. She just seemed to appear at my home during the points in my childhood when I most needed her for solace. "Puerto Ricans are different from American blacks," she told me once. "There is no racism between what you call white and black. Nobody even considers the marriages interracial." She then pointed out the difference in color between my father and mother. "You never noticed that," she said, "because you were not raised with that hang-up."

10   Aunt Aurelia passed away before I could follow up on her observation. But she had made an important point. It's why I never liked the attitude that says I should be exclusive to one race.

11   My behavior toward this race thing pegged me as an iconoclast of sorts. Children from mixed marriages, from my experience, also share this attitude.

If I have to beat the label of iconoclast because the world wants people to be in set categories and I don't want to, then I will.

12   A month before Aunt Aurelia died, she saw I was a little down about the whole race thing, and she said, "Roberto, don't worry. Even if—no matter what you do—black people in this country don't, you can always depend on white people to treat you like a black."

Reading-to-Write Questions

1. **Content:** How does the dialogue contribute to the essay?

2. **Arrangement:** Why do you think Santiago closed his essay with a quotation from Aunt Aurelia?

3. **Style:** Notice the line "Acting black. Looking black. Being a real black." Is this series of fragments effective? If so, why?

4. _____

    _____

    _____

Suggested Topics

1. **Observation:** What do the phrases "Acting black. Looking black. Being real black" mean to you? (audience = offspring from interracial or Hispanic marriages)

2. **Critique:** Santiago argues that he should not have to choose between Black and Puerto Rican. Many Americans born to interrracial couples have advanced the same argument. Consequently, the U.S. Census Bureau now allows a person to select more than one racial category (see Trent's essay). Is this a good idea? (audience = U.S. Census Bureau)

3. **Synthesis:** According to Santiago, culture determines one's identity in Puerto Rico, but in the continental U.S. race matters more. Should it? For contrasting ideas, see Hurston's, Staples', Trent's, and Bates's essays. Make sure you define key terms. (audience = Latinos)

4. _____

    _____

    _____

Background Readings: MIXED RACE

Root, Maria P. *Racially Mixed People in America*. Newbury Park, CA: Sage, 1992.

_____. *The Multiracial Experience: Racial Borders as the New Frontier*. London: Sage, 1996.

Tizard, Barbara. *Black, White, or Mixed Race?: Race and Racism in the Lives of Young People of Mixed Parentage*. London and New York: Routledge, 1993.

Williamson, Joel. *New People: Miscegenation and Mulattoes in the United States*. Baton Rouge, LA: Louisiana State UP, 1996.

Wilson, Anne. *Mixed Race Children: A Study of Identity*. London and Boston: Allen & Unwin, 1987.

Zack, Naomi, ed. *American Mixed Race: The Culture of Microdiversity*. Lanham: Rowman & Littlefield, 1995.

_____

_____

_____

Recommended Literature: William Wells Brown, *Clotel, or The President's Daughter* (novel)

Charles Chesnutt, *The Wife of His Youth and Other Stories of the Color Line* (short stories)

There's No Box to Account for Our History

Sydney Trent

After reporting and/or editing for the Virginian-Pilot, Philadelphia Inquirer, *and* Miami Herald, *Sydney Trent joined the staff of* The Washington Post. *As Deputy Maryland Editor, she wrote the following op-ed article for the March 25, 2001 edition of the newspaper. In this commentary, she explains why she considers her adopted daughter "black," even though the child's birth mother was white. In the process, she interrogates the meaning of the words* black, mulatto, *and* biracial.

————————————

1   It was big news across the country. Tallies released by the U.S. Census Bureau earlier this month showed that 7 million people had selected the new option of checking more than one racial category, declaring themselves multiracial.

2   But that number was barely worthy of a headline in our household. My mother pronounced it a gross undercount.

3   It's all a lie, she said. Black people in this country have been racially mixed for hundreds of years. What's different now, she maintains, is that the government is *allowing* us to be what we've always been.

4   Reasoning the way I suspect many African Americans did, my mother wasn't about to change the way she thought about herself and her family just because some government Rip Van Winkle finally woke up. When the census form arrived in the mail last spring, she checked just one box: "black, African American or Negro." As did I, without hesitation, for myself, and then for my young daughter.

5   I'd thought through Alexandra's racial identity three years ago when her birth mother placed her in my arms, with desperate faith that my husband and I would guide this almond-skinned, curly-haired baby lovingly through life. In the simplest terms, Alex's birth mother is white, as is my husband. Her birth father is African American, as am I.

6   How could I put Alex in a separate category from myself? The answer, though imperfect I know, was clear enough to me. I could not. It would be a false distinction.

7   From the stories my parents told me as I grew up, I know that I am the product of African slaves, of slavemasters of European descent—Scottish, French and Welsh among them—and of Native Americans. Alex is another version of the same. We are not unusual. Most of us who call ourselves African American are, to one degree or another, some combination of those three groups. And, like many blacks, my family arrived at that mixture in a horrible way, one most people would rather forget. Our ancestors were raped.

8   This fact of what went on during slavery goes a long way toward explaining white America's willful amnesia when it comes to the history of mixed-race blacks—this notion that to be biracial, or multiracial, is something new, born of our freedom to love and marry across a narrowing racial divide.

9   In truth, more than a century ago, my great-grandmother Sally Johns, daughter of a slavemaster, would have been counted in the census as a "mulatto," a category for those who were three-eighths to five-eighths black. And following this painstaking calculation by the government, she would have been distinguished from a quadroon, someone one-quarter black, and an octoroon, a person who was one-eighth black.

10   By 1930, these racial categories had been abandoned, due in part to a fear that they would encourage the mixing of the races. In their place we got the one-drop rule—one drop of black blood and you were counted as black. As my mother now puts it, it's as if we were given *permission* to forget our mixed-race history. And now, with the opportunity to mark more than one box on the census form, we've been given permission to acknowledge it.

11   So my decision to identify my daughter as black has much to do with my rejection of the census as the arbiter of who we as African Americans are. How I perceive myself does not change because Uncle Sam changes the rules again.

12   But there are other reasons as well. I want Alex to know that as an African American of mixed-racial ancestry she is not hanging on the precipice of history. My family and our ancestors, the black half of her birth family and their ancestors, and millions of other African Americans have come before her. We have always been who we are, no matter how others wished to see us. As Langston Hughes wrote in his 1942 poem "Harlem Sweeties," we African Americans are and have always been "blush of the rose" to "blackberry cordial."

13   I also agree with many African Americans that racism is not a thing of the past. Despite this new multiracial awareness, America's new immigrants soon realize who is at the bottom of the totem pole. So we have learned to look war-

ily at those who visibly share our African roots but choose not to identify with them. Are they merely employing the racial rules of their native cultures, or are they disowning the bonds they have with us?

14   And it is the racism that still thrives in our society that makes many African Americans question the motives of those who call themselves biracial, or those parents who underscore their children's mixed-race heritage. In emphasizing the mix, we wonder, are they teaching children to be proud of all facets of their heritage—or are they really just trying to deemphasize the blackness?

15   This biracial stuff started when *white* women began giving birth to mixed-race babies, my mother maintains.

16   So I emphasize Alex's blackness, hoping she will not be tempted to devalue it, that she will be able to withstand the cultural whisperings that still tell us white is better.

17   At some point, however, my mother and I part ways, she looking over her shoulder at our family history, I straining to see ahead into Alex's future. I know that my daughter's life will not be my mother's, or my own.

18   I try to explain to my mother some of the things that make this true. Alex is growing up with a white parent in the house, my husband Bruce, with whom she will surely also wish to identify. Like me, he knows the logic of calling Alex African American is imperfect, but he understands the compromise I'm making between truth and history.

19   My mother points out that my great-grandmother Sally was grudgingly reared by the white slavemaster who fathered her, but never saw herself as anything but black. Nor did her son, my grandfather, Vernon Johns, a civil rights pioneer with fair skin and straight features.

20   But then I think of something else. My ancestors did not grow up in integrated schools, in integrated neighborhoods. They did not attend the birthday parties of the white kids across the street; their parents did not entertain white friends and colleagues in their homes. They did not date whites, they did not marry them. They were not raised in homes with one black parent and one white parent who openly loved them, and each other.

21   My ancestors likely did not encounter people who proudly proclaimed themselves biracial or multiracial. They, like my mother and, to some extent, myself, were not granted permission to choose.

22   I await the day when Alex comes home to tell me that she played with the children of another interracial couple and those kids call themselves biracial. "Why then," I imagine she might ask me, "am I black?"

23   I'll respond by sharing with her the meaning of the word "black" in America. I'll tell her about her great-great grandmother Sally, and her great-grandfather Vernon, and about her birth father's family, with a little bit of everything thrown in, too. I'll point to her Aunt Beth, her Aunt Margot, her Uncle Jay— and my mother, who raises her when I am at work. I'll show her a mirror.

24   But in the end, I'll make sure she knows she has my permission to define herself in the way that feels most right to her. Whatever that may be.

25   Embrace the future, Alex. Just don't forget what you're leaving behind.

Reading-to-Write Questions

1. **Content:** Compare Morrison's and Trent's essays. What is similar about the way they present history?

2. **Arrangement:** This article consists of many short paragraphs because it was formatted for the narrow columns of a newspaper. How do you think Trent would have constructed the paragraphs if she had been typing the essay for a book?

3. **Style:** At the end of the essay, Trent suddenly bypasses the reader to address her daughter. How did you react to this shift?

4. _____

   _____

   _____

Suggested Topics

1. **Observation:** Look up the findings of the Human Genome Project, talk to an anthropology professor, or read recent anthropological research on race. How do scientists define race? How significant is it genetically? (audience = participants in a school workshop on diversity)

2. **Critique:** How does Trent define the Census Bureau's phrase "black, African American or Negro"? Is her definition adequate? (audience = Census Bureau)

3. **Synthesis:** How might other authors respond to Trent's definition of "black" and "African American"? Consider the views of Ture, Hurston, and Santiago. (audience = other readers of *Revelations*)

4. _____

   _____

   _____

Background Readings: MIXED RACE

See the reading list for Roberto Santiago's essay.

Student Essay:
BROADENING THE DEFINITION
OF "BLACK"

Bakesta King

(1996)

1   Extract the athletic ability, the musical inclination, rhythm, and soul from the modern African American. Are there any other characteristics which distinguish blacks from any other race? Can "black" be defined by such insufficient means? In "The Handicap of Definition," William Raspberry intensely explores a topic most individuals, especially blacks, take too lightly. He describes how the definition of "black" is limited to the stereotypes created by black subcultures. Raspberry questions the notion that hard work, proper speech, and preparation for long-term goals are "white," while exceptional basketball skills, soulful singing, and rhythmic ability are "black" (167).

2   Raspberry ranks this "handicap of definition" with the traditional burdens of racism and economic deprivation. He specifically pinpoints successful whites who have benefited from their "black" talent, while they marvel at the assumption that their style is equivalent to that of blacks. On the contrary, a white person in a corporate position may feel offended by the label of "black" characteristics (167).

3   There is certainly nothing wrong with possessing talent, but why must blacks be limited to the non-academic, non-professional fields, while whites are categorized with businesslike, professional attitudes and habits? The success of so many black entertainers and athletes creates a narrow definition of "black" success.

4   Raspberry also cites the indoctrination of this concept in our children, a major issue of the essay. How can we instill in children that they can excel in math and compete on a level with the whites and even the Chinese? Raspberry suggests that we associate strength, courage, and determination to excel with slave ancestors, deeming these values "quintessentially black" (168).

5   I feel that black people are traditionally rooted with a grand sense of style, rhythm, and soul. Everything done that is considered "black" is done with soulful mannerisms unique to our race. I do not believe that blacks should be

limited to or wholly defined by these terms, but we must keep in mind that we have a style all our own, conventionalized over hundreds of years. We cannot simply throw away these years of establishing our creative spirit. On the other hand, we must also diversify ourselves with academic, professional, and corporate attitudes to broaden the definition of "black."

6   Today, other cultures are proving that blacks are trendsetters. I open a magazine and see white girls with dreads. I turn on the radio and hear white musical artists imitating soulful musical styles. I've even heard that young people in Tokyo enjoy listening to D.C.-originated Go-Go music. Most people, specifically blacks, define these adaptations by these other cultures as "acting black," when, in essence, no one can "act black."

7   "Black" is a state of mind—pride, strength, respect for oneself and his/her people—not a walk, style of dress, hairstyle, or athletic skill. "Black" isn't defined by "poppin' fingers, eatin' chicken, and drinkin' Kool-Aid." Although members of some black subcultures display these habits, our people, as a whole, have evolved since the "singin' and dancin' and showboatin'" days.

8   I fully agree with William Raspberry that we must instill in our children that they, too, are academically compatible with any other race (168). We need to encourage them not to limit themselves, so that a young black male who has the ability to master his skills on the basketball court can additionally master scientific equations; so that a young black female who manipulates her body in stylistic, soulful, sultry dance can also manipulate mathematical strategies.

9   For the most part, black people have worked hard for centuries in all that we do, and as time progresses we should utilize that time by expounding on the betterment and diversity of our race. We should be able to excel in any area we pursue, not just those in which we are expected to.

Works Cited

Raspberry, William. "The Handicap of Definition." *Revalations*. Ed. Teresa M. Redd. 3rd ed. Needham Heights, MA: Simon & Schuster, 1997. 167–168

Student Essay:
CLEANING HOUSE
Leah Smith
(2000)

Black is pride; black is shame.
Black is unity; black is discord.
Black is success; black is failure.
Black is law-abiding; black is criminal.
Black is respectful; black is irreverent.

———————————

1   Blacks and whites have been brought up to believe that being "Black" means being disrespectful, dishonest, and disgraceful. The common train of thought is that blacks can only play sports and entertain. True, blacks dominate the sports and entertainment industries, but we must realize the word "Black" does not fit within well-defined parameters. It has the opportunity to expand well beyond previous thoughts and expectations. The keys to defining Blackness are perception, presentation, practice, and purification.

2   Those who cannot experience Blackness rely on perception. Therefore, their definition of "Black" will be based upon the blacks they encounter. Examine these two instances: A young black male attends a predominantly white high school, associates with mostly white students, and is at the top of his class; while a young white male attends a predominantly black inner-city high school but chooses not to associate with the students. In the former example, the white students and teachers are exposed daily to a positive version of Blackness. To these observers, "Black" symbolizes achievement, dedication, and politeness. At the same time, however, the white student in the reverse situation is bombarded with negative representations of "Black." He observes fights *between* blacks, trouble caused *by* blacks, and negligence *of*

blacks by the school system. To him, "Black" symbolizes failure, criminality, and abandonment.

3   Because perception is a factor, presentation becomes of utmost importance. For example, when asked to choose between two boxes with identical contents, my younger sister will always opt for the brightly decorated box rather than the dented and ripped box. "Black," like anything else, must be properly presented to be correctly defined. Perhaps the current definition of "Black" has arisen from many years of improper presentation on the behalf of blacks. Many have not understood the true meaning of Blackness and have therefore created a misleading image. This image has overshadowed the positive images of Blackness that others portray. So the positive image, like the dented and ripped box, is often skipped or considered second best.

4   In "The Handicap of Definition," William Raspberry proclaims that "enthusiastic practice" will ensure the redefinition of "Black" (168). He utilizes a basketball analogy. According to Raspberry, black youngsters tend to play basketball better because they assume that they can master the game, "so they practice constantly to prove themselves right" (168). If, instead of basketball, young blacks mastered "their mathematical reasoning, their elocution, and their attitudes," the definition of black would encompass a new realm (168). How will this change be brought about?

5   Change is not possible without dedication. A mighty struggle will have to take place in order to change years of misconception on behalf of blacks as well as whites. But before a change can be visible without, a change must be made within. Our own psyche has to undergo a purification equivalent to the spring cleaning of a house. Old stereotypes must be swept out the window; previous expectations have to be dusted from the tabletops of our minds; outdated assumptions should be mopped from the floor of America's consciousness. Then, and only then, can the change occur.

6   Despite popular opinion, "Black" does not have to bear negative connotations. Through untiring work, we can achieve a new definition for ourselves. We, as black people, are the only ones who can control perception through an appropriate presentation, diligent practice, and self-purification. However, amid the myriad of possibilities, one simple fact must be in the forefront of our minds: "Black" is what you make it.

Works Cited

Raspberry, William. "The Handicap of Definition." *Revelations*, 3rd ed. Ed Teresa M. Redd. Needham Heights, MA: Simon & Schuster, 1997. 167–170.

*the seeds
and fruit of racism:
cause-effect*

I been rebuked and I been scorned,
I been rebuked and I been scorned,
Chillun, I been rebuked and I been scorned,
I'se had a hard time, sho's you born.

from the spiritual "I Been Rebuked
and I Been Scorned"

Black vs. Blue:
Time for a Cease-Fire?
Meta Carstarphen

A winner of the Jesse H. Neal Award for feature writing, Meta Carstarphen is a freelance writer and professor of journalism. She has co-edited a collection of essays entitled Sexual Rhetoric: Media Perspectives on Sexuality, Gender, and Identity. *In addition, she has contributed essays, short stories, and poems to periodicals. This essay, dated 1989, discusses the causes of tension between African Americans and the police.*

---

1   When the red and blue flashing lights reflected off my rearview mirror, I froze. Still moving, the tires still turning, my car was momentarily driverless. Instinctively, I slowed to an uneasy halt by the side of a small street, in the dark, waiting. With a sideways and cautious glance, I watched the uniformed stranger walk—no, swagger—toward me. I hadn't been speeding. I hadn't run through any red lights. I hadn't violated any traffic law as far as I knew. That sure knowledge, however, did not give me confidence. Instead, I braced myself cautiously and prepared to say or do nothing that might upset him. For <u>anything could happen, anything, when white police and black civilians cross paths</u>.   thesis

2   <u>Strife, even violence, between white policemen and African Americans seems to be an ever-present reality, unlimited by time or locality</u>. In Dallas, Texas, a young white officer died after being shot by a black vagrant, and this incident sparked tensions which threatened to tear the city asunder. Reports surfaced that the mainly black inner city onlookers cheered the mentally unstable assailant on to assault Officer Glen Chase. With this discovery, police   problem

199

administrators decried the entire incident as evidence that police were not supported by the very communities which needed them most. Black officials, meanwhile, used the same occurrence as proof that a history of racist actions by Dallas police had so hardened the residents that unequivocal support of the "blue" was impossible.

3   In Miami, Florida, a white Hispanic officer shot an unarmed black motorcyclist whose death provoked riots, fires, and protests in the black neighborhood where it occurred. While community leaders fought to appease the residents' anger and prod the Chief of Police into retributive action against Officer Lozano, they noted the irony. In the face of high unemployment and fiscal restraints, the city of Miami had just spearheaded a massive resettlement project for Central American refugees that appeared to give them so easily the economic assistance that was utterly lacking for its poorest citizens. Officer Lozano's assault of an unarmed black, they said, was just one more proof of the system's assault against its black residents.

4   More and more, contentious relations between police departments and black residents are surfacing. What is more alarming than the frequency of these events are the similarities. Change the players and the results still remain the same: police actions involving African Americans in a dispute, regardless of the issue, are tinged by racial tensions. The humanity of both the police officer and black citizen evaporates, leaving only mutual targets in their places.

5   When did police officers become symbols of evil instead of representatives of good in the black community? Frankly, if there has ever been a time of harmony between the two, most blacks are unaware of it. In 1966, as a result of earlier surveys conducted for *Newsweek* by political pollster Louis Harris, two of the magazine's staffers wrote *Black and White: A Study of U.S. Racial Attitudes Today*. Taken by 1000 African Americans and 1200 whites, the surveys posed similar questions to both groups to gauge their perceptions about the society and its major institutions. One striking element showed the disparity of opinion between blacks and whites over how helpful, or harmful, local authorities were to blacks.

6   According to the survey, 58 percent of the whites polled felt local authorities were "more helpful" to blacks than not; only 35 percent of the black respondents felt that way. When pointedly questioned about local police, only 26 percent of the blacks felt that law enforcement officials were "more helpful" to them, whereas 74 percent were either not sure or decidedly convinced that the police were "more harmful" to blacks.

7   Such a high level of mistrust among blacks had its roots in widespread   cause patterns of frustrating experiences with police. So similar were these interactions across a variety of black communities throughout the country that, in 1968, a special task force created by President Lyndon B. Johnson brought special attention to this problem. Dubbed *The Kerner Report*, this groundbreaking study, issued by the National Advisory Commission on Civil Disorders, noted that strained police-community relations contributed much during the mid-sixties to the series of racial riots which had just rocked the nation:

> All major outbursts of recent years ... were
> precipitated by arrests of Negroes by white
> police for minor offenses.... Thus, to many
> Negroes, police have come to symbolize
> white power, white racism and white repres-
> sion. And the fact is that many police do
> reflect and express these white attitudes.
> (200)

8   Until the civil rights movements of the fifties and the sixties culminated in
instigating significant legislation—most notably the Civil Rights Act of 1964—
segregation blocked most blacks from the mainstream of virtually every
aspect of American society. What the new age of integration inherited, despite
its promise of better days ahead, was an ominous legacy of exclusion and mistrust.

9   No two areas reflected this estrangement more than <u>housing</u> and <u>jobs</u>. For   causes
blacks, this usually meant that no matter how much money they may have
had, they were prevented from buying houses outside predominantly black
neighborhoods. And their sons living in those neighborhoods who grew up
playing "cops and robbers" may have rudely discovered in manhood that real
careers in law enforcement were closed to them because of their color.

10   A context eventually developed that seemed unchanging. Crimes committed in black neighborhoods by black criminals were to be stopped by white
police in blue uniforms, who usually only saw black people in times of crisis,
or in handcuffs. On the other hand, blacks were quite used to interacting with
whites in positions of authority, whites who represented a system that seemed
determined to separate them into their respective places. The white police officer, especially if his actions and words were aggressive or brutal, was just
another reminder of the same. However, because he could enter their neighborhoods more freely than blacks could enter his, he became an even more
menacing personal threat.

11   In the sixties, one of the most strident voices expressing this enmity was
that of the Black Panther Party, which argued that passive, though organized
resistance by blacks to social and political inequities was not enough. Instead,
the Black Panthers advocated aggressive, even armed, defense of black life
and property against white authorities. And, the Panthers charged, no one
seemed to be more identified with all that was wrong and perverse in America than her police officers.

12   By 1969, the Black Panther's Minister of Information, Eldridge Cleaver, was
a key party member who had become famous for explaining the party philosophy through published articles and books. In one of them, *Post-Prison Writings
& Speeches,* Cleaver described his perception of police/community relations in
Oakland, California:

> The notorious, oppressive, racist and brutal
> Oakland Police Department is at the heart of

202 *revelations: an anthology of expository essays by and about blacks*

> the matter. This Gestapo force openly and fla-
> grantly terrorizes the black people of Oak-
> land.... The OPD has increased its patrols
> of the black community to the saturation
> point and become like a sword buried in the
> heart of the people. The Black Panther Party
> intended to remove that sword. (101–2)

13   This was not a sentiment felt only by an eccentric group of hotheads, ex-
cons, and radicals as the Black Panther members were often portrayed.
Repeated experiences of brutality and corruption by police convinced most
blacks that law enforcement meant separate and unequal treatment.

14   Over the years since the turbulent times of the Black Panthers, urban riots,
and "race" studies, little seems to have improved. Recently, just outside of Los
Angeles in the decidedly upscale community of Long Beach, California, a
"sting" operation was deliberately planned. Designed to capture some truths
about white police behavior toward black civilians, the experiment yielded
chilling results. A black motorist (and undercover police officer) did not have
to drive long in the predominantly white neighborhoods before he was
noticed and stopped by a white officer. The motorist, without provocation,
was harassed and assaulted by the officer as a nearby hidden TV camera
recorded it all, including the uniformed officer smashing the undercover officer's head through a plate glass window.

15   But there may be hope. Just 35 miles north of the sprawling metropolitan
area of Dallas, another small community is attempting a change. In the university city of Denton, an integrated team of seven officers formed the core of
a new, volunteer initiative: "C.O.P.," for <u>Community-Oriented Policing</u>. Con-   solution
trary to traditional police practices, C.O.P. members try to allay black residents' latent suspicions about police with a different set of experiences. C.O.P.
officers knock on doors in the city's predominantly black neighborhoods, meet
the residents, learn their first names, listen to their concerns. As for the African
American community members, they hope to prevent their neighborhoods
from becoming another potential battleground between black and white,
between the police and the citizens.

16   Perhaps change is possible. My own encounter with a white police officer
ended surprisingly. After the obligatory check of license and insurance, the
officer told me why I had been stopped. He had observed that both of my
brake lights had been out and thought perhaps I had been unaware of that
fact. He gave me no ticket, no citation. In the friendliest of voices, he advised
me to repair the lights "for my own safety." And, if I ever see him again, the
first thing I do may be to smile instead of panic. Perhaps, just perhaps, change
is possible.

Works Cited

Cleaver, Eldridge. *Post-Prison Writings & Speeches.* New York: Putnam, 1981.

Doe, Jane, and John Doe. *Black and White: A Study of U.S. Racial Attitudes Today.* New York: Newsweek, 1966.

National Advisory Commission on Civil Disorders. *The Kerner Report.* Washington, DC: GPO, 1968.

Reading-to-Write Questions

1. **Content:** What types of evidence does Carstarphen cite?

2. **Arrangement:** Outline the problem-cause-solution structure of the essay.

3. **Style:** In the opening paragraph how does Carstarphen manipulate language in order to build suspense?

4. _____

    _____

    _____

Suggested Topics

1. **Observation:** Have you or a friend ever had a confrontation with the police? If so, describe the incident. Then, consider the remote and immediate causes of the confrontation. (audience = police)

2. **Critique:** Carstarphen believes that the relationship between African Americans and the police might improve. Are you as optimistic? Citing examples from the media and your own neighborhood, explain why you are or are not hopeful. (audience = Carstarphen's readers)

3. **Synthesis:** Consider how the predicament Staples describes in his essay contributes to the tensions Carstarphen discusses. (audience = op-ed page of a local newspaper)

4. _____

    _____

    _____

Background Readings: BLACKS AND THE POLICE

Anderson, John, and Hilary Hevenor. *Burning Down the House: MOVE and the Tragedy of Philadelphia.* New York: Norton, 1987.

Cannon, Lou. *Official Negligence: How Rodney King and the Riots Changed Los Angeles and the LAPD.* New York: Times Books, 1997.

Cashmore, Ernest, and Eugene McLaughlin. *Out of Order? Policing Black People.* London and New York: Routledge, 1991.

Dudley, William, ed. *Police Brutality.* Current Controversies Series. San Diego, CA: Greenhaven Press, 1991.

Fogelson, Robert M., comp. *Los Angeles Riots.* Salem, NH: Ayer, 1969.

Madhubuti, Haki. *Why L.A. Happened: Implications of the '92 Los Angeles Rebellion.* Chicago: Third World Press, 1993.

Morris, Terry. *No Justice No Peace: From Emmett Till to Rodney King.* Brooklyn, NY: Africentric Productions, 1993.

Ogletree, Charles J. *Beyond the Rodney King Story: An Investigation of Police Conduct in Minority Communities.* Boston: Northeastern UP, 1995.

_____

_____

_____

Recommended Literature: David Henderson, "Keep on Pushing" in Jones and Neal's *Black Fire* (poem)

Bobb Hamilton, "Poem to a Nigger Cop" in Jones and Neal's *Black Fire* (poem)

Langston Hughes, "Bop" from *The Best of Simple* (sketches)

Don L. Lee (Haki Madhubuti), "One-Sided Shoot-Out" from *We Walk the Way of the New World* (poem)

Ann Petry, *The Narrows* (novel)

Black Men and Public Space
Brent Staples

Although he is a psychologist by training, Brent Staples has had a successful career as a journalist, writing for both magazines and newspapers, including the editorial board of The New York Times. *He has also published a memoir,* Parallel Time: Growing Up in Black and White. *In the following essay, Staples discusses the suspicion Black men arouse in public, identifying the effects on himself as well as on those who fear him. Originally entitled "Just Walk on By," the essay first appeared in* Ms. Magazine *in September 1986.*

———————

1   My first victim was a woman—white, well dressed, probably in her late twenties. I came upon her late one evening on a deserted street in Hyde Park, a relatively affluent neighborhood in an otherwise mean, impoverished section of Chicago. As I swung onto the avenue behind her, there seemed to be a discreet, uninflammatory distance between us. Not so. She cast back a worried glance. To her, the youngish black man—a broad six feet two inches with a beard and billowing hair, both hands shoved into the pockets of a bulky military jacket—seemed menacingly close. After a few more quick glimpses, <u>she picked up her pace and was soon running in earnest</u>. Within seconds she disappeared into a cross street.   effect

2   That was more than a decade ago. I was twenty-two years old, a graduate student newly arrived at the University of Chicago. It was in the echo of that terrified woman's footfalls that <u>I first began to know the unwieldy inheritance I'd come into—the ability to alter public space in ugly ways</u>. It was clear that   thesis

she thought herself the quarry of a mugger, a rapist, or worse. Suffering a bout of insomnia, however, I was stalking sleep, not defenseless wayfarers. As a softy who is scarcely able to take a knife to a raw chicken—let alone hold one to a person's throat—<u>I was surprised, embarrassed, and dismayed all at once</u>. Her flight made me feel like an accomplice in tyranny. It also made it clear that I was indistinguishable from the muggers who occasionally seeped into the area from the surrounding ghetto. That first encounter, and those that followed, signified that a vast, unnerving gulf lay between nighttime pedestrians—particularly women—and me. And I soon gathered that <u>being perceived as dangerous is a hazard in itself</u>. I only needed to turn a corner into a dicey situation, or crowd some frightened, armed person in a foyer somewhere, or make an errant move after being pulled over by a policeman. Where fear and weapons meet—and they often do in urban America—there is always the possibility of death.

effect

effect

3   In that first year, my first away from my hometown, <u>I was to become thoroughly familiar with the language of fear</u>. At dark, shadowy intersections, I could cross in front of a car stopped at a traffic light and elicit the *thunk, thunk, thunk, thunk* of the driver—black, white, male, or female—<u>hammering down the door locks</u>. On less traveled streets after dark, I grew accustomed to but never comfortable with <u>people crossing to the other side</u> of the street rather than pass me. Then there were the <u>standard unpleasantries with policemen, doormen, bouncers, cabdrivers, and others</u> whose business it is to screen out troublesome individuals *before* there is any nastiness.

others' responses:

effect

effect
effect

4   I moved to New York nearly two years ago and I have remained an avid night walker. In central Manhattan, the near-constant crowd cover minimizes tense one-on-one street encounters. Elsewhere—in SoHo, for example, where sidewalks are narrow and tightly spaced buildings shut out the sky—things can get very taut indeed.

5   After dark, on the warrenlike streets of Brooklyn where I live, I often see <u>women who fear the worst from me. They seem to have set their faces on neutral, and with their purse straps strung across their chests bandolier-style, they forge ahead</u> as though bracing themselves against being tackled. I understand, of course, that the danger they perceive is not a hallucination. Women are particularly vulnerable to street violence, and young black males are drastically overrepresented among the perpetrators of that violence. Yet these truths are no solace against the kind of alienation that comes of being ever the suspect, a fearsome entity with whom pedestrians avoid making eye contact.

effect

6   Over the years, <u>I learned to smother the rage I felt at so often being taken for a criminal</u>. Not to do so would surely have led to madness. I now take precautions to make myself less threatening. <u>I move about with care</u>, particularly late in the evening. <u>I give a wide berth</u> to nervous people on subway platforms during the wee hours, particularly when I have exchanged business clothes for jeans. If I happen to be entering a building behind some people who appear skittish, <u>I may walk by, letting them clear the lobby</u> before I return, so

his response:

effect
effect

effect

as not to seem to be following them. <u>I have been calm and extremely congenial</u>   effect
on those rare occasions when I've been pulled over by the police.

7   And on late-evening constitutionals I employ what has proved to be an
excellent tension-reducing measure: <u>I whistle melodies from Beethoven and</u>   effect
<u>Vivaldi and the more popular classical composers</u>. Even steely New Yorkers
hunching toward nighttime destinations seem to relax, and occasionally they
even join in the tune. Virtually everybody seems to sense that a mugger
wouldn't be warbling bright, sunny selections from Vivaldi's *Four Seasons*. It is
my equivalent of the cowbell that hikers wear when they know they are in
bear country.

Reading-to-Write Questions

1. **Content:** Why is Staples' lead paragraph deliberately misleading?

2. **Arrangement:** Study the paragraph that begins "In that first year. . . ." How is it constructed?

3. **Style:** What expressive verbs does Staples select?

4. _____

   _____

   _____

Suggested Topics

1. **Observation:** Interview an African American male and write a case study of the psychological impact the criminal stereotype has had upon him. (audience = White women)

2. **Critique:** Staples lists the precautions he takes to make himself less threatening to pedestrians. Do his tactics evade the problem? Would you recommend a different solution? If so, propose a solution and predict the effects on African American men and the community. (audience = African American males in your class)

3. **Synthesis:** Staples concedes that "young black males are drastically over-represented among the perpetrators of [street] violence." Why? Explore some of the causes, turning to West's essay for ideas. (audience = African American high school males)

4. _____

   _____

   _____

Background Readings: BLACK MEN

Black, Daniel. *Dismantling Black Manhood.* New York: Garland, 1997.

Blount, Marcellus, and George Cunningham, eds. *Representing Black Men.* New York: Routledge, 1996.

Evans, Brenda J. *Black Males in the United States.* Washington, DC: American Psychological Association, 1988.

Gary, Lawrence, ed. *Black Men.* Beverly Hills, CA: Sage, 1981.

Harper, Phillip Brian. *Are We Not Men? Masculine Anxiety and the Problem of African American Identity.* New York: Oxford UP, 1996.

Hutchinson, Earl Ofari. *The Assassination of the Black Male Image.* New York: Simon & Schuster, 1996.

Madhubuti, Haki. *Black Men: Obsolete, Single, Dangerous?* Chicago: Third World Press, 1990.

_____, and Maulana Karenga, eds. *Million Man March/Day of Absence: A Commemmorative Anthology.* Chicago: Third World Press: 1996.

Pullman, Wesley. *African American Men in Crisis: Proactive Strategies for Urban Youth.* New York: Garland, 1995.

Staples, Robert. *Black Masculinity: The Black Man's Role in American Society.* San Francisco: Black Scholars, 1982.

Stecopoulos, Harry. *Race and the Subject of Masculinities.* Durham, NC: Duke UP, 1997.

White, Joseph, and James Cones, III. *Black Man Emerging: Facing the Past and Seizing a Future in America.* New York: W.H. Freeman, 1999.

_____

_____

_____

Recommended Literature: Ralph Ellison, *Invisible Man* (novel)

Richard Wright, *Native Son* (novel)

August Wilson, *King Hedley II* (play)

Excuse Me, Your Race Is Showing
Karen Grigsby Bates

Freelance writer Karen Grigsby Bates has penned columns for the Los Angeles Times, *articles for various magazines, and even a novel (*Plain Brown Wrapper*) and an etiquette book for African Americans (*Basic Black: Home Training for Modern Times*). While planning the etiquette book, Bates "happened upon a mother lode" of racial slights that African Americans too often endure. With her co-author, Karen Elyse Hudson, she discusses some of these "racial slings and arrows" (and how to handle them) in their guide. Bates points out the effects of such slights in the following essay, which was featured in the January 22, 1997 issue of* The Washington Post.

———————————

1   A friend of mine recently insisted that Chris Darden was wrong when he claimed the now-infamous "N-word" as the "nastiest, the most despicable word in the English language." Not for my friend. "Oh hell, I get called that every day, one way or another," he snorted. "That's hardly even distracting; it's the price we pay for being black in America. No, what sets me off is the A-word."

2   Come again?

3   "The A-word. If you end up seeing me waving a gun in a parking lot on 'Hard Copy,' it's because some white person has called me 'articulate' again and I couldn't take it anymore."

4   He's kidding—mostly. My friend is a big man, burly-framed and dark in hue. And although he's polite to the point of being courtly, many white people still cross the street when they see him, or clutch the straps of their shoulder bags more tightly. He is black and male in America and that, as he noted, is the price of the ticket.

5   He also speaks the King's English in a mellifluous baritone—which surprises and delights some white people with whom he comes into contact, so much so that they feel compelled to share their relief and amazement: "When you interviewed me on the telephone, I had no idea you were black. . . . You're so *articulate!*" Depending on how he feels that day, he may or may not let them know that he finds this "compliment" offensive, and why.

6   As Lorraine Hansberry once wryly told James Baldwin: "I love being black, Jimmy, but sometimes it can be so complicated." Amen. It can become even more complicated trying to explain the drip-drip of small indignities we black Americans experience daily. I happened upon a mother lode of such slights last year when Karen E. Hudson and I decided to write an etiquette book addressed to the black community's needs. While pondering what to include, we agreed that, while not standard to etiquette books, race had to be addressed somewhere. Our community's fortunes don't rise or fall on which fork is used when, but our survival—economic and sometimes even literal— well may depend on how we respond to the local police when we're arbitrarily stopped, or how we react at work when someone farther up the organization food chain tells a joke that is clearly racist (even though, of course, the joke-teller does not consider himself to *be* racist). The etiquette of race relations became an important part of our book.

7   As word began to leak out that we were interested in including racially uncomfortable situations with which our readers might be faced, the suggestions flew in via fax, phone and e-mail. We heard from CEOs who, on business trips, had had car keys slapped in their hands outside their hotels in the mistaken assumption that they were valets. Of a former first lady's press secretary who, when browsing posh boutiques, is routinely asked "Does this come in size 8?" by other shoppers who carelessly presuppose that since she is black, she must, ergo, be there to serve. Of affluent diners who showed up ready to claim a table they had reserved at a chic restaurant, only to be told "there must be some mistake" by the flustered maitre d'. Of successful business people and entertainers who must ask white colleagues to hail taxis for them if they're in a rush, because their tight schedules don't allow them to waste 20 minutes watching empty, on-duty cabs pass them by.

8   It is ironic, and painful, that having won the major battles of the first civil rights movement—the right to vote; the right (in theory, anyway) to live wherever one can afford a home; the integration of our public schools—children of this movement must now learn to battle a different kind of segregation, a mental apartheid that pigeonholes us in this decade almost as effectively as de jure segregation did our predecessors three decades ago.

9   And these seemingly petty slights have consequences beyond raising the blood pressure of black Americans, although that is certainly one result. Cumulatively, they exacerbate race relations at large. The constant trickle of racial indignities to which we are routinely subjected serves to make little things bigger than they are on surface inspection. That nice brown lady in the designer suit, who has spent her adult lifetime building bridges to other communities, didn't snap because the luxe cosmetics salesperson in an upscale department store frostily ignored her while serving non-brown customers who came after her; but the saleswoman's thinly veiled rudeness may have pushed a normally mild-mannered person over the edge into a public demonstration of rage.

10   The fiftysomething black janitor at a white-shoe law firm who normally just ignores young associates' condescending attempts at faux camaraderie ("Yo, Jonesy, what up?") and suddenly snarls "My name is *Mr.* Jones!" is simply reacting to cumulative weeks, or years, of being overlooked and underestimated. The lawyer who vows to vote for Al Sharpton or Marion Barry (insert the appropriate political bogeyman here) "to send a message to Them," even though she works among and has extremely cordial relations with "Them," is simply signaling "enough already."

11   Racial faux pas also make the substance of our racial problems that much harder to talk about. It's logical to assume that people will not discuss race if they don't feel safe in the environment in which the discussion takes place. What one can ask, and how far one can press in the asking, are important boundaries to establish. "Are both your parents black?" may be borderline for some black folks, forgivable even, given the tremendous physical variety that exists in the African American community. But to challenge the answer—"It's so unusual to see black people your color" (unusual for *whom*?) "Are you sure both your parents are black?"—is just plain rude. Much like the presumption that all black people look alike, the notion that we think alike is ridiculous and insulting. "It is an absolute certainty," a single friend of mine said, smiling thinly, "that if a white co-worker offers to hook me up with a brother—usually the one brother she knows—we will have nothing in common except, of course, the thing that made her think of him for me in the first place."

12   In the end, integration, as Harvard's Henry Louis Gates Jr., has often noted, is a two-way street: It's not just about us assimilating into your mainstream, it's about the mainstream respecting those things that make us different. My co-author and I wrote about the etiquette of race relations because we wanted our community to have suggestions for how to cope with the racial slings and arrows we encounter all too often. But if those slings and arrows weren't employed in the first place, we would not have had to include the section. Perhaps it's time for an etiquette book to teach the finer points of race relations to the white community at large—which might, eventually, lead to some constructive conversations about how we can all move to improve race relations in this country.

Reading-to-Write Questions

1. **Content:** How many anecdotes does Bates cite as evidence of racism? Why does she cite so many?

2. **Arrangement:** Can you identify the problem-solution structure of the essay? Where does Bates present the problem? Where does she discuss possible solutions?

3. **Style:** When does Bates employ understatement and sarcasm?

4. _____

   _____

   _____

Suggested Topics

1. **Observation:** Present your own series of "racial faux pas" and analyze the effects. (audience = Whites who unwittingly commit such faux pas)

2. **Critique:** A White reader might accuse Bates of making much ado about nothing, insisting that African Americans carry a chip on their shoulders. Anticipating such an argument, write a letter to the editor of *The Washington Post* to defend or attack Bates's argument. (audience = readers of the *Post*'s letters to the editor).

3. **Synthesis:** Bates attributes these racial slights to "a different kind of segregation, a mental apartheid that pigeonholes us in this decade almost as effectively as de jure segregation did our predecessors three decades ago." Write an essay about the causes and/or effects of this "mental apartheid," incorporating material from essays by Raspberry, Davis, C. Steele, or Carter. (audience = readers of the *Post*'s letters to the editor)

4. _____

   _____

   _____

Background Readings: RACISM IN AMERICA

Bell, Derrick. *Faces at the Bottom of the Well: The Permanence of Racism.* New York: Basic Books, 1992.

Bender, David, ed. *Racism in America. Opposing Viewpoints Series.* San Diego: Greenhaven Press, 1991.

Berry, Mary Frances. *Black Resistance/White Law: A History of Constitutional Racism in America.* rev. ed., New York: A. Lane, 1994.

Cose, Ellis. *Color-blind: Seeing Beyond Race in a Race-Obsessed World.* New York: HarperCollins, 1997.

Davis, Angela Y. *Women, Race, and Class.* New York: Random House, 1981.

Entman, Robert, and Andrew Rojecki. *The Black Image in the White Mind: Media and Race in America.* Chicago: University of Chicago Press, 2000.

Faison, Edward, Jr. *Racism, the Inevitable in America.* New York: Vantage Press, 1987.

Feagin, Joe R. *Living with Racism: The Black Middle-Class Experience.* Boston: Beacon Press, 1994.

Finkenstaedt, Rose. *Face-to-Face: Blacks in America: White Perceptions and Black Realities.* New York: William Morrow, 1994.

Hacker, Andrew. *Two Nations: Black and White, Separate, Hostile, Unequal.* 2nd ed. New York: Ballantine Books, 1995.

Rothenberg, Paula S. *Racism and Sexism: An Integrated Study.* New York: St. Martin's Press, 1988.

Steele, Shelby. *The Content of Our Character: A New Vision of Race in America.* New York: St. Martin's, 1990.

Thernstrom, Stephan, and Abigail Thernstrom. *America in Black and White: One Nation, Indivisible.* New York: Simon & Schuster, 1997.

Weinberg, Meyer. *Racism in the United States.* New York: Greenwood Press, 1990.

_____

_____

_____

The Best Black
Stephen Carter

With the 1991 release of his autobiographical collection, Reflections of an Affirmative Action Baby, *Stephen Carter became a leading figure in the controversy about affirmative action. A lawyer and professor, Carter has continued to write about public issues, namely in his books* The Culture of Disbelief, Civility: Manners, Morals, and the Etiquette of Democracy, *and* God's Name in Vain: How Religion Should and Should Not Be Involved in Politics. *In the following selection, excerpted from* Reflections, *Carter identifies the causes and effects of the "best black syndrome," the practice of distinguishing between the best qualified candidate and the best qualified* black *candidate.*

———————————

1   We are measured by a different yardstick: *first black, only black, best black.* The best black syndrome is cut from the same cloth as the implicit and demeaning tokenism that often accompanies racial preferences: "Oh, we'll tolerate so-and-so at our hospital or in our firm or on our faculty, because she's the best black." Not because she's the best-qualified candidate, but because she's the best-qualified *black* candidate. She can fill the black slot. And then the rest of the slots can be filled in the usual way: with the best-*qualified* candidates.

2   This dichotomy between "best" and "best black" is not merely something manufactured by racists to denigrate the abilities of professionals who are not white. On the contrary, the durable and demeaning stereotype of black people

as unable to compete with white ones is reinforced by advocates of certain forms of affirmative action. It is reinforced, for example, every time employers are urged to set aside test scores (even, in some cases, on tests that are good predictors of job performance) and to hire from separate lists, one of the best white scorers, the other of the best black ones. It is reinforced every time state pension plans are pressed to invest some of their funds with "minority-controlled" money management firms, even if it turns out that the competing "white" firms have superior track records.[1] It is reinforced every time students demand that universities commit to hiring some pre-set number of minority faculty members. What all of these people are really saying is, "There are black folks out there. Go and find the best of them." And the best black syndrome is further reinforced, almost unthinkingly, by politicians or bureaucrats or faculty members who see these demands as nothing more than claims for simple justice.

3   Successful black students and professionals have repeatedly disproved the proposition that the best black minds are not as good as the best white ones, but the stereotype lingers, even among the most ardent friends of civil rights. In my own area of endeavor, academia, I hear this all the time from people who should know better. It is not at all unusual for white professors, with no thought that they are indulging a demeaning stereotype, to argue for hiring the best available professors of color, whether or not the individuals on whom that double-edged mantle is bestowed meet the usual appointment standards. I put aside for the moment the question of the fairness of the standards, for the white people I am describing have few doubts about *that;* I have in mind white people who argue with straight face for the hiring of black people *they themselves* do not believe are good enough to be hired without extra points for race. For example, one prominent law professor, a strong and sincere proponent of racial diversity, sent me a list of scholars in his field who might be considered for appointment to the Yale faculty. The first part of the list set out the names of the best people in the field; the second part, the names of people who were so-so; and the last part, the names of the leading "minorities and women" in the field, none of whom apparently qualified (in his judgment) for even the "so-so" category, let alone the best. I know that my colleague acted with the best of intentions, but the implicit invitation offered by this extraordinary document was to choose between diversity and quality. I suspect that to this day he is unaware of any insult and actually believes he was advancing the cause of racial justice.

4   "No responsible advocate of affirmative action," argues Ira Glasser, "opposes merit or argues . . . that standards should be reduced in order to meet affirmative action goals."[2] Perhaps not; but the language of standards

---

[1] See, for example, the account of the debate in Maryland in *Bond Buyer,* 31 July 1991, p. 32.

[2] Ira Glasser, "Affirmative Action and the Legacy of Racial Injustice," in *Eliminating Racism: Profiles in Controversy,* ed. Phyllis A. Katz and Dalmas A. Taylor (New York: Plenum Press, 1988), pp. 341, 350.

and merit is slippery at best. I am reminded of a conversation I had some years ago with a veteran civil rights litigator who, concerned at charges that affirmative action sometimes results in hiring unqualified candidates, drew a sharp distinction between *unqualified* and *less qualified*. An employer, he mused, does not have to hire the *best* person for the job, as long as everyone hired is *good enough* to do the job. Consequently, he reasoned, it is perfectly fine to require employers to hire black applicants who are less qualified than some white applicants, as long as the black candidates are capable of doing the job. A tidy argument in its way, but, of course, another example of an almost unconscious acceptance of a situation in which an employer is made to distinguish between the best black candidates and the best ones.

5   Even our sensible but sometimes overzealous insistence that the rest of the nation respect the achievements of black culture might reinforce the depressing dichotomy: if we insist, as often we must, that others appreciate "our" music and "our" literature, we should not be surprised if those others come to think of the best of our music and the best of our literature as distinct from the best music and the best literature. Indeed, this is the implication of Stanley Crouch's vigorous argument (on which I here express no view) that white critics accept a level of mediocrity from black artists, filmmakers, and writers that they would never tolerate from creative people who are white.[3]

6   The best black syndrome creates in those of us who have benefited from racial preferences a peculiar contradiction. We are told over and over that we are among the best black people in our professions. And in part we are flattered, or should be, because, after all, those who call us the best black lawyers or doctors or investment bankers consider it a compliment. But to professionals who have worked hard to succeed, flattery of this kind carries an unsubtle insult, for we yearn to be called what our achievements often deserve: simply the best—no qualifiers needed! In *this* society, however, we sooner or later must accept that being viewed as the best blacks is part of what has led us to where we are; and we must further accept that to some of our colleagues, black as well as white, we will never be anything else.

---

[3]Stanley Crouch, *Notes of a Hanging Judge* (New York: Oxford University Press, 1990).

Reading-to-Write Questions

1. **Content:** What would the essay lose if Carter dropped the anecdotes about the prominent law professor and the civil rights litigator?

2. **Arrangement:** Outline Paragraph 2 to highlight the topic sentence and to isolate the groups (the causes) that reinforce the "best black syndrome."

3. **Style:** What stylistic technique does Carter employ to tie together the causal factors in Paragraph 2?

4. _____

   _____

   _____

Suggested Topics

1. **Observation:** Do you suspect that you were once hired or admitted because you were the "best black" candidate (or one of a few)? If so, how did this suspicion affect you? (audience = the organization that hired or admitted you)

2. **Critique:** A self-styled "Affirmative Action Baby," Carter benefited from the very syndrome he criticizes. Does he have a right to complain when so many other African Americans could not get a foot in the doors that the "best black syndrome" opened for him? (audience = Carter's readers)

3. **Synthesis:** How does the "best-black syndrome" contribute to the intellectual performance gap discussed in C. Steele's essay? (audience = a faculty search committee)

4. _____

   _____

   _____

Background Readings: THE PSYCHOLOGY OF AFFIRMATIVE ACTION

Blanchard, Fletcher, and Faye Crosby. *Affirmative Action in Perspective.* New York: Springer-Verlag, 1989.

Bowen, William, and Derek Bok. *The Shape of the River.* Princeton: Princeton UP, 1998.

Chavez, Lydia. *The Color Bind: California's Battle to End Affirmative Action.* Berkeley: University of California Press, 1998.

Coate, Stephen. *Will Affirmative Action Policies Eliminate Negative Stereotypes?* Boston: Department of Economics, Boston University, 1992.

Feinberg, Walter. *On Higher Ground: Education and the Case for Affirmative Action.* New York: Teachers College Press, 1998.

McWhorter, John. *Losing the Race: Self-Sabotage in Black America.* New York: The Free Press, 2000.

_____

_____

_____

Race and the Schooling
of Black Americans
Claude Steele

Through careful experimentation, Stanford psychologist Claude Steele has challenged all those who believe that African Americans tend to score lower on tests because of genetic inferiority. Such people, he argues below, perpetuate the negative stereotypes that can cause black underachievement. In this essay, first published in The Atlantic Monthly *in 1992, Steele builds his causal argument from the results of experiments that he and his colleagues conducted.*

---

1   The buildings had hardly changed in the thirty years since I'd been there. "There" was a small liberal-arts school quite near the college that I attended. In my student days I had visited it many times to see friends. This time I was there to give a speech about how racial and gender stereotypes, floating and abstract though they might seem, can affect concrete things like grades, test scores, and academic identity. My talk was received warmly, and the next morning I met with a small group of African-American students. I have done this on many campuses. But this time, perhaps cued by the familiarity of the place, I had an experience of déjà vu. The students expressed a litany of complaints that could have come straight from the mouths of the black friends I had visited there thirty years earlier: the curriculum was too white, they heard too little black music, they were ignored in class, and too often they felt slighted by faculty members and other students. Despite the school's recruitment efforts,

they were a small minority. The core of their social life was their own group.
To relieve the dysphoria, they went home a lot on weekends.

2   I found myself giving them the same advice my father gave me when I was
in college: lighten up on the politics, get the best education you can, and move
on. But then I surprised myself by saying, "To do this you have to learn from
people who part of yourself tells you are difficult to trust."

3   Over the past four decades African-American college students have been
more in the spotlight than any other American students. This is because they
aren't just college students; they are a cutting edge in America's effort to integrate itself in the thirty-five years since the passage of the Civil Rights Act.
These students have borne much of the burden for our national experiment in
racial integration. And to a significant degree the success of the experiment
will be determined by their success.

4   Nonetheless, throughout the 1990s the national college-dropout rate for
African-Americans has been 20 to 25 percent higher than that for whites.
Among those who finish college, the grade-point average of black students is
two-thirds of a grade below that of whites.

5   A recent study by William Bowen and Derek Bok, reported in their book *The
Shape of the River,* brings some happy news: despite this underachievement in
college, black students who attend the most selective schools in the country go
on to do just as well in postgraduate programs and professional attainment as
other students from those schools. This is a telling fact in support of affirmative action, since only these schools use affirmative action in admissions. Still,
the underperformance of black undergraduates is an unsettling problem, one
that may alter or hamper career development, especially among blacks not
attending the most selective schools.

6   Attempts to explain the problem can sound like a debate about whether
America is a good society, at least by the standard of racial fairness, and maybe
even about whether racial integration is possible. It is an uncomfortably finger-
pointing debate. Does the problem stem from something about black students
themselves, such as poor motivation, a distracting peer culture, lack of family
values, or—the unsettling suggestion of *The Bell Curve*—genes? Or does it
stem from the conditions of blacks' lives: social and economic deprivation, a
society that views blacks through the lens of diminishing stereotypes and low
expectations, too much coddling, or too much neglect?

7   In recent years this debate has acquired a finer focus: the fate of middle-
class black students. Americans have come to view the disadvantages associated with being black as disadvantages primarily of social and economic
resources and opportunity. This assumption is often taken to imply that if you
are black and come from a socioeconomically middle-class home, you no
longer suffer a significant disadvantage of race. "Why should the son of a
black physician be given an advantage in college admission over the son of a
white delivery-truck driver?" This is a standard question in the controversy
over affirmative action. And the assumption behind it is that surely in today's

society the disadvantages of race are overcome when lower socioeconomic status is overcome.

8   But virtually all aspects of underperformance—lower standardized-test scores, lower college grades, lower graduation rates—persist among students from the African-American middle class. This situation forces on us an uncomfortable recognition: that beyond class, something racial is depressing the academic performance of these students.

9   Some time ago I and two colleagues, Joshua Aronson and Steven Spencer, tried to see the world from the standpoint of these students, concerning ourselves less with features of theirs that might explain their troubles than with features of the world they see. A story I was told recently depicts some of these. The storyteller was worried about his friend, a normally energetic black student who had broken up with his longtime girlfriend and had since learned that she, a Hispanic, was now dating a white student. This hit him hard. Not long after hearing about his girlfriend, he sat through an hour's discussion of *The Bell Curve* in his psychology class, during which the possible genetic inferiority of his race was openly considered. Then he overheard students at lunch arguing that affirmative action allowed in too many underqualified blacks. By his own account, this young man had experienced very little of what he thought of as racial discrimination on campus. Still, these were features of his world. Could they have a bearing on his academic life?

10   My colleagues and I have called such features "stereotype threat"—the threat of being viewed through the lens of a negative stereotype, or the fear of doing something that would inadvertently confirm that stereotype. Everyone experiences stereotype threat. We are all members of some group about which negative stereotypes exist, from white males and Methodists to women and the elderly. And in a situation where one of those stereotypes applies—a man talking to women about pay equity, for example, or an aging faculty member trying to remember a number sequence in the middle of a lecture—we know that we may be judged by it.

11   Like the young man in the story, we can feel mistrustful and apprehensive in such situations. For him, as for African-American students generally, negative stereotypes apply in many situations, even personal ones. Why was that old roommate unfriendly to him? Did that young white woman who has been so nice to him in class not return his phone call because she's afraid he'll ask her for a date? Is it because of his race or something else about him? He cannot know the answers, but neither can his rational self fully dismiss the questions. Together they raise a deeper question: Will his race be a boundary to his experience, to his emotions, to his relationships?

12   With time he may weary of the extra vigilance these situations require and of what the psychologists Jennifer Crocker and Brenda Major have called the "attributional ambiguity" of being on the receiving end of negative stereotypes. To reduce this stress he may learn to care less about the situations and activities that bring it about—to realign his self-regard so that it no longer depends

on how he does in the situation. We have called this psychic adjustment "disidentification." Pain is lessened by ceasing to identify with the part of life in which the pain occurs. This withdrawal of psychic investment may be supported by other members of the stereotype-threatened group—even to the point of its becoming a group norm. But not caring can mean not being motivated. And this can have real costs. When stereotype threat affects school life, disidentification is a high price to pay for psychic comfort. Still, it is a price that groups contending with powerful negative stereotypes about their abilities—women in advanced math, African-Americans in all academic areas—may too often pay.

Stereotype Threat Versus Self-Fulfilling Prophecy

13 Another question arises: Do the effects of stereotype threat come entirely from the fear of being stereotyped, or do they come from something internal to black students—self-doubt, for example?

14   Beginning with George Herbert Mead's idea of the "looking-glass self," social psychology has assumed that one's self-image derives in large part from how one is viewed by others—family, school, and the broader society. When those views are negative, people may internalize them, resulting in lower self-esteem—or self-hatred, as it has been called. This theory was first applied to the experience of Jews, by Sigmund Freud and Bruno Bettelheim, but it was also soon applied to the experience of African-Americans, by Gordon Allport, Frantz Fanon, Kenneth Clark, and others. According to the theory, black students internalize negative stereotypes as performance anxiety and low expectations for achievement, which they then fulfill. The "self-fulfilling prophecy" has become a commonplace about these students. Stereotype threat, however, is something different, something external: the situational threat of being negatively stereotyped. Which of these two processes, then, causes the results of our experiments?

15   Joshua Aronson, Michael Lustina, Kelli Keough, Joseph Brown, Catherine Good, and I devised a way to find out. Suppose we told white male students who were strong in math that a difficult math test they were about to take was one on which Asians generally did better than whites. White males should not have a sense of group inferiority about math, since no societal stereotype alleges such an inferiority. Yet this comment would put them under a form of stereotype threat: any faltering on the test could cause them to be seen negatively from the standpoint of the positive stereotype about Asians and math ability. If stereotype threat alone—in the absence of any internalized self-doubt—was capable of disrupting test performance, then white males taking the test after this comment should perform less well than white males taking the test without hearing the comment. That is just what happened. Stereotype threat impaired intellectual functioning in a group unlikely to have any sense of group inferiority.

16   In science, as in the rest of life, few things are definitive. But these results are pretty good evidence that stereotype threat's impairment of standardized-test performance does not depend on cueing a pre-existing anxiety. Steven Spencer, Diane Quinn, and I have shown how stereotype threat depresses the performance of accomplished female math students on a difficult math test, and how that performance improves dramatically when the threat is lifted. Jean-Claude Croizet, working in France with a stereotype that links poor verbal skills with lower-class status, found analogous results: lower-class college students performed less well than the upper-class college students under the threat of a stereotype-based judgment, but performed as well when the threat was removed.

17   Is everyone equally threatened and disrupted by a stereotype? One might expect, for example, that it would affect the weakest students most. But in all our research the most achievement-oriented students, who were also the most skilled, motivated, and confident, were the most impaired by stereotype threat. This fact has been under our noses all along—in our data and even in our theory. A person has to care about a domain in order to be disturbed by the prospect of being stereotyped in it. That is the whole idea of disidentifica-tion—protecting against stereotype threat by ceasing to care about the domain in which the stereotype applies. Our earlier experiments had selected black students who identified with verbal skills and women who identified with math. But when we tested participants who identified less with these domains, what had been under our noses hit us in the face. None of them showed any effect of stereotype threat whatsoever.

18   These weakly identified students did not perform well on the test: once they discovered its difficulty, they stopped trying very hard and got a low score. But their performance did not differ depending on whether they felt they were at risk of being judged stereotypically.

Why Strong Students Are Stereotype-Threatened

19   This finding, I believe, tells us two important things. The first is that the poorer college performance of black students may have another source in addition to the one—lack of good preparation and, perhaps, of identification with school achievement—that is commonly understood. This additional source—the threat of being negatively stereotyped in the environment—has not been well understood. The distinction has important policy implications: different kinds of students may require different pedagogies of improvement.

20   The second thing is poignant: what exposes students to the pressure of stereotype threat is not weaker academic identity and skills but stronger academic identity and skills. They may have long seen themselves as good students—better than most. But led into the domain by their strengths, they pay an extra tax on their investment—vigilant worry that their future will be compromised by society's perception and treatment of their group.

21   This tax has a long tradition in the black community. The Jackie Robinson story is a central narrative of black life, literature, and journalism. *Ebony* mag-

azine has run a page for fifty years featuring people who have broken down one or another racial barrier. Surely the academic vanguard among black college students today knows this tradition—and knows, therefore, that the thing to do, as my father told me, is to buckle down, pay whatever tax is required, and disprove the damn stereotype.

22   That, however, seems to be precisely what these students are trying to do. In some of our experiments we administered the test of ability by computer, so that we could see how long participants spent looking at different parts of the test questions. Black students taking the test under stereotype threat seemed to be trying too hard rather than not hard enough. They reread the questions, reread the multiple choices, rechecked their answers, more than when they were not under stereotype threat. The threat made them inefficient on a test that, like most standardized tests, is set up so that thinking long often means thinking wrong, especially on difficult items like the ones we used.

23   Philip Uri Treisman, an innovator in math workshops for minority students who is based at the University of Texas, saw something similar in his black calculus students at the University of California at Berkeley: they worked long hours alone but they worked inefficiently—for example, checking and rechecking their calculations against the correct answers at the back of the book, rather than focusing on the concepts involved. Of course, trying extra hard helps with some school tasks. But under stereotype threat this effort may be misdirected. Achievement at the frontier of one's skills may be furthered more by a relaxed, open concentration than by a strong desire to disprove a stereotype by not making mistakes.

24   Sadly, the effort that accompanies stereotype threat exacts an additional price. Led by James Blascovich, of the University of California at Santa Barbara, we found that the blood pressure of black students performing a difficult cognitive task under stereotype threat was elevated compared with that of black students not under stereotype threat or white students in either situation.

25   In the old song about the "steel-drivin' man," John Henry races the new steam-driven drill to see who can dig a hole faster. When the race is over, John Henry has prevailed by digging the deeper hole—only to drop dead. The social psychologist Sherman James uses the term "John Henryism" to describe a psychological syndrome that he found to be associated with hypertension in several samples of North Carolina blacks: holding too rigidly to the faith that discrimination and disadvantage can be overcome with hard work and persistence. Certainly this is the right attitude. But taken to extremes, it can backfire. A deterioration of performance under stereotype threat by the skilled, confident black students in our experiments may be rooted in John Henryism.

26   This last point can be disheartening. Our research, however, offers an interesting suggestion about what can be done to overcome stereotype threat and its detrimental effects. The success of black students may depend less on expectations and motivation—things that are thought to drive academic performance—than on trust that stereotypes about their group will not have a limiting effect in their school world.

How to Reduce Stereotype Threat

27   Putting this idea to the test, Joseph Brown and I asked, How can the usual detrimental effect of stereotype threat on the standardized-test performance of these students be reduced? By strengthening students' expectations and confidence, or by strengthening their trust that they are not at risk of being judged on the basis of stereotypes? In the ensuing experiment we strengthened or weakened participants' confidence in their verbal skills, by arranging for them to have either an impressive success or an impressive failure on a test of verbal skills, just before they took the same difficult verbal test we had used in our earlier research. When the second test was presented as a test of ability, the boosting or weakening of confidence in their verbal skills had no effect on performance: black participants performed less well than equally skilled white participants. What does this say about the commonsense idea that black students' academic problems are rooted in lack of self-confidence?

28   What did raise the level of black students' performance to that of equally qualified whites was reducing stereotype threat—in this case by explicitly presenting the test as racially fair. When this was done, blacks performed at the same high level as whites even if their self-confidence had been weakened by a prior failure.

29   These results suggest something that I think has not been made clear elsewhere: when strong black students sit down to take a difficult standardized test, the extra apprehension they feel in comparison with whites is less about their own ability than it is about having to perform on a test and in a situation that may be primed to treat them stereotypically. We discovered the extent of this apprehension when we tried to develop procedures that would make our black participants see the test as "race-fair." It wasn't easy. African-Americans have endured so much bad press about test scores for so long that, in our experience, they are instinctively wary about the tests' fairness. We were able to convince them that our test was race-fair only when we implied that the research generating the test had been done by blacks. When they felt trust, they performed well regardless of whether we had weakened their self-confidence beforehand. And when they didn't feel trust, no amount of bolstering of self-confidence helped.

30   Policies for helping black students rest in significant part on assumptions about their psychology. As noted, they are typically assumed to lack confidence, which spawns a policy of confidence-building. This may be useful for students at the academic rearguard of the group. But the psychology of the academic vanguard appears different—underperformance appears to be rooted less in self-doubt than in social mistrust.

31   Education policy relevant to non-Asian minorities might fruitfully shift its focus toward fostering racial trust in the schooling situation—at least among students who come to school with good skills and high expectations. But how should this be done? Without particulars this conclusion can fade into banality, suggesting, as Alan Ryan has wryly put it in *Liberal Anxieties and Liberal*

Education, that these students "will hardly be able to work at all unless everyone else exercises the utmost sensitivity to [their] anxieties." Sensitivity is nice, but it is an awful lot to expect, and even then, would it instill trust?

32   That is exactly what Geoffrey Cohen, Lee Rosa, and I wondered as we took up the question of how a teacher or a mentor could give critical feedback across the "racial divide" and have that feedback be trusted. We reasoned that an answer to this question might yield insights about how to instill trust more broadly in the schooling environment. Cohen's hunch was that niceness alone wouldn't be enough. But the first question had to be whether there was in fact a racial divide between teachers and students, especially in the elite college environment in which we worked.

33   We set up a simple experiment. Cohen asked black and white Stanford students one at a time to write essays about their favorite teachers, for possible publication in a journal on teaching. They were asked to return several days later for feedback on their essays. Before each student left the first writing session, Cohen put a Polaroid snapshot of the student on top of his or her essay. His ostensible purpose was to publish the picture if the essay was published. His real purpose was to let the essay writers know that the evaluator of their writing would be aware of their race. When they returned days later, they were given constructive but critical feedback. We looked at whether different ways of giving this feedback engendered different degrees of trust in it.

34   We found that neither straight feedback nor feedback preceded by the "niceness" of a cushioning statement ("There were many good things about your essay") was trusted by black students. They saw these criticisms as probably biased, and they were less motivated than white students to improve their essays. White students took the criticism at face value—even as an indication of interest in them. Black students, however, faced a different meaning: the "ambiguating" possibility that the criticism was motivated by negative stereotypes about their group as much as by the work itself. Herein lies the power of race to make one's world insecure—quite apart from whatever actual discrimination one may experience.

35   But this experiment also revealed a way to be critical across the racial divide: tell the students that you are using high standards (this signals that the criticism reflects standards rather than race), and that your reading of their essays leads you to believe that they can meet those standards (this signals that you do not view them stereotypically). This shouldn't be faked. High standards, at least in a relative sense, should be an inherent part of teaching, and critical feedback should be given in the belief that the recipient can reach those standards. These things go without saying for many students. But they have to be made explicit for students under stereotype threat. The good news of this study is that when they *are* made explicit, the students trust and respond to criticism. Black students who got this kind of feedback saw it as unbiased and were motivated to take their essays home and work on them even though this was not a class for credit. They were more motivated than any other group of students in the study—as if this combination of high stan-

dards and assurance was like water on parched land, a much needed but seldom received balm.

Reassessing the Test-Score Gap

36   There is, of course, another explanation for why black college students haven't fared well on predominantly white campuses: they aren't prepared for the competition. This has become an assumption of those who oppose affirmative action in college admissions. Racial preference, the argument goes, brings black students onto campuses where they simply aren't prepared to compete.

37   The fact most often cited in support of the underpreparation explanation is the lower SAT scores of black students, which sometimes average 200 points below those of other students on the same campus. The test-score gap has become shorthand for black students' achievement problems. But the gap must be assessed cautiously.

38   First, black students have better skills than the gap suggests. Most of the gap exists because the proportion of blacks with very high SAT scores is smaller than the corresponding proportions of whites and Asians. Thus when each group's scores are averaged, the black average will be lower than the white and Asian averages. This would be true even if the same admissions cut-off score were used for each group—even if, for example, affirmative action were eliminated entirely. Why a smaller proportion of blacks have very high scores is, of course, a complex question with multiple answers, involving, among other things, the effects of race on educational access and experience as well as the processes dwelt on in this article. The point, though, is that blacks' test-score deficits are taken as a sign of underpreparation, whereas in fact virtually all black students on a given campus have tested skills within the same range as the tested skills of other students on the campus.

39   In any case, the skills and preparation measured by these tests also turn out not to be good determinants of college success. As the makers of the SAT themselves tell us, although this test is among the best of its kind, it measures only about 18 percent of the skills that influence first-year grades, and even less of what influences subsequent grades, graduation rates, and professional success.

40   Indulge a basketball analogy that my colleagues Jay Rosner and Lee Ross and I have developed. Suppose that you were obliged to select a basketball team on the basis of how many of ten free throws a player makes. You'd regret having to select players on the basis of a single criterion. You'd know that free-throw shooting involves only a few of the skills that go into basketball—and, worse, you'd know that you'd never pick a Shaquille O'Neal.

41   You'd also wonder how to interpret a player's score. If he made ten out of ten or zero out of ten, you'd be fairly confident about making a judgment. But what about the kid who makes five, six, or seven? Middling scores like these could be influenced by many things other than underlying potential for free-throw shooting or basketball playing. How much practice was involved? Was

the kid having a good or a bad day? Roughly the same is true, I suggest, for standardized-test scores. Are they inflated by middle-class advantages such as prep courses, private schools, and tours of European cathedrals? Are they deflated by race-linked experiences such as social segregation and being consistently assigned to the lower tracks in school?

42   In sum, black college students are not as underprepared in academic skills as their group score deficit is taken to suggest. The deficit can appear large, but it is not likely to be the sole cause of the troubles they have once they get on campus.

43   Showing the insufficiency of one cause, of course, does not prove the sufficiency of another. My colleagues and I believed that our laboratory experiments had brought to light an overlooked cause of poor college performance among non-Asian minorities: the threat to social trust brought about by the stereotypes of the larger society. But to know the real-life importance of this threat would require testing *in situ*, in the buzz of everyday life.

44   To this end Steven Spencer, Richard Nisbett, Kent Harber, Mary Hummel, and I undertook a program aimed at incoming first-year students at the University of Michigan. Like virtually all other institutions of higher learning, Michigan had evidence of black students' underachievement. Our mission was clear: to see if we could improve their achievement by focusing on their transition into college life.

45   We also wanted to see how little we could get away with—that is, to develop a program that would succeed broadly without special efforts. The program (which started in 1991 and is ongoing) created a racially integrated "living and learning" community in a 250-student wing of a large dormitory. It focused students on academic work (through weekly "challenge" workshops), provided an outlet for discussing the personal side of college life (through weekly rap sessions), and affirmed the students' abilities (through, for example, reminding them that their admission was a vote of confidence). The program lasted just one semester, although most students remained in the dormitory wing for the rest of their first year.

46   Still, it worked: it gave black students a significant academic jump start. Those in the program (about 15 percent of the entering class) got better first-year grades than black students outside the program, even after controlling for differences between these groups in the skills with which they entered college. Equally important, the program greatly reduced underperformance: black students in the program got first-year grades almost as high as those of white students in the general Michigan population who entered with comparable test scores. This result signaled the achievement of an academic climate nearly as favorable to black students as to white students. And it was achieved through a concert of simple things that enabled black students to feel racially secure.

47   One tactic that worked surprisingly well was the weekly rap sessions—black and white students talking to one another in an informal dormitory setting, over pizza, about the personal side of their new lives in college. Participation

in these sessions reduced students' feelings of stereotype threat and improved grades. Why? Perhaps when members of one racial group hear members of another racial group express the same concerns they have, the concerns seem less racial. Students may also learn that racial and gender stereotypes are either less at play than they might have feared or don't reflect the worst-feared prejudicial intent. Talking at a personal level across group lines can thus build trust in the larger campus community. The racial segregation besetting most college campuses can block this experience, allowing mistrust to build where cross-group communication would discourage it.

48   Our research bears a practical message: even though the stereotypes held by the larger society may be difficult to change, it is possible to create niches in which negative stereotypes are not felt to apply. In specific classrooms, within specific programs, even in the climate of entire schools, it is possible to weaken a group's sense of being threatened by negative stereotypes, to allow its members a trust that would otherwise be difficult to sustain. Thus when schools try to decide how important black-white test-score gaps are in determining the fate of black students on their campuses, they should keep something in mind: for the greatest portion of black students—those with strong academic identities—the degree of racial trust they feel in their campus life, rather than a few ticks on a standardized test, may be the key to their success.

Reading-to-Write Questions

1. **Content:** Steele describes numerous experiments, omitting many of the details that would have been mandatory had he been writing for a scientific journal. Why does Steele omit these details?

2. **Arrangement:** Throughout his essay, Steele poses question after question. How do the questions contribute to the coherence of the essay?

3. **Style:** Steele writes that the "combination of high standards and assurance" is "like water on parched land, a much needed but seldom received balm." Would this simile be appropriate in a scientific journal? Why or why not?

4. _____

_____

_____

Suggested Topics

1. **Observation:** Survey a sample of students on your campus to ascertain whether they felt a stereotype threat when they were taking the SATs. Then use your data to support or call into question Steele's causal analysis. (audience = African American students preparing for the SATS)

2. **Critique:** Steele claims that stereotype threat plays a significant role in the performance of achievement-oriented black students. Do you think he is exaggerating the importance of this factor? (audience = Steele's *Atlantic Monthly* readers)

3. **Synthesis:** Combine concepts from Steele's, Raspberry's, and McWhorter's essays to identify three possible causes of the black-white academic achievement gap. (audience = PTA)

4. _____

_____

_____

Background Readings: BLACK ACADEMIC ACHIEVEMENT

See the reading list for William Raspberry's essay.

Losing the Race
John McWhorter

In 2000, when John McWhorter released his book Losing the Race: Self-Sabotage in Black America, *he touched off an explosion of criticism and praise. His previous books (e.g.,* The Word on the Street *and* Spreading the Word*) had focused on linguistics, the subject he had been teaching at the University of California, Berkeley. However, in* Losing the Race, *he ventures into the heated debate about race and education: He attributes African American students' underachievement to self-enforced separatism, a sense of victimhood, and anti-intellectualism. In this excerpt from the book, he critiques Claude Steele's study of African American students' academic performance (see the preceding essay) and concludes that stereotype threat is not a significant cause of the problem.*

---

1   In a widely publicized study in 1992, Claude Steele showed that black students at Stanford did better on various SAT-like verbal aptitude test samples when they were not required to indicate their race or when the test was not presented as measuring racial ability. Less well-known is that these were only one part of the experiment, much of which showed that even when the students were neither required to indicate their race nor presented with the tests as measures of racial ability, they performed less well when the tests were

presented as measuring intellectual ability than when it was simply presented as examining "the psychological factors involved in solving verbal problems."

2   What these experiments suggest is that black students' school performance is hindered by self-doubts brought on by the stereotype of black mental inferiority, and it quickly became accepted in many quarters that "Stereotype Threat" was a major factor in black students' lagging school performance, particularly those performing at relatively higher levels. Predictably, this study has been marshaled to bolster the wisdom that black children are *kept* from doing well in school rather than *disinclined* to, and that what must be addressed in order to make black students do better in school is the societal racism behind the stereotype.

3   Claude Steele's experiments rather clearly show that black students do less well in contexts where the stereotype of black mental inferiority looms. However, we can be sure that any human being's performance would suffer under equivalent conditions, as has been shown to be the case for women—and even for white men when given tests billed as measuring their abilities against Asians' (another part of Claude Steele's study). Our question, then, is how *important* this factor might be in black students' performance *here in the real world*—where they are never required to indicate their race on their schoolwork, and are only rarely threatened so explicitly with racial stereotypes in the course of being assigned schoolwork.

4   Of course, Claude Steele's point is that the overall impact of the stereotype "in the air" interferes with black performance. Here one might again ask why this isn't thought to be so crippling for women, but then the answer could be that the stereotype of mental weakness regarding black students is stronger and more deeply entrenched than the one regarding women. There is an argument there. But this is not the only difference between (white and Asian) female students and black ones. Namely, there is a certain smugness and insouciance about many black students' lack of engagement in school (at private schools, Berkeley, and sometimes Stanford, not just in Harlem or South Central) which one does not often encounter in, for example, white women, and which strikes me less as fear than as active dismissal. It is much easier on the soul to return always to racism to explain black underperformance. I tried to for years, because we would all prefer not to criticize a culture that has suffered so much for so long. But I suspect that many of those who are indignant upon hearing explanations that stray too far from victimhood would see things differently if they could spend just a few days watching the expression on many black students' faces when finding out that they are expected to internalize new ways of thinking for a class rather than simply memorize concrete facts—a slightly amused, quietly disbelieving smirk. I have watched this smirk all of my life, come to realize its meaning and rootedness in black identity itself as I got older, and can richly attest that it is as likely from a doctor's daughter as from a UPS deliveryman's son.

5   It is tempting to surmise that the smirk is a defense mechanism masking frustration, but where, then, is that smirk on other children's faces? I have almost

never seen that smirk on a white or Asian student's face, even when their confidence problems were quite clear. Confidence problems create a look of trepidation. A cultural hallmark creates a smile.

6   Thus the traditional approach to this issue that Claude Steele's study reflects, that black students want to learn but are thwarted from doing so, is not the usual case. When students cannot remember someone's name or career highlight two weeks after the person has been singled out for a ten-minute eulogy and then discussed, illustrated, and shown on video, when a university student writes me a biographical book report after I have said innumerable times that biographies would not be acceptable, when a student writes two incoherent sentences as the answer to an essay question and hands her test in with a smile, the problem is not confidence. There is an obvious fundamental detachment from learning itself.

7   Tracing the black scholarly lag to a lack of confidence is also another example of a tendency to suppose that black students are the only ones on earth who can be expected to excel only under ideal conditions. Without denying that "Stereotype Threat" has some effect (I have felt it on occasion), we must ask why we suppose that black students are incapable of rising above this whereas students of various other backgrounds rise above obstacles much more concrete. It would be nothing less than unusual if, for example, a fourteen-year-old Vietnamese immigrant did not feel some trepidation in an American school when he was still learning the language, not at home in the surrounding culture, physically smaller than the average American his age, and even found himself teased and harassed by American kids. Imagine going to high school in Vietnam, with little hope of ever returning to the United States, and thus with one's fortunes in future life hinging entirely upon one's performance immersed in a language vastly different from yours, which even after six months you can only understand when spoken slowly. Some might object that a stereotype of mental dimness is somehow more of a barrier to learning than a linguistic difference—but then would not many of them at the same time support claims like the Oakland School Board's that black children are hindered from learning to read by the small differences between Black and standard English? If black children are barred from learning to read, and thus learning in general, by the fact that they say *I'm a answer dat person firs'* instead of *I'm going to answer that person first,* then surely we can muster some empathy for the Vietnamese child whose rendition of that same sentence at home is *Tôi sẽ trà lòi cho ngùòi dó truòc!*

8   Then some might argue that a stereotype of mental inferiority is more crippling than anything this Vietnamese student undergoes—but upon what grounds? How comfortable would we be telling this student to his face that having been wrenched from one's homeland to make one's way in a country where one is inarticulate and physically small, and where his efforts to assimilate into American peer culture often create sharp frictions with his parents, is somehow less of a sociological burden than being associated with mental mediocrity (and even being occasionally trailed in stores)?

9   Crucially, these confidence problems are not seen as a sentence for scholarly mediocrity outside of the black community. Every year I have a few Asian immigrant students in my larger classes who dutifully ask me questions in their foreign accents after class, having missed a word or cultural reference; students like this are legion in California, and they tend to be good ones. They, like women and so many students of other backgrounds, overcome these problems as often as not, even if some get stalled.

10   In short, certainly racial stereotypes undermine confidence, but confidence cannot be a *significant* reason why even black children of doctors and lawyers make the lowest average grades and test scores in the United States. The minimal effect stereotyping has on so many other students, and the particular tenor of so many black students' attitude toward school, simply do not square with an analysis claiming that confidence is the heart, or even one of the hearts, of the problem we face. To argue that confidence is anything more than a background factor sits well in the Victimologist groove, but only at the expense of implying that black children are congenitally mentally inferior or possess a tragic dearth of emotional strength. None of us could name a whole ethnic group stalled permanently by mere problems with confidence, and if this were what holds black students back, the gap between white and black students would have virtually closed twenty years ago, with the underprivileged minority creating a small lag.

Notes

"Stereotype Threat" studies: Claude M. Steele, "Race and the Schooling of Black America," Atlantic Monthly, April 1992; Claude M. Steele, "Thin Ice: "Stereotype Threat" and Black College Students," Atlantic Monthly, August 1999; Claude M. Steele and Joshua Aronson, "Stereotype Threat and the Intellectual Test Performance of African Americans," Journal of Personality and Social Psychology 69: 797-811; Claude M. Steele and Joshua Aronson, "Stereotype Threat and the Test Performance of Academically Successful African Americans," The Black-White Test Score Gap, ed. Christopher Jencks and Meredith Phillips, Washington, DC: Brookings Institution Press, 1998, pp. 401–27.

Reading-to-Write Questions

1. **Content:** Steele gathers evidence from experiments to bolster his claims. What types of evidence does McWhorter present to challenge Steele?

2. **Arrangement:** Where does McWhorter summarize Steele's work, and why does he choose this order?

3. **Style:** Why is the title of McWhorter's book an excellent example of "double entendre"?

4. _____

   _____

   _____

Suggested Topics

1. **Observation:** Based on his classroom observations, McWhorter attributes many black students' underachievement to a "fundamental detachment from learning itself." What have *you* observed at school? Construct your own causal analysis by citing specific cases from your college and secondary school. (audience = students attending your high school)

2. **Critique:** Critique McWhorter's critique of Steele's conclusions. Does McWhorter marshal adequate counterevidence? Is his comparison of Vietnamese and African American students appropriate? Is *he* stereotyping? (audience = McWhorter's readers)

3. **Synthesis:** Compare Raspberry's and McWhorter's views on the causes of black academic underachievement. (audience = PTA)

4. _____

   _____

   _____

Background Readings: BLACK ACADEMIC ACHIEVEMENT

See the reading list for William Raspberry's essay.

Student Essay:
AN UNNECESSARY FEAR
J. Strong, III
(1996)

1   Coming from the deep South as I did, I never realized just what a difference location would mean. In the South, hospitality and friendliness are alive and well. But here on the streets of Washington, DC, I find myself in the middle of a totally different scenario. To walk these streets is to be seen as a criminal. People of all kinds would rather cross the street than pass by a black man for fear of getting robbed or mugged. Being perceived as a criminal totally destroys the already slight chance of receiving any type of friendliness or hospitality from anyone—white, black, male, or female.

2   To leave home in the South only to realize that I am less than welcome here creates a reaction somewhat akin to culture shock. I have come to realize that every black man has had this experience at one time or another. Nevertheless, neither this realization nor my Southern upbringing is enough to prevent me from feeling the same as any other black man when faced with this same situation.

3   A black man who finds himself in my position, the cause of nothing short of terror in others, may experience a false sense of joy as a result of his ability to frighten others. This joy may be misguided, but it is present nevertheless. For the average black man, authority is a thing almost alien to him. Being feared by others seemingly places him in authority, especially where whites are involved. Fear from the white man reminds the black man of a time when the roles were reversed and the black man lived in perpetual fear of the white man. The fear from the white woman only serves to make the black man feel ever more superior, even to the extent of being master of all things.

4   This misguided joy does not last long, gradually giving way to anger. The white man expects the black man to hurt him, thereby causing the black man's grief. Out of this grief comes the desire to hurt the white man. But resorting to violence would be the very reaction the white man expects. Knowing this, the black man's only recourse is to do the opposite, subsequently turning his anger inward.

5   In turning his anger on himself, the black man searches for reasons why he seems to threaten the white man. He seeks to change these offenders. Maybe he attempts to appear more cheerful and happy or even change his physical appearance. Brent Staples, a noted psychologist, documents his own attempts at such a change in his essay "Black Men and Public Space." He began to whistle a tune from Vivaldi in order to seem less likely to do others harm (223). Some black men may even go so far as to try to become as much like the white man as possible to disarm him.

6   After all of his attempts have failed, the black man finds himself in a deep sorrow. He realizes at last that no amount of changing he does will alter his situation. Now the questions begin to run through his head. He wonders why no one can see him for who he is rather than who he seems to be. He wonders how and when his people made the transition from being kings and queens to being perceived as thieves and murderers. Finally, he ponders one still unanswerable question: Will we ever be seen as potential doctors, lawyers, and writers instead of only being seen as potential killers and muggers? Good question.

Works Cited

Staples, Brent. "Black Men and Public Space." *Revelations.* Ed. Teresa M. Redd, 3rd ed. Needham Heights, MA: Simon & Schuster, 1997. 221–23.

Student Essay:
THE VICTIM
Naomi Porterfield
(1996)
Journal Entry

1   Briskly walking down Georgia Avenue in the cold, dark and desolate night, I had my mind set on my final destination: home. As I reached the halfway point, I heard a masculine voice behind me: "Hey, baby. Come over here." Not surprised, I continued walking, gradually picking up my pace. The quiet winds were suddenly disturbed by the sound of the heavy feet of a large black man behind me. I quickly glanced back and noticed that the distance between us was less than I desired. Without hesitation, I transformed my brisk walk into a jog.

2   There was that moment, however, when I thought that perhaps I was being paranoid. Then the relevant statistics ran through my mind. How many other women had assumed that the black "weirdo" on the corner would mind his own business—and never made it home? How many times did young college students ignore the dangers of their environment to accomplish the task at hand and never finish, at the harmful hands of a black man? It was at this point that I decided I did not want to become another statistic.

3   The question then remaining was the intent of the black man walking behind me. Maybe he found me attractive and just wanted the chance to talk. Maybe he was just repeating the rhetoric black men often use at the sight of a female and forgot about it. The problem was that I could not forget about it. I had the responsibility to protect myself from the mugging, rape, or other sort of harm I had heard about.

4   I continued my jog down the street, holding on to my backpack like the last breath of air. I am not sure what happened to the man walking behind me. When I safely reached the comfort of my dorm room, I was so glad that I had not become another victim. Looking back, I must ask myself the ultimate question: Was I the victim, or was he?

the enemy within

Browns and yellers,
All have fellers,
Gentlemen prefer them light.
Wish I could fade,
Can't make the grade,
Nothin' but dark days in sight.

from "(What Did I Do to Be So) Black and Blue?"
by Thomas "Fats" Waller, Andy Razaf,
and Harry Brooks

Light Skin Versus Dark Skin
Clarisse Jones

Addressing "a painful topic that many blacks would rather not confront," Clarisse Jones exposes poignant instances of intrarracial color prejudice in this essay from the October 1995 issue of Glamour Magazine. *A Pulitzer-Prize-winning journalist, Jones has published many other essays in periodicals such as* The New York Times, Vibe, *and* Essence.

---

1   I'll never forget the day I was supposed to meet him. We had only spoken on the phone. But we got along so well, we couldn't wait to meet face-to-face. I took the bus from my high school to his for our blind date. While I nervously waited for him outside the school, one of his buddies came along, looked me over, and remarked that I was going to be a problem, because his friend didn't like dating anybody darker than himself.

2   When my mystery man—who was not especially good-looking—finally saw me, he took one look, uttered a hurried hello, then disappeared with his smirking friends. I had apparently been pronounced ugly on arrival and dismissed.

3   That happened nearly fifteen years ago. I'm thirty now, and the hurt and humiliation have long since faded. But the memory still lingers, reinforced in later years by other situations in which my skin color was judged by other African Americans—for example, at a cocktail party or a nightclub where light-skinned black women got all the attention.

4   A racist encounter hurts badly. But it does not equal the pain of "colorism"—being rejected by your own people because your skin is colored cocoa and not cream, ebony and not olive. On our scale of beauty, it is often the high yellows—in the lexicon of black America, those with light skin—whose

looks reap the most attention. Traditionally, if someone was described that way, there was no need to say that person was good-looking. It was a given that light was lovely. It was those of us with plain brown eyes and darker skin hues who had to prove ourselves.

5   I was twelve, and in my first year of junior high school in San Francisco, when I discovered dark brown was not supposed to be beautiful. At that age, boys suddenly became important, and so did your looks. But by that time—the late 1970s—black kids no longer believed in that sixties mantra, "Black is beautiful." Light skin, green eyes, and long, wavy hair were once again synonymous with beauty.

6   Colorism—and its subtext of self-hatred—began during slavery on plantations where white masters often favored the lighter-skinned blacks, many of whom were their own children. But though it began with whites, black people have kept colorism alive. In the past, many black sororities, fraternities, and other social organizations have been notorious for accepting only light-skinned members. Yes, some blacks have criticized their lighter-skinned peers. But most often in our history, a light complexion has been a passport to special treatment by both whites *and* blacks.

7   Some social circles are still defined by hue. Some African Americans, dark and light, prefer light-skinned mates so they can have a "pretty baby." And skin-lightening creams still sell, though they are now advertised as good for making blemishes fade rather than for lightening whole complexions.

8   In my family, color was never discussed, even though our spectrum was broad—my brother was very light; my sister and I, much darker. But in junior high, I learned in a matter of weeks what had apparently been drummed into the heads of my black peers for most of their lives.

9   Realizing how crazy it all was, I became defiant, challenging friends when they made silly remarks. Still, there was no escaping the distinctions of color.

10   In my life, I have received a litany of twisted compliments from fellow blacks. "You're the prettiest dark-skinned girl I have ever seen" is one; "you're pretty for a dark girl" is another.

11   A light-complexioned girlfriend once remarked to me that dark-skinned people often don't take the time to groom themselves. As a journalist, I once interviewed a prominent black lawmaker who was light-skinned. He drew me into the shade of a tree while we talked because, he said, "I'm sure you don't want to get any darker."

12   Though some black people—like film-maker Spike Lee in his movie *School Daze*—have tried to provoke debate about colorism, it remains a painful topic many blacks would rather not confront. Yet there has been progress. In this age of Afrocentrism, many blacks revel in the nuances of the African American rainbow. Natural hairstyles and dreadlocks are in, and Theresa Randle, star of the hit film *Bad Boys,* is only one of several darker-skinned actresses noted for their beauty.

13   That gives me hope. People have told me that color biases among blacks run too deep ever to be eradicated. But I tell them that is the kind of attitude

that allows colorism to persist. Meanwhile, I do what I can. When I notice that a friend dates only light-skinned women, I comment on it. If I hear that a movie follows the tired old scenario in which a light-skinned beauty is the love interest while a darker-skinned woman is the comic foil, the butt of "ugly" jokes, I don't go see it. Others can do the same.

14   There is only so much blacks can do about racism, because we need the cooperation of others to make it go away. But healing ourselves is within our control.

15   At least we can try. As a people we face enough pain without inflicting our own wounds. I believe any people that could survive slavery, that could disprove the lies that pronounced them less than human, can also teach its children that black is beautiful in all of its shades.

16   Loving ourselves should be an easy thing to do.

Reading-to-Write Questions

1. **Content:** Jones published this essay in *Glamour,* a mainstream American magazine. Do you think the content of her essay is appropriate for her racially mixed audience? Or do you think she should have published the essay in a Black magazine such as *Essence*?

2. **Arrangement:** Can you identify a problem-solution structure in this loosely organized essay?

3. **Style:** Jones substitutes "ugly" for "dead" to produce the bitingly humorous phrase "pronounced ugly on arrival." Use her technique to transform another cliché.

4. _____

    _____

    _____

Suggested Topics

1. **Observation:** Interview a dark-skinned African American and write a case study of his/her psychological struggle with "colorism." (audience = light-skinned African Americans)

2. **Critique:** Jones believes that African Americans can eliminate colorism while others fear that "color biases among blacks run too deep ever to be eradicated." Whose side would you take? Why? (audience = African American student union)

3. **Synthesis:** How do Ford's confessions in his essay illustrate the problem Jones faces? (audience = readers of *Glamour* or *Essence* magazine)

4. _____

    _____

    _____

Background Readings: INTRARACIAL COLOR PREJUDICE

Dansby, Pearl Gore. "Black Pride in the Seventies: Fact or Fantasy?" *Black Psychology*. Ed. Reginald L. Jones. New York: Harper & Row, 1980. 71–80.

Grier, William H., and Price M. Cobbs. "Marriage and Love." *Black Rage*. New York: Banta/Basic Books, 1969. 63–85.

Russell, Kathy. *The Color Complex: The Politics of Skin Color among African Americans*. New York: Harcourt Brace Jovanovich, 1992.

Scales-Trent, Judy. *Notes of a White Black Woman: Race, Color, Community*. University Park, PA: Pennsylvania State UP, 1995.

_____

_____

_____

Recommended Literature: Charles Chesnutt, *The Wife of His Youth and Other Stories of the Color Line* (short stories)
Wallace Thurman, *The Blacker the Berry* (novel)
Ernest Gaines, *Catherine Carmier* (novel)
Gwendolyn Brooks, *Maud Martha* (novel)
Mary Mebane, *Mary* (autobiography)

Straightening Our Hair
bell hooks

Few contemporary scholars have published as many books about Blacks and women as the feminist, poet, cultural critic, and professor bell hooks (née Gloria Jean Watkins). Since 1989, she has produced, on average, a book a year, including Ain't I A Woman: Black Women and Feminism, Talking Back: Thinking Feminist, Thinking Black, Black Looks: Race and Representation, Sisters of the Yam: Black Women and Self-Recovery, Feminist Theory, *and* Salvation: Black People and Love. *In the essay below, printed first in* Z Magazine *in 1988, hooks contrasts the psychological, economic, and political implications of pressing Black hair, "getting a perm," and "going natural."*

---

1   On Saturday mornings we would gather in the kitchen to get our hair fixed, that is straightened. Smells of burning grease and hair, mingled with the scent of our freshly washed bodies, with collard greens cooking on the stove, with fried fish. We did not go to the hairdresser. Mama fixed our hair. Six daughters—there was no way we could have afforded hairdressers. In those days, this process of straightening black women's hair with a hot comb (invented by Madame C. J. Walker) was not connected in my mind with the effort to look white, to live out standards of beauty set by white supremacy. It was connected solely with rites of initiation into womanhood. To arrive at that point where one's hair could be straightened was to move from being perceived as

a child (whose hair could be neatly combed and braided) to being almost a woman. It was this moment of transition my sisters and I longed for.

2   Hair pressing was a ritual of black women's culture—of intimacy. It was an exclusive moment when black women (even those who did not know one another well) might meet at home or in the beauty parlor to talk with one another, to listen to the talk. It was as important a world as that of the male barber shop—mysterious, secret. It was a world where the images constructed as barriers between one's self and the world were briefly let go, before they were made again. It was a moment of creativity, a moment of change.

3   I wanted this change even though I had been told all my life that I was one of the "lucky" ones because I had been born with "good hair"—hair that was fine, almost straight—not good enough but still good. Hair that had no nappy edges, no "kitchen," that area close to the neck that the hot comb could not reach. This "good hair" meant nothing to me when it stood as a barrier to my entering this secret black woman world. I was overjoyed when mama finally agreed that I could join the Saturday ritual, no longer looking on but patiently waiting my turn. I have written of this ritual: "For each of us getting our hair pressed is an important ritual. It is not a sign of our longing to be white. There are no white people in our intimate world. It is a sign of our desire to be women. It is a gesture that says we are approaching womanhood . . . Before we reach the appropriate age we wear braids, plaits that are symbols of our innocence, our youth, our childhood. Then, we are comforted by the parting hands that comb and braid, comforted by the intimacy and bliss. There is a deeper intimacy in the kitchen on Saturdays when hair is pressed, when fish is fried, when sodas are passed around, when soul music drifts over the talk. It is a time without men. It is a time when we work as women to meet each other's needs, to make each other feel good inside, a time of laughter and out-rageous talk."

4   Since the world we lived in was racially segregated, it was easy to overlook the relationship between white supremacy and our obsession with hair. Even though black women with straight hair were perceived to be more beautiful than those with thick, frizzy hair, it was not overtly related to a notion that white women were a more appealing female group or that their straight hair set a beauty standard black women were struggling to live out. While this was probably the ideological framework from which the process of straightening black women's hair emerged, it was expanded so that it became a real space of black woman bonding through ritualized, shared experience. The beauty parlor was a space of consciousness raising, a space where black women shared life stories—hardship, trials, gossip; a place where one could be comforted and one's spirit renewed. It was for some women a place of rest where one did not need to meet the demands of children or men. It was the one hour some folk would spend "off their feet," a soothing, restful time of meditation and silence. These positive empowering implications of the ritual of hair pressing mediate but do not change negative implications. They exist alongside all that is negative.

5   Within white supremacist capitalist patriarchy, the social and political context in which the custom of black folks straightening our hair emerges, it represents an imitation of the dominant white group's appearance and often
indicates internalized racism, self-hatred, and/or low self-esteem. During the
1960s black people who actively worked to critique, challenge, and change
white racism pointed to the way in which black people's obsession with
straight hair reflected a colonized mentality. It was at this time that the natural
hairdo, the "afro," became fashionable as a sign of cultural resistance to racist
oppression and as a celebration of blackness. Naturals were equated with
political militancy. Many young black folks found just how much political
value was placed on straightened hair as a sign of respectability and conformity to societal expectations when they ceased to straighten their hair. When
black liberation struggles did not lead to revolutionary change in society the
focus on the political relationship between appearance and complicity with
white racism ceased and folks who had once sported afros began to straighten
their hair.

6   In keeping with the move to suppress black consciousness and efforts to be
self-defining, white corporations began to acknowledge black people and
most especially black women as potential consumers of products they could
provide, including hair-care products. Permanents specially designed for
black women eliminated the need for hair pressing and the hot comb. They not
only cost more but they also took much of the economy and profit out of black
communities, out of the pockets of black women who had previously reaped
the material benefits (see Manning Marable's *How Capitalism Underdeveloped
Black America*, South End Press). Gone was the context of ritual, of black
woman bonding. Seated under noisy hair dryers black women lost a space for
dialogue, for creative talk.

7   Stripped of the positive binding rituals that traditionally surrounded the
experience, black women straightening our hair seemed more and more to be
exclusively a signifier of white supremacist oppression and exploitation. It
was clearly a process that was about black women changing their appearance
to imitate white people's looks. This need to look as much like white people as
possible, to look safe, is related to a desire to succeed in the white world.
Before desegregation black people could worry less about what white folks
thought about their hair. In a discussion with black women about beauty at
Spelman College, students talked about the importance of wearing straight
hair when seeking jobs. They were convinced and probably rightly so that
their chances of finding good jobs would be enhanced if they had straight hair.
When asked to elaborate they focused on the connection between radical politics and natural hairdos, whether natural or braided. One woman wearing a
short natural told of purchasing a straight wig for her job search. No one in the
discussion felt black women were free to wear our hair in natural styles without reflecting on the possible negative consequences. Often older black adults,
especially parents, respond quite negatively to natural hairdos. I shared with

the group that when I arrived home with my hair in braids shortly after accepting my job at Yale my parents told me I looked disgusting.

8   Despite many changes in racial politics, black women continue to obsess about their hair, and straightening hair continues to be serious business. It continues to tap into the insecurity black women feel about our value in this white supremacist society. Talking with groups of women at various college campuses and with black women in our communities there seems to be general consensus that our obsession with hair in general reflects continued struggles with self-esteem and self-actualization. We talk about the extent to which black women perceive our hair as the enemy, as a problem we must solve, a territory we must conquer. Above all it is a part of our black female body that must be controlled. Most of us were not raised in environments where we learned to regard our hair as sensual or beautiful in an unprocessed state. Many of us talk about situations where white people ask to touch our hair when it is unprocessed then show surprise that the texture is soft or feels good. In the eyes of many white folks and other non-black folks, the natural afro looks like steel wool or a helmet. Responses to natural hairstyles worn by black women usually reveal the extent to which our natural hair is perceived in white supremacist culture as not only ugly but frightening. We also internalize that fear. The extent to which we are comfortable with our hair usually reflects on our overall feelings about our bodies. In our black women's support group, *Sisters of the Yam*, we talk about the ways we don't like our bodies, especially our hair. I suggested to the group that we regard our hair as though it is not part of our body but something quite separate—again a territory to be controlled. To me it was important for us to link this need to control with sexuality, with sexual repression. Curious about what black women who had hot-combed or had permanents felt about the relationship between straightened hair and sexual practice I asked whether people worried about their hairdo, whether they feared partners touching their hair. Straightened hair has always seemed to me to call attention to the desire for hair to stay in place. Not surprisingly many black women responded that they felt uncomfortable if too much attention was focused on their hair, if it seemed to be too messy. Those of us who have liberated our hair and let it go in whatever direction it seems fit often receive negative comments.

9   Looking at photographs of myself and my sisters when we had straightened hair in high school I noticed how much older we looked than when our hair was not processed. It is ironic that we live in a culture that places so much emphasis on women looking young, yet black women are encouraged to change our hair in ways that make us appear older. This past semester we read Toni Morrison's *The Bluest Eye* in a black women's fiction class. I ask students to write autobiographical statements which reflect their thoughts about the connection between race and physical beauty. A vast majority of black women wrote about their hair. When I asked individual women outside class why they continued to straighten their hair, many asserted that naturals don't look good on them, or that they required too much work. Emily, a favorite student with very short hair, always straightened it and I would tease and challenge

her. She explained to me convincingly that a natural hairdo would look horrible with her face, that she did not have the appropriate forehead or bone structure. Later she shared that during spring break she had gone to the beauty parlor to have her perm and as she sat there waiting, thinking about class reading and discussion, it came to her that she was really frightened that no one else would think she was attractive if she did not straighten her hair. She acknowledged that this fear was rooted in feelings of low self-esteem. She decided to make a change. Her new look surprised her because it was so appealing. We talked afterwards about her earlier denial and justification for wearing straightened hair. We talked about the way it hurts to realize the connection between racist oppression and the arguments we use to convince ourselves and others that we are not beautiful or acceptable as we are.

10   In numerous discussions with black women about hair one of the strongest factors that prevent black women from wearing unprocessed hairstyles is the fear of losing other people's approval and regard. Heterosexual black women talked about the extent to which black men respond more favorably to women with straight or straightened hair. Lesbian women point to the fact that many of them do not straighten their hair, raising the question of whether or not this gesture is fundamentally linked to heterosexism and a longing for male approval. I recall visiting a woman friend and her black male companion in New York years ago and having an intense discussion about hair. He took it upon himself to share with me that I could be a fine sister if I would do something about my hair (secretly I thought mama must have hired him). What I remember is his shock when I calmly and happily asserted that I like the touch and feel of unprocessed hair.

11   When students read about race and physical beauty, several black women describe periods of childhood when they were overcome with longing for straight hair as it was so associated with desirability, with being loved. Few women had received affirmation from family, friends, or lovers when choosing not to straighten their hair and we have many stories to tell about advice we receive from everyone, including total strangers, urging to understand how much more attractive we would be if we would fix (straighten) our hair. When I interviewed for my job at Yale, white female advisers who had never before commented on my hair encouraged me not to wear braids or a large natural to the interview. Although they did not say straighten your hair, they were suggesting that I change my hairstyle so that it would most resemble theirs, so that it would indicate a certain conformity. I wore braids and no one seemed to notice. When I was offered the job I did not ask if it mattered whether or not I wore braids. I tell this story to my students so that they will know by this one experience that we do not always need to surrender our power to be self-defining to succeed in an endeavor. Yet I have found the issue of hairstyle comes up again and again with students when I give lectures. At one conference on black women and leadership I walked into a packed auditorium, my hair unprocessed wild and all over the place. The vast majority of black women seated there had straightened hair. Many of them looked at me

with hostile contemptuous stares. I felt as though I was being judged on the spot as someone out on the fringe, an undesirable. Such judgments are made particularly about black women in the United States who choose to wear dreadlocks. They are seen and rightly so as the total antithesis of straightening one's hair, as a political statement. Often black women express contempt for those of us who choose this look.

12   Ironically, just as the natural unprocessed hair of black women is the subject of disregard and disdain we are witnessing return of the long dyed, blonde look. In their writing my black women students described wearing yellow mops on their heads as children to pretend they had long blonde hair. Recently black women singers who are working to appeal to white audiences, to be seen as crossovers, use hair implanting and hair weaving to have long straight hair. There seems to be a definite connection between a black female entertainer's popularity with white audiences and the degree to which she works to appear white, or to embody aspects of white style. Tina Turner and Aretha Franklin were trend setters; both dyed their hair blonde. In everyday life we see more and more black women using chemicals to be blonde. At one of my talks focusing on the social construction of black female identity within a sexist and racist society, a black woman came to me at the end of the discussion and shared that her seven-year-old daughter was obsessed with blonde hair, so much so that she had made a wig to imitate long blonde curls. This mother wanted to know what she was doing wrong in her parenting. She asserted that their home was a place where blackness was affirmed and celebrated. Yet she had not considered that her processed straightened hair was a message to her daughter that black women are not acceptable unless we alter our appearance or hair texture. Recently I talked with one of my younger sisters about her hair. She uses bright colored dyes, various shades of red. Her skin is very dark. She has a broad nose and short hair. For her these choices of straightened dyed hair were directly related to feelings of low self-esteem. She does not like her features and feels that the hairstyle transforms her. My perception was that her choice of red straightened hair actually called attention to the features she was trying to mask. When she commented that this look receives more attention and compliments, I suggested that the positive feedback might be a direct response to her own projection of a higher level of self-satisfaction. Folk may be responding to that and not her altered looks. We talked about the messages she is sending her dark-skinned daughters—that they will be most attractive if they straighten their hair.

13   A number of black women have argued that straightened hair is not necessarily a signifier of low self-esteem. They argue that it is a survival strategy; it is easier to function in this society with straightened hair. There are fewer hassles. Or as some folk stated, straightened hair is easier to manage, takes less time. When I responded to this argument in our discussion at Spelman by suggesting that perhaps the unwillingness to spend time on ourselves, caring for our bodies, is also a reflection of a sense that this is not important or that we do not deserve such care, in this group and others, black women talked about

being raised in households where spending too much time on appearance was ridiculed or considered vanity. Irrespective of the way individual black women choose to do their hair, it is evident that the extent to which we suffer from racist and sexist oppression and exploitation affects the degree to which we feel capable of both self-love and asserting an autonomous presence that is acceptable and pleasing to ourselves. Individual preferences (whether rooted in self-hate or not) cannot negate the reality that our collective obsession with straightening black hair reflects the psychology of oppression and the impact of racist colonization. Together racism and sexism daily reinforce to all black females via the media, advertising, etc. that we will not be considered beautiful or desirable if we do not change ourselves, especially our hair. We cannot resist this socialization if we deny that white supremacy informs our efforts to construct self and identity.

14   Without organized struggles like the ones that happened in the 1960s and early 1970s, individual black women must struggle alone to acquire the critical consciousness that would enable us to examine issues of race and beauty, our personal choices, from a political standpoint. There are times when I think of straightening my hair just to change my style, just for fun. Then I remind myself that even though such a gesture could be simply playful on my part, an individual expression of desire, I know that such a gesture would carry other implications beyond my control. The reality is: straightened hair is linked historically and currently to a system of racial domination that impresses upon black people, and especially black women, that we are not acceptable as we are, that we are not beautiful. To make such a gesture as an expression of individual freedom and choice would make me complicit with a politic of domination that hurts us. It is easy to surrender this freedom. It is more important that black women resist racism and sexism in every way; that every aspect of our self-representation be a fierce resistance, a radical celebration of our care and respect for ourselves.

15   Even though I have not had straightened hair for a long time, this did not mean that I am able to really enjoy or appreciate my hair in its natural state. For years I still considered it a problem. (It wasn't naturally nappy enough to make a decent interesting afro. It was too thin.) These complaints expressed my continued dissatisfaction. True liberation of my hair came when I stopped trying to control it in any state and just accepted it as it is. It has been only in recent years that I have ceased to worry about what other people would say about my hair. It has been only in recent years that I could feel consistent pleasure washing, combing, and caring for my hair. These feelings remind me of the pleasure and comfort I felt as a child sitting between my mother's legs feeling the warmth of her body and being as she combed and braided my hair. In a culture of domination, one that is essentially anti-intimacy, we must struggle daily to remain in touch with ourselves and our bodies, with one another. Especially black women and men, as it is our bodies that have been so often devalued, burdened, wounded in alienated labor. Celebrating our bodies, we participate in a liberatory struggle that frees mind and heart.

Reading-to-Write Questions

1. **Content:** Although she does not quantify her results or adopt a social science format, hooks reports the results of informal surveys. Underline her findings, noticing how she weaves survey results into the fabric of her essay.

2. **Arrangement:** Notice how hooks alternates between the personal and the general. Why does she open and close the essay with her personal experience?

3. **Style:** When expressing political ideas, hooks invokes what detractors might call "the jargon of revolution." Circle word choices that have a political flavor (e.g., "critical consciousness," "liberatory struggle"). Do you understand the terms? Do they help or hinder hooks's mission?

4. _____

    _____

    _____

Suggested Topics

1. **Observation:** Why do you wear your hair as you do (e.g., pressed, permed, natural, shaved, braided with or without extensions, in dreadlocks)? Does your hairstyle make a political statement? (audience = your classmates)

2. **Critique:** hooks maintains that, since the advent of the permanent, the African American "obsession with straightening black hair reflects the psychology of oppression and the impact of racist colonization." Do you think straightening black hair is always the sign of a "colonized mind"? (audience = African American women who, like hooks, refuse to straighten their hair)

3. **Synthesis:** Apply hooks's political theories to the obsession with light skin that Jones attacks in her essay. (audience = readers of *Glamour* or *Essence Magazine*)

4. _____

    _____

    _____

Background Readings: STANDARDS OF BEAUTY

Boone, Sylvia Ardyn. *Radiance from the Waters: Ideals of Feminine Beauty in Mende Art.* New Haven and London: Yale UP, 1986.

Dansby, Pearl Gore. "Black Pride in the 70s: Fact or Fantasy?" *Black Psychology.* Ed. Reginald L. Jones. New York: Harper & Row, 1980. 71–80.

Grier, William H., and Price M. Cobbs. "Achieving Womanhood." *Black Rage.* New York: Bantam/Basic Books, 1968. 31–45.

Rooks, Noliwe M. *Hair Raising: Beauty, Culture, and African American Women.* New Brunswick, NJ: Rutgers UP, 1996.

_____

_____

_____

Recommended Literature: Waring Cuney, "No Images" in Johnson's *The Book of American Negro Poetry* (poem)

Haki Madhubuti (Don L. Lee), "Mixed Sketches" from *We Walk the Way of the New World* (poem)

Toni Morrison, *The Bluest Eye* (novel)

Raymond Washington, "Freedom Hair" from *Visions from the Ghetto* (poem)

On Being Black
and Middle Class
Shelby Steele

A controversial professor of English, Shelby Steele won a National Book Critics Circle award for the essays in his book The Content of Our Character: A New Vision of Race in America. *This book was followed by* A Dream Deferred: The Second Betrayal of Black Freedom in America. *Known for his bold criticism of affirmative action, Steele continues to write about race, as he does in this excerpt from his essay "On Being Black and Middle Class," which was first published in* Commentary *in January 1988. Here, Steele contrasts his family's middle-class values with their images of lower-class African American life.*

----

1   The black middle class has always defined its class identity by means of positive images gleaned from middle- and upper-class white society, and by means of negative images of lower-class blacks. This habit goes back to the institution of slavery itself, when "house" slaves both mimicked the whites they served and held themselves above the "field" slaves. But in the sixties the old bourgeois impulse to dissociate from the lower classes (the "we-they" distinction) backfired when racial identity suddenly called for the celebration of this same black lower class. One of the qualities of a double bind is that one feels it more than sees it, and I distinctly remember the tension and strange

sense of dishonesty I felt in those days as I moved back and forth like a bigamist between the demands of class and race.

2   Though my father was born poor, he achieved middle-class standing through much hard work and sacrifice (one of his favorite words) and by identifying fully with solid middle-class values—mainly hard work, family life, property ownership, and education for his children (all four of whom have advanced degrees). In his mind these were not so much values as laws of nature. People who embodied them made up the positive images in his class polarity. The negative images came largely from the blacks he had left behind because they were "going nowhere."

3   No one in my family remembers how it happened, but as time went on, the negative images congealed into an imaginary character named Sam, who, from the extensive service we put him to, quickly grew to mythic proportions. In our family lore he was sometimes a trickster, sometimes a boob, but always possessed of a catalogue of sly faults that gave up graphic images of everything we should not be. On sacrifice: "Sam never thinks about tomorrow. He wants it now or he doesn't care about it." On work: "Sam doesn't favor it too much." On children: "Sam likes to have them but not to raise them." On money: "Sam drinks it up and pisses it out." On fidelity: "Sam has to have two or three women." On clothes: "Sam features loud clothes. He likes to see and be seen." And so on. Sam's persona amounted to a negative instruction manual in class identity.

4   I don't think that any of us believed Sam's faults were accurate representations of lower-class black life. He was an instrument of self-definition, not of sociological accuracy. It never occurred to us that he looked very much like the white racist stereotype of blacks, or that he might have been a manifestation of our own racial self-hatred. He simply gave us a counterpoint against which to express our aspirations. If self-hatred was a factor, it was not, for us, a matter of hating lower-class blacks but of hating what we did not want to be.

5   Still, hate or love aside, it is fundamentally true that my middle-class identity involved a dissociation from images of lower-class black life and a corresponding identification with values and patterns of responsibility that are common to the middle class everywhere. These values sent me a clear message: Be both an individual and a responsible citizen; understand that the quality of your life will approximately reflect the quality of effort you put into it; know that individual responsibility is the basis of freedom and that the limitations imposed by fate (whether fair or unfair) are no excuse for passivity.

6   Whether I live up to these values or not, I know that my acceptance of them is the result of lifelong conditioning. I know also that I share this conditioning with middle-class people of all races and that I can no more easily be free of it than I can be free of my race. Whether all this got started because the black middle class modeled itself on the white middle class is no longer relevant. For the middle-class black, conditioned by these values from birth, the sense of meaning they provide is as immutable as the color of his skin.

Reading-to-Write Questions

1. **Content:** How does Steele add a humorous touch to a serious subject?

2. **Arrangement:** Which pattern of comparison-contrast do you see here—point-by-point or subject-by-subject?

3. **Style:** From this excerpt, pick a simile that you like and explain why it is so effective.

4. _____

   _____

   _____

Suggested Topics

1. **Observation:** Invent an imaginary character like Sam who represents all of the values your family rejected. (audience = your roommate)

2. **Critique:** Steele claims that his family portrait of Sam, the ne'er-do-well, did not reflect his family's self-hatred even though Sam resembled a white racist stereotype of African Americans. Are you convinced? (See the selections by Malcolm X and bell hooks for two theoretical frameworks.) (audience = Steele's *Commentary* readers)

3. **Synthesis:** Compare Steele's and McCall's views of the Black middle class. (audience = students interested in African American studies)

4. _____

   _____

   _____

Background Readings: THE BLACK MIDDLE CLASS

Banner-Haley, Charles Pete. *The Fruits of Integration: Black Middle-Class Ideology and Culture, 1960–1990*. Jackson, MI: University Press of Mississippi, 1994.

Coner-Edwards, Alice F., and Jeanne Spurlock, eds. *Black Families in Crisis: The Middle Class*. New York: Bruner/Mazel, 1988.

Cose, Ellis. *The Rage of a Privileged Class*. New York: Harper Collins, 1993.

Dennis, Rutledge M. *The Black Middle Class*. Greenwich, CT: JAI Press, 1995.

Feagin, Joe R. *Living with Racism: The Black Middle-Class Experience*. Boston: Beacon Press, 1994.

Frazier, Edward Franklin. *The Black Bourgeoisie*. 1957. New York: 1st Free Press, 1997.

Fulwood, Sam, III. *Waking from the Dream: My Life in the Black Middle Class*. New York: Anchor Books, 1996.

Landry, Bart. *The New Black Middle Class*. Berkeley: University of California Press, 1988.

Ransford, H. Edward. *Race and Class in American Society: Black, Latino, Anglo.* 2nd ed. Rochester, VT: Schenkman Books, 1994.

———————————————————

———————————————————

———————————————————

Recommended Literature: Stephen Carter, *Reflections of an Affirmative Action Baby* (autobiography)

John O. Killens, *Cotillion*

Faking the Funk:
The Middle Class Black Folks
of Prince George's County
Nathan McCall

In his best-selling autobiography Makes Me
Wanna Holler, *Nathan McCall reveals how he
rose from prison to the press. Instead of "running the streets," he began "covering the streets"
for newspapers such as* The Atlanta-Journal Con-
stitution, The Virginia Pilot-Ledger Star, *and* The
Washington Post. *Thus, in the following essay
from his book* What's Going On *(1997), he analyzes the words and deeds of the Black middle
class from the perspective of someone who has
known the street as well as the suburban life. To
strengthen his analysis, he combines illustration, narration, and comparison-contrast with
cause-effect strategies.*

---

1   When the sun is out and the weather is nice, about fifteen young bloods
sometimes gather on the corner of Lake Arbor Way and Winged Foot Drive.
Maybe in their late teens, they chill on that spot, rap casually, and slyly pass
forty-ounce bottles of brew from hand to hand.

2   Of course, they sport the popular gangsta look and wear the standard street
gear: knit skullcaps pulled over their shaved heads; bulky, unlaced brogans;

and baggy sweatshirts flung over blue jeans that ride low—*real low*—on their butts.

3   In dress and manner, they could pass for a typical crew of young hustlers in Washington, D.C. And as you drive by, they even eye you warily, like leery drug dealers scoping for the Man. But cruising through there, you're struck by the realization that something's wrong with this picture. There's a major contradiction here. There's something that, well, just doesn't seem to make sense.

4   The discrepancy begins with the setting: The backdrop for the fellas is not boarded-up tenements, graffiti-marked walls, and urban blight. The backdrop is $250,000 homes with manicured lawns—houses that are sprinkled around a sprawling, well-tended community golf course and near jogging trails that circle a scenic, man-made lake.

5   In other words, this is not the rugged Chocolate City, where the gang bangers rule. This is Prince Georges County, a serene suburb of Washington. And the dudes hanging on the corner aren't desperate hoods trying to survive a hard-scrabble life; they're middle-class black kids with braces on their teeth. They're wanna-bes who are just acting out, pretending to be the gritty street warriors they see in D.C.

6   If you think *they're* a little confused, you should see their parents.

7   Their parents are the professional and business people who help make Prince Georges the richest majority-black county in the United States. By practically every barometer—income, education, and so on—used by our "social experts," they're the black crème de la crème. But like their children, they seem to be caught up in a bizarre identity crisis of some sort. And just like their offspring, their struggle is sometimes a pathetic sight.

8   In the normal scheme of things, the middle-class black people of Prince Georges County (everyone calls it P.G. for short) wouldn't be particularly noteworthy. In most ways, they're just typical Americans—or they're what we tend to think average Americans are: They're hardworking, honest folks who want the best for themselves and their families. They're good people—the kind of black folks that whites seem to get little exposure to.

9   But they are also something else. They are black America's crystal ball: Hailed by the media as a "national showcase for black achievement," P.G. is a scale model of what *is* and *is not* happening among the most promising African Americans in this splintered land. And the goings-on of brothers and sisters there offer some clues about the future, especially for the black poor, who are catching hell.

10   The middle-class blacks of Prince Georges County symbolize our greatest hope. They're part of a spontaneous, quietly budding movement that seems to be catching on everywhere. In suburbs surrounding cities such as Atlanta, Philadelphia, and Chicago, the movement consists of upwardly mobile blacks who have broken from the pattern of following white folks wherever they settle. Instead, these blacks have made a conscious decision to live among their own.

11   Unlike the movements of the past, which were in-your-face and on the streets, this one is more subtle and more instinctive. In fact, it's so low-key that you can become a part of it without even realizing it.

12   It happened that way for me several years ago, when my teenage son came to live with me in D.C. With my son so close by, the city worried me as never before: Too many people have become casualties of the crack epidemic or the out-of-control gangsterism that's made Washington seem like a war zone. So we did what lots of black folks have done: We left.

13   First, we moved in with my sister-in-law in a mostly white Virginia suburb. There, I faced the usual hassles that you encounter when living among whites: suspicious Caucasians whispering concerns to our landlord that we might bring down their property values or break into their houses and rip off their TVs.

14   Often when I left home for work at *The Washington Post*, I encountered so many wary whites on sidewalks and buses that I often was pissed off by the time I reached the office in downtown D.C. Disgusted, I decided to move someplace else, someplace where I could get away from paranoid whites.

15   That's when I heard about P.G. I was told that in some parts of the county, blacks had formed enclaves in peaceful communities as nice as you'll find any-where. I went to a place called Mitchellville, looked around, and bought a townhouse right away.

16   Before blacks moved there in large numbers, Prince Georges County was one vast cow pasture run by white, beer-bellied good old boys. Blacks began moving in around the 1970s. Two decades later, the county of 750,000 had a black majority. In 1994, blacks showed off their new political might and elected the first black county executive ever to run the place.

17   Of course, there are working-class and even some poor areas in P.G., just like anywhere else, but the county is known mostly for the large concentration of well-off blacks who have settled there. The community where I now live, known as Lake Arbor, is surrounded by others very much like it—develop-ments called Fort Washington, Kettering, Perrywood. These are sprawling, rustic neighborhoods where the median income is relatively high and the crime is low. A survey found that blacks with college degrees outnumber college-educated whites in P.G. County and that more blacks than whites live in house-holds with earnings above fifty thousand dollars. P.G. has also become a magnet for local black celebrities. Former heavyweight champion Riddick Bowe, the writer Marita Golden, and several NBA basketball stars live there.

18   Any P.G. resident will tell you what it means to feel welcome in your com-munity. Often, when I step out onto my deck and scan the woodsy landscape that fronts my neighborhood, the tranquillity of the place fills me with a deep sense of racial pride. My euphoria is prompted partly by the atmosphere, which is really nice: The townhouses where I live stand in the shadows of a lake, a golf course, and large houses. But more than that, the good feeling comes from the realization that this may be as close to heaven as I will ever get: I can

travel for a couple of miles in any direction and see mostly black folks, mostly *my* people; I can step outdoors without worrying about being insulted by some arrogant white dude who thinks I'm after his wallet; I can stroll through my neighborhood without seeing some old, blue-haired white lady clutching her bags when she sees me. In fact, when I go outdoors, my neighbors are genuinely glad to see me. They wave and say a cheerful hello.

19   Driving through my neighborhood, you can't help being impressed. And if you're not careful, you can get *really* carried away and interpret the outward appearance of things as a promising sign that we black people are finally pulling ourselves together. As the theme song for the old sitcom *The Jeffersons* went, it looks like "we're movin' on up."

20   But as the young bloods who hang on that corner demonstrate, things aren't always what they appear to be. The truth is, some blacks in P.G. County are living what one of my neighbors called an illusion of success. Their houses are impressive and their cars look expensive, but few have any real wealth to speak of. Many are not even nigger rich, though some have learned, damned well, to act the part. Although they may *look* as though they have things together, many are just groping in the dark. A schoolteacher who moved there recently from Florida told me, "They seem to have lost their focus. They're just like ostriches with their heads in the sand."

21   What she meant is that among the "successful" blacks of P.G. and, by extension, middle-class blacks everywhere, many have failed the crucial commitment test: This crowd—my generation of college-trained blacks—came up in the world with some high expectations heaped on them. We are the people expected to form the "talented tenth" that W.E.B. Du Bois imagined; we rode the shoulders of our predecessors, the civil rights protesters who fought, and sometimes sacrificed their lives, to open doors for us. We were expected to use our skills and training to take the black struggle to the next level. For a long time, it was assumed that when we got our chance, we'd figure out a way to reach back and help those poor blacks who were left in the urban trenches to fend for themselves.

22   But if the prosperous blacks in P.G. County are any indication, the huddled poor masses may just have to wait awhile. The truth is, black America's middle class is a conflicted bunch of people who are still unsure of the power they wield. Right now, they can't save the poor—they're too preoccupied trying to figure out who *they* are.

23   Despite all the material signs of progress, there's no indication that the middle-class movement will spread beyond the thriving bounds of places like P.G. County and embrace those blacks most in need of our help.

24   For one thing, there's no concrete game plan at work here. This middle-class movement is not spearheaded by the NAACP or the National Urban League or even by some charismatic leader. There's no indication that the man or woman who will be the next Martin Luther King, Jr., or Malcolm X will spring from this bunch to lead the way. You get the feeling that the college-

trained blacks with that kind of potential are too busy hustling the dollar, trying to make partner in some prominent white law firm.

25   "I think that too many of us are too tied to the system to be effective in the way that Martin and Malcolm were. Martin and Malcolm weren't beholden to the system," noted one friend, a lawyer who also lives in P.G.

26   The result is that the movement lacks direction. So the black people of Prince Georges County—and middle-class African Americans everywhere—are improvising; they're just taking the black struggle day by day.

27   As I wonder about my own role in helping the poor, I realize that the main question the black middle class faces is this: Beyond the quest for financial security and personal comfort, what, if anything, are we committed to? It's not that we don't have plenty of good, firsthand reasons to fight for the cause. A *Washington Post* story on the subject said, "Middle-class African Americans are more likely to feel they face racism than working-class and poor blacks. Nearly six in 10 middle-class blacks says they have experienced racism in the past 10 years and six in 10 say that they are concerned that they or a family member will face discrimination in the future."

28   The writer of the article, Kevin Merida, went on to say, "This unease comes at a time when many high-achieving blacks see their status threatened by corporate and government downsizing and their gains being challenged in the courts, in the political arena and in the theories of conservative scholars. As a result, though they are viewed within their race as having 'made it,' they are drawing closer politically to those who haven't."

29   Yet middle-class blacks clearly are not drawing closer to the black poor in other ways. Like cats curled up comfortably on a favorite rug, many of them live in what amounts to what the writer Sam Fulwood described as a "self-protective buppie cocoon, separate from poor blacks and all whites."

30   The blacks in Prince Georges seem to bear that out. If P.G. County is a symbol of success for the black middle class, for the poor it's also a discouraging sign of black flight. Of course, the term *black flight* makes many middle-class blacks cringe. In defense of themselves, some are quick to point out that theirs is not flight in the traditional sense of the word. (Blacks in P.G. want you to know that they're not so much running *from* something as running *to* something.)

31   Still, many middle-class blacks in P.G., and everywhere else, seem to be nagged by a deep sense of guilt about the notion that they've abandoned the poor. "I shouldn't feel guilty, because I didn't get a free ride," Bravitte Manley, a corporate lawyer, once told me. "But when you see blacks who are hopeless, you feel guilty, and you feel helpless because you don't know how to make the situation better. What most people do is try not to think about it because if you think about it, it's intellectually unjustifiable to say, *So what?*"

32   The guilt stems from the fact that for many African Americans who have come into their own in recent decades, economic success has been doubled-edged: It's brought them material comfort, but it's distanced them—physically and emotionally—from those for whom the mainstream remains out of reach.

33   In response, the so-called black underclass has created a defiant countercul-ture all its own. It has developed its own language, values, music, and—as ruthless as the drug trade may be—a self-sustaining industry. That counter-culture has evolved so swiftly and furiously, and the devastation of poverty and violence in its wake is so far-reaching, that it's left the entire nation dumb-founded. The astonishing murder rate among blacks attests to this.

34   The result is that now, in the midst of one of the toughest challenges ever to our collective survival, middle-class and poor blacks have become terribly divided. This estrangement has crippled our struggle, which once had unity. "I've been disgusted with myself because I've become very class-conscious and very mainstream," a friend once confessed to me. "I don't feel personal guilt, but I do feel ashamed that many of us who have arrived have not banded together to help the underclass. I struggle with that."

35   In P.G. County, some folks try to relieve their guilty feelings by taking up social causes. But they don't seem like the kinds of folks who'd actually go to the ghetto and work in the trenches. They're more likely to scribble a check in arm's-length support of some worthy black cause. Or they'll turn to mentor-ing and other relatively risk-free activities to convince themselves that at least they're doing *something*.

36   It doesn't help matters that some middle-class blacks secretly relish their buppie status. For such folks, even charity is a status symbol. Jackie Woods, a friend who has lived in Philly, Chicago, and D.C., told me about a gathering she attended that could easily have passed for a scene in a Tom Wolfe novel: A group of well-to-do blacks got together in an elegant high-rise apartment, drinking wine and nibbling asparagus tips and lobster while planning fund-raisers to help the homeless. "There were twenty-five people in the room, and everybody had on a thousand dollars worth of clothes," she said. "We were talking about helping the homeless, and there wasn't a homeless person in the room."

37   I truly believe that most middle-class blacks do want to help. Like me, they feel frustrated and so overwhelmed by the complex web of problems facing African Americans that they don't know where to begin. It's also true that vir-tually every element in America's black communities is pitching in. People in neighborhoods are taking to the streets to help the police fight crime. Civil rights groups are launching public relations campaigns to stop the violence. And churches, as usual, are doing their thing.

38   One battle cry that you hear more often now is the call for black suburban-ites to return and help revive the cities they've abandoned. But the option of returning poses a serious practical problem: At a time when bystanders are often caught in the cross fire of gun battles, most people with a choice are understandably reluctant to place themselves and their families at risk. For many, it's plain foolish to go back when it's clear that the people there are fighting losing battles with drug lords armed with automatic weapons.

39   The issue of whether or not to return to the city is not just about establish-ing a physical presence. Unfortunately, some middle-class blacks also consider

it necessary to distance themselves totally from the problems confronting us. In action, if not in philosophy, they subscribe to the view of Reverend Ike, the slick-haired, money-loving preacher who says, "The best thing you can do for the poor is not to become one of them."

40   So some middle-class blacks create their own strange existence, one that leaves them torn between two conflicting worlds: On the one hand, they're disillusioned by the racial realities of America, which hates blacks and the poor; on the other hand, they're still in love with the idea and the hope of achieving white folks' American dream. They're troubled by their loyalty—or lack of it—to less fortunate blacks, and yet for all their striving, for all the effort they've made to live among their own kind, the model of middle-class success that they pattern themselves on is lily-white.

41   Drive to Mitchellville Plaza, one of the many little shopping centers that have sprung up near upscale P.G. neighborhoods, and you'll see what I mean. You'll catch hints of chaotic lifestyles that reveal that some blacks haven't gotten as far away from the influence of whites as they may think they have. You'll see in their lifestyles a tangled mesh of contradictions and weird behaviors that are as confusing as the sight of bourgeois black kids hanging on a street corner, sucking brew.

42   A rush of activity flows through the shopping-center parking lot most evenings, when the professional blacks, returning from their oppressive jobs, zip to *this* shop or *that* store to pick up necessities. One by one, you see them rolling in, driving gleaming late-model Lexuses, Benzes, and Jeep Cherokees with disoriented-looking children strapped inside. Although they sport the trappings of prosperity, they don't seem happy. They look hurried and harried, tense—as uptight as the white people they emulate.

43   Every day, the frantic pattern at that shopping center repeats itself as predictably as the rising of the sun: After collecting their kids from day care and school, many parents stop first at the Blockbuster Video outlet and rent movies to baby-sit their children for the evening. From there, it's on to the McDonald's to pick up Happy Meals. Then, they head home, where the kids wolf down their high-cholesterol food and watch TV while Mama and Daddy collapse upstairs and try to catch their shortening breath.

44   It's success, white American style. It's blacks blindly caught up in the daily performance of what one writer in *The New Yorker* described as "the adrenaline surge that accompanies perhaps the fiercest desire of all these days—the desire to get ahead."

45   Although few would admit it, many of the blacks of P.G. County also pattern their lives on whites' lives in other, more subtle ways. When I first moved to the county, the complaint I heard most often was that expensive retailers, such as Macy's, Lord & Taylor, and other high-end businesses that follow white money everywhere had failed to open branches in P.G. I wondered whether those blacks really understood what they were saying: Without being aware of it, they were saying that they were upset that white retailers were refusing to come in and *exploit* them. They seemed to overlook the possibility

that white racism could provide motivation for blacks to create their own businesses.

46   Fortunately, there is a sprinkling of black businesses operating in P.G. Black entrepreneurs recently opened BET SoundStage, an elaborate black-theme restaurant owned by Black Entertainment Television. And soul-food joints are springing up everywhere.

47   But for the most part, black business development in P.G. has followed the same pattern as it follows in poor neighborhoods: There's a glut of black barbershops and hair salons, and there's a black shopping mall nearby. (You can tell the black malls by the proliferation of stores that sell gold chains, beepers, and Payless shoes.)

48   Lots of nonblacks certainly have no problem recognizing the business potential in P.G. County. In recent years, as word has spread that there's black money to be had, a rainbow of other races has stormed into the county and set up businesses. There's a Jerry's Pizza place on Central Avenue, but it's not run by anybody named Jerry. It's owned and run by a group from Pakistan, who pooled their resources and bought the franchise. There's a carryout seafood joint, where you can buy crabs by the barrel. The place is named Homeboys, but the owner is white. At Kettering Plaza, there's a place called simply Beauty Barber. There, you can buy all kinds of special products for blacks—much of it adorned with the colors and symbols of African kinte cloth. You can buy nappy Afro wigs and hair products galore that come in tall bottles that say MADE BY AFRICANS FOR AFRICANS. You can also buy products whose labels declare that they are manufactured by companies that are 100 PERCENT AFRICAN AMERICAN OWNED. But the store is run by Koreans.

49   "The Asians are like fleas on the back of a dog," one resentful friend complained. "You can't get rid of them. They follow black folks around, sucking blood, wherever they go."

50   There is a determination among the P.G. blacks to demand respect, especially from the foreigners who come to their communities and earn livelihoods off them. The problem is, their commitment to the struggle is often expressed in ways that are uniquely black bourgeois.

51   Once, they protested when Eddy's, a new Chinese takeout restaurant in Lake Arbor, refused to provide seats for customers waiting for their orders. The demonstration was cool, but it was hard to get fired up about it after seeing all those well-heeled folks out in front of the place in their monogrammed shirts and expensive suits, marching and waving protest signs.

52   On another occasion, they protested when the Giant Food store in Kettering Plaza placed magnetic detectors near the doors to catch shoplifters. One irate woman told me, "We wanted to let them know that blacks out *here* don't steal."

53   I went to the Giant and asked a black employee about the matter. He chuckled as if reflecting on the pretentious head trips that sometimes come with being black and middle-class. The employee told me that the store managers

put up the detectors after learning that in the previous year, twenty thousand dollars worth of merchandise had walked out the door.

54   At some point, neighborhood activists who met with the management demanded that the "insulting" detectors be removed, but the management refused. "I guess they lost that battle," the store employee said.

55   "Yeah," I told him. "That's not the only battle they've lost."

56   Of course, it's also a status statement among some blacks in P.G. County to imitate white folks' obsession with protecting their property values. When it comes to that property, some blacks proved they can be as racist toward their people as some white folks are. In Perrywood, when too many young black boys and men began gathering at a basketball court, distressed "activists" encouraged the police to get aggressive with them. Just as they have harassed brothers in white areas, the police began randomly confronting young black men at the court, demanding that they show proof that they live in the neighborhood.

57   And dig this. Blacks in a section of P.G. called Woodmoor, where homes run around five hundred thousand dollars, campaigned successfully to get a new zip code because the old one associated them too closely with a place called Landover, where many lower-income blacks live.

58   For all the confusion among blacks in P.G. County, there is some cause for hope. Recently, a group of black churches banded together and launched a plan to form their own banks, which would extend loans to black businesses and home buyers, who routinely get turned down by white lenders.

59   The promise of that and other, similar efforts leads you to believe—or maybe you just *want* to believe—that the professional blacks of P.G. County are going to work things out. Like middle-class black folks everywhere, they *have* to work it out. Nothing less than the future of black America depends on it.

60   For the moment, though, it looks rough for the home team. It looks confusing, as conflicting as the notion of African Americans giving lip service to the need to support black life, then acting as if they valued their property more than human beings.

61   This contradiction has been apparent sometimes in the clumsy ways they've handled problems with young people in some P.G. County neighborhoods. In Lake Arbor, when ballplayers got a little rowdy at a playground court, community activists also did the white reactionary thing—they had the basketball rims taken down without providing a gym or some other alternative recreational outlet for the young.

62   And as for the young bloods who gather sometimes on the corner to shoot the breeze and drink their brew, they've been taken care of, too. They were ordered to take their confusion somewhere else.

Reading-to-Write Questions

1. **Content:** What is McCall's thesis?

2. **Arrangement:** Notice when and where McCall refers to the "young bloods" hanging on the corner. How do his repeated references to this scene contribute to the coherence of the essay?

3. **Style:** McCall frequently infuses his Standard English sentences with the lexicon of African American Vernacular English, especially in the opening scene of his essay. Why do you think he adopts this style?

4. _____

    _____

    _____

Suggested Topics

1. **Observation:** Like a journalist, take notes while observing a neighborhood and asking yourself the questions "Who?" "What?" "When?" "Where?" "Why?" and "How?" Write a cause-effect analysis or comparison-contrast based on your observations. (audience = readers of the local newspaper)

2. **Critique:** Do you think McCall is too "hard" on the Black middle class? If so, summarize his thoughts and then explain why you disagree with him. (audience = McCall's readers)

3. **Synthesis:** Discuss African Americans' pursuit of the American Dream by contrasting the dream and the reality or by analyzing the effects. Tap the essays by McCall, S. Steele, and Ellison for ideas. (audience = low- and middle-class African American youths)

4. _____

    _____

    _____

Background Readings: THE BLACK MIDDLE CLASS

See the reading list for Shelby Steele's essay.

The Great Divide: Male vs. Female

Audrey Chapman

A national authority on male-female relation-ships, Audrey Chapman counsels singles, couples, and groups through her practice and her talk show on WHUR-FM. She has written insightfully about Black men and women in her books Seven Attitude Adjustments for Finding a Loving Man *(2001) and* Entitled to Good Loving: Black Men and Women and the Battle for Love and Power *(1995). In this excerpt from the latter, she focuses on the economic forces—real and imagined—that divide African American men and women.*

---

1   There are many who would say that there is only one reason black men and women can't get along—economics. It is no secret that black men have a difficult time in the marketplace. According to researcher Delores P. Aldridge in the work *Black Male-Female Relationships: A Resource Book of Selected Materials:* "In the last decade and a half, the median income of black males never reached two-thirds of the median income of white males. Perhaps even more striking is the fact that the income gap has repeatedly shown signs of widening. Although black females appear to compare more favorably with white females than black males with white males, in reality, they fare worse than either one of the other groups."

2   Some black men are angry because they believe black women have succeeded during the seventies and eighties at their expense. Statistics don't support their belief, but it persists just the same. The truth is that two out of three

black children are born to unmarried women, meaning that black women are struggling economically to raise children by themselves. And in terms of a paycheck, black women are *last* on the list—behind white men, white women, and black men. In 1992 the median income was $8,816 for black women and $12,962 for black men. Yet the myth persists that black women are doing well at the expense of black men.

3   One reason the myth endures is the high visibility of some black women who in recent years have risen through the corporate ranks. In 1994 the *Wall Street Journal* reported that black women professionals in corporate America outnumbered black men two-to-one. The article also noted that the ranks of professional black women grew 125 percent between 1982 and 1992 among companies reporting figures to the U.S. Equal Employment Opportunity Commission. The problem with such reports is that they fuel the debate between black men and women about who is doing better economically. Furthermore, it is grossly unfair to focus on the small group of women who have climbed the corporate ladder when huge numbers of black women are continuing to struggle.

4   In higher education, black women accounted for about 6 percent of people aged seventeen to thirty-four who were enrolled in institutions of higher learning in 1988. The figure for black men was only 4.5 percent. From 1990 to 1991, African Americans recorded a 7.1 percent gain in total enrollment in higher education. African-American women experienced a slight decline from 1990 to 1991 in the participation rates of high school graduates in college. Nonetheless, the 1991 rate of 30.9 percent reflects a 6 percent gain overall for African-American women since 1985.

5   During the 1980s, African-American female graduates showed more progress in higher-education participation than African-American male graduates. Yet thus far, the 1990s show a slight reversal in this trend. In 1991, 32.2 percent of African-American male high school graduates enrolled in college, compared with the 30.9 percent figure for females.

6   But despite obvious gains, power and the perquisites of the good life are not available to the majority of black men, and they are painfully aware of this fact. Does this lowered economic status affect how a black man deals romantically with a black woman? Remember the old adage that there's no romance without finance. This seems to be especially true in the black community. A black male college student told me that he worries about his ability to attract a "superstar sister." Without a lot of money or the appearance of some money, he believes his chances with most black women are slim.

7   Another young man, Jason, a thirty-year-old electrician who is working to complete a college degree, told me, "The sisters only want brothers who are together with a career. They won't even go out with us if we don't have a car. They want us to be making millions or they won't even talk to us. They say we are not up to par if we don't look prosperous." So unequal educational levels and imbalanced economics play a direct role in the power dynamics that go on between black men and women, eroding the passion they both long for and deserve.

Reading-to-Write Questions

1. **Content:** What role do the statistics play in the selection? How does Chapman present the statistics so that her essay does not become a "data dump"?

2. **Arrangement:** Chapman devotes the first half of the selection to statistical research and the second half to anecdotal evidence. Does the order make a difference?

3. **Style:** In the midst of her scholarly treatise, Chapman recalls the old saying "there's no romance without finance." Also, notice her use of the contraction "can't" in the first line. What do these colloquialisms achieve?

4. _____

    _____

    _____

Suggested Topics

1. **Observation:** Interview a random sample of African American undergraduates (half female, half male). What do they think divides African American men and women? Report and analyze your findings. (audience = readers of the campus newspaper)

2. **Critique:** To determine whether educational and economic status divide African American men and women, Chapman presents the opinions of two African American men who fear that African American women snub men who are not well off. How could Chapman make this part of her analysis thorough and balanced? (audience = Chapman)

3. **Synthesis:** Compare Chapman's analysis of Black male-female relationships with the Deficit-Deficiency Model described in White's essay. Does Chapman's analysis support the model? (audience = White's readers)

4. _____

    _____

    _____

Background Readings: BLACK MALE-FEMALE RELATIONSHIPS

Ali, Shahrazad. *The Blackman's Guide to Understanding the Blackwoman.* Philadelphia: Civilized Publications, 1989.

Aldridge, Delores P. *Black Male-Female Relationships: A Resource Book of Selected Materials.* Dubuque, IO: Kendall-Hunt, 1989.

Golden, Marita, ed. *Wild Women Don't Wear No Blues: Black Women Writers on Love, Men, and Sex.* New York: Doubleday, 1993.

Millner, Denene, and Nick Chiles. *Money, Power, Respect: What Brothers Think, What Sistahs Know.* New York: William Morrow, 2001.

Vanzant, Iyanla. *The Spirit of a Man: A Vision of Transformation for Black Men and the Women Who Love Them.* San Francisco: HarperSanFrancisco, 1996.

Wallace, Michelle. *Black Macho and the Myth of the Superwoman.* New York: Verson/Routledge, Chapman & Hall, 1990.

Washington, Elsie B. *Uncivil War: The Struggle Between Black Men and Women.* Chicago: Noble Press, 1996.

_____

_____

_____

Recommended Literature: Zora Neale Hurston, *Their Eyes Were Watching God* (novel)

Terry McMillan, *Waiting to Exhale* (novel)

Ntozake Shange, *for colored girls who have considered suicide/when the rainbow is enuf* (play)

Homophobia: Hip-Hop's Black Eye

Farai Chideya

Tackling tough topics ranging from politics to race, Farai Chideya has distinguished herself as a Newsweek *reporter, an MTV newswriter, a CNN political analyst, an ABC news correspondent, a syndicated columnist, and the anchor of the TV show* Pure Oxygen. *She has also published the website* www.popandpolitics.com *as well as the books* The Color of Our Future *and* Don't Believe the Hype: Fighting Cultural Misinformation about African Americans. *Among her numerous freelance articles is the following from the August 1993 issue of* Spin Magazine. *In the article, she explores the causes and effects of homophobia in the hip-hop community.*

---

1   It was the day, maybe the one day, that the unthinkable happened: Troubled trash tabloid the *New York Post* developed a social conscience. On October 24 of last year, its front page was graced with a smiling snapshot of teenage dancehall reggae artist Buju Banton—above huge black letters spelling HATE MUSIC. The snapshot was from "Boom Bye Bye," the single on which Banton proclaimed: "Two men necking/Lying in a bed . . . Get an automatic or an Uzi instead/Shoot them now."

2   A couple of months later, on the British TV show *The Word*, dancehall star Shabba Ranks supported Banton and added, "If you forfeit the laws of God

Almighty, you deserve crucifixion." The resulting attention back in the States from Ranks's statements led the *Tonight Show* to cancel a pending March booking. What landed Banton on the front page and yanked Ranks from Leno's show was an aggressive media campaign by a New York–based gay-rights group called the Gay & Lesbian Alliance Against Defamation (GLAAD), an organization whose recent successes in voicing its agenda has heated up longstanding tensions between gays and the hip-hop community. GLAAD has been somewhat successful at exacting retribution from hate-speech perpetrators; Banton, Ranks, and Marky Mark (who, also on *The Word,* supported Ranks's right to state his opinion) have all reluctantly signed to do anti-gay-bashing public service announcements on radio and TV, while even the radio stations that aired "Boom Bye Bye" offered unctuous public apologies. And each new twist in the saga has been accompanied by articles in the New York papers, as well as reports in the national media ranging from *Newsweek* to *Us.*

3   In the past, many rappers never thought twice about letting their hatred loose on the mike. Chubb Rock says, "You know I'll slap a faggot." "The Big Daddy law," says Big Daddy Kane, "is anti-faggot." Public Enemy's Flavor Flav has gone on record with antigay remarks, and Ice Cube rhymes "true niggas ain't gay." The "true niggas" Cube raps about are gangstas, the AK-47 toting, 40-swilling embodiments of urban manhood whose image sells millions of albums to black and white listeners. Gangstas—real ones, or the kind created out of thin air by a rapper's lyrical finesse—have become the street preachers of urban reality. And according to hard-core rappers, there's no room in that reality for being gay.

4   Homophobia is as American as apple pie—as witnessed by the "moral" outrage that stymied President Clinton's push to end the ban on gays in the military. And rap, of course, is not alone in its antigay lyrics. Heavy metal is, like rap, music that defines maleness for its adolescent fans, a kind of maleness that makes gays outsiders. Axl Rose, on the cusp of superstardom, sang, "Immigrants and faggots/They make no sense to me" in Guns N' Roses' "One in a Million." But there's one crucial difference between the two musical genres: Metal doesn't—and doesn't have to—shoulder the same moral and cultural weight that rap does. How many times have you seen ol' Axl interviewed about the mood of the white community? The leaders of the hip-hop nation, however, are regularly called on to represent an entire race. "Some people call R.E.M. the most important band in America," says Jonathan Van Meter, editor of the hip-hop magazine *Vibe.* "But when are they on CNN or on the cover of *Time?*" Public Enemy called rap "black America's CNN," and rappers such as the Oakland-based Paris believe the messages behind rap lyrics are not just listened to but heard. "I know they are," Paris says. "They are the reason why people listen."

5   "With the forced exile, incarceration, and execution of black leaders, rappers have become the spokesmen for the black community," says Michael Franti,

leader of Disposable Heroes of Hiphoprisy, whose "Language of Violence" is perhaps the only anti-gay-bashing rap. But a lot of these spokesmen are barely through adolescence. "When you're 16, you want to drive a car, get drunk, have sex," says Franti, who appeared on that very same British TV show one week after Shabba Ranks with the words F—— HOMOPHOBIA written on his chest. "Those are the symbolic rites of manhood, and the most important one is heterosexual virility. And the way to say you're the most virile is to say you're the least homosexual or 'soft.'"

6　　GLAAD public affairs director Donald Suggs—an African American—has taken heat for targeting primarily black artists, yet makes no apologies for his media crusade. Currently on the agenda: a postering campaign against Brand Nubian, whose "Punks Jump Up to Get Beat Down" includes the lines: "F—— up a faggot / Don't understand their ways / And I'm not down with gays." The posters, a play on the parental warning stickers, read "Societal Advisory, Homophobic Lyrics." (Brand Nubian declined to comment for this article.) "Everybody wants to talk about artistic freedom," says Suggs, "but nobody wants to talk about artistic responsibility."

7　　Suggs is battling not just individual rappers, but a whole system of belief. In the black community, as in America as a whole, many beliefs about gays have their roots in religion. Shabba Ranks stated that his comments on *The Word* were "premised upon . . . my childhood religious training." Rappers such as Buju Banton and Chubb Rock look to Christianity, too, while Cube and Brand Nubian look to Islam. Saying "the devil made me do it" is nice, but saying "God made me do it" is even better.

8　　But Suggs won't accept the homophobia, or the reasoning behind it. "There are so many things in hip hop and dancehall that are against religion: killing, adultery. If people really followed religion, half these songs wouldn't be out there." The moral authority of religion, now and throughout history, has allowed artists such as Cube and Ranks to remain mired in wrongheaded dogma without having to consider progressive change.

9　　Religious beliefs aren't the only factor shaping the conventions of the hip-hop nation: Many otherwise well-informed texts from the new doctrines of Afrocentrism play the same role. In the seminal book *Afrocentrism*, Molefi Asante calls homosexuality a trait learned from the white bourgeoisie that "makes the [gay] person evaluate his own physical needs above the teachings of national consciousness." And popular books such as *The Isis Papers* offer much the same argument: that white society emasculates black men and makes them gay.

10　　"I think effeminate traits in black men are glorified by the white media," says Paris, who formed his own label after Time Warner–owned Tommy Boy Records rejected his presidential assassination-fantasy "Bush Killa." "Prince and Michael Jackson—who are these he-women supposed to be? They cross over [to white audiences] because they're androgynous." The former Nation of Islam member adds, "I can't be the rapper in hip hop that stands up for the gay cause. It's not something I agree with, if you get down to it." But he takes pains to add, "As far as beating people down, I'm not into that. To each his or her own."

11   To Paris, the whole debate over hip hop and homophobia seems tangential. "We're getting killed, our women are being raped. Considering that we are on a collision course for destruction, the issue of homophobia is trivial." Many in the black community see gays, whom they view as socio-economically well-off, as pretenders to the uncomfortable throne of disadvantage. Being black is an instant visual distinction, but as long as gays keep their mouths shut, those who question the gay-rights agenda argue, they can live their lives free of harassment. In a May 17 *New Yorker* article, Harvard professor Henry Louis Gates, Jr., chided the black community for its lack of compassion for gay rights: "For those blacks and whites who viewed last month's march on Washington with skepticism, to be gay is merely an inconvenience; to be black is to inherit a legacy of hardship and inequity." But that standard of discrimination is flawed, Gates went on. For example, mainstream leaders, especially religious ones, can still talk about hating gays in ways that they can no longer talk about hating blacks. "In short," Gates says, "measured by their position in society, gays on the average seem privileged relative to blacks; measured by the acceptance of hostile attitudes toward them, gays are worse off than blacks."

12   The constant positioning of one group against the other is, of course, absurd, and denies the fact that many "true niggas" can be and are gay and lesbian. The fact that one of those brothers waving their hands in the air might be gay, or one of the front-row cuties in full Kente dress might snuggle up at night with the girl right next to her, is never acknowledged.

13   Even with the ubiquitous misogyny of rap, sexism is a little less openly nihilistic than homophobia. Women, after all, are always valued by the guys for some reason, even if they're the wrong ones (receptacle, breeder, "easy on the eye" sexual wallpaper). But the hip-hop nation, as defined by some of its most prominent citizens, has absolutely no use for gay men and women.

14   Many in the hip-hop community argue that stories such as the *Post*'s are driven more by antiblack sentiment than any honest regard for the good of gay America, acting as yet another excuse for the hostile mainstream media to spew antirap rhetoric. James Bernard, an editor at the *Source* and the author of an upcoming book on Ice Cube and South Central L.A., feels that the outcry over hip hop's homophobia is just good old-fashioned rap-bashing. "I'm not trying to defend particular lyrics, but I think these guys have taken more heat than they deserve," he says. "The rap industry has so many seminars on these issues." Bill Adler, a rap publicist who also produced a booklet criticizing Ice Cube for anti-Semitism, disagrees. "If you cover this topic at all," he says, "you can't help but do it justice."

15   Monica Lynch, head of Tommy Boy Records, recognizes that the media card can be played two ways. "Rap in general draws a disproportionate amount of media sensationalism," she says. "I think that there's a tremendous fear of

black males. A lot of what you hear in rap today, the bitch-ho-lyrics, is man trying to be man. And sometimes you hear the phrase 'The oppressed becomes the oppressor.' But I'm not a young black male; I try not to judge that. I would just say there's a real insecurity about their own masculinity, and they [take it out on] gays, women, or anyone else that they see as being weaker."

16 But while women have stepped up to the mike to challenge the gangsta stereotype (or to join in on their own terms), gay rappers are not allowed or not interested in entering what Lynch calls "the jousting ring" of rap. "Women, gays, Jews, Koreans; whatever [rapped about group] it may be, there may be lyrics deemed hate mongering. It's the rapper's right to be there and their right to be full of sh——. But there is always an open invitation for the next person to get on the mike and do battle and counter these things. A lot of people get bloody noses, but you've got to fight back," she says, adding she believes there could be openly gay rappers under the right circumstances.

17 But what are those circumstances? For gays and lesbians, the present lyrical atmosphere, and the lack of hardcore authenticity that gayness represents, may be too much to overcome. Could there ever be, say, a gay gangsta rapper? "I don't think so," says Paris. "No way."

18 LA rapper Yo Yo agrees. Street credibility, she says, "would be a problem, 'cause people wouldn't be able to deal with it." Yo Yo, who favors Clinton's moves to end the gay ban in the military, supports GLAAD's Antihomophobia campaigns. "If I felt like my life was in danger, I'd stand up," she says.

19 "I did this thing on my new album with [dancehall artist] Idle Joe," Yo Yo continues. "He said this word 'batty boy.' And I was singing it, singing the male part, and my friend told me what it means [the West Indian equivalent of 'faggot']. I went through this thing trying to get it off this album. I tried to have them bleep that out—I don't want anything like that on the album. But it was too late, and I feel bad about it. Society has made it so easy for people to discriminate. It's hard for you to stop it—it makes you look stupid if you say anything."

20 Gay members of the hip-hop industry are in a precarious position. Those who are openly gay often condemn homophobia, but say the lyrics don't bother them personally. Van Meter has taken his licks for being a gay white man in what is traditionally a straight black man's world. Russell Simmons, who was originally involved in the launching of *Vibe,* the Quincy Jones–Time Warner hip-hop publication, pulled out because *Vibe* "didn't hire one straight black man," he claimed in an interview with the *Washington Post.* Says Van Meter, "I guess I didn't anticipate the criticism I'd come under. But I feel that my sexuality is irrelevant, that I've adequately defended myself.

21 "The idea that hip hop is homophobic is exaggerated," he says. "If [Naughty By Nature's] Treach refers to his father who left him as a fag, he's not really calling him a fag. I love that song. I'm willing to accommodate what appears to be homophobia because I love the music so much." But songs such as [this, he] admits, "walk that line."

22   RuPaul, the skyscraper-tall black drag queen whose "Supermodel" hit No. 1 on the dance charts, has much the same attitude. "I'm not bothered by it and I thank God they have the freedom to say it," RuPaul says. "It doesn't make me lose sleep at night. Let them go on and do their own thing. They'll burn themselves out." Although RuPaul claims to have been "discriminated against by every community there is: black, white, straight, gay, lesbian," the singer doesn't place any particular emphasis on hip hop.

23   So who does hip hop's homophobia hurt? Suggs believes it contributes to rejection of and sometimes violence against gays of color. He argues that the antagonism between straight and gay blacks masks the common enemy of racism, saying: "[Straight blacks] don't realize that gay blacks are discriminated against in the white *and* gay communities." Matt Foreman, the executive director of the New York Gay and Lesbian Anti-Violence Project, which provides counseling and aid to victims of bias crimes, believes hip hop's lyrics have a deep effect on young listeners. He likens it to studies that show a correlation between depictions of violence on television and actual violent crimes. "What we know empirically is that young people, those under 18, are disproportionately the perpetrators of antigay violence," Foreman says. "Of the 662 antigay bias crimes reported to us last year, 31 percent were committed by people under 18, 52 percent by people aged 18 to 29. The popular media has a direct impact on the way young people act. It's absurd to think that a [music] group that can influence fashion across the country in profound ways doesn't have an effect on behavior. Kids will dress like them, go out and buy the clothes, but they're not listening to the lyrics?"

24   But Foreman isn't a fan of GLAAD's tactics: He thinks they're too weak. "I think we take a much more hard-line approach to this stuff than GLAAD does," he says, adding that he's never seen GLAAD's anti–Brand Nubian posters on New York's streets. "We thought they let Marky Mark off the hook too easily. My perspective is that [hip-hop] lyrics, which are homophobic both in that they're degenerating and that they're encouraging violence, are unique [in pop music] in terms of how many there are and the lack of outrage over them. We don't have any problem condemning these lyrics, urging people to boycott the record producers, but GLAAD has a problem saying that. I don't know if it's because we're right there with the people who bear the brunt of this stuff, but we just have a much more," he pauses, "*violent* attitude to these people."

25   For some targets, the perception of gayness is enough. P.M. Dawn's Prince Be was shoved off the stage of the Sound Factory in January 1992 by KRS-One (Kris Parker) of Boogie Down Productions. The attack may have had something to do with rumors about Prince Be's sexuality—as well as the fact that Be has refused to term his group's melody-suffused music "rap." "A lot of hardcore hip hop isn't down with P.M. Dawn," Prince Be says with supreme understatement. "It would be real dangerous for someone [in the hard-core community] to talk about gayness. What would have to change at the same

time would be the consciousness of the whole hip hop hard-core crowd, and of the whole world."

26   "A lot of people thought I was gay and I just wouldn't acknowledge it," he says. The question came up when he appeared on the U.K. television show *The Word,* the same show Ranks later went on. "They asked me if I was gay, and I said it doesn't matter. But then it leaked out to some people in the States, and I had to straighten it out," he recalls. "Do I like men? No. Am I gay? I don't think so. But," he laughs, "I seen *The Crying Game,* and that girl's fly!"

27   Few rappers are willing to laugh at the tension that exists around gay issues today, but some are making strides to bridge the gap between the gay and hip-hop communities. Victoria Starr, a radio programmer who is a lesbian and has a woman's music show on WBAI, shared a panel with Ice-T at the New Music Seminar two years ago. "I didn't even have to push him," she says of his public change of heart on homosexuality. "He talked about how he used to say things in concert like, 'If you have AIDS, don't clap.' Then people told him that wasn't cool. He said, 'Look, we're all victims of society, and we grow up learning these things.'"

28   "I'm working on a book on k.d. lang," says Starr. "Could she have come out five years ago? She was working in country music, which was probably as bad as rap. Hip hop is so rabidly homophobic that maybe it would kill someone's career to come out. Ninety percent of gay people could come out, but for someone in hip hop maybe that's not possible."

29   Rap music, for all its flaws, is still the CNN of black America. The problem isn't too much free speech, but not enough. The hip-hop nation, with a painful few exceptions, is unwilling to stand up and call gay-bashing rhymes wack. So now gays and lesbians are trying to break the lyrical silence. For example, GLAAD, in conjunction with the New York group Out Youth, is bringing together young gay and lesbian rappers in a competition for a cash prize. Says Suggs, "We wanted to show Brand Nubian who was out there." What's needed is an editorial from *inside* the hip-hop community that comes out strong against those who love to hate. Finding a "true nigga" who can rock the mike—and who's gay—may be the only way.

Reading-to-Write Questions

1. **Content:** What types of sources does Chideya use to illustrate her points?

2. **Arrangement:** Chideya could have started this essay with Paragraph 4, forthrightly stating that homophobia in rap music would be her focus. Instead, she opens with the Banton incident. Why?

3. **Style:** Chideya quotes heavily, so much so that at times you might feel that you are listening to a conversation instead of reading an article. What are the advantages and disadvantages of such a style?

4. _____

   _____

   _____

Suggested Topics

1. **Observation:** View MTV or BET music videos one evening and jot down the song titles and names of the hip-hop groups. Keep track of any negative references to homosexuals and women. Then write an essay classifying your findings.

2. **Critique:** At the end of her essay, Chideya suggests a remedy for homophobia in the hip-hop community: "What's needed is an editorial from _inside_ the hip-hop community that comes out strong against those who love to hate. Finding a 'true nigga' who can rock the mike—and who's gay—might be the only way." What do you think of Chideya's proposed solution? (audience = Chideya via e-mail)

3. **Synthesis:** What divides the African American community the most—homophobia, colorism, class, gender, or political affiliation? Classify these sources of intraracial conflict and then argue that one source is more significant than the others. For relevant facts, examples, and opinions, see the essays by C. Jones, McCall, Chapman, Brown, and Chideya. (audience = NAACP)

4. _____

   _____

   _____

Background Readings: BLACKS AND HOMOSEXUALITY

Boykin, Keith. *One More River to Cross: Black and Gay in America.* NY: Anchor, 1998.

Murray, Steph, and Will Roscoe, eds. *Boy-Wives and Female Husbands: Studies in African Homosexualities.* New York: St. Martin's Press, 1998.

Somerville, Siobhan. *Queering the Color Line: Race and the Invention of Homosexuality in American Culture.* Durham, NC: Duke UP, 2000.

_____

_____

_____

Recommended Literature: James Baldwin, *Giovanni's Room* and *Another Country* (novels)

E. Lynn Harris, *Abide with Me, Invisible Life, And This Too Shall Pass, Not a Day Goes By* (novels)

Becoming a Republican
Tony Brown

*Talk show host and National Public Radio com-
mentator, film director and TV/film producer,
newspaper columnist, and author of* Black Lies,
White Lies—*Tony Brown has forged a successful career in the media. In July 1991, he
stunned fans by announcing that he was
becoming a Republican. A month later he published the following explanation in the* Wall
Street Journal. *In his article, he not only explains
his decision but identifies the causes and effects
of African American rejection of the Republican
Party.*

---

1   "A veteran black TV personality and longtime battler of racism is dropping
a bombshell on his fans by ceremoniously joining the Republican Party,"
columnist Mary Papenfuss wrote in the *New York Post* last week after my
announcement on July 8 that I was ceasing to be a political independent and
was joining the party that was organized in 1854 to oppose the expansion of
slavery.

2   Blacks responded after the end of slavery by voting for the party of the man
who signed the Emancipation Proclamation, Abraham Lincoln. Blacks affili-
ated with the Republican Party, such as the remarkable Frederick Douglass, a
former slave and an abolitionist who insisted that "power concedes nothing
without a demand," emerged as national heroes. Republicans in Congress
were the architects of Reconstruction, a 10-year period of unprecedented political power for black people. They initiated the 13th Amendment, which out-
lawed slavery, the 14th Amendment, which guaranteed blacks citizenship,

and the 15th Amendment, which extended the right to vote to former slaves, as well as the Civil Rights Act of 1866.

Independent Thinking

3   Ironically, it is the right of a black to be a member of the Republican Party that is being openly questioned in 1991. And unfortunately, the First Amendment's guarantee of free speech has not been taken seriously by some black intellectuals and leaders. Many of them perpetuate an intellectual fascism and foster a totalitarian environment in which any independent thinking black who breaks lock-step with their often self-serving Democratic worldview is severely condemned, and even ostracized.

4   How did blacks move from the party that gave them civil and political rights to a previously all-white Democratic Party with a history of racist demagoguery, support for slavery and Jim Crow, and tacit approval of lynching? The movement began during the Depression, when the social programs of Franklin Roosevelt severed the close ties that blacks had felt in the Republicans. But many blacks remained loyal to the party of Lincoln: 40% of black voters voted for Dwight Eisenhower in 1956, and 32% cast their ballots for Richard Nixon in 1960. The black middle class, eager to associate itself with a message of self-sufficiency, was even more Republican: In some prosperous areas, Republicans were getting nearly 50% of the black vote as late as 1960.

5   Then Lyndon Johnson—who accomplished more for blacks legislatively than any president in American history—enacted his historic civil rights acts. Disgruntled Southern whites defected to the Republicans in the 1961 election, enabling Barry Goldwater to win such once-solid Democratic states as Mississippi, Georgia, Louisiana, South Carolina and Alabama. Tempted by these votes, the Republicans adopted a "Southern strategy," which has carried them to the White House in all but one of the elections since then. The strategy, as expounded in "The Emerging Republican Majority" by Kevin Phillips, demonstrated how Republicans could profit from racial polarization with code words like "law and order." The insidious idea behind this "Willie Hortonism" was to gain anti-black votes without appearing racist in the old Deep South style.

6   Today's near-unanimous perception among blacks that all white Republicans are racists is born out of that history—and the subsequent extension of the Southern strategy into Northern suburbs and ethnic enclaves. As a result, blacks have almost completely deserted the Republicans: In 1988, just 1% of the votes cast in the Republican presidential primaries were cast by blacks.

7   The absence of blacks from the Republican Party spells disaster for the black community. Between 1936 and 1964, when blacks voted roughly 65% Democratic to 35% Republican, both parties had to compete for their votes. Today, however, because blacks vote overwhelmingly Democratic, the Democrats can offer lip service and still count on the black vote. And because blacks have

become an almost nonexistent force in the GOP, Republicans can ignore them altogether.

8   But the absence of blacks from the Republican Party also spells long-term economic ruin for our country. We must adapt to cultural diversity as the foundation of our economic competitiveness. And it spells long-term political danger for the Republicans themselves: What the GOP is doing, or not doing, in the black ghettoes can have consequences in the white suburbs. White suburbanites could defect from the Republican fold if the party becomes stigmatized as racist. That's what moves Republicans like Sen. John Danforth (R., Mo.) to criticize the way some Republicans are exploiting the quota issue. That's why the Ripon Republicans in the 1960s warned of the danger of a strategy of racial divisiveness and promoted racial inclusion instead.

9   So, no matter how great the risk to some of us personally, we cannot allow black America to remain a one-party community in a two-party system. Nor can we permit the Republican Party to become a lily-white enclave in a heterogeneous country.

10   At one stage in history, the Democratic Party may have been the best choice for blacks. However, the Democratic policies of exclusive reliance on government programs evidently have not brought economic success to black America. As Martin Luther King, Jr., said more than 20 years ago: "New laws are not enough. The emergency we now face is economic." Blacks have an abiding faith in the philosophy of self-sufficiency, but are stuck, out of perverse necessity, with the something-for-nothing entitlement dogma of the Democrats. But the problem with depending on government is that you cannot depend on it.

11   Racism is a problem, but poverty is the primary problem facing blacks. Blacks need economic solutions. And self-help is a time-tested economic solution.

12   For example, the 350 black organizations that spend $16 billion in white-owned hotels each summer ($500 million at the Congressional Black Caucus meeting alone) discussing white racism and black poverty could cancel their 1992 conventions and use that $16 billion as a capital fund to buy hotels (at the moment, not one major hotel in America is owned by blacks) start new companies, create jobs for the poor and fund social programs in the black community.

13   In September, I am launching an effort to start 50,000 small companies in the next five years through a telephone-based loan program, using a state-of-the-art telecommunications system. Profits from calls to the businesses on the Buy Freedom 900 network will be used to provide the loans.

14   A community of 30 million people who emphasize civil rights over economic power will never have equal rights. Both civil rights and economic power are equally necessary. Neither can a black community earning $300 billion a year, the equivalent of the GNP of the ninth-richest nation in the free world, spend 95% of its money with other groups and blame them for 100% of its problems.

15   The color of freedom is green. As Adam Smith taught in "The Wealth of Nations," true freedom can come only from an intelligent and humane use of the free market system. And the party of free enterprise, despite all its potentially reversible shortcomings, is the Republican Party. If blacks want to return the Republican Party to its tradition of inclusion, they will have to join it and work from within.

Ideological Diversity

16   Since I announced my affiliation with the Republicans, a surprising number of blacks have told me they will follow my example. And all of the blacks who have spoken to me like the idea of greater ideological diversity within the black community. The statement that best typified the reaction to my becoming a Republican came from a woman at the Apollo Theater in Harlem, following my interview on WLIB, New York's black radio station.

17   "When I first heard the news, I thought you had sold out. So I had to hear an explanation from you personally. After hearing you explain, I agree with you and admire your courage. We do have to rely on self-help and we do have to be involved in both parties. But I'm not ready to become a Republican yet. I don't trust the Republican Party, but I trust Tony Brown."

Reading-to-Write Questions

1. **Content:** Could Brown have argued his case without statistics?

2. **Arrangement:** What kind of order does Brown follow?

3. **Style:** List the emotion-charged words Brown chooses to describe his Democratic critics. Does his word choice strengthen or weaken his position?

4. _____

   _____

   _____

Suggested Topics

1. **Observation:** On your campus or in your neighborhood, survey African Americans who are registered voters. Ask them whether they have joined a political party and why. Then write a causal analysis discussing the reasons for your respondents' political affiliations. (audience = recruiting committee for the Republican Party)

2. **Critique:** Brown declares that "the color of freedom is green." Summarize his argument and then explain why you agree or disagree. (audience = college seniors at their graduation ceremony)

3. **Synthesis:** Use facts from Bennett's essay to show how 19th Century African Americans fulfilled Brown's philosophy of self-help. Then suggest how African Americans today could emulate their actions. (audience = an African American fraternity or sorority)

4. _____

   _____

   _____

Background Readings: BLACK ENTERPRISE

Dingle, Derek. *Black Enterprise: Titans of the B.E. 100s: Black CEOs Who Redefined and Conquered American Business.* New York: J. Wiley, 1999.

Graves, Earl. *How to Succeed in Business without Being White: Straight Talk on Making It in America.* New York: Harper-Business, 1997.

Hutchinson, Earl Ofari. *The Myth of Black Capitalism.* New York: Monthly Review Press, 1970.

Johnson, John, with Lerone Bennett, Jr. *Succeeding Against the Odds.* New York: Warner Books, 1989.

Lewis, Reginald, and Blair S. Walker. *Why Should White Guys Have All the Fun?* New York: John Wiley & Sons, 1995.

Marable, Manning. *How Capitalism Underdeveloped Black America.* Boston: South End Press, 1983.

Woodard, Michael. *Black Entrepreneurs in America: Stories of Struggle and Success.* New Brunswick, NJ: Rutgers UP, 1997.

Student Essay:
THE ORIGINS AND INTENTIONS
OF COLORISM
Daud Cole
(2000)

1   For 200 years, Blacks were challenged with the task of living in slavery. For 200 years, they endured racism and tyranny at its most wicked levels. After slavery was abolished in 1865, we were freed from the shackles of racial oppression, or so we thought. Ironically, following this emancipation, blacks began to subject themselves to a form of interracial racism commonly referred to as "Colorism." Colorism is the attitude or practice among African Americans of discriminating against other African Americans because their "skin is colored cocoa and not cream, ebony and not olive" (Jones 240). Since blacks were subjected to 200 years of racism by another people, one would be inclined to wonder how blacks, after being legally freed from these practices, could subject themselves to such racism again. The problem is not that simple, however. The seeds of Colorism lie in social doctrines implanted by slave-owners into the minds of their slaves.

2   To begin with, color was simply one of a series of differences among slaves that slaveowners emphasized as a means of mind control. The infamous speech given by the slaveowner Willie Lynch in 1712 to a group of slaveowners spells this out loud and clear. Lynch states, "I have outlined a number of differences among the slaves and I take these differences and make them bigger" (1). Besides color, there were many other differences that slaveowners placed significance on, including age, intelligence, and one's status on the plantation, just to name a few. Lynch also explains why he uses these particular differences: "I use fear, distrust, and envy for control purposes" (1). He goes on to state that "the Black slave after receiving this indoctrination shall carry on and will become self-refueling and self-generating for hundreds of years, maybe thousands" (2). This may only come to pass, he adds, once the blacks "love, respect, and trust only us" (2). The plan laid down by Lynch is a calculated attempt to control the minds of slaves, a strategy that is designed to build trust and dependence on whites, further perpetuating the oppression of

blacks. This method is effective whether the institution of slavery is in place or not.

3   This mind-control technique infiltrated the dynamics of slave life, instigating the "house nigger" vs. "field nigger" conflict. It pitted the slave who worked in the house against the slave who worked in the fields. The reason why this holds any relevance to this discussion is that "house niggers" had a strong tendency to be light complexioned while "field niggers" were everybody else, including the dark-skinned slaves. As Clarisse Jones explains, "white masters often favored the lighter-skinned blacks, many of whom were their own children" (240). Thus, light-skinned blacks were more likely to secure the less strenuous jobs—the jobs in the master's house.

4   "House niggers" were envied but at the same time despised by all the other slaves. It was widely believed that those who worked in the Big House led easier, more comfortable lives. They were allowed to sleep in the house, they ate the master's leftovers, and they did not have to work in the field all day doing hard, laborious work. Because the "house niggers" (light-skinned blacks) were in such close contact with their master, they often developed personal relationships with him (X 290). Many of these slaves thought that their master loved them more than the other slaves. (Why they thought that they were loved at all is beyond me.) Because of this, light-skinned slaves were notorious for leaking information about slave escapes and uprisings, attempting to gain admiration from their masters.

5   Colorism has proven to be steadfast in its intentions. It has been about 150 years since Reconstruction, yet the evidence that Colorism still exists is very strong. We see it every day when black women straighten their hair. Straightening their hair is a thinly disguised attempt to imitate white people's looks, to become more white (hooks 247). Hopefully, in due time we will eradicate these stereotypes and prejudices. According to Willie Lynch, however, we still have hundreds of years to go before this can happen.

Works Cited

hooks, bell. "Straightening Our Hair." *Revelations*. Ed. Teresa M. Redd. 3rd ed. Needham Heights, MA: Simon & Schuster, 1997. 245–51.

Jones, Clarisse. "Light Skin Versus Dark Skin." *Revelations*. Ed. Teresa M. Redd. 3rd ed. Needham Heights, MA: Simon & Schuster, 1997. 239–241.

Lynch, William. "Let's Make a Slave." 1712. Rpt. by The Black Arcade Liberation Library, 1970. 28 Oct. 2000. <http://www.ehhs.cmich.edu/~rlandrum/lynch.htm>.

X, Malcolm. "Message to the Grassroots." *Revelations*. Ed. Teresa M. Redd. 3rd ed. Needham Heights, MA: Simon & Schuster, 1997. 289–91.

Student Essay:
STRUGGLE OF A GENTLEMAN
Shay Gilliam
(1996)

1   "If you don't learn anything else, learn to respect women" were the first words of advice that my grandmother gave to me about relationships. "If you learn to respect them, then everything else will fall into place." I contrasted these words of wisdom with what I learned from my major childhood sources of information—mass media and my friends—and came out with the major confusion that is still continuing today. My grandmother instilled in me that women are to be put on a pedestal and treated with the utmost respect. But television and music, on the other hand, placed the "dog" in me.

2   Growing up in a household full of women (a grandmother, mother, aunt, and two little cousins), I learned how to be compassionate and how to be tender and loving towards women and still be the man of the house. Even though I missed all the manly things (fishing, camping, and watching girls walk by with my father), I learned things about women that I might not have learned living in an all-male environment. Knowing that one day I could turn into the "enemy" in the battle with the male chauvinistic point of view, my female relatives tried to make me into a gentleman and have me as a major ally to tell my little cousins the evil of men firsthand. Even though the gentleman in me did not always shine, as I went out into the world I found that there was no other way to treat a Nubian Queen.

3   Though I have the nature of a gentleman, there is still that person inside me who wants to be with every woman he can, to disrespect women by calling them "bitches" and "hoes" or any other name besides their own. (I found out that calling women these names in their aura was suicidal.) Not to offend my "brothas" and say that this is how all men are, but most do think along these lines. Besides my womanly influence, I grew up around male companions, and it seems as though all of them wanted to be male prostitutes and be with as many girls as they could . . . this is what television brought into my life and the lives of my peers. Characters such as Dolomite and Shaft glorified this mentality of "doggin'" women. Along with pornography, most people in my generation grew up with this state of mind and figured it was the right way.

4   Television was not the only fiend implanting this mindset into my age group. Rap songs were and still are major influences. Culprits like Calvin "Snoop Doggy Dogg" Broadus, Eric "Eazy-E" Wright and Tupac "2PAC" Shakur, Craig "The Notorious B.I.G." Wallace, Luther "Uncle Luke" Campbell, Too Live Crew, and many others released songs with lyrics like "bitches ain't sh_t but hoes and tricks. . . ." (Calvin "Snoop Doggy Dogg" Broadus), "I don't trust these hoes, I keep 'em in flavas like Timbos. . . ." (Craig "The Notorious B.I.G." Wallace), and "all respect to those who break they necks to keep they hoes in check. . . ." (Tupac "2PAC" Shakur). This made it appear morally correct to put down women and to use their beautiful bodies only for sexual acts (oral and traditional).

5   The things that I have learned from my parents, peers, and other sources of knowledge have developed me into a well-rounded young man. Though I know some things about my beautiful black princesses, there are still many things that I get confused about. I cannot understand why, when girls like a guy, they seem to want to play it off and act like they don't. Also, no matter how well-mannered I am to them, women are always flocking to the "dog pound" for men. Then when they are treated inappropriately and/or are called wrongful names, they get mad and call *all* men dogs. These are just a couple of my reasons for conflict with women. Should I be taken under and be thrown into the ranks of the "common dog," or should I struggle and be alone until women find out about my commodities? I know the answers to my own questions: I love women too much to purposely dishonor them by changing my lifestyle. So far it seems as though my grandmother was wrong. Things have not worked out, and discouragement is on my shoulder. The way things are going, it seems I will never find that special young lady who will ease my confusion.

mother tongue

. . . how choose
Between this Africa and the English tongue I love?
Betray them both, or give back what they give?

from "A Far Cry from Africa" by Derek Walcott

Black English: A Discussion
Karen Webb

Linguist Karen Webb is Dean of the School of Education at Alliant University. Over the years she has written journal articles and textbook chapters about sociolinguistics and second-language acquisition. The following essay, written in 1991, is an outgrowth of her research and teaching. In the essay, she classifies Black English as a language and sorts its features into three categories: phonological, syntactic, and semantic.

---

1   YES! Black English is a language. This is my response to my students' most frequently asked linguistics question. Black English and controversy seem synonymous in the African-American community. The varied language experiences that our speech communities provide reflect images as diverse as our diaspora and as common as our ancestry. For some the images are literary, the haunting truth in James Baldwin's "Sonny's Blues":

> "It ain't a question of being a good boy,"
> Mama said, "nor of his having good sense. It
> ain't only the bad ones, nor yet the dumb
> ones that gets sucked under."

2   The emotional bonding that Lucille Clifton describes in "Sisters" is made cogent by the use of a variety of Black English:

> me and you be sisters.
> we be the same. . . .
> me and you

got babies
got thirty-five
got black
let our hair go back
be loving ourselves
be loving ourselves
be sisters.
only where you sing
i poet.

3   The wisdom of Mama in "Sonny's Blues" is not obscured by a plural subject in agreement with a singular verb form; nor is the pride of two sisters lost due to the use of the invariant "be". Yet language attitudes are not solely based on semantic clarity. Other images arise from our experiences and are poignant in their reality—the urban rap, a grandmother's wisdom, or a Sunday sermon. Whatever the image, our perceptions about languages and the people who speak them are learned and are culture bound. In reality Black English is rule governed with roots in the languages of West Africa and has semantically influenced other English varieties (Turner 1949, Wolfram and Fasold 1974, Smitherman 1977).

4   Language perceptions and attitudes about speech communities are the result of our reactions to the pronunciation of words (phonology), our ability to abstract meaning from what is said (semantics) and our understanding of the grammatical rules underlying the structure of the language (syntax). Linguists do not judge whether a language is "good" or "bad", "right" or "wrong". What linguists do judge is whether there are rules for phonology, semantics and syntax in a communication system. When such rules exist, a language exists. In most varieties of Black English these rules are based on the Niger-Kordofanian sub family of languages (Turner 1949, Smitherman 1977) and reflect an evolution from the African linguistic heritage of our ancestors, through the creolization process which occurred on southern plantations (Dillard 1977) and was defined by the regional migration patterns of our journeys. It is not only the pronunciation and meaning and usage of the speech forms to which we react, but also the prosodic features—the intonation, pitch and inflection of language. Moreover, in the case of Black English, attitudes are formed in response to the nomenclature—the suggestion that sets of linguistic features are representative of the communication medium of all Black people and that there is one set of these linguistic features. Therefore Africanized English, Ebonics and other terms appear in sociolinguistic literature—attempts to more accurately describe the language's history rather than the speech community. Regardless of nomenclature, attitudes and passions are formed based on the positive or negative opinions related to combinations of categories of linguistic features. It is these opinions which prompt the question "Is Black English a language?" Exploration of a representative set of categories will make the answer affirmative.

5   All varieties of Black English are rule governed. The most salient and recognizable phonological features are

1. the inflection of open syllables evident in consonant cluster reduction (except = 'cep)

2. the devoicing of single voiced consonants and loss of voiceless consonants, nasals and liquids in that position (desk = des')

3. the absence of interdental fricatives ƀ and ঽ (teeth = teef, the = da)

4. the pronunciation of r and 1 in medial and final positions becomes an "uh" sound (sister = sistuh, help = hep)

5. the final sk clusters become "x" (ask = ax)

6. the hypercorrection of plural endings (tests = tesses)

7. the reduction of "going" to "goin'"

8. the primary stress on the second syllable shifts to the first syllable (police = PO-lice).

6   These are certainly not all of the phonological features of the various varieties of Black English, but they are of high frequency in both urban and rural speech communities (Stoller 1975, Smitherman 1977, Alexander 1985). The most distinguishing grammatical features of the language are

1. the use of the invariant "be" for permanent conditions (She be workin')

2. the absence of the "be" copula for temporary conditions (He sick today)

3. the completive aspect with "done" (I done finish my work)

4. the absence of the third person singular "s" in the present tense (Mary have it)

5. the third person singular "s" with plural number subjects (They gets to me)

6. the absence of irregular past participles (They have came)

7. multiple negation (Wasn't nobody in the house)

8. the use of the pronoun "it" to introduce an utterance (It a boy over there)

9. the hypercorrection of irregular plurals and possessives (men = mens, mine = mines).

7   The listing of syntactic and phonological categories is not to suggest that the majority of Black English dominant speakers use all the features in their

speech. A speaker may have the phonological but not the syntactic, or may be proficient in a combination of the following semantic features:

1. the use of circumlocution or parable to identify a concept

2. the use of context to convey meaning (He go to bed las' night)

3. the selected use of stress or intonation patterns

4. emphasis on the creativity of language style and usage (derivational morphemes, rap).

8   Semantically when information cues are fully comprehended, the information is processed in memory to be repeated or to be recalled later. If the information is unfamiliar to the listener or unintelligible to the listener, the language may not be processed; attitudes toward the speaker and the language are made. Therefore, language is often used as a code to include or exclude an audience. In reality each society makes that decision, often using language as the excuse for misunderstanding and non-communication.

9   Yes! Black English is a language and it is the first language of many African-Americans, but not all. It is a language with its own rules and audience as are academic English and the competitive English of the professions.

10   The knowledge of one does not preclude the mastery of another, nor must the process diminish the proficiency of the first language. Our brains have the capacity for mastery of many languages and language varieties; when we do so we unlock the culture and logic of a people. Your ideas, which reflect the rich images of our ancestry, deserve global expression.

References

Baldwin, J. "Sonny's Blues" in *Going to meet the man*. New York: Bantam Books, 1965.

Brooks, C. K. (Ed.). *Tapping potential: English language arts for Black learners*. Urbana: National Council of Teachers of English, 1985.

Carroll, J. B. "What grammar is in the brain?" In D. L. Horton & J. J. Jenkins (Eds.), *Perception of language*. Columbus, Ohio: Charles E. Merrill Publishing, 1971.

Clifton, L. *An ordinary woman: Poems by Lucille Clifton*. New York: Random House, 1974.

Dillard, J. L. *Black English: Its history and usage in the United States*. New York: Vintage Books, 1972.

Smitherman, G. *Talkin and testifyin: The language of Black America*. Boston: Houghton Mifflin, 1977.

Stoller, P. (Ed.). *Black American English: Its background and its usage in the schools and in literature.* New York: Dell, 1975.

Turner, L. *Africanisms in the Gullah dialect.* Ann Arbor, Michigan: University of Michigan Press, 1949.

Wolfram, W. & Fasold, R. W. *The study of social dialects in American English.* Englewood Cliffs, N. J.: Prentice-Hall, 1974.

Reading-to-Write Questions

1. **Content:** Webb has to explain a technical subject—linguistics—to a lay audience. How does she make her explanation clear?

2. **Arrangement:** Why does Webb *list* the features in each category?

3. **Style:** In her introductory and concluding paragraphs, Webb uses first-person and second-person pronouns (e.g., *my, we, your*). What impression do these pronouns create?

4. _____

   _____

   _____

Suggested Topics

1. **Observation:** Question your classmates about their use of Black English, listing examples. Then, borrowing Webb's categories—phonological, grammatical, syntactic—classify the examples from your survey data. (audience = classmates)

2. **Critique:** Based on her definition of a language, Webb classifies Black English as a language. Find or formulate another definition of a language and argue that Webb misclassifies Black English according to the new definition. (audience = Webb's readers)

3. **Synthesis:** After reading the essays by Barras and Traylor, describe three types of attitudes toward Black English. (audience = people attending a panel discussion on Ebonics)

4. _____

   _____

   _____

Background Readings: BLACK ENGLISH

Andrews, Malachi, and Paul T. Owens. *Black Language.* Los Angeles: Seymour-Smith, 1973.

Bailey, Guy, Natalie Maynor, and Patricia Cukor-Avila, eds. *The Emergence of Black English: Text and Commentary.* Amsterdam and Philadelphia: J. Benjamins, 1991.

Baugh, John. *Beyond Ebonics: Linguistic Pride and Racial Prejudice.* New York: Oxford UP, 2000.

_____. *Black Street Speech: Its History, Structure, and Survival.* Austin, TX: University of Texas Press, 1983.

Dillard, J. L. *Black English: Its History and Usage in the United States.* New York: Vintage, 1972.

Labov, William. *Language in the Inner City: Studies in the Black English Vernacular.* Philadelphia: University of Pennsylvania Press, 1972.

McWhorter, John. *Spreading the Word: Language and Dialect in America.* Portsmouth: Heinemann, 2000.

Mufwene, Salikoko, John Rickford, Guy Bailey, and John Baugh, eds. *African American English.* London: Routledge, 1998.

Rickford, John. *African American Vernacular English: Features, Evolution, Educational Implications.* Malden, MA: Blackwell Publishers, 1999.

_____, and Russell Rickford. *Spoken Soul: The Story of Black English.* New York: Wiley, 2000.

Smitherman, Geneva. *Talkin and Testifyin: The Language of Black America.* Detroit: Wayne State UP, 1977.

_____. *Talkin' That Talk: Language, Culture, and Education in African America.* London: Routledge, 2000.

Wolfram, Walter A. *Dialects and American English.* Englewood Cliffs, NJ: Prentice Hall & Center for Applied Linguistics, 1991.

Recommended Literature: Toni Cade Bambara, "My Man Bovanne" from *Gorilla, My Love* (short story)

Keith Gilyard, *Voices of the Self* (autobiography)

Alice Walker, *The Color Purple* (novel)

White English in Blackface, or Who Do I Be?

Geneva Smitherman

Known for her ardent defense of language rights, Geneva Smitherman has led the struggle to gain recognition for Black English for over 20 years. A distinguished professor of linguistics, she has analyzed Black English in her books Talkin' and Testifyin': The Language of Black America, Black Talk: Words and Phrases from the Hood to the Amen Corner, *and, more recently,* Talkin' That Talk, *a retrospective collection of her essays. From* Talkin' That Talk *comes her landmark essay "White English in Blackface, or Who Do I Be?," which first appeared in* The Black Scholar *in 1973. The essay is one of her earliest attempts to define and write in Black English, "to tell as well as show the power of Black speech." In the last section, reprinted below, Smitherman explains that, in addition to its own grammar and vocabulary, the "Black Idiom" (BI) encompasses a distinctive rhetorical style. She compares the sacred and secular variations of this style and identifies five distinguishing characteristics.*

---

1   Black verbal style exists on a sacred-secular continuum, as represented by the accompanying scheme [see table below]. The model allows us to account for the many individual variations in black speech, which can all be located at some point along the continuum.

2   The sacred style is rural and Southern. It is the style of the black preacher and that associated with the black church tradition. It tends to be more emotive and highly charged than the secular style. It is also older in time. However, though I've called it "sacred," it abounds in secularisms. Black church service tends to be highly informal, and it ain't nothin for a preacher to get up in the pulpit and, say, show off what he's wearing: "Y'all didn't notice the new suit I got on today, did y'all? Ain the Lord good to us. . . ."

3   The secular style is urban and Northern, but since it probably had its beginnings in black folk tales and proverbs, its *roots* are Southern and rural. This is the street culture; the style found in barbershops and on street corners in the black ghettos of American cities. It tends to be more cool, more emotionally restrained than sacred style. It is newer and younger in time and only fully evolved as a distinct style with the massive wave of black migration to the cities.

4   Both sacred and secular styles share the following characteristics:

5   1. *Call and Response.*   This is basic black oral tradition. The speaker's solo voice alternates or is intermingled with the audience's response. In the sacred style, the minister is urged by the congregation's Amen's, That's right, Reverend's, or Preach Reverend's. One also hears occasional Take your time's when the preacher is initiating his sermon, the congregation desiring to savor every little bit of this good message they bout to hear. (In both sacred and secular political rap styles, the "Preach Reverend" is transposed to "Teach Brother.") In the secular style, the response can take the form of a back-and-forth banter between the speaker and various members of the audience. Or the audience might manifest its response in giving skin (fives) when a really down verbal point is scored. Other approval responses include laughter and phrases like "Oh, you mean, nigger," "Get back, nigger," "Git down, baby," etc.

SACRED	SECULAR
Political Rap Style	*Political Rap Style*
Examples: Jesse Jackson	*Examples:* Malcolm X
Martin Luther King	Rap Brown
Political Literary Style	*Political Literary Style*
Examples: Barbara Ann Teer's	*Examples:* Don Lee
National Black Theater	Last Poets
Nikki Giovanni's "Truth Is	
on Its Way"	

Sacred and Secular Black Verbal Styles

6   2. *Rhythmic Pattern.*   I refer to cadence, tone, and musical quality. This is a pattern that is lyrical, sonorous, and generally emphasizing sound apart from sense. It is often established through repetition, either of certain sounds or words. The preacher will get a rhythm going, conveying his message through sound rather than depending on sheer semantic import. "I-I-I-I-I-Oh-I-I-Oh, yeah, Lord-I-I-heard the voice of Jesus saying. . . ." Even though the secular style is characterized by rapidity, as in the toasts (narrative tales of bad niggers and they exploits like Stag-O-Lee, or bad animals and they trickeration, like the Signifying Monkey), the speaker's voice tone still has that rhythmic, musical quality, just with a faster tempo.

7   3. *Spontaneity.* ⸢Generally, the speaker's performance is improvisational, with the rich interaction between speaker and audience dictating and/or directing the course and outcome of the speech event.⸣Since the speaker does not prepare a formal document, his delivery is casual, nondeliberate, and uncontrived. He speaks in a lively, conversational tone, and with an ever-present quality of immediacy. All emphasis is on process, movement, and creativity of the moment. The preacher says "Y'all don wont to hear dat, so I'm gon leave it lone," and his audience shouts, "Naw, tell it Reverend, tell it!," and he does. Or, like, once Malcolm [X] mentioned the fact of his being in prison, and sensing the surprise of his audience, he took advantage of the opportunity to note that all black people were in prison: "That's what American means: prison."

8   4. *Concreteness:*   The speaker's imagery and ideas center around the empirical world, the world of reality, and the contemporary Here and Now. Rarely does he drift off into esoteric abstractions; his metaphors and illustrations are commonplace and grounded in everyday experience. Perhaps because of his concreteness, there is a sense of identification with the event being described or narrated, as in the secular style where the toast-teller's identity merges with that of the protagonist of his tale, and he becomes Stag-O-Lee or Shine; or when the preacher assumes the voice of God or the personality of a Biblical character. Even the experience of being saved takes on a presentness and rootedness in everyday life: "I first met God in 1925. . . ."

9   5. *Signifying.*   This is a technique of talking about the entire audience or some member of the audience either to initiate verbal "war" or to make a point hit home. The interesting thang bout this rhetorical device is that the audience is not offended and realizes—naw, expects—the speaker to launch this offensive to achieve this desired effect. "Pimp, punk, prostitute, Ph.D.—all the P's— you still in slavery!" announces the Reverend Jesse Jackson. Malcolm puts down the nonviolent movement with: "In a revolution, you swinging, not singing." (Notice the characteristic rhythmic pattern in the above examples— the alliterative poetic effect of Jackson's statement and the rhyming device in Malcolm's.)

10   An analysis of black expressive style, such as presented here, should facilitate the construction of a performance instrument to measure the degree of command of the style of any given BI speaker. Linguists and educators sincerely interested in black education might be about the difficult, complex business of

devising such a "test," rather than establishing linguistic remediation programs to correct a nonexistent remediation. Like in any other area of human
activity, some BI rappers are better than others, and today's most effective
black preachers, leaders, politicians, writers are those who rap in the black
expressive style, appropriating the ritual framework of the Oral Tradition as
vehicle for the conveyance of they political ideologies. Which brings me back
to what I said from Jump Street. The real heart of this language controversy
relates to/is the underlying political nature of the American educational system. Brother Frantz Fanon is highly instructive at this point. From his "Negro
and Language," in *Black Skin, White Masks:*

> I ascribe a basic importance to the phenome-
> non of language. . . . To speak means . . . above
> all to assume a culture, to support the weight
> of a civilization. . . . Every dialect is a way of
> thinking. . . . And the fact that the newly
> returned [i.e., from white schools] Negro
> adopts a language different from that of the
> group into which he was born is evidence of
> a dislocation, a separation. . . .

In showing why the "Negro adopts such a position . . . with respect to European languages," Fanon continues:

> It is because he wants to emphasize the rup-
> ture that has now occurred. He is incarnating
> a new type of man that he imposes on his
> associates and his family. And so his old
> mother can no longer understand him when
> he talks to her about his *duds,* the family's
> *crummy joint,* the *dump* . . . all of it, of course,
> tricked out with the appropriate accent.
>   In every country of the world, there are
> climbers, 'the ones who forget who they
> are,' and in contrast to them, 'the ones who
> remember where they came from.' The
> Antilles Negro who goes home from France
> expresses himself in the dialect if he wants to
> make it plain that nothing has changed.

11   As black people go moving up toward separation and cultural nationalism,
the question of the moment is not which dialect, but which culture, not whose
vocabulary but whose values, not *I am* vs. *I be,* but WHO DO I BE?

Reading-to-Write Questions

1. **Content:** List the people Smitherman refers to in order to illustrate the five characteristics of Black verbal style. What do you notice about her selection of examples?

2. **Arrangement:** What features of the text help readers anticipate what will come later?

3. **Style:** How do you feel about Smitherman's mixture of Black English and academic English?

4. _____
   _____
   _____

Suggested Topics

1. **Observation:** Which of Smitherman's stylistic features are used by African American students on your campus? Collect examples. Then, applying Smitherman's classification scheme, present the examples, category by category OR create your own classification scheme. (audience = campus newspaper)

2. **Critique:** Smitherman says "The real heart of this language controversy relates to/is the underlying political nature of the American educational system." What does she mean? Do you agree with her? (audience = Smitherman's readers)

3. **Synthesis:** Study Malcolm X's or Martin Luther King, Jr.'s selections in this book. As you read, underline stylistic features that catch your eye and sort them into Smitherman's categories. Discuss your findings. (audience = would-be orators)

4. _____
   _____
   _____

Background Readings: THE AFRICAN AMERICAN ORAL TRADITION

Abrahams, Roger D. *Talking Black.* Rowley, MA: Newbury House, 1976.

Asante, Molefi Kete. *The Afrocentric Idea.* Philadelphia: Temple UP, 1987.

Balester, Valerie. *Cultural Divide: A Study of African-American College-Level Writers.* Portsmouth, NH: Boynton/Cook, 1993.

Brown, Fahamisha Patricia. *Performing the Word: African-American Poetry as Vernacular Culture.* New Brunswick: Rutgers UP, 1999.

Folb, Edith A. *Runnin' Down Some Lines: The Language and Culture of Black Teenagers.* Cambridge, MA: Harvard UP, 1980.

If Black English Isn't a Language, Then Tell Me, What Is?

James Baldwin

James Baldwin (1924–1987) was a prolific essayist, novelist, and playwright. Some of his most famous works are his plays Blues for Mister Charlie *and* The Amen Corner; *his novels* Go Tell It on the Mountain, Giovanni's Room, *and* Another Country; *and his volumes of essays* Notes of a Native Son, The Fire Next Time, *and* Nobody Knows My Name. *In this essay, published in* The New York Times *in 1979, Baldwin explains what the word "language" means to him in order to classify Black English as a language, not merely a dialect.*

---

1   The argument concerning the use, or the status, or the reality, of black English is rooted in American history and has absolutely nothing to do with the question the argument supposes itself to be posing [The argument has nothing to do with language itself but with the *role* of language. Language, incontestably, reveals the speaker. Language, also, far more dubiously, is meant to define the other—and, in this case, the other is refusing to be defined by a language that has never been able to recognize him.]

2   People evolve a language in order to describe and thus control their circumstances, or in order not to be submerged by a reality that they cannot articulate. (And, if they cannot articulate it, they *are* submerged.) A Frenchman

319

living in Paris speaks a subtly and crucially different language from that of the man living in Marseilles; neither sounds very much like a man living in Quebec; and they would all have great difficulty in apprehending what the man from Guadeloupe, or Martinique, is saying, to say nothing of the man from Senegal—although the "common" language of all these areas is French. But each has paid, and is paying, a different price for this "common" language, in which, as it turns out, they are not saying, and cannot be saying, the same things: They each have very different realities to articulate or control.

3   What joins all languages, and all men, is the necessity to confront life, in order, not inconceivably, to outwit death: The price for this is the acceptance, and achievement, of one's temporal identity. So that, for example, though it is not taught in the schools (and this has the potential of becoming a political issue) the south of France still clings to its ancient and musical Provençal, which resists being described as a "dialect." And much of the tension in the Basque countries, and in Wales, is due to the Basque and Welsh determination not to allow their languages to be destroyed. This determination also feeds the flames in Ireland for among the many indignities the Irish have been forced to undergo at English hands is the English contempt for their language.

4   It goes without saying, then, that language is also a political instrument, means, and proof of power. It is the most vivid and crucial key to identity: It reveals the private identity, and connects one with, or divorces one from, the larger public, or communal identity. There have been, and are, times, and places, when to speak a certain language could be dangerous, even fatal. Or, one may speak the same language, but in such a way that one's antecedents are revealed, or (one hopes) hidden. This is true in France, and is absolutely true in England: The range (and reign) of accents on that damp little island make England coherent for the English and totally incomprehensible for everyone else. To open your mouth in England is (if I may use black English) to "put your business in the street": You have confessed your parents, your youth, your school, your salary, your self-esteem, and, alas, your future.

5   Now, I do not know what white Americans would sound like if there had never been any black people in the United States, but they would not sound the way they sound. *Jazz*, for example, is a very specific sexual term, as in *jazz me, baby,* but white people purified it into the Jazz Age. *Sock it to me,* which means, roughly, the same thing, has been adopted by Nathaniel Hawthorne's descendants with no qualms or hesitations at all, along with *let it all hang out* and *right on! Beat to his socks,* which was once the black's most total and despairing image of poverty, was transformed into a thing called the Beat Generation, which phenomenon was, largely, composed of *uptight,* middle-class white people, imitating poverty, trying to *get down,* to get *with it,* doing their *thing,* doing their despairing best to be *funky,* which we, the blacks, never dreamed of doing—we *were* funky, baby, like *funk* was going out of style.

6   Now, no one can eat his cake, and have it, too, and it is late in the day to attempt to penalize black people for having created a language that permits

the nation its only glimpse of reality, a language without which the nation would be even more *whipped* than it is.

7   I say that this present skirmish is rooted in American history, and it is. Black English is the creation of the black diaspora. Blacks came to the United States chained to each other, but from different tribes: Neither could speak the other's language. If two black people, at that bitter hour of the world's history, had been able to speak to each other, the institution of chattel slavery could never have lasted as long as it did. Subsequently, the slave was given, under the eye, and the gun, of his master, Congo Square, and the Bible—or, in other words, and under these conditions, the slave began the formation of the black church, and it is within this unprecedented tabernacle that black English began to be formed. This was not, merely, as in the European example, the adoption of a foreign tongue, but an alchemy that transformed ancient elements into new language: *A language comes into existence by means of brutal necessity, and the rules of the language are dictated by what the language must convey.*

8   There was a moment, in time, and in this place, when my brother, or my mother, or my father, or my sister, had to convey to me, for example, the danger in which I was standing from the white man standing just behind me, and to convey this with a speed, and in a language, that the white man could not possibly understand, and that, indeed, he cannot understand, until today. He cannot afford to understand it. This understanding would reveal to him too much about himself, and smash that mirror before which he has been frozen for so long.

9   Now, if this passion, this skill, this (to quote Toni Morrison) "sheer intelligence," this incredible music, the mighty achievement of having brought a people utterly unknown to, or despised by "history"—to have brought this people to their present, troubled, troubling, and unassailable and unanswerable place—if this absolutely unprecedented journey does not indicate that black English is a language, I am curious to know what definition of language is to be trusted.

10   A people at the center of the Western world, and in the midst of so hostile a population, has not endured and transcended by means of what is patronizingly called a "dialect." We, the blacks, are in trouble, certainly, but we are not doomed, and we are not inarticulate because we are not compelled to defend a morality that we know to be a lie.

11   The brutal truth is that the bulk of the white people in America never had any interest in educating black people, except as this could serve white purposes. It is not the black child's language that is in question, it is not his language that is despised: It is his experience. A child cannot be taught by anyone who despises him, and a child cannot afford to be fooled. A child cannot be taught by anyone whose demand, essentially, is that the child repudiate his experience, and all that gives him sustenance, and enter a limbo in which he will no longer be black, and in which he knows that he can never become white. Black people have lost too many black children that way.

12   And, after all, finally, in a country with standards so untrustworthy, a country that makes heroes of so many criminal mediocrities, a country unable to face why so many of the nonwhite are in prison, or on the needle, or standing, futureless, in the streets—it may very well be that both the child, and his elder, have concluded that they have nothing whatever to learn from the people of a country that has managed to learn so little.

Reading-to-Write Questions

1. **Content:** What sweeping generalizations does Baldwin make? Why do you think he dares to make such statements?

2. **Arrangement:** How does Baldwin tie together the sentences in his next-to-last paragraph?

3. **Style:** A lover of language, Baldwin plays with words by repeating sounds (e.g., "the argument supposes itself to be posing") and by coordinating series of words (e.g., "my brother, or my mother, or my father, or my sister"). Can you find other examples?

4. _____
    _____
    _____

Suggested Topics

1. **Observation:** Baldwin offers an unconventional definition of "language," one not found in dictionaries or linguistics textbooks. Provide an unconventional definition of another term. (general audience)

2. **Critique:** Baldwin contends that language is a political instrument. If you agree, support Baldwin's position by identifying at least three political purposes of language. For additional support, see Toni Cade Bambara's statements in Traylor's essay. (audience = unsuspecting public)

3. **Synthesis:** Drawing upon Ellison's and Traylor's essays as well as Baldwin's, classify the ways in which Black English has contributed to mainstream American English or culture. Feel free to add examples from the Background Readings (e.g., Geneva Smitherman's *Black Talk*). (audience = people attending a panel discussion on Ebonics)

4. _____
    _____
    _____

Background Readings: BLACK ENGLISH

See the list of readings for Karen Webb's essay.

What's Wrong with Black English

Rachel Jones

In 1982, when Newsweek *published the follow-ing essay in its "My Turn" column, the writer, Rachel Jones was just a sophomore at Southern Illinois University. Since then, Jones has pursued a career in journalism, and the essay has appeared in countless anthologies. Throughout the essay, Jones attacks the notion of "talking white."*

---

1   William Labov, a noted linguist, once said about the use of black English, "It is the goal of most black Americans to acquire full control of the standard language without giving up their own culture." He also suggested that there are certain advantages to having two ways to express one's feelings. I wonder if the good doctor might also consider the goals of those black Americans who have full control of standard English but who are every now and then troubled by that colorful, grammar-to-the-winds patois that is black English. Case in point—me.

2   I'm a 21-year-old black born to a family that would probably be considered lower-middle class—which in my mind is a polite way of describing a condi-tion only slightly better than poverty. Let's just say we rarely if ever did the winter-vacation thing in the Caribbean. I've often had to defend my humble beginnings to a most unlikely group of people for an even less likely reason. Because of the way I talk, some of my black peers look at me sideways and ask, "Why do you talk like you're white?"

3   The first time it happened to me I was nine years old. Cornered in the school bathroom by the class bully and her sidekick, I was offered the opportunity to

swallow a few of my teeth unless I satisfactorily explained why I always got good grades, why I talked "proper" or "white." I had no ready answer for her, save the fact that my mother had from the time I was old enough to talk stressed the importance of reading and learning, or that L. Frank Baum and Ray Bradbury were my closest companions. I read all my older brothers' and sisters' literature textbooks more faithfully than they did, and even light-weights like the Bobbsey Twins and Trixie Belden were allowed into my book-ish inner circle. I don't remember exactly what I told those girls, but I somehow talked my way out of a beating.

4   **"White pipes."** I was reminded once again of my "white pipes" problem while apartment hunting in Evanston, Ill., last winter. I doggedly made out lists of available places and called all around. I would immediately be invited over—and immediately turned down. The thinly concealed looks of shock when the front door opened clued me in, along with the flustered instances of "just getting off the phone with the girl who was ahead of you and she wants the rooms." When I finally found a place to live, my roommate stirred up old memories when she remarked a few months later, "You know, I was surprised when I first saw you. You sounded white over the phone." Tell me another one, sister.

5   I should've asked her a question I've wanted an answer to for years: how does one "talk white"? The silly side of me pictures a rabid white foam spewing forth when I speak. I don't use Valley Girl jargon, so that's not what's meant in my case. Actually, I've pretty much deduced what people mean when they say that to me, and the implications are really frightening.

6   It means that I'm articulate and well-versed. It means that I can talk as freely about John Steinbeck as I can about Rick James. It means that "ain't" and "he be" are not staples of my vocabulary and are only used around family and friends. (It is almost Jekyll and Hyde-ish the way I can slip out of academic abstractions into a long, lean, double-negative-filled dialogue, but I've come to terms with that aspect of my personality.) As a child, I found it hard to believe that's what people meant by "talking proper"; that would've meant that good grades and standard English were equated with white skin, and that went against everything I'd ever been taught. Running into the same type of mentality as an adult has confirmed the depressing reality that for many blacks, standard English is not only unfamiliar, it is socially unacceptable.

7   James Baldwin once defended black English by saying it had added "vital-ity to the language," and even went so far as to label it a language in its own right, saying, "Language [i.e., black English] is a political instrument" and a "vivid and crucial key to identity." But did Malcolm X urge blacks to take power in this country "any way y'all can"? Did Martin Luther King, Jr. say to blacks, "I has been to the mountaintop, and I done seed the Promised Land"? Toni Morrison, Alice Walker and James Baldwin did not achieve their elo-quence, grace and stature by using only black English in their writing. Andrew Young, Tom Bradley and Barbara Jordan did not acquire political power by saying, "Y'all crazy if you ain't gon vote for me." They all have full

command of standard English, and I don't think that knowledge takes away from their blackness or commitment to black people.

8   **Soulful.** I know from experience that it's important for black people, stripped of culture and heritage, to have something they can point to and say, "This is ours, *we* can comprehend it, *we* alone can speak it with a soulful flourish." I'd be lying if I said that the rhythms of my people caught up in "some serious rap" don't sound natural and right to me sometimes. But how heartwarming is it for those same brothers when they hit the pavement searching for employment? Studies have proven that the use of ethnic dialects decreases power in the marketplace. "I be" is acceptable on the corner, but not with the boss.

9   Am I letting capitalistic, European-oriented thinking fog the issue? Am I selling out blacks to an ideal of assimilating, being as much like white as possible? I have not formed a personal political ideology, but I do know this: it hurts me to hear black children use black English, knowing that they will be at yet another disadvantage in an educational system already full of stumbling blocks. It hurts me to sit in lecture halls and hear fellow black students complain that the professor "be tripping dem out using big words dey can't understand." And what hurts most is to be stripped of my own blackness simply because I know my way around the English language.

10   I would have to disagree with Labov in one respect. My goal is not so much to acquire full control of both standard and black English, but to one day see more black people less dependent on a dialect that excludes them from full participation in the world we live in. I don't think I talk white; I think I talk right.

Reading-to-Write Questions

1. **Content:** What type of evidence does Jones cite to support her case? Where does she need to identify her source of evidence?

2. **Arrangement:** Why does Jones mention the linguist William Labov in her concluding paragraph?

3. **Style:** Where does Jones use the hyphen to coin adjectives?

4. _____

_____

_____

Suggested Topics

1. **Observation:** Ask your African American peers what the phrase "talk white" means. Then write an essay evaluating the various definitions of the phrase. (audience = your peers)

2. **Critique:** Jones defines Black English as a "colorful, grammar-to-the-winds patois." Do you accept her definition? Why or why not? (audience = Jones's readers)

3. **Synthesis:** Jones challenges statements from Baldwin's essay (see the preceding essay). How do you think Baldwin should have responded to her criticism? (audience = Jones)

4. _____

_____

_____

Background Readings: BLACK ENGLISH

See the reading list for Karen Webb's essay.

The Ubiquity of Ebonics
John Rickford

Born in Guyana, Stanford University linguist John Rickford has written extensively about dialects in the U.S. and Caribbean in books such as Dimensions of a Creole Continuum *and* Sociolinguistics and Pidgin Creole Studies. *Recently, he published* African American Vernacular English *and (with his journalist son Russell)* Spoken Soul: The Story of Black English, *winner of an American Book Award. The following article, published by father and son in the March/April 2001 issue of* American Language Review, *summarizes evidence from* Spoken Soul *and responds to the Oakland School Board's controversial proposal to use Ebonics to teach Standard English. After defining Ebonics, the article classifies the many uses of Ebonics in comedy, music, preaching, and literature.*

---

1   The recently released *Kings of Comedy* movie demonstrates among other things that Ebonics is alive, accepted and appreciated within the African American community, especially in informal interaction among blacks. The routines of the film's four stars (Cedric The Entertainer, Steve Harvey, D.L. Hughley, and Bernie Mac) certainly rely extensively on black vernacular language. And the overwhelmingly black on-screen North Carolina audience

seems to relish the Kings' Ebonics, as similar audiences did during the group's live performances elsewhere over the past two years.

2   Given the widespread denial and deprecation of Ebonics during the Oakland controversy of 1996, both the vitality of the vernacular and its positive reception might come as a surprise. But as we'll argue below, summarizing evidence from our recent book, *Spoken Soul*, Ebonics in one form or another has been actively used by Black comedians, writers, preachers, actors, singers, and everyday folk for ages. And recent public disparagement of black talk is only one side of a complex love-hate relationship that African Americans and others have had with it for ages too.

3   Before we go any further, however, we need to clarify what we mean by Ebonics, or what Claude Brown, author of *Manchild in the Promised Land,* called "Spoken Soul." Contrary to popular misconception, Ebonics is not synonymous with slang, the informal and usually short-lived word-usage most characteristic of teenagers and young adults (e.g., dope "very good" or ill "very bad"). The Kings in fact use relatively little slang, consistent with their self-proclaimed "old school" status. And while they do use four-letter words and their derivatives, this is definitely not a necessary nor a defining characteristic of Ebonics.

4   The more organic Ebonics features that these popular funnymen deploy are the distinctive vernacular pronunciations, grammatical features and rhetorical patterns found among virtually all age groups and most classes within the African American community.

5   Consider grammar. In the movie, the Kings mark tense and aspect, when and how events occur, with the tools of black talk. They place invariant *be* before verbs for frequent or habitual actions ("they songs *be* havin a cause"), and use *done* for completed actions ("you *done* missed it"), and *be done* for future perfect or hypothetical events ("Lightning *be done* struck my house"). And they frequently delete *is* and *are* in sentences where standard English requires it ("Tiger __ my cousin" . . . "We __ confrontational"). As Bernie Mac noted (although not in relation to these forms): "You talk this way ain' nothin to be ashamed of."

6   Some of these features are also found in the vernacular of whites and other ethnic groups, particularly in the South, where 90% of the Black population was concentrated until the early 20th century. But as extensive linguistic research has demonstrated, they are more common in the vernacular of blacks, particularly among the working and lower class.

7   Some features, like the deletion of *is* and *are,* are rarely if ever found in white vernacular usage, particularly outside the South. As D.L. Hughley commented in the movie, "We do things different." Where these features came from is still a matter of academic debate, but African, Caribbean and English sources have all contributed.

8   And contrary to public perception, Ebonics is governed by systematic rules and restrictions, unconsciously acquired and obeyed, as all natural languages are.

9   Are the Kings of Comedy unique in their use of Ebonics? Absolutely not. Comedians like Richard Pryor and Adele Givens and Chris Rock all draw on the vernacular, often to differentiate between blacks and whites, a recurrent theme in black comedy. Twentieth century icons like Sammy Davis, Moms Mabley and Dick Gregory all did too, as did old-timers like Bert Williams and George Walker (who began performing in the 1890s). Noting its ubiquity, in fact, Redd Foxx and Norma Miller included a chapter on "black street language" in their *Redd Foxx Encyclopedia of Black Humor* (1977).

10   The musical and verbal traditions of the Black experience are also replete with the sounds and structures of Spoken Soul. This may be most obvious in the newer genres, like hiphop, as in Grammy winner Lauryn Hill's 1998 *Lost Ones*: "... did you really gain from/What you done done, it—so silly, how come?" But in 1924, Ma Rainey's blues wailed in similar grammatical grooves ("See, See, Rider, see what you done done"). So too did the old spiritual that the Howard University choir intoned at their 1997 commencement ceremony ("Lord, I done done/I done done whatcha told me ta do") moments after keynote speaker Carole Simpson had bashed Ebonics.

11   Although African American ministers include some of the most accomplished manipulators of standard English, they invariably draw on Black rhetorical patterns in their sermons, as the Reverend Martin Luther King, Jr., often did, and as the Rev. Jesse Jackson still does. Moreover, as several studies have shown, Afro-Baptist and other preachers often use Black English to add realism and drama, especially at the peaks of their sermons. Celebrated Black writers too, have drawn extensively and creatively on the Black vernacular, from Paul Laurence Dunbar (1872–1906) through Langston Hughes (1902–1967) and Lorraine Hansberry (1930–1965) to contemporaries Sonia Sanchez (b. 1934) and August Wilson (b. 1945). Some novelists, among them Alice Walker and John Widemann, have used Ebonics not just in dialogue, but in narrative text.

12   Black writers have also been among the staunchest defenders and aficionados of Black English. James Baldwin called it "this passion, this skill, this incredible music," Toni Morrison insisted that there were certain things she could not say "without recourse to my language," and June Jordan praised its "life, voice and clarity."

13   As these last comments show, it is definitely not the case that African Americans always deny and disdain what is for most of them their mother tongue. So why did the nation greet Ebonics with such vitriol and hilarity during the controversy of 1996/1997?

14   Perhaps because of the general misconception that the Oakland School Board intended to teach and accept Ebonics in the classroom. Most of the fuming and fulminating about Ebonics stemmed from the mistaken belief that it was to replace Standard English as a medium of instruction and a target for success. Actually, the Board agreed with virtually everyone else in America that their students should master mainstream English, Standard English or whatever you want to call the variety of English needed for school, formal occasions, and success in the world of work.

15   The real disagreement was about the means. The School Board's plan was to improve the teaching of the standard variety through systematic comparison and contrast with the vernacular. There is good research evidence for this approach, though the Board cited none of it. The conventional approach, favored by most Americans despite overwhelming evidence of its limitations, is to elevate and teach the standard by disparaging and trying to stamp out the vernacular.

16   But we are not convinced that African Americans want to abandon "down-home" speech and become one-dimensional mainstream speakers. Even Maya Angelou, who said in 1996 that she was "incensed" by the Ebonics resolution, has used Ebonics creatively in her poems (e.g., "The Thirteens" and "The Pusher"). And Bill Cosby, who contemptuously referred to "Igno-Ebonics" has crafted his comedic routines with soul talk (e.g., in "The Lower Tract"). Their strong negative reactions, we believe, were largely the result of their fear that students would be restricted to the vernacular.

17   Over a hundred years ago, James Weldon Johnson, who wrote the black national anthem ("Lift Every Voice and Sing") argued with his friend Paul Laurence Dunbar about the limitations of black dialect as an expressive instrument. But he had written masterful dialect poems himself (e.g. "Sence You Went Away," 1900). Johnson's love-hate relationship with the vernacular is just one manifestation of the dual consciousness ("Two souls . . . two warring ideals in one dark body") that W.E.B. DuBois identified in 1903 as a characteristic of being black in America.

18   Judging from America's wholesale consumption and enjoyment of black comedy, music and literature that is born and bred of Spoken Soul, we are not convinced that whites and other ethnic groups want to see Ebonics abandoned either, quiet as that viewpoint is kept. Certainly it is not necessary to abandon Spoken Soul to master Standard English, any more than it is necessary to abandon English to learn French, or to deprecate jazz to appreciate classical music.

19   Moreover, suggesting, as some do, that we abandon Spoken Soul and cleave only to Standard English is like proposing that we play only the white keys of a piano. The fact is that for many of our most beautiful melodies, we need both the white keys and the black. What really strikes us about the Kings of Comedy, and the other comedians, writers, singers and preachers whom we've cited in this column, is their ability to command and switch seamlessly between Spoken Soul and Standard English.

20   Developing that dynamic bi-dialecticism in young African Americans is what Oakland was essentially proposing (albeit unclearly) in 1996. It remains an achievable and laudable goal.

Reading-to-Write Questions

1. **Content:** Circle the names of all the celebrities that Rickford and Rickford cite. Do they cite enough to persuade you that Ebonics is ubiquitous?

2. **Arrangement:** Where do Rickford and Rickford adopt a classification strategy to organize their evidence?

3. **Style:** Where do Rickford and Rickford employ alliteration?

4. _____

    _____

    _____

Suggested Topics

1. **Observation:** Choose ONE of the categories (comedy, music, or literature) that Rickford and Rickford mention. Then find more examples to illustrate the role of Ebonics within that category. (audience = readers of *American Language Review*)

2. **Critique:** Rickford and Rickford believe that African Americans should not "abandon Spoken Soul and cleave only to Standard English." Do you agree? (audience = elementary schoolteachers)

3. **Synthesis:** Classify reactions to the Oakland School Board controversy, drawing upon views from Rickford and Rickford's, Barras's, and Hutchinson's essays. Then state and defend your position. (audience = Oakland School Board)

4. _____

    _____

    _____

Background Readings: BLACK ENGLISH AND SCHOOLING

See the reading list for Barras's essay.

The Fallacy of Talkin' Black
Earl Ofari Hutchinson

Syndicated columnist, political analyst, and host of a call-in radio show, Earl Ofari Hutchinson has written a shelf of books about Black America, among them The Myth of Black Capitalism, The Mugging of Black America, Black Fatherhood, *and* Blacks and Reds: Race and Class in Conflict. *Naturally, then, in 1996, when the Oakland Board of Education recognized Black English as a language, their proclamation triggered an immediate response from Hutchinson in the* San Francisco Chronicle *and, later, in the following essay. This essay appeared in Hutchinson's ninth book,* The Crisis in Black and Black *in 1998. Point by point throughout the essay, Hutchinson critiques the Board's resolutions, contrasting his views with those of Ebonics advocates.*

---

1   I was dumbstruck when I heard that the Oakland Board of Education in December 1996, voted to recognize "Black English" as a second language. I thought the debate over the use of "Black English" had pretty much died a merciful death years ago. At the height of the "black is beautiful" movement during the 1960s, it was fashionable for black militants to proudly boast that

335

when blacks "talked black," the so-called language of the ghetto, they were rejecting the white man's culture and rebelling against white authority.[1]

2   Many blacks who spoke the standard English were taunted for trying to "act white." Many black writers went through deft acrobatic circus hoops in articles trying to defend the legitimacy of "Black English." Blacks were told that this way of speaking was a survival of their African past and they should take pride in it. During the 1980s, they redubbed "Black English" with a new name, Ebonics (ebony and phonics), declared it a separate language, and demanded that educators recognize and include it in their school district's curriculum.[2]

3   The supporters of Ebonics are certainly right to criticize those teachers and school administrators that view black students who speak in an unconventional dialect as hopeless dunces who cannot be educated. This is condescension at best, and racism at worst. The humbug that blacks cannot learn like whites became a dim-witted self-fulfilling prophecy that put many black students at educational risk. The blacks that spoke this way were not dumber than whites. They simply picked up this pattern of speech in their home or from their peers on the streets.

4   However, the converts to and advocates of Ebonics still relied on a dangerous stew of stereotypes and educational as well as cultural misassumptions about blacks. They erroneously believe that most blacks communicate in the same unconventional dialect. In its resolution, the Oakland School Board repeatedly called it "the predominantly primary language" of blacks. Some black leaders even made the ridiculous and stereotypical assertion that many blacks learn this kind of talk in the home and on the streets. Many do not. There is no such thing as uniform "black talk." Blacks, as do other ethnic groups, use the full range of tones, inflections, and accents in their speech depending on their education, family background, and the region where they live.

5   Some young blacks, heavily influenced by rap, hip-hop culture, slang, and street talk, mispronounce words, misplace verb tenses, or "code switch" when they talk to each other. Many young whites, Latinos, and Asians do the same. There is no conclusive proof that "Black English," as some blacks and linguists assert, has a separate syntax, grammar, and structure that fulfill all the requirements of a separate language.

6   Some black writers and educators have gone through more tortured gyrations trying to make the case that this type of speech is a cultural survival of African linguistic and speech patterns. All the African slaves did not come from the same region, belong to the same ethnic group, share the same culture, or speak the same language. There are more than 1,000 ethnic groups in the 52 nations on the African continent. They speak hundreds of languages, and

---

[1]*Oakland Post*, December 12, p. 1.

[2]Hutchinson, "How 'Talking White' Spurred Ebonics," *San Francisco Chronicle*, December 30, 1996, p. 20.

there are thousands of regional dialects and linguistic influences. Long before the European slavers began their systematic decimation of African populations, Arabic heavily influenced many of those languages and dialects. Despite this, some Ebonics advocates even make the absurd claim that 80 percent of blacks speak "Black English."[3]

7   The Oakland School Board went much further and proclaimed "black speak" a direct derivative of West and Central African language systems—Niger-Congo languages. It sounded plausible to some. The majority of black slaves in North America did come from West and Central Africa. Some linguists agree that the Niger-Congo languages were the languages spoken throughout the region. Other linguists and Africa experts, however, have repeatedly pointed out that this is not a unitary language but a widely differentiated grouping of languages that have evolved so distinctly apart over thousands of years that many of the words, meanings, and sounds within this language grouping are totally different from each other.[4]

8   Even if it was one language, four hundred years of black acculturation in America has effectively washed out most traces of African linguistic patterns and cultural traditions. The Oakland School Board and Ebonics advocates ignored all this. They gave conflicting and muddled definitions of what they consider "Black English" and completely disregarded the class background and educational deficiencies that more likely explain why some blacks say: "He *be* going to the store," rather than "He is going to the store."[5]

9   Ebonics advocates make the dubious claim that devising new teaching methods based on Ebonics will help black students learn standard English easier. The Oakland School Board zoomed to the outer limits of inaneness by claiming that black students were doomed to fail in school unless they were "instructed" in English and their primary language (that is, Ebonics). It even made the fantastic boast that an Ebonics program would instantly "remedy" the supposedly chronic below standard test scores of black students in English.

10   Before the mass outcry forced the Oakland school officials within days to back pedal fast from the original line, they were apparently prepared to squander time and pirate money from other underfunded programs in a desperate attempt to prove that their learning theory works.

11   There is absolutely no evidence to support any of this. The Ebonics advocates base their shaky case on patchy and inconclusive studies on other language

---

[3]John Iliffe, *Africans: The History of a Continent* (London: Cambridge University Press, 1995).

[4]Roger Westcott, "African Languages and Prehistory" in Creighton Gabel and Norman R. Bennett, eds., *Reconstructing African Cultural History* (Boston: Boston University Press, 1967), pp. 45–55; Roland Oliver and J. D. Fage, *A Short History of Africa* (New York: Facts on File, 1988), pp. 17–18; "Should Black English Be Considered a Second Language?," *Jet*, January 27, 1997, p. 1216.

[5]*Los Angeles Times*, May 6, 1997, p. 1.

groups, mainly those who speak Spanish and Chinese. For several years the Los Angeles Unified School District has had a program of "special language" instruction for black and non-white students. Beyond a few anecdotal success stories, teachers and administrators have produced no measured evidence that this program has boosted the student's verbal achievement.

12   This points to one of the most gaping instances of sightlessness of the Ebonic advocates. They presume that blacks are chronic educational failures. They are not. Over eighty percent of blacks graduated from high school and nearly 35 percent were enrolled in college in 1996. In 1994, four young African-American males were awarded Rhodes Scholarships, and 300,000 young black high schoolers competed nationwide in the annual NAACP Academic, Cultural, Technological and Scientific Olympics (ACT-SO) competition. In 1995 and 1996, more African Americans grabbed the Rhodes honors.[6]

13   The Ebonics advocates also do not explain how generations of black students, like white students, mastered standard English without their teachers approaching the subject as a foreign or incomprehensible language. The answer is simple. These students were taught by teachers who were dedicated and determined that they excel in their studies. They held black students to the same educational standards and accountability as whites and in many cases they got solid results.

14   In spite of the voguish claim that black students fail because standard English is supposedly so alien to them, educators who have devised these programs during the 1980s and 1990s have proven this is a fraud: the Accelerated Schools Program, the Comer School Development Program, the Higher Order Thinking Skills Program, the IBM Writing to Read Program, the National Urban Alliance's Cognition and Comprehensive Program, Reading Recovery, the School-Based Instructional Leadership Program, and Success for All.[7]

15   These programs have had modest to spectacular success in raising the reading and achievement level of many black students. Their approaches are different but they have several things in common. They challenge students to learn, set specific goals, demand active participation of the students (and in most cases the parents), emphasize clarity of assignments, give positive and constant direction to the students, and continually monitor their progress.

16   The cruel irony is that if a white group had called blacks educational defectives and demanded that they be stacked in special programs because they cannot learn or speak standard English, they would be loudly denounced as racists. Yet whites did not make that demand. Blacks did, and they must bear a small part of the blame for hardening the suspicions of many whites that blacks are mentally inferior or social misfits who need costly and time con-

---

[6]Glen Lowry, "Blind Ignorance," *Emerge*, December 1996–January 1997, p. 65.

[7]Daniel U. Levine, "Instructional Approaches That Can Improve the Academic Performance of African-American Students," *Journal of Negro Education*, 63, Winter 1994, pp. 46–63.

suming special aids, texts, training, and remedial programs to learn. This could make even more employers believe that blacks are unstable, uncooperative, dishonest, uneducated, crime-prone, and not fit to be hired.

17   The Ebonics advocates certainly cannot be incriminated for the social and educational plight of many African Americans. This happened long before they came along. That is what made the debate over Ebonics even more heartbreaking.

18   *A final comment:* Black leaders, educators, and parents should demand quality education and greater funding for teacher training programs. They should insist that teachers and school administrators recognize, accept, and respect cultural diversity among students, and adhere to the highest educational standards in predominantly minority school districts. To argue or imply that most, many, or even all, black students cannot master standard English without a radical racially divisive overhaul of the educational system is not only a slavish bow to fringe Afrocentrism and political correctness, it is a flat-out fallacy.

19   *A happy note:* **On May 5, 1997, the Oakland school board finally came to its senses and approved a workable plan to improve the district's reading levels. It did not include Ebonics.[8]**

---

[8]*Los Angeles Times*, May 6, 1997, p. 1.

Reading-to-Write Questions

1. **Content:** Since Hutchinson is not a linguist or educational researcher, how does he attempt to buttress his claims?

2. **Arrangement:** How does Hutchinson organize this essay? In other words, before he makes a point, what does he do?

3. **Style:** Notice Hutchinson's word choice when he refers to the Oakland School Board? Which words best express his attitude?

4. _____

   _____

   _____

Suggested Topics

1. **Observation:** Go to the Linguist List of Eastern Michigan University (http://linguist.emich.edu/topics/ebonics) to read the Oakland School Board's resolutions. Then write your own summary of the Board's position. (audience = your class)

2. **Critique:** Hutchinson insists, "There is no conclusive proof that 'Black English,' as some blacks and linguists assert, has a separate syntax, grammar, and structure that fulfill all the requirements of a separate language." Has Hutchinson used the linguistic terms accurately? (See Webb's essay for help.)

3. **Synthesis:** Weave together Barras's, Jones's, and Hutchinson's arguments and contrast them with a combination of Rickford and Rickford's, Webb's, and Smitherman's. Then offer your own conclusions. (audience = high school English teachers)

4. _____

   _____

   _____

Background Readings: BLACK ENGLISH AND SCHOOLING

See the reading list for Barras's essay.

The Trouble with Ebonics
Jonetta Rose Barras

*As a newspaper columnist and author, Jonetta Rose Barras has written about a wide range of issues affecting Black Americans—from the role of Black leaders (*The Last of the Black Emperors*) to the role of Black fathers (*Whatever Happened to Daddy's Little Girl?*) The following commentary appeared in the* Washington Times *on January 3, 1997, in the midst of a national controversy about the role of Ebonics in education. Entering the fray, Barras offers her own perspective, recalling how she learned Standard English in school. In her opinion, Black English should be classified as a dialect, rather than a language.*

---

1   Oh Jesse. How you disappoint. Just when I thought you were a changed man, you change again.

2   Last month the Rev. Jesse Jackson was one of the first African-Americans to publicly admonish the Oakland, California school board for voting to consider "Ebonics" a separate language and for approving a plan to instruct teachers in the fine art of using the unconjugated form of the verb "to be," dropping consonant endings, and exchanging "th" for "d." The board and others suggest that if teachers learn "Ebonics"—a neologism that combines Ebony and phonics—they could better reach African-American students who score poorly in reading and other basic subjects. Mr. Jackson called the school board's action an "unacceptable surrender, bordering on disgrace."

3   I was excited by his departure from what would have been his standard line of "if it's black it's good" or "if black folks advocate it, it must be all right."

4   But within a few days, he reversed himself, saying, "They're not trying to teach black English as a standard language. They're looking for tools to teach children standard English, so they might be competitive." Mr. Jackson's reversal is unfortunate.

5   First, most Americans do not speak standard English—just ask the British. We all already speak a dialect; I call it "Americanese." Like the country, American English is an amalgam of dialects from around the world—words we have taken and twisted the pronunciation of, augmented the original meaning of, or simply played with to make our own.

6   Still, there are other unique dialects or patois spoken in this country that have very little to do with color, and certainly nothing to do with slave origins. Some linguists argue that each has its own distinctive pattern. For example, many Appalachians speak a dialect, and certainly no one can deny that many black and white rural Southerners speak a dialect—all their own. I am not talking accents here; I know the difference.

7   Targeting only the dialect spoken by urban blacks in some ways is discriminatory. And to accord language status only to that dialect ignores the inherent value of other dialects. Advancing Ebonics as a separate language egregiously ignores the reality of America. To be sure, ours is a Creolized culture.

8   The issue that seems to be lost on the Oakland school board—and nearly everyone who has weighed in on the topic—is this: The retention of a dialect other than "American English or Americanese" often is based on class. Yes, my friends, in capitalistic America, money still talks. Poor whites, blacks and Hispanics often retain their dialects because most don't have access to sufficient resources or educational experiences to alter their reality and thus, their language.

9   Most don't have substantial in-home libraries, which as we all know help build vocabularies. Many never get tickets, season or otherwise, to the Opera, or the Symphony—even when Bobby McFerrin guest conducts. And hardly any have the opportunity to witness any live drama or see any dance performance—even of the national ballet company of Senegal.

10   Those of us who made it out of public housing projects or the ghettos—as some call poor neighborhoods—did so not because some school board declared the dialect we spoke a separate language, but because some adult took the time to transport our minds and bodies past the boundaries of our limited experiences. I can directly attribute my rise to Ara Dozier, who didn't wait for some school board or some college professor working on a doctoral dissertation and looking for tenure to explain to her what I and others were saying. She worked around us, listened to us, and sometimes even visited our homes and communities.

11   She knew what we meant. She knew how to correct us, and she wasn't intimidated by the way we looked, wore our hair or dressed our young bodies. She stepped right up and said, I think you mean "I am not" instead of "I

ain't." She also made it clear the verb "to be" was not an unconjugated crutch, dropped in sentences on a whim.

12   While it is noble that some want to recognize the language some of us in the 'hood speak, this Ebonics stuff is mostly poppycock.

13   If some of our middle- and upper-class teachers hadn't stepped so far away from the students whose lives they are expected to guide, they wouldn't need some high-priced consultant to assist them in hearing and understanding the cry for help coming from the mouths of inner-city youth. They also would understand it will take more than a properly spoken, constructed, and expertly diagrammed sentence to reach the poor young people in Oakland or any other urban school. It takes more time, more commitment, more imagination, and a lot more love, which all seem to be in short supply these days.

14   With all due respect to Mr. Jackson and the Oakland school board, it seems that their late discovery of Ebonics and its proposed use is yet another hair-brained scheme to either extort money from governments and corporations; or another ploy to camouflage their continued failure to properly and adequately educate the young charges in their care. The Oakland school board, teachers, journalists, Mr. Jackson, and others with a newly compelling need to study dialect might search the Library of Congress, where volumes of first person slave narratives await discovery; the dialect-starved can pig out.

15   Children from low-income, working-class or poor families already face enormous obstacles in their struggle to obtain access to an unfamiliar world and become successful citizens. They don't need adults with fancy or exotic-sounding neologisms adding to their troubles.

Reading-to-Write Questions

1. **Content:** Notice how Barras has incorporated a personal anecdote in her essay. Does the anecdote drive home her point? Or could it also lend support to the Oakland School Board?

2. **Arrangement:** Why does Barras open her column with a lengthy summary before stating her position on Ebonics?

3. **Style:** At times Barras adopts a sarcastic tone. Underline the words that convey her sarcasm.

4. _____

    _____

    _____

Suggested Topics

1. **Observation:** Classify the dialects spoken on your campus or in your hometown. (audience = interested classmates)

2. **Critique:** Barras insists that "most Americans do not speak standard English." Summarize and respond to this part of her argument. (audience = readers of the letters to the editor of the *Washington Times*)

3. **Synthesis:** According to Barras, Baldwin, and Raspberry, African American children encounter different types of obstacles on the road to mastery of Standard English: socioeconomic isolation, white hatred, and a distorted sense of "blackness." Citing these authors, describe the three obstacles. (audience = undergraduate education majors)

4. _____

    _____

    _____

Background Readings: BLACK ENGLISH AND SCHOOLING

Adger, Carolyn Temple, Donna Christian, and Orlando Taylor. *Making the Connection: Language and Academic Achievement among African American Students*. Washington, DC: Center for Applied Linguistics & Delta Systems, 1999.

Balester, Valerie M. *Cultural Divide: A Study of African American College-Level Writers*. Portsmouth, NH: Boynton/Cook, 1993.

Baugh, John. *Out of the Mouths of Slaves: African American Language and Educational Malpractice*. Austin: University of Texas Press, 1999.

Brooks, Charlotte, ed. *Tapping Potential: English and Language Arts for the Black Learner*. Urbana, IL: NCTE, 1985.

Conference on College Composition & Communication. *Students' Right to Their Own Language*. Special Issue, 25 (1974).

Gilyard, Keith. *Let's Flip the Script: An African American Discourse on Language, Literature and Learning*. Detroit: Wayne State UP, 1996.

Perry, Theresa, and Lisa Delpit. *The Real Ebonics Debate: Power, Language, and the Education of African-American Children*. Boston: Beacon, 1998.

Rickford, John. *African American Vernacular English: Features, Evolution, Educational Implications*. Malden, MA: Blackwell Publishers, 1999.

_____, and Russell Rickford. *Spoken Soul: The Story of Black English*. New York: Wiley, 2000.

Smitherman, Geneva. *Talkin' That Talk: Language, Culture, and Education in African America*. London: Routledge, 2000.

Taylor, H. *Standard English, Black English, and Bidialectalism: A Controversy*. New York: P. Lang, 1989.

Van Keulen, Jean, Gloria Weddington, and Charles De Bose. *Speech, Language, Learning and the African American Child*. Boston: Allyn & Bacon, 1998.

Recommended Literature: Keith Gilyard, *Voices of the Self* (autobiography)

Black English: The Counter Narrative of Toni Cade Bambara
Eleanor Traylor

*Literary critic, professor, actress—Eleanor Tray-
lor has devoted her life to the arts and humanities in the U.S. and abroad. She has produced
countless chapters, articles, papers, and books,
including* The Humanities and Afro-American
Literary Tradition *and* Broad Sympathy: The
Howard University Oral Traditions Reader. *In
the following paper, delivered at the December
1996 meeting of the Modern Language Association, she celebrates and elucidates the language
of fiction writer Toni Cade Bambara. Bambara,
Traylor declares, countered the many misclassi-
fications of Black English by constructing a fictional universe "where language . . . loves itself."*

Old Wife: *I'ma get my walkin shoes soon, Min, cause them haints fixing to beat on
them drums with them cat bones and raise a rukus. So you just leave me
here and I'll talk to you after while. I can't stand all that commotion them
haints calling music . . . (The Salt Eaters 62)*

Min: *Old wife, what are you but a haint?*

Old Wife: *I'm a servant of the Lord, beggin your pardon.*

Min: *I know that. But you a haint. You dead ain't you?*

Old Wife: There is no death in spirit, Min, I keep tellin you [that]. Why you so hard
             headed? (SE 62)

> You [just] rip them fancy clothes off, Min, and
> thrash out into them waters, churn up all them
> bones we dropped from the old ships, churn up all
> that brine from the salty deep where our tears
> sank, and you grab them chirren by the neck and
> bop'm a good one and drag'm on back to shore and
> fling'm down and jump to it, pumping and cussing,
> fussing and cracking they ribs if ya have to to
> let'm live, Min. Cause love won't let you let'm go.
> (SE 62)

1   A sense of the wonderful—the pervasive atmosphere—informing the fictional universe of Toni Cade Bambara is achieved through a language alive with self-confidence as it invents

> ... new possibilities in formation
> new configurations to move with ... (SE 293)
> the need for legend and fable,
> for the extraordinary so big,
> the courage to pursue ... (SE 268)

It is ever alert to and adept at testing its own trustworthiness:

> ... The dream is real, my friends.
> The failure to make it work is the unreality ... (SE 126)
> It requires "exacting ceremonies," Min. (145)

It points to the way it has forever existed as music, lore, saga, poetry, oratory, rhetoric; as a core of ideas and beliefs and values and literature (*Black English* 81) and humor and fun. It is the instrument of creation itself:

> ... And God said,
> I believe I'll make me a world ...
> And God said: That's good! (Johnson 17)

It signals pride when it records its transitions as it defied and continues to defy the muzzle since the time when it said,

> ... I must navigate my way through circumstance
> that will otherwise destroy me. (Equiano et passim)
>
> ... I set out with a firm purpose to learn.
> (Douglass 275)

It expresses impish glee when it recalls its willfulness—its vulnerable though intrepid impulse to fly in the face of conventional wisdom in order to insure posterity:

> *. . . Come down off dat gate post, you little sow,*
> *lookin' dem white folks dead in dey eye, dey gon*
> *lynch you yet, git in dis house. You hear me?*
> *(Hurston)*

2   Loving its amazing powers, this language connects two interacting worlds: *Aye* (the tangible and visible world of living beings) and *Orun* (its invisible companion, the ever present otherworld of spirits, ancestors, gods.) It conflates tenses to sound in a present moment the voices of the past and the prescient voices of the yet unborn. This language is "clairvoyant, clairfeelant, clairaudient, and clairdoent" (*SE et passim*). It is the stubborn, enduring, deeply textured language of Toni Cade Bambara, alias T.C.B., alias the swamp hag, alias the loa of the yellow flowers, alias Miz Hazel, alias the "she" who with her "Afrafemcentric"—co-conspirator—"shes" of literature and of film creates a language called *she:*

> *She [had] learned to read the auras of trees and*
> *stones and plants and neighbors . . . And studied*
> *the sun's corona, the jagged petals of magnetic*
> *colors . . . And then the threads that shimmered*
> *between wooden tables and flowers and children*
> *and candles and birds . . . She could dance their*
> *dance and match their beat and echo their pitch*
> *and know their frequency as if her own . . . She*
> *knew each way of being in the world and could*
> *welcome them home again open to wholeness.*
> *(SE 48)*

3   This she-language, confident of its self-chosen, life-saving, life-enhancing, corrective, and healing purpose understands everything there is to know about the arbitrariness of signs. The questions it asks are these: who is controlling the sign? Is some glib and hypocritical HUNCa Bubba or some mean-spirited self-deprecating Miz Turner breaking the heart of Little Hazel Elizabeth Deborah Parker or Little Luther—dashing their dreams and aspirations by wielding a sign reading grown-up-common-sense-wisdom: the ability to "mis-inform, mis-direct, smoke-out, screen out, black-out, confound, contain, intimidate?" (*BE* 78) Are the children of "Bovanne's" Miz Hazel under the sign of "we hipper than you" refusing "home-tongue proficiency" (*BE* 78) in favor of some "unattached," "unobliged," "psychically immature, spiritually impoverished, and intellectually undisciplined" (*SE* 133) hype?

4   These and similar questions regarding the nature of language had received by 1972 a stunning and rigorous response from Toni Cade Bambara in an essay called "Black English" published by *The Black Child Development Institute* in a collection called *Curriculum Approaches from a Black Perspective.* In that essay, she corroborates James Baldwin, following Max Weinreich's observation that people who raise powerful armies are said to speak a language; those who do

not are said to speak a dialect. Many premises of twentieth century linguistics and semantics, of course, support this observation, but two in particular are the focus of Bambara's "Black English." One is that, in her words, "language is the single most important political institution in a culture" (78). The other is that language, as W.E.B. DuBois and other scholars laying the foundation for more recent thinkers knew it, is "a political institution that functions in the interest of the ruling class" (78). As she reminds us, the political way of looking at and speaking about language is "not the way schools approach language" (78). She continues:

> In school, we have focused on how language operates as grammar, diction, vocabulary. We have focused on language as noun (namer) not on what or who is named or on who is doing the naming; we have focused on language as verb (generator of action or situation of being) not on what kind of action is being generated or on who or what is situated in what kind of state of being. In schools we do not emphasize the real function of language in our lives: how it operates in courts, in hospitals, in schools, in the media, how it operates to perpetuate a society, maintain a social order, to reflect biases, to transmit basic values. In schools we focus on vocabulary, diction and grammar, but not on the implications of words, not on the use to which words are put. (*BE* 78)

5   In her essay, she raises the question being aired in the National Media today: "What is Black English anyway?" (77) She muses: Is it "ghettoese, a sloppy variation of proper speech" . . . is it what many teachers, Black and non-Black describe it to be, slang, profanity; a language that demonstrates the intellectual deficiencies of Black folks, or that demonstrates perhaps sheer perversity on the part of the student . . . is it, as some parents describe it, "something shameful, disgraceful, the language of low-life, unambitious folk?" . . . or "among the pedagogues," ". . . those who get their Ph.D.'s hustling Black stuff—there is the notion that the whole issue can be summed up" [in a question]: "Are Black students bidialectal or bilingual? Bidialectal meaning that the language of the home is a variation of a standard. Bilingual meaning that Black English is a language . . . *foreign*, perhaps" (*BE* 77).

Old wife: It won the Nobel, didn't it, Min. Whatever dey call dem prizes.

Min: Please, old wife, remember that you are a haint.

Old Wife: Min, your brain is a sieve. I told you ain't no death. You just pull off dat red suit and bop em.

mother tongue   *351*

6   Black English, continues Miss Bambara, "The language of our music, poetry," stories, intellectual discourses "has been maintained through the usual methods, by traditional use. It has been kept alive by our caretakers and custodians—our writers, and teachers, and singers. It is reinforced by ideological maintenance where there is a cultural aggression on our language (which has nothing to do with illiteracy of any kind). This language has persisted at great odds," she says (*BE* 83).

7   In her short fictions, collected in *Gorilla My Love* (1972), the *Sea Scabirds Are Still Alive* (1977), in *The Salt Eaters* (1980), her novel, and in the stories collected in *Deep Sightings and Rescue Missions* just published by Louis Messiah and Toni Morrison, Toni Cade Bambara perfects a narrative mode and appropriates a language which writes against the language of another narrative mode. That other has been suggested by Toni Morrison and my students as a *master narrative*, a school, an overwhelming volume of literature, theory, argument, hypothesis and accepted belief. It is a school which, finally, betrays, abandons the teacher and plunges the student into the void of homelessness.

8   Countering this school, the language of Toni Cade Bambara constructs a universe of intelligence where foolishness—a fateful handicap—is laughed to derision; this narrative universe is a place where language—in the creation of "broad sympathy, a knowledge of the world that was and is and the relation of all of us to it," as W.E.B. DuBois put it,—loves itself. It is this language with its host of contributors that Miss Bambara calls *Black English*.

Works Cited

Bambara, Toni Cade. "Black English." *Curriculum Approaches from a Black Perspective*. Atlanta: Black Child Development Institute, 1972.

_____. *The Salt Eaters*. New York: Vintage, 1992.

Douglass, Frederick. *Narrative of the Life of Frederick Douglass, an American Slave, The Classic Slave Narratives*. Ed. Henry Louis Gates, Jr. New York: Penguin, 1987.

Equiano, Olaudah. *The Interesting Narrative of the Life of Olaudah Equiano, or Gustavus Vassa, the African. The Classic Slave Narratives*. Ed. Henry Louis Gates, Jr. New York: Penguin, 1987.

Hurston, Zora Neale. *Dust Tracks on a Road, an Autobiography*. 1st. ed. Philadelphia: Lippincott, 1942.

Johnson, James Weldon, "Creation." *God's Trombones*. New York: Viking, 1927.

Reading-to-Write Questions

1. **Content:** Since Traylor's essay extols Bambara's language, the essay itself is—quite appropriately—saturated with Bambara's voice. Using a colored marker, highlight Bambara's words, noticing how Traylor merges Bambara's words with her own in the same sentence.

2. **Arrangement:** How does Traylor tie together the series of examples following the opening scene?

3. **Style:** Traylor's essay vibrates with vigorous verbs. Underline ten.

4. _____

   _____

   _____

Suggested Topics

1. **Observation:** Traylor describes Bambara's language as "a language gloriously in love with itself." Can you find more examples in this anthology of language that loves itself? Can you find examples—in other college texts, the media, official documents, and ads—of language that hates itself? Or language that does not care about itself? Write about your findings, citing examples in each of the language categories. (audience = class)

2. **Critique:** Traylor quotes Bambara's claim "In schools we do not emphasize the real function of language in our lives." Do you agree with Bambara's statement? To support or challenge it, discuss three "real" or "unreal" functions of language in schools. (audience = teachers)

3. **Synthesis:** Bambara identifies Black English as the language of African American music, poetry, and fiction. Drawing upon Traylor's examples as well as Webb's, Smitherman's, Rickford and Rickford's, and Dyson's, illustrate the role of Black English in each of these categories. (audience = European Internet correspondents)

4. _____

   _____

   _____

Background Readings: BLACK ENGLISH

See the reading list for Karen Webb's essay.

The Politics of Language
Ngugi wa Thiong'o

Bidding "farewell to English as a vehicle" for his writing, Kenyan author Ngugi wa Thiong'o delivered this lecture at Auckland University in New Zealand in a series entitled Decolonizing the Mind: The Politics of Language in African Literature *(1986). By that time he had become one of Africa's most respected literary figures, composing novels such as* Weep Not, Child *and plays such as* The Black Hermit—*in English. Now, having decided to write in his native Gikuyu and Kiswahili, in this portion of the lecture, he analyzes the effects of writing in English, the colonizer's language. In the process, he distinguishes between language as communication and language as culture, dividing each into three parts.*

———————

1   Language, any language, has a dual character: it is both a means of communication and a carrier of culture. Take English. It is spoken in Britain and in Sweden and Denmark. But for Swedish and Danish people English is only a means of communication with non-Scandinavians. It is not a carrier of their culture. For the British, and particularly the English, it is additionally, and inseparably from its use as a tool of communication, a carrier of their culture and history. Or take Swahili in East and Central Africa. It is widely used as a means of communication across many nationalities. But it is not the carrier of

a culture and history of many of those nationalities. However, in parts of Kenya and Tanzania, and particularly in Zanzibar, Swahili is inseparably both a means of communication and a carrier of the culture of those people to whom it is a mother-tongue.

2   Language as communication has three aspects or elements. There is first what Karl Marx once called the language of real life, the element basic to the whole notion of language, its origins and development: that is, the relations people enter into with one another in the labour process, the links they necessarily establish among themselves in the act of a people, a community of human beings, producing wealth or means of life like food, clothing, houses. A human community really starts its historical being as a community of co-operation in production through the division of labour; the simplest is between man, woman and child within a household; the more complex divisions are between branches of production such as those who are sole hunters, sole gatherers of fruits or sole workers in metal. Then there are the most complex divisions such as those in modern factories where a single product, say a shirt or a shoe, is the result of many hands and minds. Production is co-operation, is communication, is language, is expression of a relaxation between human beings and it is specifically human.

3   The second aspect of language as communication is speech and it imitates the language of real life, that is communication in production. The verbal signposts both reflect and aid communication or the relations established between human beings in the production of their means of life. Language as a system of verbal signposts makes that production possible. The spoken word is to relations between human beings what the hand is to the relations between human beings and nature. The hand through tools mediates between human beings and nature and forms the language of real life: spoken words mediate between human beings and form the language of speech.

4   The third aspect is the written signs. The written word imitates the spoken. Where the first two aspects of language as communication through the hand and the spoken word historically evolved more or less simultaneously, the written aspect is a much later historical development. Writing is representation of sounds with visual symbols, from the simplest knot among shepherds to tell the number in a herd or the hieroglyphics among the Agĩkũyũ gicaandi singers and poets of Kenya, to the most complicated and different letter and picture writing systems of the world today.

5   In most societies the written and the spoken languages are the same, in that they represent each other: what is on paper can be read to another person and be received as that language which the recipient has grown up speaking. In such a society there is broad harmony for a child between the three aspects of language as communication. His interaction with nature and with other men is expressed in written and spoken symbols or signs which are both a result of that double interaction and a reflection of it. The association of the child's sensibility is with the language of his experience of life.

6   But there is more to it: communication between human beings is also the basis and process of evolving culture. In doing similar kinds of things and actions over and over again under similar circumstances, similar even in their mutability, certain patterns, moves, rhythms, habits, attitudes, experiences and knowledge emerge. Those experiences are handed over to the next generation and become the inherited basis for their further actions on nature and on themselves. There is a gradual accumulation of values which in time become almost self-evident truths governing their conception of what is right and wrong, good and bad, beautiful and ugly, courageous and cowardly, generous and mean in their internal and external relations. Over a time this becomes a way of life distinguishable from other ways of life. They develop a distinctive culture and history. Culture embodies those moral, ethical and aesthetic values, the set of spiritual eyeglasses, through which they come to view themselves and their place in the universe. Values are the basis of a people's identity, their sense of particularity as members of the human race. All this is carried by language. Language as culture is the collective memory bank of a people's experience in history. Culture is almost indistinguishable from the language that makes possible its genesis, growth, banking, articulation and indeed its transmission from one generation to the next.

7   Language as culture also has three important aspects. Culture is a product of the history which it in turn reflects. Culture in other words is a product and a reflection of human beings communicating with one another in the very struggle to create wealth and to control it. But culture does not merely reflect that history, or rather it does so by actually forming images or pictures of the world of nature and nurture. Thus the second aspect of language as culture is as an image-forming agent in the mind of a child. Our whole conception of ourselves as a people, individually and collectively, is based on those pictures and images which may or may not correctly correspond to the actual reality of the struggles with nature and nurture which produced them in the first place. But our capacity to confront the world creatively is dependent on how those images correspond or not to that reality, how they distort or clarify the reality of our struggles. Language as culture is thus mediating between me and my own self; between my self and other selves; between me and nature. Language is mediating in my very being. And this brings us to the third aspect of language as culture. Culture transmits or imparts those images of the world and reality through the spoken and the written language, that is through a specific language. In other words, the capacity to speak, the capacity to order sounds in a manner that makes for mutual comprehension between human beings is universal. This is the universality of language, a quality specific to human beings. It corresponds to the universality of the struggle against nature and that between human beings. But the particularity of the sounds, the words, the word order into phrases and sentences, and the specific manner, or laws, of their ordering is what distinguishes one language from another. Thus a specific culture is not transmitted through language in its universality but in

its particularity as the language of a specific community with a specific history. Written literature and orature are the main means by which a particular language transmits the images of the world contained in the culture it carries.

9   Language as communication and as culture are then products of each other. Communication creates culture: culture is a means of communication. Language carries culture, and culture carries, particularly through orature and literature, the entire body of values by which we come to perceive ourselves and our place in the world. How people perceive themselves affects how they look at their culture, at their politics and at the social production of wealth, at their entire relationship to nature and to other beings. Language is thus inseparable from ourselves as a community of human beings with a specific form and character, a specific history, a specific relationship to the world.

10   So what was the colonialist imposition of a foreign language doing to us children?

11   The real aim of colonialism was to control the people's wealth: what they produced, how they produced it, and how it was distributed; to control, in other words, the entire realm of the language of real life. Colonialism imposed its control of the social production of wealth through military conquest and subsequent political dictatorship. But its most important area of domination was the mental universe of the colonised, the control, through culture, of how people perceived themselves and their relationship to the world. Economic and political control can never be complete or effective without mental control. To control a people's culture is to control their tools of self-definition in relationship to others.

12   For colonialism this involved two aspects of the same process: the destruction or the deliberate undervaluing of a people's culture, their art, dances, religions, history, geography, education, orature and literature, and the conscious elevation of the language of the coloniser. The domination of a people's language by the languages of the colonising nations was crucial to the domination of the mental universe of the colonised.

13   Take language as communication. Imposing a foreign language, and suppressing the native languages as spoken and written, were already breaking the harmony previously existing between the African child and the three aspects of language. Since the new language as a means of communication was a product of and was reflecting the "real language of life" elsewhere, it could never as spoken or written properly reflect or imitate the real life of that community. This may in part explain why technology always appears to us as slightly external, *their* product and not *ours*. The word "missile" used to hold an alien faraway sound until I recently learnt its equivalent in Gĩkũyũ, *ngurukuhi*, and it made me apprehend it differently. Learning, for a colonial child, became a cerebral activity and not an emotionally felt experience.

14   But since the new, imposed languages could never completely break the native languages as spoken, their most effective area of domination was the third aspect of language as communication, the written. The language of an

African child's formal education was foreign. The language of the books he read was foreign. The language of his conceptualisation was foreign. Thought, in him, took the visible form of a foreign language. So the written language of a child's upbringing in the school (even his spoken language within the school compound) became divorced from his spoken language at home. There was often not the slightest relationship between the child's written world, which was also the language of his schooling, and the world of his immediate environment in the family and the community. For a colonial child, the harmony existing between the three aspects of language as communication was irrevocably broken. This resulted in the disassociation of the sensibility of that child from his natural and social environment, what we might call colonial alienation. The alienation became reinforced in the teaching of history, geography, music, where bourgeois Europe was always the centre of the universe.

15   This disassociation, divorce, or alienation from the immediate environment becomes clearer when you look at colonial language as a carrier of culture.

16   Since culture is a product of the history of a people which it in turn reflects, the child was now being exposed exclusively to a culture that was a product of a world external to himself. He was being made to stand outside himself to look at himself.

17   Since culture does not just reflect the world in images but actually, through those very images, conditions a child to see that world in a certain way, the colonial child was made to see the world and where he stands in it as seen and defined by or reflected in the culture of the language of imposition.

18   And since those images are mostly passed on through orature and literature it meant the child would now only see the world as seen in the literature of his language of adoption. From the point of view of alienation, that is of seeing oneself from outside oneself as if one was another self, it does not matter that the imported literature carried the great humanist tradition of the best in Shakespeare, Goethe, Balzac, Tolstoy, Gorky, Brecht, Sholokhov, Dickens. The location of this great mirror of imagination was necessarily Europe and its history and culture and the rest of the universe was seen from that centre.

19   But obviously it was worse when the colonial child was exposed to images of his world as mirrored in the written languages of his coloniser. Where his own native languages were associated in his impressionable mind with low status, humiliation, corporal punishment, slow-footed intelligence and ability or downright stupidity, non-intelligibility and barbarism, this was reinforced by the world he met in the works of such geniuses of racism as a Rider Haggard or a Nicholas Monsarrat; not to mention the pronouncement of some of the giants of western intellectual and political establishment, such as Hume (". . . the negro is naturally inferior to the whites . . ."), Thomas Jefferson (". . . the blacks . . . are inferior to the whites on the endowments of both body and mind . . ."), or Hegel with his Africa comparable to a land of childhood still enveloped in the dark mantle of the night as far as the development of self-conscious history was concerned. Hegel's statement that there was nothing harmonious with humanity to be found in the African character is representative

of the racist images of Africans and Africa such a colonial child was bound to encounter in the literature of the colonial languages. The results could be disastrous.

Reading-to-Write Questions

1. **Content:** This essay is filled with definitions. List them. Are they necessary?

2. **Arrangement:** Why does Thiong'o discuss language as "a means of communication and a carrier of culture" *before* he describes the colonialist imposition of English on Kenyan children?

3. **Style:** What metaphors, similes, or analogies does Thiong'o create to clarify abstract concepts about language?

4. _____

_____

_____

Suggested Topics

1. **Observation:** Interview an African or Caribbean student who, like Thiong'o, was educated in the colonizer's language even though he or she spoke a different language at home. Compare or contrast your interviewee's experience with Thiong'o's. (audience = African American students)

2. **Critique:** Do you think that Thiong'o should have stopped writing in English? If so, draw upon his essay for support. If not, see Achebe's essay for ideas. (audience = an African writers' association)

3. **Synthesis:** Read Smitherman's and Rickford and Rickford's essays. Can you see any parallels between the linguistic dilemma of Ebonics-speaking African Americans and that of Kenyans like Thiong'o? (audience = your college's African student association)

4. _____

_____

_____

Background Readings: POSTCOLONIAL LANGUAGE

Ashcroft, Bill, Gareth Griffiths, and Helen Tiffin, eds. *The Post-Colonial Studies Reader.* London: Routledge, 1995.

Fanon, Frantz. *Black Skin, White Masks.* New York: Grove Press, 1967.

Smitherman, Geneva. *Talkin' That Talk.* London: Routledge, 2000.

_____

_____

_____

The Song of Ourselves
Chinua Achebe

Reared in an Igbo village and British school in Nigeria, Chinua Achebe gained worldwide fame with the publication of his first novel Things Fall Apart, *a picture of Igbo life in the late nineteenth century, just before the British colonized Nigeria. Since then, the novel has been translated into at least 45 languages, and Achebe has written many other novels in English, including* No Longer at Ease *and* Anthills of the Savannah. *Achebe discusses the implications of reading and writing English in the following excerpt from "The Song of Ourselves," a lecture delivered on British television and reprinted in the magazine* New Statesman & Society *in 1990. First, Achebe reveals the effect reading* English *had on him as a schoolboy by contrasting the way a British and an African writer depict Africa. Then, he contrasts the way he and certain African colleagues feel about* writing *in the language of their colonizers.*

——————————

1   Conrad's *Heart of Darkness*, first published in 1899, portrays Africa as a place where the wandering European may discover that the dark impulses and unspeakable appetites he has suppressed and forgotten through ages of

civilization may spring into life again in answer to Africa's free and triumphant savagery. In one striking passage, Conrad reveals a very interesting aspect of the question of presence. It is the scene where a French gunboat is sitting on the water and firing rockets into the mainland. Conrad's intention, high minded as usual, is to show the futility of Europe's action in Africa:

> Pop would go one of the six-inch guns; a small
> flame would dart and vanish, a tiny projectile
> would give a feeble screech—and nothing
> happened. Nothing could happen. There was
> a touch of insanity in the proceeding.

About sanity I cannot speak. But futility, good heavens, no! By that crazy act of shelling the bush, France managed to acquire an empire in West and Equatorial Africa nine to ten times its own size. Whether there was method in the madness or not, there was profit, quite definitely.

2   Conrad was giving vent to one popular conceit that Europe's devastation of Africa left no mark on the victim. Africa is presumed to pursue its dark, mysterious ways and destiny untouched by explorations and expeditions. Sometimes Africa as an anthropomorphic personage steps out of the shadows and physically annihilates the invasion—which of course adds a touch of suspense and even tragedy to Europe's enterprise. One of the best images in *Heart of Darkness* is of a boat going upstream and the forest stepping across to bar its return. Note, however, that it is the African forest that takes the action: The Africans themselves are absent.

3   Contrast Conrad's episode of the French gunboat with the rendering of an analogous incident in *Ambiguous Adventure,* a powerful novel of colonization by the Muslim writer Cheikh Hamidou Kane, from Senegal—a country colonized by the French. Conrad insists on the futility of the bombardment but also the absence of human response to it. Cheikh Hamidou Kane, standing as it were at the explosive end of the trajectory, tells a different story. The words are those of the Most Royal Lady, a member of the Diallobe aristocracy:

> A hundred years ago our grandfather, along
> with all the inhabitants of this countryside,
> was awakened one morning by an uproar
> arising from the river. He took his gun and,
> followed by all the elite of the region, he
> flung himself upon the newcomers. His heart
> was intrepid and to him the value of liberty
> was greater than the value of life. Our grand-
> father, and the elite of the country with him,
> was defeated. Why? How? Only the new-
> comers know. We must ask them: We must go
> to learn from them the art of conquering
> without being in the right.

Conrad portrays a void, Hamidou Kane celebrates a human presence and a heroic struggle.

4   The difference is very clear. You might say *that* difference was the very reason the African writer came into being. His story had been told for him and he found the telling quite unsatisfactory. I went to a good school modeled on British public schools. I read lots of English books there: *Treasure Island* and *Gulliver's Travels* and *Prisoner of Zenda*, and *Oliver Twist* and *Tom Brown's School Days* and such books in their dozens. But I also encountered Ryder Haggard and John Buchan and the rest, and their "African" books.

5   I did not see myself as an African to begin with. I took sides with the white men against the savages. In other words, I went through my first level of schooling thinking I was of the party of the white man in his hair-raising adventures and narrow escapes. The white man was good and reasonable and intelligent and courageous. The savages arrayed against him were sinister and stupid or, at the most, cunning. I hated their guts.

6   But a time came when I reached the appropriate age and realized that these writers had pulled a fast one on me! I was not on Marlowe's boat steaming up the Congo in *Heart of Darkness*. I was one of those strange beings jumping up and down on the river bank, making horrid faces.

7   That was when I said no, and realized that stories are not innocent; that they can be used to put you in the wrong crowd, in the party of the man who has come to dispossess you.

8   And talking of dispossession, what about language itself? Does my writing in the language of my colonizer not amount to acquiescing in the ultimate dispossession? This is a big and complex matter I cannot go into fully here. Let me simply say that when at the age of thirteen I went to that school modeled after British public schools, it was not only English literature that I encountered there. I came in contact also for the first time in my life with many boys of my own age who did not speak my Igbo language. And they were not foreigners, but fellow Nigerians. We lived in the same dormitories, attended the same morning assembly and classes, and gathered in the same playing fields. To be able to do all that we had to put away our different mother tongues and communicate in the language of our colonizers. This paradox was not peculiar to Nigeria. It happened in every colony where the British put diverse people together under one administration.

9   Some of my colleagues, finding this too awkward, have tried to rewrite their story into a straightforward case of oppression by presenting a happy monolingual African childhood brusquely disrupted by the imposition of a domineering foreign language. This historical fantasy demands that we throw out the English language in order to restore linguistic justice and self-respect to ourselves.

10   My position is that anyone who feels unable to write in English should follow their desires. But they must not take liberties with our history. It is simply not true that the English forced us to learn their language. On the contrary, British colonial policy in Africa and elsewhere emphasized again and again its

preference for native languages. We see remnants of that preference today in the Bantustan policies of South Africa. We chose English not because the British desired it, but because having tacitly accepted the new nationalities into which colonialism had grouped us, we needed its language to transact our business, including the business of overthrowing colonialism itself in the fullness of time.

11   Now, that does not mean that our indigenous languages should now be neglected. It does mean that these languages must coexist and interact with the newcomer now and in the foreseeable future. For me, it is not *either* English or Igbo, it is *both*. Twenty-one years ago when Christopher Okigbo, our finest poet, fell in the Biafran battlefield, I wrote for him one of the best poems I have ever written, in the Igbo language, in the form of a traditional dirge sung by his age-grade. Fifteen years ago I wrote a different kind of poem, in English, to commemorate the passing away of the Angolan poet and President, Agostinho Neto.

12   It is inevitable, I believe, to see the emergence of modern African literature as a return of celebration. It is tempting to say that this literature came to put people back into Africa. But that would be wrong because people never left Africa except in the guilty imagination of Africa's antagonists.

Reading-to-Write Questions

1. **Content:** Achebe draws heavily upon his personal experience. Does it weaken or strengthen his case? Explain why.

2. **Arrangement:** Where does Achebe reveal why he is comparing Joseph Conrad's and Cheikh Hamidou Kane's novels? Does he wait too long?

3. **Style:** Which features of the text suggest that Achebe was writing for a live audience instead of readers? Do those features make the text more or less readable?

4. _____

   _____

   _____

Suggested Topics

1. **Observation:** Interview some African students on your campus. Find out which languages they speak and when they use them. Present your findings to illustrate a point about the role of native vs. colonial languages. (audience = Americans)

2. **Critique:** Achebe forthrightly states, "It is simply not true that the English forced us to learn their language." Consult some of the background readings and other sources. Then explain why you agree or disagree with this statement. (audience = Achebe's readers)

3. **Synthesis:** Contrast Achebe's view on language with Thiong'o's. (audience = whites and blacks at a symposium on colonialism)

4. _____

   _____

   _____

Background Readings: POSTCOLONIAL LANGUAGE

See the reading list for Ngugi wa Thiong'o's essay.

Student Essay:
EBONICS CONTRIBUTES UNIQUENESS TO BLACK SOCIETY
Édouard Lénéus
(1997)

1   Perhaps it is because I am foreign to the United States that I understand so well why Ebonics is a language and should be used to help teach those children who speak it. Perhaps it is because I come from Haiti, where Creole, created from "broken languages," has evolved into a national language, that I can defend the many values of Ebonics.

2   I have had many arguments with some of my friends concerning the controversial decision of the school board in Oakland, California to classify Ebonics as a language. Though these confrontations provoke fiery conversations, my comrades' arguments against this "bastardized language," as they call it, have not proven sufficient to change my opinion.

3   They believe that Ebonics is bad English. It is evidence of laziness that a certain people refuse to conform to the norms and refuse to speak a language they hear every day on television, radio and particularly from their teachers in school. Furthermore, my friends contend that Ebonics is not a language; it is simply bad pronunciations with a mixture of constantly evolving vocabulary. They say mispronouncing words of a language while adding new words to its vocabulary does not make a new language.

4   Their most worthy argument submits that Ebonics is not a viable form of communication because it is not economically viable for the minorities (Blacks and the few Whites) who speak it. A business executive may not hire or may fire a secretary because the secretary speaks Ebonics. When talking to a customer, the secretary may pronounce words that are not proper in standard English, yet proper in Ebonics; therefore the executive may discriminate against that person by firing the employee. I am willing to concede that it is human nature to discriminate. So, my friends ask me, "What good is Ebonics to the kids or this society?"

5   Bastardization has always been part of the evolution of languages, I open in my rebuttal. Watch Shakespeare's *Hamlet* performed on the silver screen and

then speak thee of bastard's tales. Languages have always suffered a constant evolution—from a harder form to a simpler one people can speak.

6   Ebonics is a partial transformation of standard English. The notion that these individuals hear the language on TV, radio and in school does not ultimately determine if that person will speak that language. As a foreigner, I know that if I had not been immersed in the English language, not only to hear it, but also forced to speak it, I would not have learned the language as well as I have. However, even when one can hear and understand what a foreigner says, any student who has studied a foreign language for four years and is unable to speak the language because of lack of practice can identify. The point is that a student learns a language in school, but speaks differently at home. Because one is not fully immersed, a student may hear and understand standard English, but is unable to speak it.

7   Whether Ebonics is a language has not been agreed upon by all linguists. However, phonology, semantics and syntax are three traits linguists look for to distinguish a language; Ebonics has them all (Webb 74–76). Maybe Ebonics has not been standardized, but it is a language, in my opinion.

8   Granted that Ebonics is a language, again my friends ask, "What is its use to society?" Ebonics represents a piece of a group's culture—Black culture. It is rooted in the languages of West Africa and is a product of standard English with a retention of African heritage (Webb 74). Hence, its contribution has added uniqueness to Black society. The Jewish community speaks Hebrew; the Hispanic community has Spanish. If Ebonics is a language, I question why it cannot be recognized as such. Is economic viability reason enough to deny any group a part of its culture? Would we ask the Hispanics to forgo Spanish? Would we ask those of the Jewish faith to disavow Hebrew?

9   Because Ebonics represents a piece of Black culture, I see no reason why it should receive a lesser acknowledgment. As a foreigner who speaks a language once unrecognized, I hold no inferiority complex because it is a newly acknowledged language. To be educated, scholarly or otherwise, means that one has acquired this process by which one makes informed decisions. Executives and others should be of that mind-set; biases and prejudices should not be tolerated, not at the expense of any one group.

Works Cited

Webb, Karen. "Black English: A Discussion." *Revelations*. Ed. Teresa M. Redd. 3rd ed. Needham Heights, MA: Simon & Schuster, 1997. 73–77.

Student Essay:
EBONICS: A RACIAL PROFILE
Kaelie Knight
(2000)

1   Apart from our physical appearance, as African Americans, our speech also distinguishes us from other races. The origins, names, and very style of our speech have long been the subjects of many heated debates. More recently, the actions of the Oakland school board have caused the issue of our speech to fall squarely into the spotlight once more. As the debate on Black English raged nationwide, noted newspaper journalist Jonetta Rose Barras seized the opportunity to share her perspective with the masses. In an article entitled "The Trouble With Ebonics," which appeared in *The Washington Post* in 1997, Barras contends that Black English should be classified as a dialect, rather than a language. A critical analysis of Barras' work and my ongoing research led me to a realization of my own. Although Black English plays a significant role in Black communities, African Americans must recognize that it is indeed a dialect and that its use should be restricted to particular forums.

2   In 1996, statistics revealed that blacks accounted for 53 percent of the total school enrollment in Oakland. Furthermore, at that time 71 percent of all African Americans enrolled in Oakland schools were in special education programs. The average GPA of these special education students was 1.8 out of a possible 4.0. This substandard performance among African American students did not go unnoticed. On December 18, 1996, the school board of Oakland, California sparked national controversy through a resolution affirming that Americans of African descent speak a distinct African language called Ebonics, which is not a dialect of English. In addition the board suggested that Ebonics should be used to teach African American students Standard English. This action was met with scathing objections from many respected public figures including Barras. In the wake of the outcry, the school board amended the statement to remove any implication that the language had racial origins as opposed to social ones.

3   Barras' article is a direct response to Reverend Jesse Jackson's public support of the Oakland school board's attempt to have Ebonics classified as a separate language and to use it as a teaching aid. Her vehement disapproval stems

from her clearly defined position on the issue of Ebonics. In her opinion, the "standardization" of Ebonics is just another means of segregation. Barras maintains that there are ways to teach children Standard English without resorting to the use of Ebonics since it has no place in the classroom. She relates her own struggle to master Standard English in order to rise above the confines of the ghetto. More importantly, Barras recognizes that the classroom use of Ebonics can unintentionally become a stumbling block for African American youth (95–97).

4   In her fervor to emphasize the uselessness of Ebonics within the educational system, Barras inadvertently overlooks the importance of this dialect. African American vernacular English (AAVE), sometimes called Ebonics and formerly called Black English, has certain distinctive features: grammatical, semantic, and phonological. Ebonics capitalizes on the use of the unconjugated form of the verb "be," the addition of double and multiple negatives, and the lack of the third person singular "s"-ending on the present-tense verbs, as well as the shortening of words by dropping the last consonants (Webb 75). For many African Americans, it is the principal medium of communication as it is more frequently used in the home than Standard English. African American culture reflects the depth and impact of Ebonics in our community. The lyrics of our music, whether it is Soul, Rhythm and Blues or Rap, usually employ some degree of Ebonics. "Back That Thang Up" by the Hot Boys and "Where My Girls At?" by 702 are prime examples. Pulitzer Prize recipients like Gwendolyn Brooks, Alex Haley, and Alice Walker have used Ebonics in their award-winning works. The inclusion of Ebonics in "We Real Cool," *Roots*, and *The Color Purple* has made these literary treasures nonetheless popular. Barras should not forget that our speech represents a rich ancestral heritage and chronicles the history of our people. Ebonics is inextricably linked to our very identity as African Americans.

5   As much as Ebonics is an integral part of our identity, I must agree with Barras that it would be more fitting to classify it as a dialect rather than a separate language. According to linguist Karen Webb, in the article "Black English: A Discussion," language exists when the rules of phonology, syntax and semantics are observed (74). Although Webb provides ample evidence to support her claim that Ebonics is a language, I contend that it is merely a dialect. A dialect, according to *The Oxford Dictionary*, is a variety of pre-existing language. On the basis of this definition, I believe that Ebonics is aptly classified as a dialect because of its relationship to English. Barras strengthens my argument by pointing out that most Americans do not speak Standard English. Ebonics is therefore one of many dialects present in American society since varieties of a language develop depending on class, race, origin and geographical location. Further evidence that Ebonics is a dialect comes from John McWhorter, Professor of Linguistics and African American Studies at the University of California Berkeley. He states that the Oakland school board was implying that black people are incapable of learning a language which is so close to their own that it's not a different language" (Diringer and Olszewski A17). There-

fore any attempt to classify Ebonics as a separate language lacks a logical basis and is discriminatory.

6   I also agree with Barras' claim that mastery of Standard English is crucial if African American youth intend to improve their social condition. It would be naïve to ignore the fact that as African Americans we are still judged not only by the color of our skin, but also by our speech. We must recognize that there are areas, such as corporate America, in which Ebonics will not be acceptable. In fact, a recent survey revealed that professionals considered the use of the African American Vernacular as one of the most serious types of errors in the workplace (Redd 6).

7   For the most part, Barras effectively employs thought-provoking argument and sound reasoning to convey her perspective on the issue of Ebonics. Her first-hand experience lends a degree of credibility to her argument and accounts for the highly emotional nature of her article. From my analysis of Barras' works, I am convinced that there is indeed a time and place for all things under the sun—including Ebonics.

Works Cited

Barras, Jonetta Rose. "The Trouble With Ebonics." *Revelations*. 3rd ed. Ed Teresa M. Redd, Needham Heights, MA: Simon & Schuster, 1997, 95–97.

Diringer, Elliot and Lori Olszewski. "Critics May Not Understand Oakland's Goal Is to Teach Black Kids Standard English." *San Francisco Chronicle*. 21 Dec. 1996. A17. 18 Sept. 2000. *<http://englishfirst.org/ebonicsfjb.htm>*.

Redd, Teresa. "Learning With Our Students: Discovering Which Errors Matter in the Real World." Paper presented at the annual meeting of the National Council on the Teaching of English, Nashville, TN, 1998.

Webb, Karen. "Black English: A Discussion." *Revelations*. 3rd ed. Ed Teresa M. Redd. Needham Heights, MA: Simon & Schuster, 1997. 73–77.

struggle for freedom

Let a new earth rise. Let another world
be born. Let a bloody peace be written
in the sky. Let a second generation full
of courage issue forth, let a people
loving freedom come to growth, let a beauty
full of healing and a strength of final
clenching be the pulsing in our spirits
and our blood. Let the martial songs
be written, let the dirges disappear. Let
a race of men now rise and take control.

from "For My People"
by Margaret Walker

The Meaning of July Fourth for the Negro

Frederick Douglass

Despite the laws against slave literacy, Frederick Douglass (circa 1817–1895) taught himself to read and write while yet a slave. After escaping from slavery at the age of 21, he became one of the most eloquent leaders of the movement to abolish slavery, the founder and editor of the newspaper North Star, *and a U.S. diplomat in Haiti. Written with power and grace, his* Narrative of the Life of Frederick Douglass: An American Slave *is now a classic in the annals of American literature. The same eloquence shines forth from the following selection taken from a speech that Douglass delivered in 1852, before an assembly of whites in Rochester, New York, the day after Independence Day. Charging the United States with "revolting barbarity and shameless hypocrisy," Douglass describes the internal slave trade that was keeping Black Americans in captivity while white Americans were celebrating their liberty.*

---

1   What, to the American slave, is your 4th of July? I answer; a day that reveals to him, more than all other days in the year, the gross injustice and cruelty to which he is the constant victim. To him, your celebration is a sham; your boasted liberty, an unholy license; your national greatness, swelling vanity; your sounds of rejoicing are empty and heartless; your denunciation of tyrants, brass fronted impudence; your shouts of liberty and equality, hollow mockery; your prayers and hymns, your sermons and thanksgivings, with all your religious parade and solemnity, are, to Him, mere bombast, fraud, deception, impiety, and hypocrisy—a thin veil to cover up crimes which would disgrace a nation of savages. There is not a nation on the earth guilty of practices more shocking and bloody than are the people of the United States, at this very hour.

2   Go where you may, search where you will, roam through all the monarchies and despotisms of the Old World, travel through South America, search out every abuse, and when you have found the last, lay your facts by the side of the everyday practices of this nation, and you will say with me, that, for revolting barbarity and shameless hypocrisy, America reigns without a rival.

3   Take the American slave-trade, which we are told by the papers, is especially prosperous just now. Ex-Senator Benton tells us that the price of men was never higher than now. He mentions the fact to show that slavery is in no danger. This trade is one of the peculiarities of American institutions. It is carried on in all the large towns and cities in one-half of this confederacy; and millions are pocketed every year by dealers in this horrid traffic. In several states this trade is a chief source of wealth. It is called (in contradistinction to the foreign slave-trade) *"the internal slave-trade."* It is, probably, called so, too, in order to divert from it the horror with which the foreign slave-trade is contemplated. That trade has long since been denounced by this government as piracy. It has been denounced with burning words from the high places of the nation as an execrable traffic. To arrest it, to put an end to it, this nation keeps a squadron, at immense cost, on the coast of Africa. Everywhere, in this country, it is safe to speak of this foreign slave-trade as a most inhuman traffic, opposed alike to the laws of God and of man. The duty to extirpate and destroy it, is admitted even by our doctors of divinity. In order to put an end to it, some of these last have consented that their colored brethren (nominally free) should leave this country, and establish themselves on the western coast of Africa! It is, however, a notable fact that, while so much execration is poured out by Americans upon all those engaged in the foreign slave-trade, the men engaged in the slave-trade between the states pass without condemnation, and their business is deemed honorable.

4   Behold the practical operation of this internal slave-trade, the American slave-trade, sustained by American politics and American religion. Here you will see men and women reared like swine for the market. You know what is a swine-drover? I will show you a man-drover. They inhabit all our Southern States. They perambulate the country, and crowd the highways of the nation, with droves of human stock. You will see one of these human flesh jobbers, armed with pistol, whip, and bowie-knife, driving a company of a hundred

men, women, and children, from the Potomac to the slave market at New Orleans. These wretched people are to be sold singly, or in lots, to suit purchasers. They are food for the cotton-field and the deadly sugar-mill. Mark the sad procession, as it moves wearily along, and the inhuman wretch who drives them. Hear his savage yells and his blood-curdling oaths, as he hurries on his affrighted captives! There, see the old man with locks thinned and gray. Cast one glance, if you please, upon that young mother, whose shoulders are bare to the scorching sun, her briny tears falling on the brow of the babe in her arms. See, too, that girl of thirteen, weeping, *yes!* weeping, as she thinks of the mother from whom she has been torn! The drove moves tardily. Heat and sorrow have nearly consumed their strength; suddenly you hear a quick snap, like the discharge of a rifle; the fetters clank, and the chain rattles simultaneously; your ears are saluted with a scream, that seems to have torn its way to the centre of your soul! The crack you heard was the sound of the slave-whip; the scream you heard was from the woman you saw with the babe. Her speed had faltered under the weight of her child and her chains! That gash on her shoulder tells her to move on. Follow this drove to New Orleans. Attend the auction; see men examined like horses; see the forms of women rudely and brutally exposed to the shocking gaze of American slave-buyers. See this drove sold and separated forever; and never forget the deep, sad sobs that arose from that scattered multitude. Tell me, citizens, where, under the sun, you can witness a spectacle more fiendish and shocking. Yet this is but a glance at the American slave-trade, as it exists, at this moment, in the ruling part of the United States.

5   I was born amid such sights and scenes. To me the American slave-trade is a terrible reality. When a child, my soul was often pierced with a sense of its horrors. I lived on Philpot Street, Fell's Point, Baltimore, and have watched from the wharves the slave ships in the Basin, anchored from the shore, with their cargoes of human flesh, waiting for favorable winds to waft them down the Chesapeake. There was, at that time, a grand slave mart kept at the head of Pratt Street, by Austin Woldfolk. His agents were sent into every town and county in Maryland, announcing their arrival, through the papers, and on flaming *"hand-bills,"* headed cash for Negroes. These men were generally well dressed men, and very captivating in their manners; ever ready to drink, to treat, and to gamble. The fate of many a slave has depended upon the turn of a single card; and many a child has been snatched from the arms of its mother by bargains arranged in a state of brutal drunkenness.

6   The flesh-mongers gather up their victims by dozens, and drive them, chained, to the general depot at Baltimore. When a sufficient number has been collected here, a ship is chartered for the purpose of conveying the forlorn crew to Mobile, or to New Orleans. From the slave prison to the ship, they are usually driven in the darkness of night; for since the antislavery agitation, a certain caution is observed.

7   In the deep, still darkness of midnight, I have been often aroused by the dead, heavy footsteps, and the piteous cries of the chained gangs that passed

our door. The anguish of my boyish heart was intense; and I was often consoled, when speaking to my mistress in the morning, to hear her say that the custom was very wicked; that she hated to hear the rattle of the chains and the heart-rending cries. I was glad to find one who sympathized with me in my horror.

8   Fellow-citizens, this murderous traffic is, to-day, in active operation in this boasted republic. In the solitude of my spirit I see clouds of dust raised on the highways of the South; I see the bleeding footsteps; I hear the doleful wail of fettered humanity on the way to the slave-markets, where the victims are to be sold like *horses, sheep,* and *swine,* knocked off to the highest bidder. There I see the tenderest ties ruthlessly broken, to gratify the lust, caprice and rapacity of the buyers and sellers of men. My soul sickens at the sight.

> *Is this the land your Fathers loved,*
> *The freedom which they toiled to win?*
> *Is this the earth whereon they moved?*
> *Are these the graves they slumber in?*

Reading-to-Write Questions

1. **Content:** How Does Douglass make the audience experience the slave trade?

2. **Arrangement:** Douglass concludes his discourse on the internal slave trade with a verse (before he introduces a new topic in the uncut version of this speech). Why does he insert the verse there?

3. **Style:** Douglass is a master of parallelism. Copy at least two series of parallel phrases or clauses.

4. _____

   _____

   _____

Suggested Topics

1. **Observation:** Douglass exposes the hypocrisy of a slave-owning country that claims to cherish freedom. Read the national news in today's paper. Do you see anything that calls into question America's devotion to freedom? If so, contrast the country's ideals with the reality you see in the news. (audience = readers of the newspaper's op-ed section)

2. **Critique:** Douglass declares, "Go where you may, search where you will, roam through all the monarchies and despotisms of the Old World, travel through South America, search out every abuse . . . and you will say with me, that for revolting barbarity and shameless hypocrisy, America reigns without a rival." Accept Douglass's challenge: search history. Was Douglass's claim true in 1852? (audience = history majors)

3. **Synthesis:** Write an introductory paragraph that summarizes Douglass's argument and then poses the questions "What, to today's African American, is the fourth of July? Are we truly free?" State your answer in a thesis and support that thesis in subsequent paragraphs. For a range of ideas, read Brown's, McCall's, Robinson's, and West's essays. (audience = the African American community)

4. _____

   _____

   _____

Background Readings: BLACK ABOLITIONISTS

Aptheker, Herbert. *Abolitionism: A Revolutionary Movement.* Boston: Twayne, 1989.

Blackett, R.J.M. *Building an Anti-Slavery Wall: Black Americans in the Atlantic Abolitionist Movement.* Baton Rouge, LA: Louisiana State UP, 1983.

Bracey, John, August Meier, and Elliott Rudwick. *Blacks in the Abolitionist Movement.* Belmont, CA: Wadsworth, 1971.

Dillon, Merton. *Slavery Attacked: Southern Slaves and Their Allies 1619–1865.* Baton Rouge: Louisiana State UP, 1990.

Painter, Nell. *Sojourner Truth: A Life, Symbol.* New York: W.W. Norton, 1996.

Quarles, Benjamin. *Black Abolitionists.* New York: Oxford UP, 1969.

———. *Frederick Douglass.* Washington, DC: Associated Publishers, 1948. Rpt. New York: DaCapo Press, 1997.

Ripley, Peter, Roy Finbine, Michael Hembree, and Donald Yacovone, eds. *Witness for Freedom: African American Voices on Race, Slavery, and Emancipation.* 3 vols. Chapel Hill, NC: University of North Carolina Press, 1985–1991.

Walker, David. *Appeal in Four Articles.* 1830. Rpt. New York: Hill and Wang, 1995.

Yee, Shirley. *Black Women Abolitionists: A Study in Activism, 1828–1860.* Knoxville, University of Tennessee Press, 1992.

_____

_____

_____

Pilgrimage to Nonviolence
Martin Luther King, Jr.

Nobel laureate Martin Luther King, Jr. (1929–1968) began his professional life as a minister. Having committed himself to a nonviolent struggle for Blacks' civil rights, he founded the Southern Christian Leadership Conference (SCLC) to lead his crusade. In this excerpt from his book Stride Toward Freedom *(1958), King identifies six characteristics of nonviolent resistance, explaining what it is* not *as well as what it is. In the process, he discusses three types of love and defines the third type— "agape"—because it is central to an understanding of nonviolent resistance.*

———————

1   When I went to Montgomery as a pastor, I had not the slightest idea that I would later become involved in a crisis in which nonviolent resistance would be applicable. I neither started the protest nor suggested it. I simply responded to the call of the people for a spokesman. When the protest began, my mind, consciously or unconsciously, was driven back to the Sermon on the Mount, with its sublime teachings on love, and the Gandhian method of nonviolent resistance. As the days unfolded, I came to see the power of nonviolence more and more. Living through the actual experience of the protest, nonviolence became more than a method to which I gave intellectual assent; it became a commitment to a way of life. Many of the things that I had not cleared up intellectually concerning nonviolence were now solved in the sphere of practical action.

2   Since the philosophy of nonviolence played such a positive role in the Montgomery Movement, it may be wise to turn to a brief discussion of some basic aspects of this philosophy.

3   First, it must be emphasized that nonviolent resistance is not a method for cowards; it does resist. If one uses this method because he is afraid or merely because he lacks the instruments of violence, he is not truly nonviolent. This is why Gandhi often said that if cowardice is the only alternative to violence, it is better to fight. He made this statement conscious of the fact that there is always another alternative: no individual or group need submit to any wrong, nor need they use violence to right the wrong; there is the way of nonviolent resistance. This is ultimately the way of the strong man. It is not a method of stagnant passivity. The phrase "passive resistance" often gives the false impression that this is a sort of "do-nothing method" in which the resister quietly and passively accepts evil. But nothing is further from the truth. For while the nonviolent resister is passive in the sense that he is not physically aggressive toward his opponent, his mind and emotions are always active, constantly seeking to persuade his opponent that he is wrong. The method is passive physically, but strongly active spiritually. It is not passive nonresistance to evil, it is active nonviolent resistance to evil.

4   A second basic fact that characterizes nonviolence is that it does not seek to defeat or humiliate the opponent, but to win his friendship and understanding. The nonviolent resister must often express his protest through noncooperation or boycotts, but he realizes that these are not ends themselves; they are merely means to awaken a sense of moral shame in the opponent. The end is redemption and reconciliation. The aftermath of nonviolence is the creation of the beloved community, while the aftermath of violence is tragic bitterness.

5   A third characteristic of this method is that the attack is directed against forces of evil rather than against persons who happen to be doing the evil. It is evil that the nonviolent resister seeks to defeat, not the persons victimized by evil. If he is opposing racial injustice, the nonviolent resister has the vision to say that the basic tension is not between races. As I like to say to the people in Montgomery: "The tension in this city is not between white people and Negro people. The tension is, at bottom, between justice and injustice, between the forces of light and the forces of darkness. And if there is a victory, it will be a victory not merely for fifty thousand Negroes, but a victory for justice and the forces of light. We are out to defeat injustice and not white persons who may be unjust."

6   A fourth point that characterizes nonviolent resistance is a willingness to accept suffering without retaliation, to accept blows from the opponent without striking back. "Rivers of blood may have to flow before we gain our freedom, but it must be our blood," Gandhi said to his countrymen. The nonviolent resister is willing to accept violence if necessary, but never to inflict it. He does not seek to dodge jail. If going to jail is necessary, he enters it "as a bridegroom enters the bride's chamber."

7   One may well ask: "What is the nonviolent resister's justification for this ordeal to which he invites men, for this mass political application of the ancient doctrine of turning the other cheek?" The answer is found in the realization that unearned suffering is redemptive. Suffering, the nonviolent resister realizes, has tremendous educational and transforming possibilities. "Things of fundamental importance to people are not secured by reason alone, but have to be purchased with their suffering," said Gandhi. He continues: "Suffering is infinitely more powerful than the law of the jungle for converting the opponent and opening his ears which are otherwise shut to the voice of reason."

8   A fifth point concerning nonviolent resistance is that it avoids not only external physical violence but also internal violence of spirit. The nonviolent resister not only refuses to shoot his opponent but he also refuses to hate him. At the center of nonviolence stands the principle of love. The nonviolent resister would contend that in the struggle for human dignity, the oppressed people of the world must not succumb to the temptation of becoming bitter or indulging in hate campaigns. To retaliate in kind would do nothing but intensify the existence of hate in the universe. Along the way of life, someone must have sense enough and morality enough to cut off the chain of hate. This can only be done by projecting the ethic of love to the center of our lives.

9   In speaking of love at this point, we are not referring to some sentimental or affectionate emotion. It would be nonsense to urge men to love their oppressors in an affectionate sense. Love in this connection means understanding, redemptive good will. Here the Greek language comes to our aid. There are three words for love in the Greek New Testament. First, there is *eros*. In Platonic philosophy *eros* meant the yearning of the soul for the realm of the divine. It has come now to mean a sort of aesthetic or romantic love. Second, there is *philia*, which means intimate affection between personal friends. *Philia* denotes a sort of reciprocal love; the person loves because he is loved. When we speak of loving those who oppose us, we refer to neither *eros* nor *philia*; we speak of a love which is expressed in the Greek word *agape*. *Agape* means understanding, redeeming good will for all men. It is an overflowing love which is purely spontaneous, unmotivated, groundless, and creative. It is not set in motion by any quality or function of its object. It is the love of God operating in the human heart.

10   *Agape* is disinterested love. It is a love in which the individual seeks not his own good, but the good of his neighbor (I Cor. 10:24). *Agape* does not begin by discriminating between worthy and unworthy people, or any qualities people possess. It begins by loving others *for their sakes*. It is entirely "neighbor-regarding concern for others," which discovers the neighbor in every man it meets. There, *agape* makes no distinction between friend and enemy; it is directed toward both. If one loves an individual merely on account of friendliness, he loves him for the sake of the benefits to be gained from the friendship, rather than for the friend's own sake. Consequently, the best way to assure

oneself that Love is disinterested is to have love for the enemy-neighbor from whom you can expect no good in return, but only hostility and persecution.

11   Another basic point about *agape* is that it springs from the *need* of the other person—his need for belonging to the best in the human family. The Samaritan who helped the Jew on the Jericho Road was "good" because he responded to the human need that he was presented with. God's love is eternal and fails not because man needs his love. St. Paul assures us that the loving act of redemption was done "while we were yet sinners"—that is, at the point of our greatest need for love. Since the white man's personality is greatly distorted by segregation, and his soul is greatly scarred, he needs the love of the Negro. The Negro must love the white man, because the white man needs his love to remove his tensions, insecurities, and fears.

12   *Agape* is not a weak, passive love. It is love in action. *Agape* is love seeking to preserve and create community. It is insistence on community even when one seeks to break it. *Agape* is a willingness to sacrifice in the interest of mutuality. *Agape* is a willingness to go to any length to restore community. It doesn't stop at the first mile, but it goes the second mile to restore community. It is a willingness to forgive, not seven times, but seventy times seven to restore community. The cross is the eternal expression of the length to which God will go in order to restore broken community. The resurrection is a symbol of God's triumph over all the forces that seek to block community. The Holy Spirit is the continuing community creating reality that moves through history. He who works against community is working against the whole of creation. Therefore, if I respond to hate with a reciprocal hate I do nothing but intensify cleavage in broken community. I can only close the gap in broken community by meeting hate with love. If I meet hate with hate, I become depersonalized, because creation is so designed that my personality can only be fulfilled in the context of community. Booker T. Washington was right: "Let no man pull you so low as to make you hate him." When he pulls you that low he brings you to the point of working against community; he drags you to the point of defying creation, and thereby becoming depersonalized.

13   In the final analysis, *agape* means a recognition of the fact that all life is interrelated. All humanity is involved in a single process, and all men are brothers. To the degree that I harm my brother, no matter what he is doing to me, to that extent I am harming myself. For example, white men often refuse federal aid to education in order to avoid giving the Negro his rights; but because all men are brothers they cannot deny Negro children without harming their own. They end, all efforts to the contrary, by hurting themselves. Why is this? Because men are brothers. If you harm me, you harm yourself.

14   Love, *agape*, is the only cement that can hold this broken community together. When I am commanded to love, I am commanded to restore community, to resist injustice, and to meet the needs of my brothers.

15   A sixth basic fact about nonviolent resistance is that it is based on the conviction that the universe is on the side of justice. Consequently, the believer in nonviolence has deep faith in the future. This faith is another reason why the

nonviolent resister can accept suffering without retaliation. For he knows that in his struggle for justice he has cosmic companionship. It is true that there are devout believers in nonviolence who find it difficult to believe in a personal God. But even these persons believe in the existence of some creative force that works for universal wholeness. Whether we call it an unconscious process, an impersonal Brahman, or a Personal Being of matchless power and infinite love, there is a creative force in this universe that works to bring the disconnected aspects of reality into a harmonious whole.

Reading-to-Write Questions

1. **Content:** What misconceptions about nonviolence does King attack?

2. **Arrangement:** Why is the enumeration of the characteristics of nonviolence so helpful in this selection?

3. **Style:** King repeatedly employs antithesis in his sentences. Where does he juxtapose opposites (e.g., *defeat* vs. *win*) or construct grammatical contrasts (e.g., *neither . . . nor*)?

4. _____

   _____

   _____

Suggested Topics

1. **Observation:** Talk to someone who participated in the Civil Rights Movement as a nonviolent resister. In flesh-and-blood terms, explain what "nonviolent resistance" means to him or her. (audience = post-Civil Rights generation)

2. **Critique:** King declares, "To the degree that I harm my brother, no matter what he is doing to me, to that extent I am harming myself." Do you agree? Cite supporting or opposing examples. (audience = American junior high students)

3. **Synthesis:** Does King adequately address the objections Malcolm X raises in his critique of nonviolence? (See Malcolm's essay in this book). (audience = political activists on your campus)

4. _____

   _____

   _____

Background Readings: NONVIOLENT RESISTANCE

Gandhi, M. *Nonviolent Resistance.* 1951. rpt. New York: Schocken Books, 1961.

Gregg, Richard B. *The Power of Nonviolence.* 2nd ed. New York: Schocken Books, 1966.

Hare, A. Paul, and Herbert H. Blumberg, eds. *Nonviolent Direct Action: American Cases, Social and Psychological Analyses.* Washington, DC and Cleveland, OH: Corpus Books, 1968.

Jones, LeRoi (Amiri Baraka). "What Does Nonviolence Mean?" *Home: Social Essays.* New York: William Morrow, 1966. 133–154.

Kapur, Sudarshan. *Raising Up a Prophet: The African-American Encounter with Gandhi.* Boston: Beacon Press, 1992.

Lynd, Staughton, and Alice Lynd. *Nonviolence in America: A Documentary History.* Maryknoll, NY: Orbis Books, 1995.

Marable, Manning, and Leith Mullings, eds. *Let Nobody Turn Us Around: Voices of Resistance, Reform, and Renewal: An African American Anthology.* Lanham, MD: Rowman & Littlefield, 2000.

Moses, Greg. *Revolution of Conscience: Martin Luther King, Jr., and the Philosophy of Nonviolence.* New York: Guilford Press, 1997.

_____

_____

_____

Recommended Literature: Ernest Gaines, *The Autobiography of Miss Jane Pittman* (novel)

The Civil Rights Movement: What Good Was It?

Alice Walker

Most famous for her Pulitzer-Prize–winning novel The Color Purple, *Alice Walker has published collections of short stories (e.g.,* You Can't Keep a Good Woman Down), *poems (e.g.,* Revolutionary Petunias), *and essays (e.g.,* In Search of Our Mothers' Gardens), *as well as novels:* The Third Life of Grange Copeland, Meridian, The Temple of My Familiar, Possessing the Secret of Joy, *and* By the Light of My Father's Smile. *The following essay appears in the collection* In Search of Our Mothers' Gardens. *Written when she was 23 years old, this essay won first prize in the* American Scholar *essay contest and was published by that magazine in 1967. In the essay Walker defends the Civil Rights Movement, describing its profound effects on Blacks like herself.*

---

1   Someone said recently to an old black lady from Mississippi, whose legs had been badly mangled by local police who arrested her for "disturbing the peace," that the Civil Rights Movement was dead, and asked, since it was dead, what she thought about it. The old lady replied, hobbling out of his presence on her

cane, that the Civil Rights Movement was like herself, "if it's dead, it shore ain't ready to lay down!"

2   This old lady is a legendary freedom fighter in her small town in the Delta. She has been severely mistreated for insisting on her rights as an American citizen. She has been beaten for singing Movement songs, placed in solitary confinement in prisons for talking about freedom, and placed on bread and water for praying aloud to God for her jailers' deliverance. For such a woman the Civil Rights Movement will never be over as long as her skin is black. It also will never be over for twenty million others with the same "affliction," for whom the Movement can never "lay down," no matter how it is killed by the press and made dead and buried by the white American public. As long as one black American survives, the struggle for equality with other Americans must also survive. This is a debt we owe to those blameless hostages we leave to the future, our children.

3   Still, white liberals and deserting Civil Rights sponsors are quick to justify their disaffection from the Movement by claiming that it is all over. "And since it is over," they will ask, "would someone kindly tell me what has been gained by it?" They then list statistics supposedly showing how much more advanced segregation is now than ten years ago—in schools, housing, jobs. They point to a gain in conservative politicians during the last few years. They speak of ghetto riots and of the survey that shows that most policemen are admittedly too anti-Negro to do their jobs in ghetto areas fairly and effectively. They speak of every area that has been touched by the Civil Rights Movement as somehow or other going to pieces.

4   They rarely talk, however, about human attitudes among Negroes that have undergone terrific changes just during the past seven to ten years (not to mention all those years when there was a Movement and only the Negroes knew about it). They seldom speak of changes in personal lives because of the influence of people in the Movement. They see general failure and few, if any, individual gains.

5   They do not understand what it is that keeps the Movement from "laying down" and Negroes from reverting to their former silent second-class status. They have apparently never stopped to wonder why it is always the white man—on his radio and in his newspaper and on his television—who says that the Movement is dead. If a Negro were audacious enough to make such a claim, his fellows might hanker to see him shot. The Movement is dead to the white man because it no longer interests him. And it no longer interests him because he can afford to be uninterested: he does not have to live by it, with it, or for it, as Negroes must. He can take a rest from the news of beatings, killings, and arrests that reach him from North and South—if his skin is white. Negroes cannot now and will never be able to take a rest from the injustices that plague them, for they—not the white man—are the target.

6   Perhaps it is naive to be thankful that the Movement "saved" a large number of individuals and gave them something to live for, even if it did not provide them with everything they wanted. (Materially, it provided them with

precious little that they wanted.) When a movement awakens people to the possibilities of life, it seems unfair to frustrate them by then denying what they had thought was offered. But what was offered? What was promised? What was it all about? What good did it do? Would it have been better, as some have suggested, to leave the Negro people as they were, unawakened, unallied with one another, unhopeful about what to expect for their children in some future world?

7   I do not think so. If knowledge of my condition is all the freedom I get from a "freedom movement," it is better than unawareness, forgottenness, and hopelessness, the existence that is like the existence of a beast. Man only truly lives by knowing; otherwise he simply performs, copying the daily habits of others, but conceiving nothing of his creative possibilities as a man, and accepting someone else's superiority and his own misery.

8   When we are children, growing up in our parents' care, we await the spark from the outside world. Sometimes our parents provide it—if we are lucky—sometimes it comes from another source far from home. We sit, paralyzed, surrounded by our anxiety and dread, hoping we will not have to grow up into the narrow world and ways we see about us. We are hungry for a life that turns us on; we yearn for a knowledge of living that will save us from our innocuous lives that resemble death. We look for signs in every strange event; we search for heroes in every unknown face.

9   It was just six years ago that I began to be alive. I had, of course, been living before—for I am now twenty-three—but I did not really know it. And I did not know it because nobody told me that I—a pensive, yearning, typical high-school senior, but Negro—existed in the minds of others as I existed in my own. Until that time my mind was locked apart from the outer contours and complexion of my body as if it and the body were strangers. The mind possessed both thought and spirit—I wanted to be an author or a scientist—which the color of the body denied. I had never seen myself and existed as a statistic exists, or as a phantom. In the white world I walked, less real to them than a shadow; and being young and well hidden among the slums, among people who also did not exist—either in books or in films or in the government of their own lives—I waited to be called to life. And, by a miracle, I was called.

10   There was a commotion in our house that night in 1960. We had managed to buy our first television set. It was battered and overpriced, but my mother had gotten used to watching the afternoon soap operas at the house where she worked as a maid, and nothing could satisfy her on days when she did not work but a continuation of her "stories." So she pinched pennies and bought a set.

11   I remained listless throughout her "stories," tales of pregnancy, abortion, hypocrisy, infidelity, and alcoholism. All these men and women were white and lived in houses with servants, long staircases that they floated down, patios where liquor was served four times a day to "relax" them. But my mother, with her swollen feet eased out of her shoes, her heavy body relaxed in our only comfortable chair, watched each movement of the smartly coiffed

women, heard each word, pounced upon each innuendo and inflection, and for the duration of these "stories" she saw herself as one of them. She placed herself in every scene she saw, with her braided hair turned blond, her two hundred pounds compressed into a sleek size-seven dress, her rough dark skin smooth and *white*. Her husband became "dark and handsome," talented, witty, urbane, charming. And when she turned to look at my father sitting near her in his sweat shirt with his smelly feet raised on the bed to "air," there was always a tragic look of surprise on her face. Then she would sigh and go out to the kitchen looking lost and unsure of herself. My mother, a truly great woman who raised eight children of her own and half a dozen of the neighbors' without a single complaint, was convinced that she did not exist compared to "them." She subordinated her soul to theirs and became a faithful and timid supporter of the "Beautiful White People." Once she asked me, in a moment of vicarious pride and despair, if I didn't think that "they" were "jest naturally smarter, prettier, better." My mother asked this: a woman who never got rid of any of her children, never cheated on my father, was never a hypocrite if she could help it, and never even tasted liquor. She could not even bring herself to blame "them" for making her believe what they wanted her to believe: that if she did not look like them, think like them, be sophisticated and corrupt-for-comfort's-sake like them, she was a nobody. Black was not a color on my mother; it was a shield that made her invisible.

12   Of course, the people who wrote the soap-opera scripts always made the Negro maids in them steadfast, trusty, and wise in a home-remedial sort of way; but my mother, a maid for nearly forty years, never once identified herself with the scarcely glimpsed black servant's face beneath the ruffled cap. Like everyone else, in her daydreams at least, she thought she was free.

13   Six years ago, after half-heartedly watching my mother's soap operas and wondering whether there wasn't something more to be asked of life, the Civil Rights Movement came into my life. Like a good omen for the future, the face of Dr. Martin Luther King, Jr., was the first black face I saw on our new television screen. And, as in a fairy tale, my soul was stirred by the meaning for me of his mission—at the time he was being rather ignominiously dumped into a police van for having led a protest march in Alabama—and I fell in love with the sober and determined face of the Movement. The singing of "We Shall Overcome"—that song betrayed by nonbelievers in it—rang for the first time in my ears. The influence that my mother's soap operas might have had on me became impossible. The life of Dr. King, seeming bigger and more miraculous than the man himself, because of all he had done and suffered, offered a pattern of strength and sincerity I felt I could trust. He had suffered much because of his simple belief in nonviolence, love, and brotherhood. Perhaps the majority of men could not be reached through these beliefs, but because Dr. King kept trying to reach them in spite of danger to himself and his family, I saw in him the hero for whom I had waited so long.

14   What Dr. King promised was not a ranch-style house and an acre of manicured lawn for every black man, but jail and finally freedom. He did not promise

two cars for every family, but the courage one day for all families everywhere to walk without shame and unafraid on their own feet. He did not say that one day it will be us chasing prospective buyers out of our prosperous well-kept neighborhoods, or in other ways exhibiting our snobbery and ignorance as all other ethnic groups before us have done; what he said was that we had a right to live anywhere in this country we chose, and a right to a meaningful well-paying job to provide us with the upkeep of our homes. He did not say we had to become carbon copies of the white American middle class; but he did say we had the right to become whatever we wanted to become.

15   Because of the Movement, because of an awakened faith in the newness and imagination of the human spirit, because of "black and white together"—for the first time in our history in some human relationship on and off TV—because of the beatings, the arrests, the hell of battle during the past years, I have fought harder for my life and for a chance to be myself, to be something more than a shadow or a number, than I had ever done before in my life. Before, there had seemed to be no real reason for struggling beyond the effort for daily bread. Now there was a chance at that other that Jesus meant when He said we could not live by bread alone.

16   I have fought and kicked and fasted and prayed and cursed and cried myself to the point of existing. It has been like being born again, literally. Just "knowing" has meant everything to me. Knowing has pushed me out into the world, into college, into places, into people.

17   Part of what existence means to me is knowing the difference between what I am now and what I was then. It is being capable of looking after myself intellectually as well as financially. It is being able to tell when I am being wronged and by whom. It means being awake to protect myself and the ones I love. It means being a part of the world community, and being *alert* to which part it is that I have joined, and knowing how to change to another part if that part does not suit me. To know is to exist: to exist is to be involved, to move about, to see the world with my own eyes. This, at least, the Movement has given me.

18   The hippies and other nihilists would have me believe that it is all the same whether the people in Mississippi have a movement behind them or not. Once they have their rights, they say, they will run all over themselves trying to be just like everybody else. They will be well fed, complacent about things of the spirit, emotionless, and without that marvelous humanity and "soul" that the Movement has seen them practice time and time again. "What has the Movement done," they ask, "with the few people it has supposedly helped?" "Got them white-collar jobs, moved them into standardized ranch houses in white neighborhoods, given them nondescript gray flannel suits?" "What are these people now?" they ask. And then they answer themselves, "Nothings!"

19   I would find this reasoning—which I have heard many, many times from hippies and nonhippies alike—amusing if I did not also consider it serious. For I think it is a delusion, a cop-out, an excuse to disassociate themselves from a world in which they feel too little has been changed or gained. The real question, however, it appears to me, is not whether poor people will adopt the

middle-class mentality once they are well fed; rather, it is whether they will ever be well fed enough to be able to choose whatever mentality they think will suit them. The lack of a movement did not keep my mother from *wishing* herself bourgeois in her daydreams.

20   There is widespread starvation in Mississippi. In my own state of Georgia there are more hungry families than Lester Maddox would like to admit—or even see fed. I went to school with children who ate red dirt. The Movement has prodded and pushed some liberal senators into pressuring the government for food so that the hungry may eat. Food stamps that were two dollars and out of the reach of many families not long ago have been reduced to fifty cents. The price is still out of the reach of some families, and the government, it seems to a lot of people, could spare enough free food to feed its own people. It angers people in the Movement that it does not; they point to the billions in wheat we send free each year to countries abroad. Their government's slowness while people are hungry, its unwillingness to believe that there are Americans starving, its stingy cutting of the price of food stamps, make many Civil Rights workers throw up their hands in disgust. But they do not give up. They do not withdraw into the world of psychedelia. They apply what pressure they can to make the government give away food to hungry people. They do not plan so far ahead in their disillusionment with society that they can see these starving families buying identical ranch-style houses and sending their snobbish children to Bryn Mawr and Yale. They take first things first and try to get them fed.

21   They do not consider it their business, in any case, to say what kind of life the people they help must lead. How one lives is, after all, one of the rights left to the individual—when and if he has an opportunity to choose. It is not the prerogative of the middle class to determine what is worthy of aspiration. There is also every possibility that the middle-class people of tomorrow will turn out ever so much better than those of today. I even know some middle-class people of today who are not *all* bad.

22   I think there are so few Negro hippies because middle-class Negroes, although well fed, are not careless. They are required by the treacherous world they live in to be clearly aware of whoever or whatever might be trying to do them in. They are middle class in money and position, but they cannot afford to be middle class in complacency. They distrust the hippie movement because they know that it can do nothing for Negroes as a group but "love" them, which is what all paternalists claim to do. And since the only way Negroes can survive (which they cannot do, unfortunately, on love alone) is with the support of the group, they are wisely wary and stay away.

23   A white writer tried recently to explain that the reason for the relatively few Negro hippies is that Negroes have built up a "super-cool" that cracks under LSD and makes them have a "bad trip." What this writer doesn't guess at is that Negroes are needing drugs less than ever these days for any kind of trip. While the hippies are "tripping," Negroes are going after power, which is so

much more important to their survival and their children's survival than LSD and pot.

24   Everyone would be surprised if the Israelis ignored the Arabs and took up "tripping" and pot smoking. In this country we are the Israelis. Everybody who can do so would like to forget this, of course. But for us to forget it for a minute would be fatal. "We Shall Overcome" is just a song to most Americans, *but we must do it*. Or die.

25   What good was the Civil Rights Movement? If it had just given the country Dr. King, a leader of conscience, for once in our lifetime, it would have been enough. If it had just taken black eyes off white television stories, it would have been enough. If it had fed one starving child, it would have been enough.

26   If the Civil Rights Movement is "dead," and if it gave us nothing else, it gave us each other forever. It gave some of us bread, some of us shelter, some of us knowledge and pride, all of us comfort. It gave us our children, our husbands, our brothers, our fathers, as men reborn and with a purpose for living. It broke the pattern of black servitude in this country. It shattered the phony "promise" of white soap operas that sucked away so many pitiful lives. It gave us history and men far greater than Presidents. It gave us heroes, selfless men of courage and strength, for our little boys and girls to follow. It gave us hope for tomorrow. It called us to life.

27   Because we live, it can never die.

Reading-to-Write Questions

1. **Content:** Reread Walker's description of her mother's fascination with soap operas. What details make the description so painfully ironic?

2. **Arrangement:** In which paragraphs does Walker use parallel structure to tie together the sentences of a paragraph?

3. **Style:** Where does Walker effectively coordinate three or more words or phrases in a series?

4. _____

    _____

    _____

Suggested Topics

1. **Observation:** Interview a Black and a White who lived during the Civil Rights Movement, but did not participate in the protests. Discuss the effects the Movement had on them. (audience = younger generation)

2. **Critique:** Speaking of Martin Luther King, Jr., Walker recalls, "I saw in him the hero for whom I had waited so long." Do you agree that King is a hero? (Define the word *hero* first.) (audience = King's admirers, including Walker)

3. **Synthesis:** Even in 1967, when Walker wrote this essay, critics questioned the value of the Civil Rights Movement by pointing to persistent segregation in education, employment, and housing. Now that many African Americans are advocating self-segregation (see Williams' essay), do you think the Movement is finally dead? (audience = student volunteers for a voter registration drive)

4. _____

    _____

    _____

Background Readings: THE CIVIL RIGHTS MOVEMENT

Blumberg, Rhoda Lois. *Civil Rights: The 1960s Freedom Struggle.* rev. ed. Boston: Twayne/G.K. Hall, 1991.

Branch, Taylor. *Parting the Waters: America in the King Years (1954–1963).* New York: Touchstone/Simon & Schuster, 1988.

Carson, Clayborne et al., eds. *The Eyes on the Prize Civil Rights Reader: Documents, Speeches, and Firsthand Accounts from the Black Freedom Struggle, 1954–1990.* New York: Penguin, 1990.

King, Martin Luther, Jr. *I Have a Dream: Writings and Speeches That Changed the World.* Glenview, IL: Scott Foresman, 1992.

Kosof, Anna. *The Civil Rights Movement and Its Legacy.* New York: Watts, 1989.

Macedo, Stephen, ed. *Reassessing the Sixties: Debating the Political and Cultural Legacy.* New York: W. W. Norton, 1997.

Meacham, Jon, ed. *Voices in Our Blood: America's Best on the Civil Rights Movement.* New York: Random House, 2001.

Williams, Juan. *Eyes on the Prize: America's Civil Rights Years, 1954–1967.* NY: Viking Penguin, 1987.

_____

_____

_____

Recommended Literature: Ann Moody, *Coming of Age in Mississippi*
                         (autobiography)
                         Alice Walker, *Meridian* (novel)

Message to the Grass Roots
Malcolm X

Before he assumed his Muslim name, Malcolm X (1925–1965) was Malcolm Little, a street hustler who was at times a dope dealer, numbers runner, drug addict, and robber. While imprisoned for burglary, he turned to Islam and books for a new direction in his life—and found it. After his release from jail, he became a minister in the Nation of Islam and a spokesman for many Black Americans. In 1965, assassins cut short his life, a life he had recorded with Alex Haley in The Autobiography of Malcolm X. *However, interest in Malcolm X's speeches— some of which are collected in* Malcolm X Speaks—*has long outlived him. The passage below comes from one of those speeches, "Message to the Grass Roots," delivered to the Northern Grass Roots Leadership Conference at a Baptist Church in Detroit in 1963. In his fiery and colorful style, Malcolm X explains black nationalism by contrasting "house Negroes" and "field Negroes."*

---

1   If you're afraid of back nationalism, you're afraid of revolution. And if you love revolution, you love black nationalism.

2   To understand this, you have to go back to what the young brother here referred to as the house Negro and the field Negro back during slavery. There were two kinds of slaves, the house Negro and the field Negro. The house Negroes—they lived in the house with master, they dressed pretty good, they ate good because they ate his food—what he left. They lived in the attic or the basement, but still they lived near the master; and they loved the master more than the master loved himself. They would give their life to save the master's house—quicker than the master would. If the master said, "We got a good house here," the house Negro would say, "Yeah, we got a good house here." Whenever the master said "we," he said "we." That's how you can tell a house Negro.

3   If the master's house caught on fire, the house Negro would fight harder to put the blaze out than the master would. If the master got sick, the house Negro would say, "What's the matter, boss, *we* sick?" *We* sick! He identified himself with his master, more than his master identified with himself. And if you came to the house Negro and said, "Let's run away, let's escape, let's separate," the house Negro would look at you and say, "Man, you crazy. What you mean, separate? Where is there a better house than this? Where can I wear better clothes than this? Where can I eat better food than this?" That was that house Negro. In those days he was called a "house nigger." And that's what we call them today, because we've still got some house niggers running around here.

4   This modern house Negro loves his master. He wants to live near him. He'll pay three times as much as the house is worth just to live near his master, and then brag about "I'm the only Negro out here." "I'm the only one on my job." "I'm the only one in this school." You're nothing but a house Negro. And if someone comes to you right now and says, "Let's separate," you say the same thing that the house Negro said on the plantation. "What you mean, separate? From America, this good white man? Where you going to get a better job than you get here?" I mean, this is what you say, "I ain't left nothing in Africa," that's what you say. Why, you left your mind in Africa.

5   On that same plantation, there was the field Negro. The field Negroes—those were the masses. There were always more Negroes in the field than there were Negroes in the house. The Negro in the field caught hell. He ate leftovers. In the house they ate high up on the hog. The Negro in the field didn't get anything but what was left of the insides of the hog. They call it "chitt'lings" nowadays. In those days they called them what they were—guts. That's what you were—gut-eaters. And some of you are still gut-eaters.

6   The field Negro was beaten from morning to night; he lived in a shack, in a hut; he wore old, castoff clothes. He hated his master. I say he hated his master. He was intelligent. That house Negro loved his master, but that field Negro—remember, they were in the majority, and they hated the master. When the house caught on fire, he didn't try to put it out; that field Negro prayed for a wind, for a breeze. When the master got sick, the field Negro prayed that he'd die. If someone came to the field Negro and said, "Let's sep-

arate, let's run," he didn't say "Where we going?" He'd say, "Any place is better than here." You've got field Negroes in America today. I'm a field Negro. The masses are the field Negroes. When they see this man's house on fire, you don't hear the little Negroes talking about "*our* government is in trouble." They say, "*The* government is in trouble." Imagine a Negro: "*Our* government"! I even heard one say "*our* astronauts." They won't even let him near the plant—and "*our* astronauts"! "*Our* Navy"—that's a Negro that is out of his mind, a Negro that is out of his mind.

7   Just as the slavemaster of that day used Tom, the house Negro, to keep the field Negroes in check, the same old slavemaster today has Negroes who are nothing but modern Uncle Toms, twentieth-century Uncle Toms, to keep you and me in check, to keep us under control, keep us passive and peaceful and nonviolent. That's Tom making you nonviolent. It's like when you go to the dentist, and the man's going to take your tooth. You're going to fight him when he starts pulling. So he squirts some stuff in your jaw called novocaine, to make you think they're not doing anything to you. So you sit there and because you've got all of that novocaine in your jaw, you suffer—peacefully. Blood running all down your jaw, and you don't know what's happening. Because someone has taught you to suffer—peacefully.

8   The white man does the same thing to you in the street, when he wants to put knots on your head and take advantage of you and not have to be afraid of your fighting back. To keep you from fighting back, he gets these old religious Uncle Toms to teach you and me, just like novocaine, to suffer peacefully. Don't stop suffering—just suffer peacefully. As Rev. Cleage pointed out, they say you should let your blood flow in the streets. This is a shame. You know he's a Christian preacher. If it's a shame to him, you know what it is to me.

9   There is nothing in our book, the Koran, that teaches us to suffer peacefully. Our religion teaches us to be intelligent. Be peaceful, be courteous, obey the law, respect everyone; but if someone puts his hand on you, send him to the cemetery. That's a good religion. In fact, that's old-time religion. That's the one that Ma and Pa used to talk about: an eye for an eye, and a tooth for a tooth, and a head for a head; and a life for a life. That's a good religion. And nobody resents that kind of religion being taught but a wolf, who intends to make you his meal.

10   This is the way it is with the white man in America. He's a wolf—and you're sheep. Any time a shepherd, a pastor, teaches you and me not to run from the white man and, at the same time, teaches us not to fight the white man, he's a traitor to you and me. Don't lay down a life all by itself. No, preserve your life, it's the best thing you've got. And if you've got to give it up, let it be even-steven.

Reading-to-Write Questions

1. **Content:** Why does Malcolm X compare the philosophy of nonviolence to novocaine? In other words, how does this comparison help him reach his audience?

2. **Arrangement:** Malcolm X intertwines two types of contrasts in this selection: field vs. house and slave vs. modern. Which pattern does he follow—subject by subject or point by point?

3. **Style:** Find examples of the "sharp turns of phrase, the euphony and rhythm" that, according to Bradley (see his essay), established the rhetorical style of protest movements of the 1960s and 1970s.

4. _____

   _____

   _____

Suggested Topics

1. **Observation:** Do you see Malcolm's "house Negroes" and "field Negroes" on campus today? If so, describe their appearance, slogans, and actions. (audience = op-ed page of your campus newspaper)

2. **Critique:** Summarize Malcolm's message. Then consider whether he is guilty of unfair stereotyping. (audience = students who revere Malcolm X)

3. **Synthesis:** Compare Malcolm X's depiction of house Negroes to S. Steele's depiction of his middle-class family. Were the Steeles "house Negroes"? (audience = middle-class African Americans)

4. _____

   _____

   _____

Background Readings: BLACK NATIONALISM

Abraham, Kinfe. *Politics of Black Nationalism.* Trenton, NJ: Africa World Press, 1992.

Carlisle, Rodney P. *The Roots of Black Nationalism.* Port Washington, NY: Kennifkat, 1975.

Carmichael, Stokely, and Charles Hamilton. *Black Power: The Politics of Liberation in America.* New York: Random House, 1967.

Cone, James H. *Martin & Malcolm & America: A Dream or a Nightmare.* Maryknoll, NY: Orbis Books, 1991.

Jones, LeRoi (Amiri Baraka). *Home: Social Essays.* New York: William Morrow, 1966.

Ovenden, Kevin. *Malcolm X: Socialism and Black Nationalism.* London: Bookmarks, 1992.

Stuckey, Sterling, ed. *The Ideological Origins of Black Nationalism.* Boston: Beacon Press, 1972.

Van Deburg, William, ed. *Modern Black Nationalism: From Marcus Garvey to Louis Farrakhan.* New York: New York UP, 1997.

Recommended Literature: Toni Cade Bambara, *The Salt Eaters* (novel)

                               Haki Madhubuti (Don L. Lee), *The Book of Life* (poetry)

The Star That Went Astray
David Bradley

Best known for his documentary novel The Chaneysville Incident, *David Bradley is a professor of English who has published articles in a variety of periodicals, including* Esquire Magazine *and the* New York Arts Journal. *The following essay comes from the December 1983 issue of* Esquire. *Here Bradley profiles Malcolm X, presenting both the similarities and the differences between Martin Luther King, Jr. and the Black Muslim leader. Elsewhere in the essay, Bradley discusses the effects Malcolm X had on him as well as on the Civil Rights, Black Power, and antiwar movements of the 1960s and 1970s.*

---

1   Martin Luther King, Jr. should have been my hero. I was a middle-class black kid, the son of a preacher, carefully trained in the Ways I Should Go: Christianity, the Protestant Ethic, the social responsibility and respectability prescribed by W.E.B. Du Bois for the Talented Tenth—that cadre of "colored, college-bred men" whose mission, Du Bois wrote, would be to keep the black masses from "brooding over the wrongs of the past and the difficulties of the present, so that all their energies may be bent toward a cheerful striving and cooperation with their white neighbors." I should have been inspired by another middle-class black kid—also the son of a preacher, a product of Atlanta and Atlanta University, the very city and institution that inspired

Du Bois's thoughts—who became a white-shirted revolutionary, the most brightly shining example of Christian idealism this nation has ever produced.

2   But Martin Luther King, Jr. left me cold. For me there was something missing in both him and his philosophy. I did not know what. I could only say (as I once did to my father in a moment of ill-advised and quickly withdrawn candor) that King knew more of Christ and Gandhi than he did of white people—at least the ones of my acquaintance.

3   That insight came to me after I read King's "Letter from Birmingham Jail," in which he expressed a disappointment with the lack of activity of the white moderates. Then, dimly and intuitively, I saw that King's ideas were based on the belief that there existed in American society a moral white majority that would be disgusted by the actions of an immoral white minority against a passive black minority and that would take swift and correct action. Clearly a fallacy.

4   I could not so quickly analyze King's philosophy when I first read "Letter from Birmingham Jail." But then I came across a wholly irreverent but deadly accurate evaluation of King's adoption of Gandhi's philosophy: "Gandhi was a big dark elephant sitting on a little white mouse. King was a little black mouse sitting on top of a big white elephant." When I read that, I knew not only what I had been trying to say but that, in the expression of the thought, there was a mighty intelligence at work. I had found my hero. He was Malcolm Little, aka Detroit Red, Satan, El-Hajj Malik El-Shabazz—Malcolm X.

5   For someone like me to identify with someone like Malcolm was not as far-fetched as it might sound. In fact, the similarities between Malcolm and King are almost bizarre, given the popular perception that their natures were totally different—that King was a master of cool intellectual protest, while Malcolm was a thoughtless firebrand. Both were born in the latter part of the 1920s, Malcolm in 1925, King four years later. Both of their fathers were Georgia Baptist preachers, and both had the early and intense exposure to Christian teaching that such parentage implies. Both had below-standard secondary educations, which forced them to play educational catch-up: Malcolm leaving school in the eighth grade; King, on entering college, having only an eighth-grade reading level. Despite that, both were voracious readers and scholars, primarily of religion and philosophy—both were especially familiar with the writings of Thoreau. Both became ministers as well as scholars, in faiths that emphasized discipline, hard work, abstention from vice, and public service; both were married, with children; both were pilgrims abroad, King having journeyed to Gandhi's India, Malcolm having become, like all good Muslims, a pilgrim to Mecca; both were assassinated when they were just about forty.

6   Their dissimilarities, however, were crucial. King was a child of relative privilege, his family affluent, fixed, secure, traditionally nuclear. Malcolm grew up in poverty, in a family that moved frequently and was finally broken up after his father's death and his mother's dissolution into insanity. King was a product of the urban South, Malcolm of the North, with experience in rural,

suburban, and hard-core urban settings. King's educational handicaps did not interfere with a traditional pattern of study; Malcolm was a dropout. King was a product of black schools until after he received his B.A.; Malcolm knew the dubious benefits of school integration first-hand. In addition to his Baptist training, Malcolm had experience with other religions. His mother, before her breakdown, became a Seventh-Day Adventist, a sect whose practices pre-adapted him to the laws of Islam. But, perhaps most significantly, unlike King, Malcolm had experience not just with poverty but with the entire underside of American society. A street hustler who graduated from shoe-shine boy to dope seller, numbers runner, burglar, drug addict, zoot-suiter, chaser of morally depraved white women, jiver, hipster, and convict, Malcolm knew the welfare system, the criminal justice system, the practical workings of American society that contradicted idealistic theory.

7   He was also the living embodiment of every negative stereotype popularly associated with the American black. As Carl Rowan, then the head of the United States Information Agency, said in response to foreign eulogizing of Malcolm, "All this about an ex-convict, ex-dope peddler who became a racial fanatic."

8   What Rowan, and almost all of America, failed to understand was that Malcolm's life was truer than King's, his experience more broad and typical. King was the prototype of the New Negro, Malcolm the stereotype Nigger. King was a saint (a woman tried to stab him through the heart; the surgeon who closed the wound set his sutures in the pattern of a cross), Malcolm a sinner (inspired by his atheism, remarkable even in a prison, his fellow inmates named him "Satan"). King said the good things that middle-class black and white America wanted to hear said; Malcolm said what no one in any establishment wanted said. On subject after subject, Malcolm kicked ass.

9   On the idea that blacks should develop as immigrant groups had: "Everything that comes out of Europe, every blue-eyed thing, is already an American. And as long as you and I have been over here, we aren't Americans yet. They don't have to pass civil rights legislation to make a Polack an American." On the hypocrisy surrounding the position of blacks in America: "I'm not going to sit at your table and watch you eat, with nothing on my plate, and call myself a diner." On blacks and the American heritage: "We didn't land on Plymouth Rock. It landed on us." On white influence in the civil rights movement: "The white man pays Reverend Martin Luther King, subsidizes Reverend Martin Luther King. . . ." On nonviolence as a way of life: "If they make the Klan nonviolent, I'll be nonviolent." On nonviolence as a universal tactic: ". . . if he only understands the language of a rifle, get a rifle. If he only understands the language of a rope, get a rope. But don't waste time talking the wrong language to a man if you really want to communicate with him." On King's reliance on the promise of protection by federal officials from white southern officials: ". . . asking the fox to protect you from the wolf." In speaking this way, with ideas that sprang from the same works of philosophy and religion as King's ideas,

but in an idiom that came from earthier experience, Malcolm spoke in a pungent voice for many blacks, especially those least likely to themselves be articulate, least likely to have access to public attention.

10   Malcolm certainly was articulate and he certainly got attention, probably contributing to acceptance of King. Malcolm was the horrible alternative. King was aware of this effect and used it, referring to Malcolm repeatedly by warning that a failure to redress black grievances might force blacks into more-violent actions, while acknowledging, at the same time, that business leaders had become "prepared to tolerate change in order to avoid costly chaos."

11   Malcolm was the spokesman of that chaos. For although the Nation of Islam had been around since the Thirties, it was not until 1959 that it was represented by a regular publication, *Muhammad Speaks,* a creation of Malcolm's. And it was also not until 1959 that the Nation received nationwide media attention. That year CBS aired the documentary *The Hate That Hate Produced.* An inflammatorily edited piece of yellow journalism (even Malcolm described it as being "edited to increase the shock mood" and likened public reaction to "what happened back in the 1930s when Orson Welles frightened America with . . . an invasion by 'men from Mars'"), the CBS program featured Malcolm and thrust him into the public spotlight. In part because Elijah Muhammad had declared him a Muslim spokesman, in part because it was Malcolm who had pushed the Muslim faith into media-conscious urban centers of the East—Boston, Philadelphia, then New York—but mainly because his style of expression brought the kind of provocative drama into a live talk-show studio that King could offer only on taped news broadcasts, by 1963, when King spoke of the positive effect of the violent alternative, Malcolm had become the symbol of that alternative. Although the Nation of Islam, which had come to be called the Black Muslims, was not and never had been violent, and in fact strictly eschewed violence save in self-defense, Malcolm chose to go along with the media representation.

12   Why he went along was never entirely clear. In his *Autobiography* he claims to have been motivated by a desire to defend the Nation of Islam and Elijah Muhammad from the false image presented in *Life, Look, Time, Newsweek,* and nearly every major media outlet in America. However, it is true that he spoke repeatedly to the white media and was, by design, untempered in speech. And he was as aware of some of his effect on the nonviolent struggle as King was, for he told King's wife while King was jailed in Selma: "If the white people realize what the alternative is, perhaps they will be more willing to hear Dr. King."

13   Which is not to say that Malcolm's strident pronouncements had no effect on the civil rights movement. For it was at the time of his greatest prominence (greater television presence in 1963 than King) that elements of the movement began to espouse Malcolm-like rhetoric and ideas. The planning of the Mississippi Freedom Summer of 1964 was complicated by the notion that it should be a black struggle carried on without white assistance. Non-violence was seen as a tactical option rather than a moral imperative; in the wake of the

triple killing of civil rights workers near Philadelphia, Mississippi, the field workers of both the Student Nonviolent Coordinating Committee and the Congress of Racial Equality asserted their right to wear guns for self-protection. Later, SNCC also adopted Malcolm's position opposing military service for blacks, coining the slogan "Hell no, we won't go," which became the rallying cry of the antidraft movement, and pushing King to consider and oppose the Vietnam War, as Malcolm had done years before.

14   Within the Nation of Islam, Malcolm's influence waned, due to jealousy, specifically that of Elijah Muhammad. Yet Malcolm's prominence made the Muslims prominent, bringing in a wave of converts and making the Muslim dreams of economic independence more a reality and the Muslim programs of rehabilitation more effective than ever before. These dreams and programs were models for those of other groups, such as the Republic of New Africa and the Black Panthers, whose leaders found that there was a new acceptance in publishing for words written from prison because of the success of Malcolm's *Autobiography*.

15   Indeed, Malcolm established the rhetorical style that became the hallmark of the various movements of the late Sixties and Seventies. While the antidraft and antiwar movements drew their strategic and tactical models from the nonviolent civil rights movement, their rhetoric, like that of later black groups, was poured hot from the mold of Malcolm rather than beaten in the shape of King's learned, lofty dissertations. From Malcolm came sharp turns of phrase, the euphony and rhythm that gave Eldridge Cleaver "If you're not part of the solution, you're part of the problem" and H. Rap Brown "Violence is as American as cherry pie."

16   At the time of his death, Malcolm's influence was only beginning to be felt. Then he was still popularly seen as a madman, a racist, a man of violence. King, with ironic self-righteousness, considering the circumstances of his own demise, on the occasion of Malcolm's assassination said Malcolm was a victim of the violence that had spawned him.

17   Precisely what Malcolm was the victim of is hard to say. He himself spoke of the danger from other Muslims. "Any number of former brothers felt they would make heroes of themselves in the Nation of Islam if they killed me. . . . No one would kill you quicker than a Muslim if he felt that's what Allah wanted him to do." But assassinations are not always done quickly. Although the likelihood of international involvement has been widely denied, Malcolm was establishing ties with black leaders in Africa and with Muslim leaders in the Middle East. These connections, especially the Middle Eastern ones, which transcended racial lines and which involved a region in which American foreign policy and economic interests were greatly concerned, surely would have made Malcolm's death a source of some relief to many. We do not know who killed Malcolm. We do know that of the four great political assassinations of the Sixties, Malcolm's was most clearly a conspiracy.

18   And it was a successful conspiracy. For not only did it result in Malcolm's death but that death obscured what is perhaps the greatest importance of

Malcolm as a man, a leader, and an example: that by the time he died, Malcolm had changed.

19   That change was totally unexpected, in fact virtually impossible, given the racial and social theories of the day. Those theories held that once blacks allowed themselves to leave the high road of moral purity, exemplified by Christian forbearance and *agape* love, once they began to hate their oppressors, they would be lost to hopeless, mindless rage. But Malcolm negated that. "In the past," he said after his pilgrimage to Mecca, "yes, I have made sweeping indictments of *all* white people. I never will be guilty of that again—as I know now that some white people *are* truly sincere, that some truly are capable of being brotherly toward a black man."

20   Impossible as it supposedly was, such a change might have been acceptable had it been simply extreme (America would have loved to have Malcolm recant). But Malcolm insisted on *developing*. He did not give up his hating or his accusation of racism. He simply learned to hate institutions: "Here in America, the seeds of racism are so deeply rooted in the white people collectively, their belief that they are 'superior' in some way is so deeply rooted, that these things are in the national white subconsciousness. . . . The white man's racism toward the black man here in America is what has got him in such trouble all over this world, with other non-white peoples. . . . That's why you've got all of this trouble in places like Viet Nam."

21   Malcolm's new ideas were, like many of his ideas, ahead of his time. Fortunately, by means of texts of speeches, interviews, and the tapes from which Alex Haley would create his *Autobiography,* Malcolm spoke beyond his time into an era and to ears, like mine, that were able to understand him and needed to.

22   For while many of his pronouncements seem silly, overly rhetorical, and extreme, he not only made them and admitted to them but he meant them and moved beyond them. His experience encompassed that of so many of us. His example applies to so many of us. He experienced, as every black does, the alienation, isolation, deprivation, elimination, exploitation, and subjugation that is dished out by American society. He saw, as every thinking person must see, the terror of racism, the awesome depth of its roots, the awful subtlety of its poisoned fruit. He felt, as every human person must feel, rage and despair and hatred so powerful as to warp the mind. He acknowledged the damage he had suffered. But he survived. Not just physically. Emotionally. Spiritually. He survived.

23   To any of us who have at times allowed the pain to defeat us and have wondered, while in the throes of it, if this were the anguish of death, to any of us who have succumbed to the feelings and feared that this was a madness from which we could not recover, to any of us who know we could never, because of our lacking or its lacking, follow a philosophy of saintly forbearance, to any of us who have hated so thoroughly that we have wondered if we could ever love again, Malcolm's example did make and continues to make more than a difference. It gives us hope.

Reading-to-Write Questions

1. **Content:** Why does Bradley cite his personal experience in the introduction to his profile of Malcolm X?

2. **Arrangement:** How does Bradley organize his discussion of Malcolm X's and Martin Luther King's similarities and differences?

3. **Style:** Find instances where Bradley uses the same one or two words to begin consecutive sentences? What effects are produced by the repetition of sentence beginnings?

4. _____

   _____

   _____

Suggested Topics

1. **Observation:** Ask White and Black students for their impressions of Malcolm X. Then compare and/or contrast their views. (audience = classmates)

2. **Critique:** Bradley states, ". . . I saw that King's ideas were based on the belief that there existed in American society a moral white majority that would be disgusted by the actions of an immoral white minority against a passive black minority and that would take swift and correct action. Clearly a fallacy." Is King's reasoning fallacious as Bradley contends? Or has Bradley misinterpreted King's philosophy? (audience = Bradley)

3. **Synthesis:** Contrast Bradley's and Early's reactions to Malcolm X. (audience = students interested in learning more about Malcolm X)

4. _____

   _____

   _____

Background Readings: MALCOLM X

Clarke, John Henrik, ed. *Malcolm X: The Man and His Ideas.* New York: Macmillan, 1969.

Cone, James H. *Martin and Malcolm and America.* Maryknoll, NY: Orbis Books, 1991.

Dyson, Michael Eric. *Making Malcolm: The Myth and Meaning of Malcolm X.* New York: Oxford UP, 1996.

Ellis, Carl F. *Malcolm: The Man Behind the X.* Chattanooga, TN: Accord, 1993.

Gallen, David. *Malcolm X: As They Knew Him.* New York: Carroll & Graf, 1992.

Leader, Edward Roland. *Understanding Malcolm X: The Controversial Changes in His Political Philosophy.* New York: Vantage Press, 1993.

Perry, Bruce. *Malcolm: The Life of a Man Who Changed Black America.* Barrytown, NY: Station Hill, 1990.

Strickland, William. *Malcolm X: Make It Plain.* New York and London: Penguin, 1994.

X, Malcolm. *Malcolm X Speaks.* New York: Merit, 1965.

_____. *Malcolm X: By Any Means Necessary.* Ed. George Breitman. New York: Pathfinder, 1970.

_____. *Malcolm X: The Last Speeches.* Ed. Bruce Perry. New York: Pathfinder, 1989.

_____ with Alex Haley. *The Autobiography of Malcolm X.* New York: Random House, 1964.

Recommended Literature: Baraka, Amiri (LeRoi Jones), "A Poem for Black Hearts" in *Black Magic Poetry* (poem)

N.R. Davidson, *El Hajj Malik* (play)

Larry Neal, "Malcolm X—An Autobiography" in Jones and Neal's *Black Fire* (poem)

Revolutionary Struggle
Assata Shakur

A member of the Black Liberation Army, Assata Shakur (born Joanne Chesimard) began her struggle against capitalism and imperialism in the sixties. Initially, she joined the Black Panthers and soon became a target of government intelligence and police agencies. After she quit the party, she went into hiding ("underground") to evade the police. Although she was arrested seven times from 1971–1973, the charges in six cases led to acquittal or were dismissed because of lack of evidence. However, on May 2, 1973, she was arrested and forced to await trial in jail until 1977, when she was finally convicted as an accomplice to the murder of a white state trooper. Two years later, she escaped from prison, eventually making her way to Cuba, where she received political asylum and published her autobiography, Assata *(1987). In the following excerpt, she describes life as a fugitive in the Black Liberation Army and explains what a "revolutionary war" is and is not.*

---

1   I was surprised to find that the Black Liberation Army was not a central-ized, organized group with a common leadership and chain of command.

Instead, there were various organizations and collectives working out of different cities, and in some of the larger cities there were often several groups working independently of each other. Many members of the various groups had been forced into hiding as a result of the extreme police repression that took place during the late sixties and early seventies. Some had serious cases, some had minor ones, and others, like me, were just wanted for "questioning."

2   Sisters and brothers joined these groups because they were committed to revolutionary struggle in general and armed struggle in particular and wanted to help build the armed movement in amerika. It was the strangest feeling. People i used to run into at rallies were now in hiding, sending messages that they wanted to hook up. Sisters and brothers from just about every revolutionary or militant group in the country were either rotting away in prison or had been forced underground. Everyone i talked to was interested in taking the struggle to a higher level. But the question was how. How to bring together all those people scattered around the country into an organized body that would be effective in struggling for Black liberation.

3   It became evident, almost from the beginning, that consolidation was not a good idea. There were too many security problems, and different groups had different ideologies, different levels of political consciousness and different ideas about how armed struggle in amerika should be waged. On the whole, we were weak, inexperienced, disorganized, and seriously lacking in training. But the biggest problem was one of political development. There were sisters and brothers who had been so victimized by amerika that they were willing to fight to the death against their oppressors. They were intelligent, courageous and dedicated, willing to make any sacrifice. But we were to find out quickly that courage and dedication were not enough. To win any struggle for liberation, you have to have the way as well as the will, an overall ideology and strategy that stem from a scientific analysis of history and present conditions.

4   Some of the groups thought they could just pick up arms and struggle and that, somehow, people would see what they were doing and begin to struggle themselves. They wanted to engage in a do-or-die battle with the pig power structure in amerika, even though they were weak and ill prepared for such a fight. But the most important factor is that armed struggle, by itself, can never bring about a revolution. Revolutionary war is a people's war. And no people's war can be won without the support of the masses of people. Armed struggle can never be successful by itself; it must be part of an overall strategy for winning, and the strategy must be political as well as military.

5   Since we did not own the TV stations or newspapers, it was easy for the news media to portray us as monsters and terrorists. The police could terrorize the Black community daily, yet if one Black person successfully defended himself or herself against a police attack, they were called terrorists. It soon became clear to me that our most important battle was to help politically mobilize, educate, and organize the masses of Black people and to win their minds and hearts. It was inconceivable that we could survive, much less win anything, without their support.

6   Every group fighting for freedom is bound to make mistakes, but unless you study the common, fundamental laws of armed revolutionary struggle you are bound to make unnecessary mistakes. Revolutionary war is protracted warfare. It is impossible for us to win quickly. To win we have got to wear down our oppressors, little by little, and, at the same time, strengthen our forces, slowly but surely. I understood some of my more impatient sisters and brothers. I knew that it was tempting to substitute military for political struggle, especially since all of our aboveground organizations were under vicious attack by the FBI, the CIA, and the local police agencies. All of us who saw our leaders murdered, our people shot down in cold blood, felt a need, a desire to fight back. One of the hardest lessons we had to learn is that revolutionary struggle is scientific rather than emotional. I'm not saying that we shouldn't feel anything, but decisions can't be based on love or on anger. They have to be based on the objective conditions and on what is the rational, unemotional thing to do.

7   In 1857 the u.s. supreme kourt ruled that Blacks were only three-fifths of a man and had no rights that whites were bound to respect. Today, more than a hundred and twenty-five years later, we still earn less than three-fifths of what white people earn. It was plain to me that we couldn't look to the kourts for freedom and justice anymore than we could expect to gain our liberation by participating in the u.s. political system, and it was pure fantasy to think we could gain them by begging. The only alternative left was to fight for them, and we are going to have to fight like any other people who have fought for liberation.

Reading-to-Write Questions

1. **Content:** Shakur claims that the media distorted the story of the Black Liberation Army. How does she attempt to convince you that her account is accurate?

2. **Arrangement:** Where does Shakur employ comparison-contrast to organize ideas within paragraphs?

3. **Style:** Why do you think Shakur spells "court" and "America" as she does? Why doesn't she consistently capitalize "U.S." or the first-person pronoun "I"?

4. _____

   _____

   _____

Suggested Topics

1. **Observation:** Find out which revolutionary parties meet on your campus. Attend one of their meetings or solicit their literature to discover how they define "revolutionary struggle." Then write a definition essay to inform other students. (audience = your classmates)

2. **Critique:** Shakur writes, "The police could terrorize the Black community daily, yet if one Black person successfully defended himself or herself against a police attack, they were called terrorists." Consult the background readings for Shakur's and Carstarphen's essays to determine how accurately Shakur has described the relationship between Blacks and the police in the late sixties and early seventies.

3. **Synthesis:** Shakur states, "It was plain to me that we couldn't look to the courts for freedom and justice any more than we could expect to gain our liberation by participating in the U.S. political system, and it was pure fantasy to think we could gain them by begging." Contrast Shakur's position with King's, Brown's, and Robinson's. (audience = student activists)

4. _____

   _____

   _____

Background Readings: BLACK REVOLUTIONARY STRUGGLE

Carmichael, Stokely, and Charles Hamilton. *Black Power: The Politics of Liberation in America.* 2nd ed. New York: Vintage Books, 1992.

Cleaver, Eldridge. *Soul on Ice.* New York: McGraw-Hill, 1968.

James, Joy, ed. *The Angela Y. Davis Reader.* Malden, MA: Blackwell, 1998.

McCartney, John. *Black Power Ideologies: An Essay in American Political Thought.* Philadelphia: Temple UP, 1992.

Nkrumah, Kwame. *Handbook of Revolutionary Warfare.* New York: International Publishers, 1968.

Seale, Bobby. *Seize the Time: The Story of the Black Panther Party and Huey P. Newton.* 1970. Rpt. Baltimore, MD: Black Classic Press, 1991.

Student Essay:
UNFAIR CRITICISM
Theryn Knight
(1996)

1   In his comparison and contrast essay "The Star That Went Astray," David Bradley tells of his preference for the life and teachings of Malcolm X over those of Martin Luther King, Jr. Bradley is not fair to Dr. King in his criticism of him, for the essay was, for the most part, a glorification of the ideas of Malcolm X. Over seventy-five percent of the article praised Malcolm, and what little space Bradley did save to dedicate to King was reserved only for negative comments that were not at all balanced by an equal mention of his positive accomplishments, which were severely and conspicuously absent.

2   For example, Bradley's negative connotations are evident when he describes King with such words as "beaten," "lofty," "ironic self-righteousness" (299). On the other hand, he describes Malcolm with phrases such as "hot" (299), "a mighty intelligence" (296), "ahead of his time" (300). At one point during Bradley's eulogy, he even trivializes the breadth of King's experience: "But, perhaps most significantly, unlike King, Malcolm had experience not just with poverty but with the entire underside of life" (297). Bradley goes on to state that "Malcolm's life was truer than King's" simply because King was a middle-class black who didn't grow up in the ghetto with the rest of the blacks as the white media would have the public and Bradley believe (297). David Bradley is blatantly biased, and this can be shown through an unobjective comment at the start of his essay: "King knew more of Christ and Gandhi than he did of white people" (296).

3   Surprisingly, Bradley was evenhanded in his handling of one aspect: King's abridged biography was true and objective. However, this one exception to the rule in no way makes Bradley's criticism of Martin Luther King, Jr. fair.

Works Cited

Bradley, David. "The Star That Went Astray." *Revelations*. Ed. Teresa M. Redd. 3rd ed. Needham Heights, MA: Simon & Schuster, 1997. 295–300.

Student Essay:
TRUE FREEDOM
Kenyatta Miles
(1996)

1   The Civil Rights Movement was a struggle for freedom. Many of the luxuries we now take for granted were virtually nonexistent fifty or sixty years ago. Our parents, grandparents, and great-grandparents made many sacrifices to ensure our freedom. Although their efforts were not in vain, African-Americans are still not completely, truly free. Even after the deaths of many black protestors, we are still not free to dream, we are still not free to make our dreams a reality, and we are still not free to simply be.

2   In the 1800s, African-Americans were not only fighting against physical bondage but they had to fight against mental bondage as well. Slavery was a horrible institution that robbed us of our lives, our freedom, and our history. At that time, it was generally believed that if we were freed (that is, in a physical sense), everything else would fall into place.

3   In the 1950s and 1960s, we found that white America had found other ways to keep us in bondage. Although some schools were integrated, those black students privileged enough to attend white schools were threatened and sometimes physically mistreated. But as time progressed, we conquered the institution of segregation, yet we still face an even stronger opponent—racism. The evils of racism permeate every aspect of society from education to entrepreneurship, and until we defeat it, we can never achieve a state of true freedom.

4   Even if one considers the large number of successful black people in America, including Oprah Winfrey, Michael Jordan, Michael Jackson and Louis Farrakhan, we still must realize that our children dream of being as successful as these celebrities. However, our society convinces them that successful black people are only one in a million and that their dreams can never be made a reality and all they can do is dream. A mentality of black inferiority stifles and prohibits their growth and development and hinders many from making positive contributions to society. Unless we support and encourage our children, brothers, sisters, nieces, and nephews to pursue their dreams, they will grow up doubting themselves and their ability to achieve all of their goals. Through

fighting the concept of black inferiority, we will help the next generation become better able and more prepared to deal with racism more effectively.

5   Another issue that prohibits African-Americans from living in a state of true freedom is the lack of funding for black businesses. When blacks decide to go into business for themselves, it takes a great deal of effort to convert that childhood dream into a reality that is tangible enough for someone else to invest money in it. Until we begin to support each other and give back to the communities that gave so much to us, black America cannot become economically independent and we will not be free.

6   After we dream and we work to make those dreams a reality, it is very disappointing to see black people in positions of power who have forgotten the communities from which they came. It is equally disappointing to find that the people we work so hard to support and uplift no longer respect us. When African-Americans are in the limelight, they find themselves under scrutiny by the entire black community. We will never be free to be until we achieve the kind of freedom that does not make it easier to criticize than it is to contribute. We will never be free to be until we achieve the kind of freedom that does not make the rich even richer while the poor become poorer. We will never be free to be until we achieve the kind of freedom that encourages children to dream big things that may be difficult (but not impossible) to attain instead of small endeavors that pose no challenge. We will never be free to be until we achieve the kind of freedom that allows us to celebrate our history while looking to a better future. We will never be free to be until we achieve the kind of freedom that urges us to support one another in a united cause as opposed to everyone "doing their own thing." Only then will we be truly free to dream, free to make our dreams a reality, and simply free to be.

a question of progress

Sometimes in life
things seem to be moving
and they are not
and they are not
there.

from "To Don at Salaam"
by Gwendolyn Brooks

A Slow Walk of Trees
Toni Morrison

The first African American woman to win the Nobel Prize for literature, Toni Morrison has written the novels The Bluest Eye, Sula, Song of Solomon, Tar Baby, Beloved, Jazz, *and* Paradise. *She has also authored a play (*Dreaming Emmett*) and numerous essays, some collected in the volumes* Playing in the Dark *and* Racing Justice. *First published on July 4, 1976, the following essay appeared in* The New York Times Magazine *in commemoration of the U.S. bicentennial. In this essay Morrison contrasts how her grandparents and parents felt about racism in the U.S. Proceeding person-by-person and point-by-point, she highlights the differences between the genders and between the generations.*

---

1   His name was John Solomon Willis, and when at age 5 he heard from the old folks that "the Emancipation Proclamation was coming," he crawled under the bed. It was his earliest recollection of what was to be his habitual response to the promise of white people: horror and an instinctive yearning for safety. He was my grandfather, a musician who managed to hold on to his violin but not his land. He lost all 88 acres of his Indian mother's inheritance to legal predators who built their fortunes on the likes of him. He was an unreconstructed black pessimist who, in spite of or because of emancipation, was convinced for 85 years that there was no hope whatever for black people in this country. His rancor was legitimate, for he, John Solomon, was not only an

artist but a first-rate carpenter and farmer, reduced to sending home to his family money he had made playing the violin because he was not able to find work. And this during the years when almost half the black male population were skilled craftsmen who lost their jobs to white ex-convicts and immigrant farmers.

2   His wife, however, was of a quite different frame of mind and believed that all things could be improved by faith in Jesus and an effort of the will. So it was she, Ardelia Willis, who sneaked her seven children out of the back window into the darkness, rather than permit the patron of their sharecropper's existence to become their executioner as well, and headed north in 1912, when 99.2 percent of all black people in the U.S. were native-born and only 60 percent of white Americans were. And it was Ardelia who told her husband that they could not stay in the Kentucky town they ended up in because the teacher didn't know long division.

3   They have been dead now for 30 years and more and I still don't know which of them came closer to the truth about the possibilities of life for black people in this country. One of their grandchildren is a tenured professor at Princeton. Another, who suffered from what the Peruvian poet called "anger that breaks a man into children," was picked up just as he entered his teens and emotionally lobotomized by the reformatories and mental institutions specifically designed to serve him. Neither John Solomon nor Ardelia lived long enough to despair over one or swell with pride over the other. But if they were alive today each would have selected and collected enough evidence to support the accuracy of the other's original point of view. And it would be difficult to convince either one that the other was right.

4   Some of the monstrous events that took place in John Solomon's America have been duplicated in alarming detail in my own America. There was the public murder of a President in a theater in 1865 and the public murder of another President on television in 1963. The Civil War of 1861 had its encore as the civil-rights movement of 1960. The torture and mutilation of a black West Point Cadet (Cadet Johnson Whittaker) in 1880 had its rerun with the 1970's murders of students at Jackson State College, Texas Southern and Southern University in Baton Rouge. And in 1976 we watch for what must be the thousandth time a pitched battle between the children of slaves and the children of immigrants—only this time, it is not the New York draft riots of 1863, but the busing turmoil in Paul Revere's home town, Boston.

5   Hopeless, he'd said. Hopeless. For he was certain that white people of every political, religious, geographical and economic background would band together against black people everywhere when they felt the threat of our progress. And a hundred years after he sought safety from the white man's "promise," somebody put a bullet in Martin Luther King's brain. And not long before that some excellent samples of the master race demonstrated their courage and virility by dynamiting some little black girls to death. If he were here now, my grandfather, he would shake his head, close his eyes and pull out his violin—too polite to say, "I told you so." And his wife would pay atten-

tion to the music but not to the sadness in her husband's eyes, for she would see what she expected to see—not the occasional historical repetition, but, *like the slow walk of certain species of trees from the flatlands up into the mountains*, she would see the signs of irrevocable and permanent change. She, who pulled her girls out of an inadequate school in the Cumberland Mountains, knew all along that the gentlemen from Alabama who had killed the little girls would be rounded up. And it wouldn't surprise her in the least to know that the number of black college graduates jumped 12 percent in the last three years: 47 percent in 20 years. That there are 140 black mayors in this country; 14 black judges in the District Circuit, 4 in the Courts of Appeals and one on the Supreme Court. That there are 17 blacks in Congress, one in the Senate; 276 in state legislatures—223 in state houses, 53 in state senates. That there are 112 elected black police chiefs and sheriffs, 1 Pulitzer Prize winner; 1 winner of the Prix de Rome; a dozen or so winners of the Guggenheim; 4 deans of predominantly white colleges. . . . Oh, her list would go on and on. But so would John Solomon's sweet sad music.

6   While my grandparents held opposite views on whether the fortunes of black people were improving, my own parents struck similarly opposed postures, but from another slant. They differed about whether the moral fiber of white people would ever improve. Quite a different argument. The old folks argued about how and if black people could improve themselves, who could be counted on to help us, who would hinder us and so on. My parents took issue over the question of whether it was possible for white people to improve. They assumed that black people were the humans of the globe, but had serious doubts about the quality and existence of white humanity. Thus my father, distrusting every word and every gesture of every white man on earth, assumed that the white man who crept up the stairs one afternoon had come to molest his daughters and threw him down the stairs and then our tricycle after him. (I think my father was wrong, but considering what I have seen since, it may have been very healthy for me to have witnessed that as my first black-white encounter.) My mother, however, *believed* in them—their possibilities. So when the meal we got on relief was bug-ridden, she wrote a long letter to Franklin Delano Roosevelt. And when white bill collectors came to our door, it was she who received them civilly and explained in a sweet voice that we were people of honor and that the debt would be taken care of. Her message to Roosevelt got through—our meal improved. Her message to the bill collectors did not always get through and there was occasional violence when my father (self-exiled to the bedroom for fear he could not hold his temper) would hear that her reasonableness had failed. My mother was always wounded by these scenes, for she thought the bill collector knew that she loved good credit more than life and that being in arrears on a payment horrified her probably more than it did him. So she thought he was rude because he was white. For years she walked to utility companies and department stores to pay bills in person and even now she does not seem convinced that checks are legal tender. My father loved excellence, worked hard (he held three jobs at

once for 17 years) and was so outraged by the suggestion of personal slackness that he could explain it to himself only in terms of racism. He was a fastidious worker who was frightened of one thing: unemployment. I can remember now the dooms day-cum-graveyard sound of "laid off" and how the minute school was out he asked us, "Where you workin'?" Both my parents believed that all succor and aid came from themselves and their neighborhood, since "they"—white people in charge and those not in charge but in obstructionist positions—were in some way fundamentally, genetically corrupt.

7   So I grew up in a basically racist household with more than a child's share of contempt for white people. And for each white friend I acquired who made a small crack in that contempt, there was another who repaired it. For each one who related to me as a person, there was one who in my presence at least, became actively "white." And like most black people of my generation, I suffer from racial vertigo that can be cured only by taking what one needs from one's ancestors. John Solomon's cynicism and his deployment of his art as both weapon and solace, Ardelia's faith in the magic that can be wrought by sheer effort of the will; my mother's open-mindedness in each new encounter and her habit of trying reasonableness first; my father's temper, his impatience and his efforts to keep "them" (throw them) out of his life. And it is out of these learned and selected attitudes that I look at the quality of life for my people in this country now. These widely disparate and sometimes conflicting views, I suspect, were held not only by me, but by most black people. Some I know are clearer in their positions, have not sullied their anger with optimism or dirtied their hope with despair. But most of us are plagued by a sense of being worn shell-thin by constant repression and hostility as well as the impression of being buoyed by visible testimony of tremendous strides. There *is* repetition of the grotesque in our history. And there *is* the miraculous walk of trees. The question is whether our walk is progress or merely movement. O.J. Simpson leaning on a Hertz car *is* better than the Gold Dust Twins on the back of a soap box. But is "Good Times" better than Stepin Fetchit? Has the first order of business been taken care of? Does the law of the land work for us?

Reading-to-Write Questions

1. **Content:** How does Morrison grab and keep the attention of her readers? Throughout the essay how does she break the monotony of the statistics?

2. **Arrangement:** Where does Morrison follow a subject by subject pattern? Where does she proceed point by point?

3. **Style:** Morrison's diction is fresh. Can you find examples of her original word choice?

4. _____

   _____

   _____

Suggested Topics

1. **Observation:** Compare or contrast your parents' and/or grandparents' views on the progress of African Americans. (audience = Morrison's audience, i.e., the readers of *The New York Times Magazine*)

2. **Critique:** Morrison wrote this essay in commemoration of the U.S. bicentennial. Do you think it fits the occasion? Why or why not? (audience = editor of *The New York Times Magazine*)

3. **Synthesis:** With additional evidence from Chapman's and Bates's essays, compare or contrast the progress of African American men vs. African American women in the struggle against racial barriers. (audience = U.S. government officials)

4. _____

   _____

   _____

Background Readings: THE PROGRESS OF AFRICAN AMERICANS

Banerji, Sanjukta. *Deferred Hopes: Blacks in Contemporary America.* New York: Advent Books, 1987.

Bell, Derrick, *Faces at the Bottom of the Well: The Permanence of Racism.* New York: Basic Books, 1992.

Boamah-Wiafe, Daniel. *The Black Experience in Contemporary America.* Omaha, NE: Wisdom, 1990.

Cashman, Sean Dennis. *African-Americans and the Quest for Civil Rights, 1900–1990*. New York: New York UP, 1991.

Coleman, Jonathan. *Long Way to Go: Black and White in America*. Chicago: University of Chicago Press, 2000.

Cross, Theodore L. *The Black Power Imperative: Racial Inequality and the Politics of Nonviolence*. New York: Faulkner, 1984.

Garwood, Alfred N., ed. *Black Americans: A Statistical Sourcebook*. Boulder, CO: Numbers & Concepts, 1990.

Jackson, James S. *Life in Black America*. Newbury Park, CA: Sage, 1991.

Levine, Michael L. *African Americans and Civil Rights: From 1619 to the Present*. Phoenix, AZ: Onyx Press, 1996.

McWhorter, John. *Losing the Race: Self-Sabotage in Black America*. New York: The Free Press, 2000.

Pinkney, Alphonso. *The Myth of Black Progress*. Cambridge and New York: Cambridge UP, 1984.

Simms, Margaret C., ed. *Black Economic Progress: An Agenda for the 1990s*. Washington, DC: The Joint Center for Political Studies, 1988.

Thernstrom, Stephan, and Abigail Thernstrom. *America in Black and White: One Nation, Indivisible*. New York: Simon & Schuster, 1997.

Weinberg, Meyer. *Racism in the United States*. New York: Greenwood Press, 1990.

Recommended Literature: Ernest Gaines, *The Autobiography of Miss Jane Pittman* (novel)

Alex Haley, *Roots* (docunovel)

Langston Hughes, *Montage of a Dream Deferred* (poetry)

James Weldon Johnson, "Lift Every Voice and Sing" in the Abingdon Press edition of *Songs of Zion* (lyric)

Is My "Post-Integration" Daughter Black Enough?

Patrice Gaines-Carter

The author of this essay, Patrice Gaines-Carter, is a newspaper reporter and veteran of the Civil Rights Movement. Written in the form of a letter, the essay first appeared as a newspaper article in The Washington Post *in 1985. Throughout the essay Gaines-Carter contrasts the experiences and attitudes of her daughter's generation with those of her generation, a generation that had to fight for integration. Gaines-Carter also describes her experiences and attitudes in her autobiography,* Laughing in the Dark.

My dearest Daughter:

1   Something's been troubling me for the past two years. I jokingly call it the "Post-Integration Blues." Actually, it's no laughing matter.

2   I get it every time something happens like last month when I said to you, "Martin Luther King's birthday is coming up and we're going to do something special like attend a memorial service." You looked at me with total disdain and said, "Momma, that's the only day I'll get to sleep late."

3   When you say things like that, I take them personally. I know that I shouldn't, but I hurt. I take it as rejection of all that my generation of Blacks fought for, yet I know that is not how you intended it.

4   I don't want you to let King's birthday go by without remembering what he stood for. Although you are 16, I want you to fight racism. I want you to march

at the South African Embassy, and even if you can't, I want you to be aware that someone else is marching.

5   We've discussed this. You told me just recently, "Just because we don't march doesn't mean we don't know it's Dr. King's birthday." Still, I hurt, and wonder: What happened to my little girl who could barely print, but wrote the governor of North Carolina to ask him to "free the Wilmington 10?"

6   See, at 35, I come from a generation of marchers. I do not understand inaction. In fact, it frightens me. I do not trust it. You think my distrust is paranoia; I understand. It is because you have not seen what I have seen. At my segregated school in Beaufort, S.C., everything—our buses, books, desks—was hand-me-downs from the White school. On cold days we wore our coats in class because the heat didn't always work. The White children passed us in their new buses, on their way to their new school.

7   You have never known such. You ride a shiny school bus to a nine-year-old school that is thoroughly integrated. "Momma, we just don't put the emphasis on Black and White that you do," you told me the other day, adding, "But when we are in school, I do end up hanging with my friends, who just happen to be Black. Everybody does the same thing, so that Black people end up on one side and White people on another."

8   That wasn't exactly what I wanted to hear either, believe it or not. I was part of a busing plan that helped integrate DuVal Senior High School in Greenbelt, just a couple of miles from your school. I suffered at that school. I felt like a stranger in a foreign land because I was one of 50 Black students out of about 2,000 pupils. Some of the Black students adapted well; I did not. I pacified myself by imagining I was a sacrificial lamb, being used so that generations of Blacks after me would receive benefits I had been denied.

9   My payback, I figured, would be the lives of those Black children who came after me. They would ride new buses and go to new schools. They would not sit in unheated classrooms. They would do all of this because of integration. They would do all of this without assimilating, without becoming like the people we were fighting or, in other words, "They would never act White."

10   You would probably say I am overreacting. I wonder if what I want isn't impossible. You think that you don't "act White," and mostly you're right. But changes can creep up so slowly and in such small ways.

11   For instance, you watch music videos for hours at a time and seem pleased at what you see. When I look at them, what I notice is that the Black women who are featured as lovers are light-skinned Black women with long, straight hair—women who look like they're White.

12   My generation watched television shows that seldom showed Blacks. We fought hard to get Blacks on television; then we fought harder to get all shades of Black people shown: dark chocolate, saffron cinnamon, blue-black and ginger. I don't see these colors in your videos—certainly not the ones meant to be physically attractive.

13   What bothers me is that you don't seem to miss the shades of color. To me, to not miss them is, in a way, to not act Black. It is like returning to the days when only Lena Horne, with her light skin and narrow nose, was considered a beautiful Black woman—by Blacks and Whites. It is like returning to days when women like Cicely Tyson, your grandmother and your great-grandmother, with their ebony skin and wide noses, were considered ugly because their features were different from those of White women. To not accept all of the shades of Black beauty is one step from "acting White."

14   I don't know when I first caught this Post-Integration Blues. It was around the first time I heard strange music coming from your room. The door was closed, but I knocked and you allowed me to peep in.

15   "What is it?" I asked, pointing to the stereo.

16   "I like that song," you said, hardly looking up from your book.

17   "Who is it? Sounds like somebody White."

18   "It's Cyndi Lauper," you replied, explaining that she was a new rock 'n' roll star.

19   "Cyndi who?" I asked.

20   You mumbled something, but by that time I was blue again. I was thinking about a time when Black people listened to music that had what I call a definite beat, a time when you could really tell a Black recording artist from a White one. I left the room floating on memories of songs by Frankie Lyman and the Teenagers, Ben E. King and James Brown. Soul Music.

21   While music and marching and television seem insignificant, they are not. It is the tiny threads of life that weave a whole history of a people. As far as I am concerned we are dealing with the continued existence of Black people. I want you to know this without knowing the pain. I wish I could push history into your consciousness simply by pressing the palm of my hand against your chest.

22   Every time I think I might suffer a total breakdown from the Post-Integration Blues, something happens to give me strength. This strength comes in ironic ways, too, like last November when you got called "nigger" for the first time.

23   You should have seen your face when you told me about it. You said you were working at the drive-in window at McDonald's and this man was at the window, waiting for his food and staring at you in a strange way. You asked if you could help him and he said, "No, I'm just looking at a nigger about to give me my food."

24   You threw the food in his car and the young Black woman working with you, who had not heard the man, screamed, "You're going to lose your job!"

25   "Momma," you told me, "I didn't care about the job. But I was too stunned to say anything to him."

26   In the old days I would have been ready to find the man and shoot him, but here I was thankful and slightly amused. "I am just amazed that it took 16 years," I said. "The first time somebody called me nigger I was too young to understand what they meant."

27   Sure, the fact that it took 16 years for you to be called a "nigger" was a sign of how some things have changed for the better. But it gave me strength for another reason: I also couldn't help feeling that it won't hurt your generation to get called "nigger" at least once to your face.

28   Every time somebody called me "nigger," I became more determined to not let up, to keep on coming, to march, to fight, to succeed. In your generation, I don't see that determination to march or fight. I think you need some reminders of what this country could easily return to unless we all fight daily.

29   I thought about the difference in our worlds on the night in July 1984 when your cousin Christopher was born. He struggled to come into this world on the very night that Jesse Jackson spoke at the Democratic National Convention.

30   I was in the delivery room with his mother and I went back and forth from wiping her brow and telling her, "Okay now, breathe, 1–2–3; that's good," to crying over the fact that I had lived long enough to see a Black man considered a serious presidential candidate.

31   When I think of Christopher now, I wonder: What will life be like for a young Black boy born into a world where a Black man has already run for president?

32   I first assumed Christopher's life would be better, then the Post-Integration Blues set in, and I looked at my blue self, who has marched and picketed, and said, "Do not assume anything." That is what frightens me about your own generation. I sometimes think you take too much for granted.

33   I am torn. I don't want you to live on the razor's edge as I did in South Carolina, when I couldn't enter certain doors, drink from certain water fountains or eat a meal sitting down at any restaurant downtown. But I don't want you to forget either. I'm afraid if you haven't lived on the razor's edge you forget you can bleed.

34   I am encouraged by incidents like the one when you came home a couple of weeks ago and in a disgusted voice said, "My history teacher didn't even know who Louis Farrakhan is, momma."

35   Maybe my words aren't just flying around your head. You have caught some of what I've been saying. Anyway, it's not just you who triggers my blues, but a lot of Black children.

36   For instance, remember when I took my friend's 12-year-old son, David-Askia, to the movie? Well, while we were sitting there waiting for the film to begin, I started telling him about how when I lived in Beaufort, S.C., in 1962, Black people could only sit in the balcony of the theater.

37   "We used to throw popcorn and ice from our sodas down on the White kids," I said. "There would always be two empty rows just under the edge of the balcony, since none of the White kids wanted to sit there and have to duck all the time."

38   "That was dumb, to throw things down on people," David-Askia said.

39   "It seems dumb now but it wasn't dumb if that was the only way you could get back at them," I said.

40   "Anyway," he said, turning to give me a puzzled look, "you can see better in the balcony."

41   "True," I told him. "But you only know that if you have had the chance to sit everywhere in the theater." He's so young, I'm not sure he understood what I was saying.

42   I hope you do.

With love,
Momma

Reading-to-Write Questions

1. **Content:** Although this letter is addressed to Gaines-Carter's daughter, what makes you think that it is addressed to a wider audience?

2. **Arrangement:** Because of the narrowness of the newspaper column, Gaines-Carter's essay contains numerous short paragraphs. How would you paragraph the essay if it appeared in a book?

3. **Style:** Now and then Gaines-Carter uses an unusually short sentence. Find the sentences. Do you think the short sentences are effective?

4. _____

   _____

   _____

Suggested Topics

1. **Observation:** Conduct interviews or a survey on campus to determine how politically active your fellow students are. Do they march and picket? Do they write letters of complaint to officials and newspaper editors? Do they participate in organizations or projects to uplift the community? (audience = campus newspaper)

2. **Critique:** Gaines-Carter writes, "That is what frightens me about your own generation. I sometimes think you take too much for granted." Are Gaines-Carter's fears well founded? If you conducted the interviews or survey recommended above, compare your findings with Gaines-Carter's claims about the Post-Integration Generation. (audience = African American college students)

3. **Synthesis:** Contrast Gaines-Carter's definition of "acting white" with the definition that (according to Raspberry) is held by many African American youths. (audience = African American high school students)

4. _____

   _____

   _____

Background Readings: THE POST-INTEGRATION GENERATION

Allen, Walter, Edgar Epps, and Nesha Haniff. *College in Black and White: African American Students in Predominantly White and in Historically Black Public Universities.* Albany: SUNY Press, 1991.

Banner-Haley, Charles Pete. *The Fruits of Integration: Black Middle-Class Ideology and Culture, 1960–1990.* Jackson, MI: University Press of Mississippi, 1994.

Bowser, Benjamin P., ed. *Black Male Adolescents: Parenting and Education in Community Context.* Lanham, MD: UP of America, 1991.

Claerbaut, David P. *Black Student Alienation: A Study.* San Francisco: R & Research Associates, 1978.

Edwards, Audrey K., and Craig K. Polite. *Children of the Dream: The Psychology of Black Success.* New York: Doubleday, 1992.

Epps, Edgar G. "The Impact of School Desegregation on Aspirations, Self-Concepts and Other Aspects of Personality." *Black Psychology.* Ed. Regnald L. Jones. New York: Harper & Row, 1980. 231–243.

McWhorter, John. *Losing the Race: Self-Sabotage in Black America.* New York: The Free Press, 2000.

Patchen, Martin. *Black-White Contact in Schools: Its Social and Academic Effects.* W. Lafayette, IN: Purdue UP, 1982.

Patterson, Orlando. *The Ordeal of Integration.* Washington, DC: Civitas/Counterpoint, 1997.

Peterson, Marvin W., et al. *Black Students on White Campuses: The Impact of Increased Black Enrollments.* Ann Arbor, MI: Survey Research Center, Institute for Social Research, University of Michigan, 1978.

Wicker, Tom. *Tragic Failure: Racial Integration in America.* New York: William Morrow, 1996.

Recommended Literature: Stephen Carter, *Reflections of an Affirmative Action Baby* (autobiography)
Trey Ellis, *Platitudes* (novel)

Private School, Private Pain
Patricia Elam Ruff

*Her twenty-fifth high school reunion compelled
Patricia Elam Ruff, a commentator for National
Public Radio, to recall her days as a Black
"token" in a "lily white" private school in the
1960s. In the following article, printed in* The
Washington Post *on February 23, 1997, Ruff
laments that the predicament of Black students
in private schools today reminds her of the isolation she felt thirty years before.*

1   Today's public schools, especially those in the District, are handicapped by budget crises, bulging classrooms, bureaucracies and violence. And so while many African American parents received fine public school educations them-selves, more and more of them are beginning to realize that public education is not so fine for their children. In the words of Steven Wright, a history teacher who sent six of his seven children to private schools, "Public schools prepare students to graduate; private schools prepare them to be leaders of tomor-row." While public schools must pluck the weeds before they can tend to the garden, private schools can get right down to planting seeds and watching them grow.

2   The most beautiful gardens have all kinds of flowers, but that variety does not come naturally to private schools. In most, black students are still a tiny minority, and thus vulnerable to isolation, unreasonable scrutiny and scram-bled identities. For black students, a private school education has a cost above and beyond the tuition. I paid that price when I integrated a private girls' school in Boston more than 30 years ago. Now I find my son and his black pri-vate school peers reliving much of my history.

3   I couldn't sleep the night before attending my 25th reunion at Winsor, the school where I was one of four black girls who broke the color bar. Ellen and Pam, two of my fellow trailblazers in Winsor's class of 1971, also had restless nights. None of us had been back to Winsor since graduation, and Pam and I had actually decided against attending the reunion until Ellen called with her idea of forming a panel to discuss our memories. Our panel would be entitled "Red, Black and White"; red and white being Winsor's school colors and black, of course, being us.

4   Seated in front of the mostly white audience, we black women begin reminiscing about penetrating the land of white privilege. In 1964, when we were 10 years old, Ellen and I entered Winsor's fifth grade. Pam came the next year. I tell our audience that most of our class did not know many black people, other than their maids and chauffeurs. Our new classmates would ask us questions they didn't dare ask their household help. "Can you wash your color off? Do you sing 'We Shall Overcome' at dinnertime?" We were unprepared for these queries and had no idea why we were being asked.

5   Those seated in front of us sit rapt and visibly moved. Unexpectedly, my eyes fill and I notice many in the audience are tearful, too.

6   Ellen remembers us taking the entrance exam in the school library with a group of white girls staring at us through glass windows. "Look at the black girls," she heard them say. "It was then," she notes, "that I knew what it was like to be an animal in a zoo." She rubs her hands together in her lap, gazing at a safe place on the wall in front of her.

7   Thirty years later, African American students in mostly white D.C.–area private schools say they, too, sometimes feel on display as they field questions about whether all of Southeast is a ghetto or how they wash their hair while it's braided. Although the number of black students in private schools has certainly grown since I was in school, for the past three years it has hovered between 9 percent and 20 percent, according to the Black Student Fund. The only local school that surpasses these numbers is the Newport School in Kensington, where more than 40 percent of its students are African American.

8   At many private schools, the numbers often translate into a single black student in a class—which renders that student, willing or not, a spokesman. "Last year we were talking about slavery and the teacher wanted me to speak for the whole race," says Asiatu Lawoyin, who is currently the only African American in the senior class at the Field School in Northwest Washington. "Then in history someone didn't understand the relationship between Martin Luther King, Malcolm X and Elijah Muhammad. The teacher asked me to explain it, and I asked, 'Why are you putting me on the spot?' But he forced me to answer the question."

9   Some black students fear that if they make a mistake, they embarrass not just themselves but their race; that makes the pressure, already intense in rigorous private schools, even more so. "There were times when I was scared to speak up, unless I was sure I had the right answer, for fear that I might reinforce negative stereotypes that blacks aren't as smart as whites," says Brandye

Lee, a 1996 graduate of Sidwell Friends. Many African American parents told me that while their children's grades are fine, their evaluations indicate that they need to speak up more in class.

10   Black students' school experience becomes defined by their difference. Lee, who also attended the Potomac School in McLean, says that she felt alienated most of the time. "At Potomac I didn't fit in with white kids. They pretended I did until school dance time—there were no black boys so I didn't dance. I was constantly looking for acceptance among my white peers."

11   I remember frantically, sometimes painfully, trying to comb the coarseness out of my hair so it would hang down, like that of my classmates, straight and lank against my face. Later I rebelled against that ideal by wearing a large afro—and deciding to forgo college because it wasn't "relevant to my authentic blackness." (I took a year off after graduation during which I realized my blackness would be best authenticated by attending college.)

12   I see similar gropings for identity among the students I talk to now, including the shunning of their "blackness." Kui Price, who left the Bullis School in Potomac three years ago to return to public school, says that she "got caught up in going to [whites'] country clubs and bar mitzvahs. I was living their life. Every weekend was like a fantasy. I'd be really happy and then really disappointed when I went home because it wasn't the kind of house they had." At a recent dance at Madeira, students told me, the black boys would dance only with white girls.

13   Other black students decide that preserving their blackness means rejecting "white values"—such as ambition. Some black parents take their children out of public school to escape just that anti-achievement ethic, but it may end up being magnified at a predominantly white school, where black students feel compelled to assert their "realness," whether by not studying or hanging with their homeboys on the street.

14   In doing so, they are partly questing for acceptance from their public school peers. "In my Southeast neighborhood," Brandye Lee says, "I was constantly teased for 'sounding white' or 'acting white.'" Lee's family helped her stay balanced, but not all kids are so fortunate. Some consciously switch from school culture to neighborhood culture as soon as they get home.

15   I tell the reunion audience I don't have any memories of blatant racism, but there were always painful reminders of my separateness. When I, the only black student in my English class, was asked to read a passage from "Huckleberry Finn," I scanned the page to make sure there were no "Nigger Jims." But of course there was one, sitting at the end of the paragraph, pompous and taunting. I remember how fast my heart was beating, how I planned to skate across the words and render them inaudible, how desperately I didn't want to cry. But when I said those two words it was as if I were Nigger Jim and the whole class knew it.

16   Even though black children should be taught not to let racism hold them back or keep them from taking responsibility for their actions, black parents do a disservice if they don't prepare their children for racism. Kui was told

that she had "nasty nigger hair" by a sixth-grade classmate when she was at Bullis.

17   Black students need to help each other through these times, but unfortunately, school administrations and white students sometimes disdain black students' efforts to comfort one another. Instead of understanding the healing it allows, white folk seem threatened by the self-segregation of African Americans. At Holton-Arms in Bethesda, which Lawoyin attended for three years, she says "when the black girls sat together at one table, the white girls would talk about us. But it was our one chance to be together and discuss what was going on. It was survival."

18   Black students need each other all the more because there are usually few black faculty members for them to turn to. Most private schools have 6 percent to 10 percent black faculty—an improvement over my school days, but still a discouraging statistic.

19   The parents and students I talked to suggest that some private schools seem to look for black teachers who check their blackness at the school door. While schools may be more comfortable with this kind of teacher, they need to realize that both black and white students would benefit from contact with grownups who do not try to play their blackness down or make it more palatable for white folk.

20   I met two African American teachers, Abe Wehmiller at Bullis and Brian King at Maret, who both sought careers in independent schools because they had no one they could relate to when they were in private school. These men, while obviously chock-full of knowledge, are also "keeping it real" and commanding respect from their students, black and white. "I taught a class with only one black student," King recalls, "and when we were studying slavery I could see the tears in his eyes. Years ago, at Georgetown Day, I was the boy. The difference was I was there for him."

21   Because of his own experience at an independent school, Wehmiller understands the importance of go-gos (dances featuring black go-go music) to black students at Bullis. "There was resistance [by the school administration] because of misconceptions about them attracting violence and hoodlums," he says. Wehmiller went to bat for the black students. "I explained . . . how important it was for the black kids who come into this other world every day to have an opportunity to feel like insiders for the first time, to share something from their world for once." The school agreed.

22   My school visits suggest to me that most schools are striving to change, and some are making tangible strides. Winsor now has 30 black students out of 399, and 11 black faculty and administrators out of 100. But I'd like to see every school follow Newport's lead and determine to have 50 percent African American enrollment, then do the same with the faculty. If private schools are truly creating future leaders, then their students must be prepared to overcome the racial divide rather than perpetuate it. Reflecting the general population isn't enough; our children need the strength of critical mass.

23   "Would you send your children to a school like Winsor?" someone at my reunion asks. Not like it was then, I tell them. Pam, Ellen and I all have children in private schools because we know the caliber of the education can't be matched, but we also know we have to work extra hard to keep our children grounded, happy and proud of who they are, and that we must stay active in their schools.

24   My mother is in the audience, and I see the pain etched in her face. She speaks, telling the audience who she is. "I felt I could take care of affirming the heritage. I didn't realize the pain would have such lasting effects, fueling rage and rebellion in Patricia. I don't know that I would make the same decision now... I hoped that my grandchildren would not be facing the same situation, but they are."

25   As a parent now, I understand that my parents felt a responsibility to provide the best education they could. And in some ways they succeeded: I breezed through college, learned how to write well, do thorough research and study in an organized fashion. And I learned not to be intimidated when I find myself in the minority, as I did in law school, graduate school and many other settings.

26   I know now that not only black students benefit from diverse education. As our panel wrapped up, a white former classmate rose. "I just want to say that you guys enriched our class. . . . You made our class aware. You guys stood up and said these things are bad and you changed things. You said white is not the only good color. Thank you," she says.

27   After the panel, other former classmates rush to me in tears, saying things like, "I'm so sorry if I said anything stupid to you back then." I tell them not to worry, it wasn't their fault, they didn't know any better.

28   But their parents and the school should have. As Barbara Patterson, president of the Black Student Fund, says, "Someone should be making sure that black children feel as good about their blackness as white children feel about their whiteness . . . the reality is that there's no tuition deduction for what's missing."

Reading-to-Write Questions

1. **Content:** Although you might label this article as a "personal essay," Ruff does not rely solely upon personal experience. What other types of evidence does she present?

2. **Arrangement:** Are you confused by Ruff's shifts back and forth between the past and present? If not, why?

3. **Style:** What pattern of images does Ruff introduce in the opening paragraphs of the article? Is the imagery effective?

4. _____

    _____

    _____

Suggested Topics

1. **Observation:** If you are an African American who attended a predominantly white private school, compare your experience to Ruff's. If you are not, interview one and compare his/her experience to Ruff's. Are there signs of progress? (audience = African American parents who might send their children to predominantly white private schools)

2. **Critique:** Were you surprised to discover that, despite her complaints, Ruff had enrolled her son in a predominantly white private school? Are her words and her actions contradictory? (audience = Ruff's *Post* readers)

3. **Synthesis:** Ruff feels that sometimes self-segregation is essential for survival at a predominantly white private school. Contrast her views with Gaines-Carter's and Williams'. (audience = African American students at predominantly white private schools)

4. _____

    _____

    _____

Background Readings: THE POST-INTEGRATION GENERATION

See the reading list for Patrice Gaines-Carter's essay.

Why Segregation Seems So Seductive
Juan Williams

Born in Panama, Juan Williams has estab-
lished his career in the U.S. as a national corre-
spondent and columnist for The Washington Post.
For his newswriting, he has won awards from
The Washingtonian Magazine, *the Washington-*
Baltimore News Guild, and the Education Writers
of America. He recently wrote the book Thurgood
Marshall: American Revolutionary. *However, he*
is probably best known for his book Eyes on the
Prize: America's Civil Rights Years, 1954–1967,
which was released in 1987 with the PBS televi-
sion series. Mindful of the sacrifices and aims of
the Civil Rights Movement, Williams penned the
following essay to oppose Black self-segregation.
Presenting contrasts as well as causes and effects,
the essay, dated January 24, 1994, appeared in
The Washington Post.

---

1   When I won scholarships to go to a white prep school and then a select
white college, my black neighbors in Brooklyn were bursting with pride.
There was no question about whether I should accept the offers. The only
question was whether a kid from a poor black neighborhood could compete at
these fancy institutions with students from rich families that provided them

with everything from tutors to world travel. Neither of my parents graduated from high school, much less college, and the pressure was on to handle the white world so as to prove that black people were just as capable if given an equal opportunity.

2   I am meeting many bright young black people who say they hear a very different message from their black neighbors. Today's message is: stay home in the name of racial unity, or at least go to a historically black college, no matter if it's inferior to white colleges now open to black students. Self-segregation is in.

3   Forty years ago this May, the Supreme Court ruled that segregation in public school was unconstitutional. The ruling was a triumph for Thurgood Marshall and his associates at the NAACP Legal Defense Fund but also for an idea—integration. That idea has dominated black American strategies for achieving economic, political, and social rights since Reconstruction. It was a lifelong dream that Martin Luther King gave voice to from the steps of the Lincoln Memorial thirty-one years ago. Today, the efforts of Marshall and King remain honored, but the idea they championed is under assault from what might seem an unlikely camp—black America.

4   To William Sampson, who now heads Chicago United, a prestigious, interracial group of business and civic leaders, the drive for integration is itself a subtle form of racism. "Integration has curious underpinnings," says Sampson, a former professor of sociology at Northwestern University. "To be for integration is to believe that blacks and Hispanics are deprived if we can't be around white folks. That is the essence of racism."

5   Harold W. Cruse, professor emeritus of Afro-American studies and history at the University of Michigan, agrees. Cruse's influential books, *Plural but Equal* and *The Crisis of the Negro Intellectual,* argue that the civil rights establishment was wrong to promote integration as an ideal. He makes a pragmatic case: "No point in us crusading under that banner," says Cruse. "It's not a question of integration being right or wrong. The issue is that sociologically, psychologically, biologically, and racially it is not going to happen, . . . never mind that we have more integration than forty years ago, more civil rights. Integration is humanly impossible because groups do not disappear."

6   A large part of the argument against integration is that its benefits have been limited to two groups: middle-class blacks ready to take advantage of integration's opportunities and working-class blacks who, if lucky enough to have strong families and good schools, moved into the rapidly expanding black middle class. But, say critics, poor blacks, battling unemployment and bad schools, have been sacrificed to this preoccupation with integration.

7   This argument is made by black leaders at both ends of the political spectrum. Robert Woodson, whose National Center for Neighborhood Enterprise tries to help poor blacks become self-sufficient, argues that poverty programs, urban renewal, and forced busing for integration have hurt poor black neighborhoods, businesses, and pride.

8   Look, says Woodson, "at the results. Look at black communities left behind, the people left behind. Integration was embraced by middle-class blacks who

sought proximity to whites as synonymous with progress. Integration meant they could stay at the Sheraton or work for IBM. Low-income blacks and entrepreneurs are not concerned with that, they are concerned with the integrity of their black institutions. The Jews got it right. They fought for desegregation—no quotas on the numbers of Jews admitted to professional schools . . . but they maintained Yeshiva and Brandeis. Black leaders go around half the time insisting anything all-black is bad. That's why our children are engaged in this frenzy of self-hate."

9   These new voices sound strange to those, like Kenneth Clark, who fought alongside leaders such as Marshall, former NAACP leader Roy Wilkins, and labor leader A. Philip Randolph to dismantle legal segregation. Today's black critics of integration "are misguided, wrong, and terribly sad people," says Clark, the renowned psychologist who travelled south to test black children in segregated schools during the 1940s. Clark found that black children in those schools developed deep inferiority complexes and internalized the concept of white superiority. That research was cited by the Supreme Court in its landmark 1954 *Brown* v. *Board of Education* decision outlawing school segregation.

10   Today's fault-finders, says Clark, now seventy-nine, are simply trying to pretend that the fact that much of America remains segregated is by their choice. "I think segregation of any kind is racist and I am against racism whether you say you like it or not," says Clark. Segregation "is damaging to the individual, damaging to the society's claim to justice, and damaging to whites as well as blacks."

11   What about calls from leading black voices for all-black schools for boys who are failing and dropping out of traditional schools? What about complaints that black businesses and newspapers, even illegal numbers operations, have died under integration? Clark is unmoved: "What they are telling me is that they have been segregated and part of the damage done to them is that they have feelings of inadequacy. They don't want to compete. They feel inferior." Clark even questions the rationale for support of historically black colleges.

12   "Integration is still the point," agrees John Hope Franklin, the eminent historian at Duke University. "What has happened is that some have grown frustrated as the opposition has stiffened and the ground has shifted. . . . It's not only that we don't have integration, but we have no equality in segregation."

13   Some, such as Michael Meyers, head of the New York Civil Rights Coalition, contend that support for segregation in black America is not a serious school of thought but "a fashion, a fashion of racial separatism."

14   "Everyone has slipped into talking about segregation as the practical and pragmatic thing to do because it is the easy thing to do," says Meyers. "More and more people really do believe that skin color determines personality, culture, and even intelligence. The racialists among civil rights activists have propagated that myth. It's the same myth put out by the white segregationists, but the black segregationists have forgotten that. They have no idea of the history

and insidious use of segregation so they are all kowtowing to the segregation-
ist line as practical."

15   Meyers, a former assistant director of the NAACP, notes the irony of seeing
the organization turn away from interracial adoptions: "They'd rather have a
black child in a foster home or orphanage than with a white family because
they now believe in race. . . . Can you believe that!" Meyers also criticizes the
Afrocentric education movement as offering an escape to those who fear they
can't compete in mainstream America.

16   Whatever the merits of the neosegregationist argument, some research suggests little progress against segregation since the *Brown* decision. In the 1992
book *American Apartheid: Segregation and the Making of the Underclass,* authors
Douglas S. Massey and Nancy A. Denton conclude that black racial segregation remains the prime cause of black poverty and disadvantage. Moreover,
they argue, segregation "did not just happen—it was manufactured by whites
through a series of self-conscious actions and purposeful institutional arrangements that continue today."

17   The heart of segregation in the '90s, say Massey and Denton, is residential.
Even middle-class blacks do not do as well as middle-class whites or middle-
class members of ethnic groups, the authors found, because they "live in
neighborhoods that are far less advantageous." Massey argues that middle-
income blacks who move to a predominantly black county may find that
whites withdraw, housing values decline, and tax hikes are needed to maintain the same level of services. Thus, middle-class blacks there would be at an
economic disadvantage compared to whites of the same class in a predominantly white county.

18   Similar findings about the current state of segregation come from the
National School Boards Association, which reported last month that racial
segregation in schools is increasing to the extent that 78 percent of black and
Hispanic students are now in schools with overwhelmingly minority enrollments. "The civil rights impulse of the '60s is dead in the water, and the ship is
floating backwards toward the shoals of racial segregation," Gary Orfield,
who ran the Harvard-based study for the school boards association, told
reporters.

19   Most of integration's critics stress that they, like Marshall, Randolph,
Wilkins, and King, oppose forced segregation. But they want to honor the idea
of pluralism—not integration. As Woodson puts it, he wants the right to go to
an all-black church and live in an all-black neighborhood if he chooses to.

20   Alan Keyes, a former Maryland GOP senatorial candidate who is now a
talk-show host, argues that segregation is the "wrong word to describe people
of similar backgrounds congregating, getting together to express their natural
affinity." But what if whites congregate to the exclusion of blacks? Keyes
responds that such get-togethers are not about keeping anyone out. All should
be welcome if they choose to come. That sounds nice, but will individuals of
both races really be free to choose if both groups agree to condone the racial
divide?

21   Some neosegregationists have come to their position less from preference than from a hardheaded recognition of the challenges faced by black America. Spencer Holland, director of the Center for Educating African-American Males at Morgan State University, for example, runs a program for black boys at three public schools in Baltimore and at a Washington school. "The problem I have with the old guard is that we can't use their tactics in the '90s," says Holland. "I'm fifty-four years old. I know what the old guard did and what they sacrificed. But . . . integration tactics don't matter to the lives of the children I deal with. We black people have to take care of these black children now."

22   "I don't want to dump on the integration thrust—it opened up wonderful opportunities for my generation and gave us a platform," says Jeff Howard, president of the Efficacy Institute, a Massachusetts group that works with schools and service agencies to improve the education and care of black children. "But it's not about integration now. It's about building up our own institutions to successfully prepare our children. . . . If the first movement was to end segregation and the second movement was to get civil rights, then I think we are ready for a third movement in which black people focus on taking care of our kids."

23   But taking care of black children includes providing them with a place in an increasingly multicultural and competitive America. That means encouraging black children to believe in their abilities, to dare to get into the mainstream and compete as equals. Those who see integration as passé unwittingly leave open the door of racial separatism.

24   In a society where blacks still live with the social ostracism that comes from a legacy of being seen as less than fully human, encouraging black separatism is an extremely high-risk strategy. By providing a convenient rationale for those whites who, statistics show, are aggressively pushing away from blacks, it is almost sure to weaken the larger society's efforts to allow disadvantaged black people to escape the islands of violence, bad schools, and unemployment on which they are stranded. As I look back on my life, and that of Martin Luther King, I can't help but conclude that integration—no matter how difficult to pursue, no matter how frustratingly slow to achieve—is far better than voluntary segregation, an idea that the very worst racist would be all too happy to live with.

Reading-to-Write Questions

1. **Content:** Williams constructs a conversation among his sources. To understand how he creates such a synthesis, list his sources (by name) under PRO and CON.

2. **Arrangement:** Why does Williams devote seven of the first eight paragraphs to his opponents' views?

3. **Style:** Notice how Williams introduces the many quotations in his article. What sentence structures does he use in addition to the usual "He says" structure?

4. _____

    _____

    _____

Suggested Topics

1. **Observation:** If you are an African American attending a historically Black college, how do you justify your self-segregation? On the other hand, if you are attending a predominantly white college, report on the ways that ethnic minorities segregate themselves on campus. (audience = seniors applying to colleges)

2. **Critique:** In a letter to the editor, summarize Williams' position against Black self-segregation. Then explain why you oppose or support his position. (audience = Williams' *Post* readers)

3. **Synthesis:** Williams believes that Black children need to compete with other Americans. Would self-segregation necessarily feed the stereotype threat that C. Steele describes? (audience = parents considering sending their children to all-black schools)

4. _____

    _____

    _____

Background readings: THE POST-INTEGRATION GENERATION

See the reading list for Patrice Gaines-Carter's essay.

Thoughts of Restitution
Randall Robinson

As founder and president of the organization TransAfrica, lawyer Randall Robinson played a leading role in the international movement to free Nelson Mandela and end apartheid in South Africa. Recently, he launched a new campaign—to seek reparations for slavery. Therefore, in 2000, after publishing his memoir Defending the Spirit, *he wrote* The Debt: What America Owes to Blacks. *According to Robinson, the aim of* The Debt *is "to stimulate, not sate. To pose the question. To invite the debate. To cause America to compensate after three and a half centuries, for a long-avoided wrong." In the excerpt below, Robinson explains why African Americans should demand reparations and how the fight for reparations could transform African Americans in the process.*

Short of a revolution, the likelihood that blacks today will obtain direct payments in compensation for their subjugation as slaves before the Emancipation Proclamation, and their exploitation as quasi-citizens since, is no better than it was in 1866, when Thaddeus Stevens recognized that his bright hope of

> "forty acres and a mule" for every freedman had vanished "like the baseless fabric of a vision."
>
> [Derrick Bell]

1   If Bell is right that African Americans will not be compensated for the massive wrongs and social injuries inflicted upon them by their government, during and after slavery, then there is *no* chance that America can solve its racial problems—if solving these problems means, as I believe it must, closing the yawning economic gap between blacks and whites in this country. The gap was opened by the 246-year practice of slavery. It has been resolutely nurtured since in law and public behavior. It has now ossified. It is structural. Its framing beams are disguised only by the counterfeit manners of a hypocritical governing class.

2   For twelve years Nazi Germany inflicted horrors upon European Jews. And Germany paid. It paid Jews individually. It paid the state of Israel. For two and a half centuries, Europe and America inflicted unimaginable horrors upon Africa and its people. Europe not only paid nothing to Africa in compensation, but followed the slave trade with the remapping of Africa for further European economic exploitation. (European governments have yet even to accede to Africa's request for the return of Africa's art treasures looted along with its natural resources during the century-long colonial era.)

3   While President Lincoln supported a plan during the Civil War to compensate slave owners for their loss of "property," his successor, Andrew Johnson, vetoed legislation that would have provided compensation to ex-slaves.

4   Under the Southern Homestead Act, ex-slaves were given six months to purchase land at reasonably low rates without competition from white southerners and northern investors. But, owing to their destitution, few ex-slaves were able to take advantage of the homesteading program. The largest number that did were concentrated in Florida, numbering little more than three thousand. The soil was generally poor and unsuitable for farming purposes. In any case, the ex-slaves had no money on which to subsist for months while waiting for crops, or the scantest wherewithal to purchase the most elementary farming implements. The program failed. In sum, the United States government provided no compensation to the victims of slavery.

5   Perhaps I should say a bit here about why the question of reparations is critical to finding a solution to our race problems.

6   This question—and how blacks gather to pose it—is a good measure of our psychological readiness as a community to pull ourselves abreast here at home and around the world. I say this because no outside community can be more interested in solving our problems than we. Derrick Bell suggested in his review of Bittker's book *[The Case for Black Reparations]* that the white power structure would never support reparations because to do so would operate

against its interests. I believe Bell is right in that view. The initiative must come from blacks, broadly, widely, implacably.

7   But what exactly will black enthusiasm, or lack thereof, measure? There is no linear solution to any of our problems, for our problems are not merely technical in nature. By now, after 380 years of unrelenting psychological abuse, the biggest part of our problem is inside us: in how we have come to see ourselves, in our damaged capacity to validate a course for ourselves without outside approval.

8   The issue here is not whether or not we can, or will, win reparations. The issue rather is whether we will fight for reparations, because we have decided for ourselves that they are our due. In 1915, into the sharp teeth of southern Jim Crow hostility, Cornelius J. Jones filed a lawsuit against the United States Department of the Treasury in an attempt to recover sixty-eight million dollars for former slaves. He argued that, through a federal tax placed on raw cotton, the federal government had benefited financially from the sale of cotton that slave labor had produced, and for which the black men, women, and children who had produced the cotton had not been paid. Jones's was a straightforward proposition. The monetary value of slaves' labor, which he estimated to be sixty-eight million dollars, had been appropriated by the United States government. A debt existed. It had to be paid to the, by then, ex-slaves or their heirs.

9   Where was the money?

10   A federal appeals court held that the United States could not be sued without its consent and dismissed the so-called Cotton Tax case. But the court never addressed Cornelius J. Jones's question about the federal government's appropriation of property—the labor of blacks who had worked the cotton fields—that had never been compensated.

11   Let me try to drive the point home here: through keloids of suffering, through coarse veils of damaged self-belief, lost direction, misplaced compass, sh—faced resignation, racial transmutation, black people worked long, hard, killing days, years, centuries—and they were never *paid*. The value of their labor went into others' pockets—plantation owners, northern entrepreneurs, state treasuries, the United States government.

12   Where was the money?

13   Where *is* the money?

14   There is a debt here.

15   I know of no statute of limitations either legally or morally that would extinguish it. Financial quantities are nearly as indestructible as matter. Take away here, add there, interest compounding annually, over the years, over the whole of the twentieth century.

16   Where is the money?

17   Jews have asked this question of countries and banks and corporations and collectors and any who had been discovered at the end of the slimy line holding in secret places the gold, the art, the money that was the rightful property

of European Jews before the Nazi terror. Jews have demanded what was their due and received a fair measure of it.

18   Clearly, how blacks respond to the challenge surrounding the simple demand for restitution will say a lot more about us *and do a lot more for us* than the demand itself would suggest. We would show ourselves to be responding as any normal people would to victimization were we to assert collectively in our demands for restitution that, for 246 years and with the complicity of the United States government, hundreds of millions of black people endured unimaginable cruelties—kidnapping, sale as livestock, deaths in the millions during terror-filled sea voyages, backbreaking toil, beatings, rapes, castrations, maimings, murders. We would begin a healing of our psyches were the most public case made that whole peoples lost religions, languages, customs, histories, cultures, children, mothers, fathers. It would make us more forgiving of ourselves, more self-approving, more self-understanding to see, *really see,* that on three continents and a string of islands, survivors had little choice but to piece together whole new cultures from the rubble shards of what theirs had once been. And they were never made whole. And never compensated. Not one red cent.

19   Left behind to gasp for self-regard in the vicious psychological wake of slavery are history's orphans played by the brave black shells of their ancient forebears, people so badly damaged that they cannot *see* the damage, or how their government may have been partly, if not largely, responsible for the disabling injury that by now has come to seem normal and unattributable.

20   Until America's white ruling class accepts the fact that the book never closes on massive unredressed social wrongs, America can have no future as one people. Questions must be raised, to American private, as well as, public institutions. Which American families and institutions, for instance, were endowed in perpetuity by the commerce of slavery? And how do we square things with slavery's modern victims from whom all natural endowments were stolen? What is a fair measure of restitution for this, the most important of all American human rights abuses?

Reading-to-Write Questions

1. **Content:** Being a lawyer, Robinson often bases his argument on precedent. Where does he use this strategy?

2. **Arrangement:** Robinson repeats the question "Where is the money?" as if it were a refrain in a song. How does this question contribute to the coherence of the passage?

3. **Style:** Why does Robinson choose the metaphor "keloids of suffering"?

4. _____

   _____

   _____

Suggested Topics

1. **Observation:** Robinson's friend Ibrahim Gassama reported that "when the issue of reparations is raised among white professors, many of whom are otherwise liberal, it is met with silence." Find out for yourself. Ask some white Americans about reparations and classify their reactions. (audience = African Americans)

2. **Critique:** Robinson predicts, "Until America's white ruling class accepts the fact that the book never closes on massive unredressed social wrongs, America can have no future as one people." Explain why you agree or disagree with this statement. (audience = Robinson's readers)

3. **Synthesis:** Cite examples from Douglass's and Franklin and Moss's descriptions of American slavery to support Robinson's call for reparations. (audience = U.S. Congress)

4. _____

   _____

   _____

Background Readings: REPARATIONS FOR BLACKS

Bittker, Boris. *The Case for Black Reparations.* New York: Random House, 1973.

D'Orso, Michael. *Like Judgment Day: The Ruin and Redemption of a Town Called Rosewood.* New York: G.P. Putnam's Sons, 1996.

Oubre, Claude. *Forty Acres and a Mule: The Freedman's Bureau and Black Land Ownership.* Baton Rouge, LA: Louisiana State UP, 1978.

_____

_____

_____

Nihilism in Black America
Cornel West

The subject of profiles in Time *and* Newsweek, *Cornell West is a professor of Afro-American Studies and the Philosophy of Religion at Harvard University. He has earned a reputation as a public intellectual through his riveting oratory and his thought-provoking books. Among the titles are* Prophetic Fragments, Breaking Bread *(with bell hooks),* Race Matters, *and, more recently (with Henry Louis Gates, Jr.),* The Future of the Race *and* The African American Century. *It is his 1993 best-seller* Race Matters *that contains the selection presented here. In this excerpt, West defines* nihilism, *investigates its causes, and explores possible solutions to the problem.*

---

1   The proper starting point for the crucial debate about the prospects for black America is an examination of the nihilism that increasingly pervades black communities. *Nihilism is to be understood here not as a philosophic doctrine that there are no rational grounds for legitimate standards or authority; it is, far more, the lived experiences of coping with a life of horrifying meaninglessness, hopelessness, and (most important) lovelessness.* The frightening result is a numbing detachment from others and a self-destructive disposition toward the world. Life without meaning, hope, and love breeds a cold-hearted, mean-spirited outlook that destroys both the individual and others.

2   Nihilism is not new in black America. The first African encounter with the New World was an encounter with a distinctive form of the Absurd. The initial black struggle against degradation and devaluation in the enslaved circumstances of the New World was, in part, a struggle against nihilism. In fact, the major enemy of black survival in America has been and is neither oppression nor exploitation but rather the nihilistic threat—that is, loss of hope and absence of meaning. For as long as hope remains and meaning is preserved, the possibility of overcoming oppression stays alive. The self-fulfilling prophecy of the nihilistic threat is that without hope there can be no future, that without meaning there can be no struggle.

3   The genius of our black foremothers and forefathers was to create powerful buffers to ward off the nihilistic threat, to equip black folk with cultural armor to beat back the demons of hopelessness, meaningless, and lovelessness. These buffers consisted of cultural structures of meaning and feeling that created and sustained communities; this armor constituted ways of life and struggle that embodied values of service and sacrifice, love and care, discipline and excellence. In other words, traditions for black surviving and thriving under usually adverse New World conditions were major barriers against the nihilistic threat. These traditions consist primarily of black religious and civic institutions that sustained familiar and communal networks of support. If cultures are, in part, what human beings create (out of antecedent fragments of other cultures) in order to convince themselves not to commit suicide, then black foremothers and forefathers are to be applauded. In fact, until the early seventies black Americans had the lowest suicide rate in the United States. But now young black people lead the nation in the rate of increase in suicides.

4   What has changed? What went wrong? The bitter irony of integration? The cumulative effects of a genocidal conspiracy? The virtual collapse of rising expectations after the optimistic sixties? None of us fully understands why the cultural structures that once sustained black life in America are no longer able to fend off the nihilistic threat. I believe that two significant reasons why the threat is more powerful now than ever before are the saturation of market forces and market moralities in black life and the present crisis in black leadership. The recent market-driven shattering of black civil society—black families, neighborhoods, schools, churches, mosques—leaves more and more black people vulnerable to daily lives endured with little sense of self and fragile existential moorings.

5   Black people have always been in America's wilderness in search of a promised land. Yet many black folk now reside in a jungle ruled by a cutthroat market morality devoid of any faith in deliverance or hope for freedom. Contrary to the superficial claims of conservative behaviorists, these jungles are not primarily the result of pathological behavior. Rather, this behavior is the tragic response of a people bereft of resources in confronting the workings of U.S. capitalist society. Saying this is not the same as asserting that individual black people are not responsible for their actions—black murderers and rapists should go to jail. But it must be recognized that the nihilistic threat con-

tributes to criminal behavior. It is a threat that feeds on poverty and shattered cultural institutions and grows more powerful as the armors to ward against it are weakened.

6   But why is this shattering of black civil society occurring? What has led to the weakening of black cultural institutions in asphalt jungles? Corporate market institutions have contributed greatly to their collapse. By corporate market institutions I mean that complex set of interlocking enterprises that have a disproportionate amount of capital, power, and exercise a disproportionate influence on how our society is run and how our culture is shaped. Needless to say, the primary motivation of these institutions is to make profits, and their basic strategy is to convince the public to consume. These institutions have helped create a seductive way of life, a culture of consumption that capitalizes on every opportunity to make money. Market calculations and cost-benefit analyses hold sway in almost every sphere of U.S. society.

7   The common denominator of these calculations and analyses is usually the provision, expansion, and intensification of *pleasure*. Pleasure is a multivalent term; it means different things to many people. In the American way of life pleasure involves comfort, convenience, and sexual stimulation. Pleasure, so defined, has little to do with the past and views the future as no more than a repetition of a hedonistically driven present. This market morality stigmatizes others as objects for personal pleasure or bodily stimulation. Conservative behaviorists have alleged that traditional morality has been undermined by radical feminists and the cultural radicals of the sixties. But it is clear that corporate market institutions have greatly contributed to undermining traditional morality in order to stay in business and make a profit. The reduction of individuals to objects of pleasure is especially evident in the culture industries—television, radio, video, music—in which gestures of sexual foreplay and orgiastic pleasure flood the marketplace.

8   Like all Americans, African-Americans are influenced greatly by the images of comfort, convenience, machismo, femininity, violence, and sexual stimulation that bombard consumers. These seductive images contribute to the predominance of the market-inspired way of life over all others and thereby edge out nonmarket values—love, care, service to others—handed down by preceding generations. The predominance of this way of life among those living in poverty-ridden conditions, with a limited capacity to ward off self-contempt and self-hatred, results in the possible triumph of the nihilistic threat in black America.

9   A major contemporary strategy for holding the nihilistic threat at bay is a direct attack on the sense of worthlessness and self-loathing in black America. This *angst* resembles a kind of collective clinical depression in significant pockets of black America. The eclipse of hope and collapse of meaning in much of black America is linked to the structural dynamics of corporate market institutions that affect all Americans. Under these circumstances black existential

angst derives from the lived experience of ontological wounds and emotional scars inflicted by white supremacist beliefs and images permeating U.S. society and culture. These beliefs and images attack black intelligence, black ability, black beauty, and black character daily in subtle and not-so-subtle ways. Toni Morrison's novel, *The Bluest Eye,* for example, reveals the devastating effect of pervasive European ideals of beauty on the self-image of young black women. Morrison's exposure of the harmful extent to which these white ideals affect the black self-image is a first step toward rejecting these ideals and overcoming the nihilistic self-loathing they engender in blacks.

10   The accumulated effect of the black wounds and scars suffered in a white-dominated society is a deep-seated anger, a boiling sense of rage, and a passionate pessimism regarding America's will to justice. Under conditions of slavery and Jim Crow segregation, this anger, rage, and pessimism remained relatively muted because of a well-justified fear of brutal white retaliation. The major breakthroughs of the sixties—more physically than politically—swept this fear away. Sadly, the combination of the market way of life, poverty-ridden conditions, black existential *angst,* and the lessening of fear of white authorities has directed most of the anger, rage, and despair toward fellow black citizens, especially toward black women, who are the most vulnerable in our society and in black communities. Only recently has this nihilistic threat—and its ugly inhumane outlook and actions—surfaced in the larger American society. And its appearance surely reveals one of the many instances of cultural decay in a declining empire.

11   What is to be done about this nihilistic threat? Is there really any hope, given our shattered civil society, market-driven corporate enterprises, and white supremacism? If one begins with the threat of concrete nihilism, then one must talk about some kind of *politics of conversion.* New models of collective black leadership must promote a version of this politics. Like alcoholism and drug addiction, nihilism is a disease of the soul. It can never be completely cured, and there is always the possibility of relapse. But there is always a chance for conversion—a chance for people to believe that there is hope for the future and a meaning to struggle. This chance rests neither on an agreement about what justice consists of nor on an analysis of how racism, sexism, or class subordination operate. Such arguments and analyses are indispensable. But a politics of conversion requires more. Nihilism is not overcome by arguments or analyses; it is tamed by love and care. Any disease of the soul must be conquered by a turning of one's soul. This turning is done through one's own affirmation of one's worth—an affirmation fueled by the concern of others. A love ethic must be at the center of a politics of conversion.

12   A love ethic has nothing to do with sentimental feelings or tribal connections. Rather it is a last attempt at generating a sense of agency among a downtrodden people. The best exemplar of this love ethic is depicted on a number of levels in Toni Morrison's great novel *Beloved.* Self-love and love of others are both modes toward increasing self-valuation and encouraging political resis-

tance in one's community. These modes of valuation and resistance are rooted in a subversive memory—the best of one's past without romantic nostalgia—and guided by a universal love ethic. For my purposes here, *Beloved* can be construed as bringing together the loving yet critical affirmation of black humanity found in the best of black nationalist movements, the perennial hope against hope for transracial coalition in progressive movements, and the painful struggle for self-affirming sanity in a history in which the nihilistic threat *seems* insurmountable.

13 The politics of conversion proceeds principally on the local level—in those institutions in civil society still vital enough to promote self-worth and self-affirmation. It surfaces on the state and national levels only when grass-roots democratic organizations put forward a collective leadership that has earned the love and respect of and, most important, has proved itself *accountable* to these organizations. This collective leadership must exemplify moral integrity, character, and democratic statesmanship within itself and within its organizations.

14 Like liberal structuralists, the advocates of a politics of conversion never lose sight of the structural conditions that shape the sufferings and lives of people. Yet, unlike liberal structuralism, the politics of conversion meets the nihilistic threat head-on. Like conservative behaviorism, the politics of conversion openly confronts the self-destructive and inhumane actions of black people. Unlike conservative behaviorists, the politics of conversion situates these actions within inhumane circumstances (but does not thereby exonerate them). The politics of conversion shuns the limelight—a limelight that solicits status seekers and ingratiates egomaniacs. Instead, it stays on the ground among the toiling everyday people, ushering forth humble freedom fighters—both followers and leaders—who have the audacity to take the nihilistic threat by the neck and turn back its deadly assaults.

Reading-to-Write Questions

1. **Content:** Why does West bother to define the word *pleasure?*

2. **Arrangement:** Label the problem-cause-solution structure of this text.

3. **Style:** Clearly, West is a theologian. Where does he inject biblical imagery?

4. _____

    _____

    _____

Suggested Topics

1. **Observation:** Do you see signs of "market morality" on your campus? If so, write an essay defining and illustrating this term. (audience = student government)

2. **Critique:** West claims that "the major enemy of black survival in America has been and is neither oppression nor exploitation but rather the nihilistic threat—that is, loss of hope and absence of meaning." Explain why you agree or disagree with West. (audience = West's readers)

3. **Synthesis:** West credits African American foremothers and forefathers with warding off nihilism by creating "religious and civic institutions that sustained familial and communal networks of support." Cite examples from White's and Bennett's essays to illustrate West's point. (audience = students in an African American history class)

4. _____

    _____

    _____

Background Readings: THE PROGRESS OF AFRICAN AMERICANS

See the reading list for Toni Morrison's essay.

Student Essay:
THAT EXTRA SOMETHING
Jonathan Howard
(2000)

1   "I am woman. Hear me roar!" This has been a battle cry to promote the
strength of modern-day women. However, women have exhibited unparal-
leled displays of inner strength on several occasions throughout time. Toni
Morrison breathes life into this topic with her essay "A Slow Walk of Trees" by
presenting the steadfast character of her mother and grandmother. Women of
today are showing the same characteristics—only in a different time period.
No matter the era, women have shown traits of stability and substance that
have held families together.

2   Morrison's parents and grandparents were from time periods in which race
relations were at their worst. Racism, segregation, and Jim Crow mentalities
served as templates for difficulty in black families and communities. Jobs were
never secure, families were always struggling, and life in general was difficult
in black households. The men of these various families were taking psychological abuse from an unmercifully harsh white society. They were in constant
danger of losing their lives to racially motivated violence as well as living
through the frustration of not knowing whether their jobs would be taken and
given to a person of lighter complexion. These are only a few of the reasons
women were so heavily relied upon to be the adhesive in the family structure.

3   Morrison's mother and grandmother held a certain something within them
that every person who graces this earth should have. Unfortunately, most
people cannot decipher what exactly it is. We can only see the effects of it.
Morrison's mother and grandmother, as many women of their times did,
rooted themselves in Jesus Christ and used that special gift within to keep the
family operating as a tight and prosperous unit. Ardelia Willis, Morrison's
grandmother, sneaked seven children out of a window in order to escape a
dangerous situation, only to move from their destination because the teacher
in the new town did not know long division. Morrison's mother was tenacious
enough to take on the President of the United States when it came to the quality of the food provided for her family. And to think that women worldwide

are exhibiting tendencies such as these on a daily basis. Although men possess many qualities that promote the family's general welfare and sanctity, women, as shown in Morrison's essay, contain an indescribable gift for love and care that spreads over the family and beyond.

4   In my opinion, this concept holds true in the case of the modern-day African-American family. There is one distinctive difference between the time periods: more so now than in the past, women are having to support the family without the help of a male counterpart. Today, women, especially those of African-American ancestry, are being left with the burden of being the sole provider for the family. Some of these women must work two or three jobs in order to provide the necessities for their families. It takes strength of mind, body, and soul to withstand such a tiresome rotation. In addition to the financial situation, they are being asked to cook, clean, and wash when they reach home. It is an endless cycle that slowly but surely breaks a person down. Many times the children are so young that they cannot help the mother with household duties, leaving the woman without aid. Numerous single-parent households are forced to swallow what pride they have and rely on federal aid. This process is not as easy as some people make it out to be. It is a sacrifice that sometimes has to be made in order to survive. I have seen firsthand how a struggling family can stretch food and resources further in a week than most households can do in a single day. "By any means necessary"—this is the battle cry of these women. Everything done is for the family's betterment and survival.

5   Not included in the financial situation are the duties of parenthood. The mother has to provide love, care, and nurturing for her children. She also has to project a positive attitude no matter how bleak the financial situation. In my opinion, the toughest duty she has is that of teaching boys how to be men. This is a difficult objective when there is a male figure in the household—imagine when there is not. A single mother has to teach a young child how to be something that she is not. I am a product of such a household and can testify to the difficulties my mother encountered raising me. The important part is that she did not give up when the times got hard. No matter what happened, she kept trying to teach me to be a responsible and positive young man. She always told me that she was more than just my mother; it took me awhile to totally comprehend what she meant, but it is all clear now. She was *both* parents to me; she was better at one than the other, but she did a great job at both. Although some single mothers claim to occupy the father's positions in the household, they cannot and never will be the same as the genuine article. Yet this does not stop women from providing the knowledge, love, and strength needed for the transition from adolescence into manhood.

6   Although multiple trends have come and gone and come back again in society, there has been one steadfast entity throughout time: strong women. Being a young man, I do not know what it is like to be a woman. What I do know is that it is not easy. Without strong women in their lives, countless men would

not be as successful or stable as they are. Women are the backbones of the family, regardless of generation, time period, or race.

Works Cited

Morrison, Toni. "A Slow Walk of Trees." *Revelations.* 3rd ed. Teresa M. Redd. Needham Heights, MA: Simon & Schuster, 1997. 307–312.

Student Essay

LIVING ON THE RAZOR'S EDGE

Shaton Sanderson

(2000)

1   Since our ancestors' debut in the United States, the African-American race has been plagued with problems. Our first problem was slavery. Next, we were "free," yet we still did not have the same freedoms as people with white skin. The new century presents us with so many problems that we need to rank them in order of least-to-most important so that we can efficiently correct them. Most of these problems—for example, colorism, stereotypes, and the "post-integration" syndrome—affect us every single day of our lives. However, although colorism and stereotyping need to be addressed, my generation's "post-integration syndrome" is the most significant problem our community faces today.

2   Colorism is a problem that triggers conflict among light- and dark-skinned African Americans. The standard of beauty within the African-American community seems to be someone with light skin and long or wavy hair. This concept can be traced to slavery, when the master's daughter was thought to be most beautiful. This image, at first, seems to be a mere preference. Yet the underlying effects of this standard are deep. African-Americans with darker skin begin to feel inferior. Moreover, being rejected by people within your race, as Clarisse Jones suggests in her essay "Light Skin Versus Dark Skin," hurts much more that an external racist encounter.

3   While colorism poses a problem, so do the stereotypes of what it means to be black. These stereotypes have coerced black people into accepting limited views about their capability in life. For example, William Raspberry explains in his essay "The Handicap of Definition" that society views African-Americans as being good at only "athletics, entertainment, and sexual performance" (167). Sadly enough, this stereotype discourages us from developing "positive ethnic traditions" (168). Although we as a race are good at these things, the impression is that these are the only things we are good at. This stereotype restricts us from excelling in areas that are "conducive to success" outside of our stereotypical fields (168). Unfortunately, becoming successful outside our proposed areas is seen as "acting white." What black person wants that?

4   As overwhelming as these two issues may seem, there is an even more pressing problem. Patrice Gaines-Carter's letter "Is My 'Post-Integration' Daughter Black Enough?" exposes the most significant problem in African-American society today. In this essay, Gaines-Carter explains how bad she feels when her daughter fails to acknowledge what past generations worked so hard to achieve. She gives examples of times, such as Martin Luther King, Jr.'s birthday, when her daughter responded "with total disdain" to the notion of attending a memorial service (313). She wants her daughter to "fight the power," stay true to her race, and celebrate all shades of blackness. However, she knows a struggle was already fought so that her daughter wouldn't be required to fight.

5   My generation's "post-integration syndrome" is a colossal problem because it allows us to forget our ancestors' struggle for freedom. Their struggle began from a destitute beginning called slavery, and they offered many sacrifices to make sure our generation could enjoy the gift of freedom. Some fought physically: they shed their blood so that future generations could succeed. Some fought politically: they organized boycotts, sit-ins, and marches to prove that they were more than ready for the challenge. Some fought mentally: they spoke to congregations and wrote literature on the inhumane and immoral situations in which those "former" masters and mistresses forced African Americans to live.

6   Slowly but surely, changes came about. Each generation had a little more freedom. Then came my generation with our "post-integration syndrome." It is the biggest problem facing our community because it hinders us from continuing our progress. Every opportunity society has to offer still is not available to black people. Our "privileges" can be taken away as easily as it was hard to get them. If that happens, we will be in the same destitute position where our ancestors started.

7   At a superficial glance, it may seem as if the African-American community has only insignificant problems, but actually it's the opposite. Colorism and stereotyping can be classified as two of the most important problems and should be addressed accordingly. However, the "post-integration syndrome" is the most lethal problem. My generation must be compelled to continue to fight for the precious freedoms our ancestors yearned for and embraced once received. We must continue to fight for and uphold justice because it can be taken away just as it was "given" to us. Gaines-Carter told her daughter, "If you haven't lived on the razor's edge, you forget you can bleed" (316). At any point, my generation runs the risk of being cut by the razor. We must live as if we are on its edge daily.

Works Cited

Gaines-Carter, Patricia. "Is My 'Post-Integration' Daughter Black Enough?" *Revelations.* Ed. Teresa M. Redd. 3rd ed. Needham Heights, MA: Simon & Schuster, 1997. 313–315.

Jones, Clarisse. "Light Skin Versus Dark Skin." *Revelations.* Ed. Teresa M. Redd. 3rd ed. Needham Heights, MA: Simon & Schuster, 1997. 239–241.

Raspberry, William. "The Handicap of Definition." *Revelations.* Ed. Teresa M. Redd. 3rd ed. Needham Heights, MA: Simon & Schuster, 1997. 167–168.